Advance Praise for
Smart Girls in the 21st Centu
Understanding Talented Girls and Women

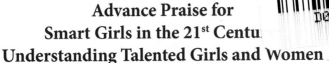

Over the past 40 years, Barbara Kerr, Ph.D., has established herself as the definitive authority on the unique characteristics and development of smart girls and the particular challenges and dilemmas they confront as they seek to build meaningful and satisfying lives. In this fully rewritten, updated volume, Smart Girls in the 21st Century: Understanding Talented Girls and Women, *Kerr and co-author Robyn McKay, Ph.D., once again cut to the very core of what it means to be a smart girl or woman in a culture that does not yet fully embrace the. While celebrating progress made, the opening of new opportunities, and the rich variety of roles adopted by today's smart girls, Kerr and McKay are quick to point out the inequality and obstacles that remain and the most promising paths forward.*
A must read for all who care about the health and well-being of smart girls and the society in which they live.
> ~ Rebecca McMillan, Founder, The Brain Café, Founder,
> Gifted Homeschoolers' Forum Online, and Senior Editor,
> The Creativity Post

Barbara Kerr and Robyn McKay forge a highly original perspective on women's talent development based on a multi-disciplinary, intergenerational review of research. In the course of this book, they tackle knotty issues like how to differentiate passion associated with eminence from other psychological variables that have been discussed in relation to high performance or giftedness
I was glad to be reminded of the joys I experienced from first reading Smart Girls, Gifted Women, *and just as I did then, I plan to apply their insights to my own work.*
> ~ Rena F. Subotnik, Ph.D., Director, Center for Psychology in
> Schools and Education, American Psychological Association

Smart Girls in the 21st Century *shines a much-needed spotlight on an issue that is rarely openly discussed in our society—the finding and nurturance of smart, creative, and talented girls and women. As this book masterfully shows, smart girls don't just exist in a vacuum; like everyone else, smart girls require engagement, love, support, belonging, and opportunities for optimal development and individual flourishing. Ignoring the message of this book has*

deep consequences for society, and the unfortunate loss of brilliance among at least half of the human population.
> ~ Scott Barry Kaufman, Ph.D., Scientific Director,
> The Imagination Institute, University of Pennsylvania

In a time when widely-reported research shows that being a "smart" girl is not a ticket to a happy life, Kerr and McKay have stepped in to provide a framework for understanding who talented girls and women are. Smart Girls in the 21ˢᵗ Century: Understanding Talented Girls and Women *addresses a complex, and often controversial, web of issues and solutions that help parents, educators, and mentors of bright girls and women understand themselves and how they can grow to optimal development.*
> ~ Heidi Molbak, M.S., N.C.C., Founder and President,
> Seed Started Educational Consulting for Gifted and Twice-Exceptional Students

Kudos for the clever analogy of intelligent girls to bees at their functional levels in the hive. The breadth of the intelligences of smart females is as complex as the honey-combed hive itself. The richness of this comparison reveals the largely untapped female mind. The need for strong women to mentor intelligent young women cannot be ignored as they find their place in the hive of society.
> ~Audrey Borden, M.P.A., Founder and President
> of MyGiftedGirl.com

Smart Girls in the 21ˢᵗ Century *melds powerful interviews with females, research, and theoretical models into a roadmap to support and guide parents, educators, policy makers, and women along a productive life course. In my clinical judgment and as a female, this easily accessible and beautifully researched book should be read by every educator and parent.*
> ~ Trudi Y. Taylor, Ph.D., N.C.C., Private Counseling Practice

Smart Girls in the 21st Century

Understanding Talented Girls and Women

Barbara Kerr, Ph.D.
and
Robyn McKay, Ph.D.

Great Potential Press, Inc.

Smart Girls in the 21ˢᵗ Century: Understanding Talented Girls and Women
Edited by: Jessica Atha
Interior design: The Printed Page
Cover design: Hutchison-Frey
Cover painting: Jeanie Tomanek, *Cypress Days,*
www.paulscottfineart.com

Published by Great Potential Press, Inc.
1325 N. Wilmot Road, Suite 300
Tucson, AZ 85712
www.greatpotentialpress.com

18 17 16 15 14   5 4 3 2 1

At the time of this book's publication, all facts and figures cited are the most current available. All telephone numbers, addresses, and website URLs are accurate and active; all publications, organizations, websites, and other resources exist as described in this book; and all have been verified as of the time this book went to press. The author(s) and Great Potential Press make no warranty or guarantee concerning the information and materials given out by organizations or content found at websites, and we are not responsible for any changes that occur after this book's publication. If you find an error or believe that a resource listed here is not as described, please contact Great Potential Press.

Library of Congress Cataloging-in-Publication Data
Kerr, Barbara A.
    [Smart girls, gifted women.]
    Smart girls in the 21st century : understanding talented girls and women / Barbara Kerr, Ph.D., Robyn McKay, Ph.D.
        pages cm
    Revised and enlarged edition of the authors's Smart girls two, 1995.
    Includes bibliographical references and index.
    ISBN-13: 978-1-935067-25-2 (pbk.)
    ISBN-10: 1-935067-25-7 (pbk.)
    1. Gifted girls. 2. Gifted women. 3. Gifted women--Longitudinal studies. 4. GIfted women--Biography. 5. Gifted women--Employment. 6. Self-actualization (Psychology) 7. Achievement motivation in women--Case studies. 8. Success--Case studies. I. McKay, Robyn. II. Title.
    BF723.G52K48 2014
    155.3'330879--dc23
                    2013038580

To Monica Steffes, a smart girl on her way to
becoming a mighty woman.
And to Grace Claiborn.

*"The untold want by life and land ne'er granted,
Now Voyager, sail thou forth to seek and find." —*Walt Whitman

Barbara

To the Smart Girls at ASU's Herberger Academy,
especially Alayzha, Katie, Grace, Tyera, Jasmine, and Kimberly;
to the ASU WiSE leadership team, especially Kayla, Hannah,
and Barbara. I'm so grateful that you all are a part of my life.

Robyn

Table of Contents

Foreword   xiii

Preface   xvii

Acknowledgments   xxv

Chapter 1. Smart + Girl: A Beehive of Definitions of Intelligence   1
  Smart is...   2
    High Intelligence   2
    Creativity   4
    Intelligence, Creativity, Task Commitment, and More   5
    Precocious Math or Verbal Abilities   7
    Multiple Intelligences   8
    General *and* Specific Abilities   9
    Emotional Intelligence   9
    Specific Personality Characteristics   10
    Spiritual Intelligence   13
  The Beehive of Smart Girls   15
    Worker Bees: The Professionals   18
    Forager Bees: The Scholars   18
    Honey Bees: Teachers, Leaders, Counselors   19
    Procreator Bees: Innovators   19
    The Queen Bees: Visionaries   21
  The Many Paths toward Fulfillment of Talent   22

Chapter 2. Generations of Smart Girls and Women   25
  The First Generation: Termites and Girl Geniuses   25
  Leta Hollingworth   27

The Second Generation: From Rosie the Riveter to
    the Problem that Had No Name   29
The Third Generation: Post-Sputnik Girls   32
The Fourth Generation: Generation X Smart Girls   33

Chapter 3. Smart Girls, Millennial Girls   37
What Does It Mean to Be a Girl in the New Millennium?   37
    The Bad News   38
    The Good News   42
Smart Girl Profile | Alyssa, age 14   45
In Her Own Words by Alyssa   46

Chapter 4. Eminent Women   49
Conditions of Eminence for Women   52
J. K. Rowling | Writer   55
Tina Fey | Award-Winning Actress, Writer, Producer,
    Comedienne   59
Jennifer Hudson | Award-Winning Vocalist and Actress   64
Malala Yousafzai | Pakistani Schoolgirl, Education Activist
    for Girls   67
Sheryl Sandberg | American Business Woman & Leader   71
Sonia Sotomayor | First Latina U.S. Supreme Court Justice   76
Margarethe Cammermeyer | Expert on Women's and
    LGBT Issues in the Military   82
Jane Goodall | Anthropologist   88

Chapter 5. What We Can Learn from Eminent Women's Lives   95
Loss of a Parent or Loved One   95
Early Interest in and Time Spent Learning   96
Connection to a Master Teacher   97
A Love of Solitude   97
Highly Developed Career Identity   98
Boundaries   99
Resistance to Stereotype Threat   100
Resistance to the Culture of Romance   100
Financial Independence   101
Egalitarian Relationships and Flexible Childrearing   101
Falling in Love with an Idea   102

Chapter 6. Smart Young Girls   **103**
  Early Signs   103
  Asynchrony   104
  Early Reading   105
  Smart Girl Profile | CJ, age 2   106
  When to Start School and Special Lessons   107
  First Friends   112
  Smart Girl Profile | Sidney, age 5   114
  The Princess Industrial Complex   114
  Preschool Years: What Little Bees Need   117

Chapter 7. Smart Girls: The Flowers That Bloom in the Spring   **119**
  In Schools   120
  The Worst Schools: Poverty, Violence, Despair   120
  Those Who Survive   121
  Average Schools   122
  The Best of the Best: Special Schools for Gifted Children   125
  What about Homeschooling?   127
  Home and Away—Busy as a Bee   132
  Girl Power and Its Products   133
  Alone Time   137
  Imaginative Play   138
  Nature   138
  The Friendship of Books   138

Chapter 8. The Adolescent Smart Girl   **141**
  The Change   141
  Middle School Malaise   144
  Talent Search to the Rescue   147
  Skipping High School   148
  Secondary School and Preparing for College   149
  Growing Identity and a Sense of Purpose   150
  The Role of Advanced Placement, International Baccalaureate,
    and Honors Programs   151
  Dual Enrollment   153
  Romance, Intimacy, and Sexuality   153
  Avoiding Danger Zones   157
  When Smart Girls Fail   159
    Tara, age 14   159
    Jenna, age 15   161

Planning for College—Or Alternatives   162
Academically Talented Girls   162
What about Women's Colleges?   165
Creatively Gifted Girls   166
Art and Design Colleges   166
Musical Conservatories   167
Technology   167
Writing Programs   168
Emotionally Intelligent Girls: Healers and Leaders   168
DIY Education, Gap Year, and World Wide Education   169
The Gap Year   170
Smart Girl Profile| Jasmine, age 15   172
In Her Own Words by Jasmine   173
Conclusion   174

**Chapter 9. Smart Women in College: Danger Zones and Paths
for Success   175**
A Paradoxical Combination of Characteristics   176
The Party Pathway   177
Smart Girl Profile | Nika, age 21   179
The Striver Pathway   180
Smart Girl Profile | Carlie, age 18   181
The Engaged Pathway   182
Smart Girl Profile | Katie, age 23   184
In Her Own Words by Katie   184
The Creative Pathway   185
Hope for the Future: A New Generation of Smart Young
    Women in STEM   186
What Is Being Done to Attract and Retain Women in STEM?   188
WiSE Leadership for Women   189
Smart Girl Profile |Anna, age 20   192
Smart Girl Profile | Sonia, age 21   193

**Chapter 10. Lean In or Opt Out? The Evolution of Adult Smart
Women   195**
20s: Full Steam Ahead   195
    And then, Marriage   196
Smart Women in Their 30s: Exhaustion and Extreme Jobs   199
    Leaving Science   199
    Innate Differences? Ridiculous!   200

Just Choices and Preferences? Hardly   201
The Home Front and the Support Needed   203
Growing Thorns in the Arts   203
Business, Politics, and Professions   205
Opting Out   207
Shame and Disillusionment vs. Opting In—With Support   207
The Mommy Wars   208
The Lucky Ones   210
40s: The Midlife Crisis and the Journey into the Self   211
Midlife Crisis   211
Dissatisfaction, Restlessness, and Spiritual Awakening   214
Smart Women in their 50s and 60s—Giftedness Will Have its Way   217
Entrepreneurship—Leaving the Organization   217
Smart Girl Profile | Sara, age 60   218
Smart Girl Profile | Tessa, age 51   218
Adapting, Creating New Narratives, Finding Meaning   219
Elderly Smart Women   221
Conclusion   223

Chapter 11. Twice-Exceptional Girls   **225**
Overlapping Profiles of Behaviors   225
Giftedness Masking Disability   226
Different Behaviors in Different Contexts   227
Learning about Twice-Exceptional Girls   227
Caution in Using Gifted-Specific Theories of Development   228
A Different Face of ADHD   229
Mood Disorders   231
Anxiety Disorders   234
Autism Spectrum Disorders   237
Getting Help for Twice-Exceptional Girls   237
Focus on the Giftedness or Talent   237
Read and Become Educated   238
Slow Down and Breathe   239

Chapter 12. Privilege, Power, and Talent: Minority Smart Girls   **241**
The Special Case of Race   243
African-American Smart Girls   243
Native American Smart Girls   246
Hispanic-American Smart Girls   247
Asian-American Smart Girls   250

Socioeconomic Status (SES) 253
Sexual Orientation 254
Attractiveness 255
The Power of Religion 257
The Geography of Opportunity: Urban, Rural, and
    Suburban Lives 259
The Importance of Social and Cultural Capital 260

Chapter 13. Passion: What Lights the Smart Girl's Fire? 263
Is Passion Just Task Commitment? 264
Is Passion Explained by Overexcitabilities Theory? 264
Is It Mindset? 266
Is It Grit? 269
Is It Flow? 270
In Love with an Idea 271
Self-Actualization and Optimal Development 273

**Chapter 14. A New Model of Talent Development for Smart
    Girls and Women** 279
Foundations 280
    Demographics and Distance from Privilege 280
    Abilities + Personality + Values 281
    Love of an Idea: Curiosity, Engagement, Passion, Vocation 283
Filters 284
    Legal Rights 284
    Gender Role and Gender Relations 284
    Social and Cultural Capital 285
    Educational and Career Opportunities 286
    Talent Domain 287
Sphere 287
    Personal 287
    Public 289

**Chapter 15. Suggestions to Guide Gifted Girls and Women
    toward Optimal Development** 291
For Parents | The Preschool Years 291
Kindergarten through Fifth grade 293
Middle School 294
Older Adolescence 296
College Years 298

Advice for Smart Girls in Elementary and Middle School   299
Advice for Smart Teens   300
Advice for College and Graduate School Women   303
Adult Smart Women   306
Recommendations for Professionals who Work with
     Gifted Women   308

Chapter 16. Conclusion   311
First, We Have to Find Them   312
We Need to Challenge Them   313
We Need to Guide Them   313
We Need to Love Them   314
We Need to Let Them Alone   314

References   317

Endnotes   337

Index   351

About the Authors   367

Table of Figures

Figure 1.1. Beehive of Smart Girls   17

Figure 14.1. A Model of Talent Development for Smart Girls
and Women   280

Foreword

From the time I was very young, I felt different, but I always had some understanding of why and I've always had places I *do* fit. Even though I'm not a stellar student, I've always been able to enjoy learning. I've always had ways to keep myself engaged and opportunities to discover new people, places, things, and ideas. What was missing for quite some time was the spark, the accident that got me to walk out of my comfort zone and onto the uncharted path.

For those who don't know me, I'm a 12-year-old girl, writer, speaker, and activist. If someone had told me a year ago that I would have thousands of readers, invitations to speak at events, and national media attention, I never would have believed them.

I don't match the mental picture many people have of what a "smart girl" is supposed to be like. I like fashion and pop culture. You're far more likely to find me watching a reality show than a documentary. I never considered myself to be a smart girl either. I always knew I was different, but I wasn't *that* girl. Being that girl involved expectations that I could never live up to. Even if I did manage to meet some of the expectations, it would only lead to more expectations I could never meet.

I remember being in preschool and being met with blank stares from the other kids when they couldn't understand my games. I don't remember learning how to read, but my first memories of reading involved bringing a book with me somewhere and someone inevitably asking, "Are you *reading* that?" When I would talk to people, even when I thought I was just talking normally, I would be met with the reaction, "WOW!"

I learned to be quiet. I didn't want to stand out. Standing out meant people would expect me to be *that* girl. My perfectionism kept me from thinking much of anything I ever did was good enough. Things never met the expectations I had of how they were supposed to be. I thought of my life in terms of things I would do "someday" at some undetermined point in the future.

My parents realized very early that I was not typical and sought information to help me. Most importantly, they always shared this information with me. I always knew why I felt out of place and seemed to experience and think about things differently. I knew what options I had in terms of my education.

Homeschooling has made it possible for me to have a lot of freedom to learn and experience the world. I've taken formal courses and done independent study, and this has enabled me to discover how I learn and what works and doesn't work for me. I've always had input into planning my education, and almost total control now that I'm older. This has made me feel more connected to and invested in what I'm doing.

Having places like Geeksboro, a local café with events like board game night and movie nights, to hang out at and participating in community theater has allowed me to interact with a wide variety of people and make friends across age barriers. Organizations like Davidson Young Scholars have enabled me to meet people my age who are also extremely gifted.

One day, I decided to join some friends in a protest against a museum in Jacksonville, Florida, that refused to renew the family membership because the family was a same-sex couple. I had been following a writer who was covering the events as they unfolded and saw how he used his writing to get others involved. Equality is an issue I am passionate about and I wondered if people would be interested in the story from my point of view. I wrote the first thing I ever shared outside of my family and close friends, "What I Did On My Summer Vacation," put it out through social media, and thousands of people liked and shared it. I decided I would keep going. I started paying more attention to what was going on around me, finding myself in the issues, and using my voice.

I accidentally discovered an outlet for me to be me. I've always liked to write, but never thought about writing about politics or social issues. My rebellious, humorous, sarcastic, creative, curious nature is something that is an asset in my work instead of being a detriment as it would in many classrooms. When I discover one fact, it leads me to want to find another, then another. Then I get to make connections, not only between facts but between issues and pop culture, between people, and between issues and ways to take action. Many of those characteristics of gifted children you read about are things I get to use on a daily basis.

Taking the first step down that unmapped path was the best decision I ever made. Not only have I been able to inspire and make a difference in the lives of others, I've made a difference in my own life. Sometimes, the biggest obstacles in our path are the ones we place there ourselves. Over the last year, I've learned many things that can't be found in a textbook or a lesson plan.

As I continue on my journey, I continue to meet other travelers along the path. My colleagues and mentors treat me as an equal and are the best teachers I've ever had. We celebrate our successes together and we're there for each other when we're feeling frustrated, stuck, or defeated. I've made so many friends who share my passions and have shared their passions with me. Most importantly, I've come to understand the power in ordinary people coming together to make a difference and the impact this can have.

I've learned that when other people have expectations, I'm not obligated to live up to them. I can set my own goals and I'm the one who is responsible for meeting them. I've learned that if I fail, even in front of thousands of people, I'm still going to wake up the next morning. When I look at other people's work, now I think of it in terms of how I can improve and what I can learn instead of focusing on feeling inferior. I've learned how to deal with attention and accept it as something that I can use to bring focus to ideas.

I don't have to be *that* girl. Being *this* girl is not only enough, it's exactly who I'm supposed to be in this moment. I've learned that the journey is even more important than the destination and that if you're brave enough to take that first step, sometimes the path leads to places you never imagined.

I have seen a great deal of myself in this book, from the characteristics of smart girls to my early experiences and things that have helped me along the way. I've also had the opportunity to learn about the experiences of women who have traveled further along the path than I have. It's empowering to know that so many other women have struggled in the same ways I've struggled and that there are so many options for me as I continue to grow and change.

To educators reading this book, I know many of you are invested in providing all you can to your gifted students. I know that many times, you are limited by things outside of your control in what you can offer. It is my hope that you will take the information and shared experiences here and use them to help the gifted girls you encounter learn to be comfortable with and confident in who they are. Providing the most advanced work isn't always as important as providing the right kind of work to help your students discover their own path.

To parents, I understand that many of you are struggling alongside your gifted girls. My parents have been on their own journey in their efforts to support me as I grow. I hope that you will give your daughters the opportunity to read this book or share with them what you learn in ways appropriate for their stage of development. Even if they appear as though the information isn't having an impact, it is.

Most importantly, to other smart girls reading this book, yes—you *are* a smart girl. You don't have to be *that* girl, or *this* girl, or anything other than *you*. You are exactly who you are supposed to be in this moment. You are enough. Break out of your comfort zone and allow the great accidents of life to happen to you. When you feel like you don't fit in anywhere, remember that there are places you do fit. Sometimes, you just have to keep looking or keep traveling alone for just a little while until you reach your next oasis. Never stop looking for those opportunities that allow you to be you. When you have a crazy idea that doesn't work out quite as you expected, don't quit. The next crazy idea that works out in unexpected ways might just take you in directions you never dreamed possible.

"Who is that girl I see, staring straight back at me?" This question is central to the story of Mulan, a uniquely clever girl who felt out of place but who discovered her inner strength despite all odds. We have to allow our reflections to show who we are inside and not worry about living up to the mental pictures of others. Our collective journey is one that involves giving others the opportunity to discover their own reflection. As we move forward together through the 21st century, we can look into the unknown not with fear but with hope, confidence, and excitement because the women who have come before us have made our path just a little bit easier to travel.

Now it's our turn.

Madison Kimrey
http://functionalhumanbeing.blogspot.com/

Preface

On an early November morning in a large St. Louis hotel conference room, a crowd was already beginning to gather. Six former classmates and I from the city's Sputnik-era gifted school stepped up to the dais. We were there to talk about our education, our careers, and our families. At 59 years old, we all had vivid memories of the extraordinary full-time gifted education program that had shaped our lives.

We were there to try to explain what happened to us and other Post-Sputnik gifted kids. After the Russians sent the first satellite into space, the United States was swept with the fear that we would not be able to win the space race unless we could train our children with the same academic rigor as the Russian children had in their schools. In defense of the nation, gifted education was suddenly awash in funding. Model schools like ours sprung up around the United States. At nine years old, I took the Stanford-Binet intelligence test. I remember vividly the grey-haired lady, the odd puzzles, and the many challenging questions. A letter came a few months later to my house, telling my parents I had been selected to attend the Major Learning Classes at a new school far away, in the nice part of St. Louis. I lived in a blue-collar neighborhood between Irish Dogtown and the Italian Hill and went to an old school that smelled like baloney and tennis shoes. Only one other girl I knew was selected from my neighborhood—Big Mary. She was tall, beautiful, brilliant, and mean. I was proud to be selected, but terrified that the rest of my childhood would be spent standing on the bus stop and going to school with Big Mary.

We were told on the first day that we would need to work harder in school than we had ever worked before. We would have four hours of home-work every night. Our teacher, Miss Marcus, said we would learn math and science at an accelerated pace, so that by high school we would be doing college level work. We would learn to speak French fluently because it was the language of civilization. We would learn speed reading, so that we could read all the nation's newspapers before breakfast, like President Kennedy. We would learn to appreciate the great works of art and music.

For me, a strange, tangle-haired little girl who had spent all her recesses, after school hours, and summers reading, this was like being invited to the best party in the world—a never ending feast of learning. Four hours of homework? In science, math, literature, French, and art? Bring it on!

My teacher continued. "Why do you think we are doing all of this for you children?" she asked us. Full stop. Silence. Then, in a whisper, she said, "Because right now the Russians and Chinese are training their children to take over the free world. And it's your job to stop them. You children are our hope and our dream of the future. You are the Leaders of Tomorrow."

We did indeed have an extraordinary education, as well as an intro-duction to the kind of social and cultural knowledge that would propel us from the working class to the upper middle class. I would have a chance to have a different life from the girls in my neighborhood who got pregnant at 16 and went to work in the donut shops and Dairy Queens of South St. Louis. Unfortunately, being told that we were the Leaders of Tomorrow was the extent of our career guidance. By 17, my mind was full of the knowledge of Western civilization, but nobody told me what to do with it. I received a full scholarship to Bryn Mawr College, but all I knew about it was that it was a girls' college, and I thought it might be too much like Catholic school. So I chose the University of Missouri, where my boyfriend was going, and muddled along changing majors (and boyfriends) every six months and specializing in living fully in the 60s. I worked in a communal crisis center, counseling people on bad LSD trips, in trouble with the draft, or in need of birth control information. The psychology professors who dropped in to study us (or enjoy the ambiance of the commune) encouraged me to go to graduate school in psychology. And so began my resentful, lackluster journey through narrow boredom of graduate school and into a sad little non-tenure track academic position in Nebraska, where my husband had a real professor job.

Ten years after graduation, I grudgingly decided to go to my high school reunion to see the people I hadn't seen in all those years. I assumed they were all astronauts, senators, and biochemists curing cancer. They were not. The men were succeeding in exactly the professions they had intended; they were doctors, lawyers, accountants, business leaders, scientists, and engineers. The women were mostly homemakers, teachers, and nurses, with a few professionals. I wouldn't have given much thought to the strangeness of finding all those brilliant women—the ones who sat in the smart row of desks while I was consigned to the almost-dumb row—leading such ordinary lives.

I was cornered in the bar, however, by Big Mary, who was still big, beautiful, and scary. "You're a psychology professor, huh? So at this Harvard of the prairie where you work, do you do research?" I mumbled something about vocational guidance, counseling process, blah, blah, blah—and she stopped me cold with a glare. "So why don't you do some real research? Why don't you find out why we're not the Leaders of Tomorrow?" I always did what Big Mary told me to do, and this time was no exception. Somehow, something was awakening in me, something that had slept for years, a taunting curiosity, a taste of the hunger for knowledge that had driven me as a child to read, read, read. I wanted to know the answer to her question. I wanted to know why we women weren't the Leaders of Tomorrow.

Since that day, I have followed that question. I wrote the first *Smart Girls, Gifted Women* in a wild rush toward some kind of truth about gender and genius. *Smart Boys* eventually followed. That led me into research on intelligence, personality, creativity, achievement, and self-actualization—as well as into the other half of the story of human potential: privilege, power, equity, and justice. I decided to follow up on the smart girls in my class after our 10th reunion—the first revision of *Smart Girls*. The search for an understanding of the fate of the promising children, the future Leaders of Tomorrow, became the idea with which I fell in love, and the passion that has carried me through in many times of private and professional upheaval.

So there we were, at our 20th reunion, men and women with spreading waists, graying hair, and wry smiles, talking to educators about our education as little kids. We talked about how lucky we had been, as blue-collar kids, to have access to the kind of school where we could be challenged by tough and caring teachers; where we went to the symphony, on architecture tours, and to the planetarium and the zoo for hands-on science lessons. We marveled at the way the daily, dreaded rapid reading lessons had actually made us speed readers, and how the French lessons, from an early age, had opened up a world of languages. We mused about the twists and turns our lives had taken—goals achieved as well as dreams deferred. I reviewed the findings of the first edition of *Smart Girls* and of *Smart Boys,* asking, "Did we fulfill the expectations of our special designation as gifted?" That we had shared a remarkable education we were sure of; what we were uncertain about was whether we had, indeed, become the Leaders of Tomorrow that our teachers had told us we would become. Looking at my clever, kindly classmates telling about careers composed of choice and chance, of loves lost and found, and lives of thoughtful service, it was apparent that we had all, at the very least, learned to be the leaders of ourselves.

After the presentation, the five women went to lunch at a nearby restaurant to catch up on what was for some of us, the last 40 years. From the first minute, we were weaving our stories together. We roared at memories of our teachers trying to contain the bursting imaginations of 30 gifted kids who were bent on staging Sherlock Holmes in French, trying to move the clock hands toward recess psychically, and writing a racy novel about class romances. We exclaimed with joy or shed tears on learning about a sudden divorce, a career exploding into success, an unexpected pregnancy, a devastating depression.

Finally, we talked about the first book, *Smart Girls*. Jeri said, "I was so mad at you when I read it. I was a homemaker at the time, and I felt so put down when you quoted research about gifted women being happier when they had a career. Later, though, when I got divorced and gradually worked up to my job as a vice president of marketing, I realized—well, I *am* happier now that I am so challenged every day." Sharon added, "I didn't really relate to the book that much because I went on thinking I wasn't really all that gifted. Nobody really knew about the special school, and I just went underground into an ordinary life. Then I had two amazing, gifted daughters. And somehow, seeing how awful their education was compared to mine made me realize how important it is to do something—something special—to keep my girls' dreams alive."

We noticed that the shadows of the tall buildings outside had now engulfed the street. A chilly, dark November evening had fallen around us and we discovered that we had talked all day. Only Mary had been somewhat quiet—until now, at the end, when she carefully and quietly began to speak. This majestic woman whom we called Big Mary in awe and fear wanted to know if I had found any answers.

The answer I found could be summed up like this. We were too well adjusted for our own good. We were so smart that we applied our intelligence only to those paths that were deemed socially acceptable for women; we used our brains to fit in, rather than to lead. Mary who had, perhaps, struggled the hardest against the barriers—little family encouragement, early marriage and difficult divorce, and poverty—had found meaning in becoming an advocate for gifted children and a leader in the state National Organization for Women. She said, "It was all true. And what you said in that book is as important now as it was then. But now you need to write another book—about *this* generation of gifted girls." So here it is, Mary. A third book. Not a revision, but a totally new book, for a totally new generation of smart girls.

—Barbara Kerr

A Note from Robyn

Since Barbara's friend Mary was so influential in Barbara's work, I decided to write this letter to Mary. I'd like for her to know the influence she has had on my life and on the next generation of smart girls, too.

Dear Mary,

You should know that you have a rare gift—not for telling Barbara what to do (lots of people try to do that!), but for inspiring her to explore what has become a lifetime of research. Since I came to the party late, I'll make my introductions here.

I was born in 1970—a year of love-ins, sit-ins, riots, the Black Panthers, Abbey Hoffman and the Chicago Seven. Remember when Janice Joplin died, the Beatles broke up, and four Kent State students were killed? I was just a baby.

My babysitters were hippie homecoming queens. The adults in my life discussed "Tricky Dick" Nixon over dinner. And by the time the war in Vietnam ended, I had memorized my multiplication tables and taught myself the American Sign Language alphabet. I wanted to be a doctor when I grew up. And someday write a book.

I was 10 in 1980 when the Cold War, the Iran hostage crisis, Reaganomics, and a distant threat of nuclear crisis underpinned all of life. Yet I was captivated by the women's movement. In social studies class, I got into a fight with the boys who said that Sandra Day O'Connor didn't belong in the U.S. Supreme Court, and later that year I wrote about the Equal Rights Amendment. Thanks in part to my parents' good humor, I wore a T-shirt emblazoned with an iron-on decal that established, "Anything boys can do, girls can do better." (Mary, you of all people, might be able to imagine the boats I rocked.)

When I was growing up, there was little mention of giftedness. Nonetheless, in sixth grade I met with the school psychologist who administered an IQ test. Afterwards, I continued as I always had: reading books beyond my grade level and being teased by my friends for getting good grades. I knew that hard work was important, but struggled to understand why writing, reading, and English didn't feel like hard work. On the other hand, math felt like very hard work. I began to think that I must be lazy since my efforts to study weren't paying off (or maybe I just got bored). But in the early 1980s, girls' performance in science and math had become the focus of school interventions, which was good for me. It turned out that I loved the scientific method. Being in the lab amid microscopes, flasks, and chemicals felt like home, a place I could relax, focus, and explore. In seventh grade, I won 3rd place in the county science fair. Science and research were my constant focus during high school.

Growing up in South Dakota left me both hungry for broader perspectives and vaguely apologetic for having grown up in a place that seemed so far removed from both coasts—not just from radical movements but also from culture, opportunity, and ideas. During my junior year of high school, I ordered a subscription to *Vanity Fair* and spent hours perusing the pages, feeling at once sophisticated and naïve as I realized how little of the content I could truly connect with. That year, I continued with the piano lessons I'd started as a child and added creative writing and photography to my class schedule. I began to understand myself as a creative person.

I graduated third in my high school class and had all the markings of one of the high-achieving young women Barbara wrote about in the first *Smart Girls.* Though I longed to go to college in California, I wound up with a basketball and academic scholarship at a private Catholic women's college in Omaha, Nebraska, where I began studying biology and pre-med.

My life spun off course just after starting college. In the first semester of freshman year, I'd fallen in love with a boy from my hometown; my mom and dad separated after 20 years of marriage; and I contracted Epstein-Barr virus, which began a long bout of mononucleosis. The adjustment to college life alone would have been enough to create minor symptoms of depression and anxiety. The physical illness, combined with psychosocial stressors, led to what would become years of undiagnosed, at times debilitating, depression, anxiety, and panic.

I was 500 miles from home, and no one who knew me grasped what was happening. I struggled to get out of bed so that I could attend classes. There were times when the panic was so extreme that I'd have to call my dad, who was able to help me regain a momentary sense of calm. I began to question my ability to achieve my goals. I thought I was dumb. I thought I was lazy. My academic performance was uneven at best: I failed French and communications, got Cs in calculus, and As in psychology. I watched my younger sisters excel in their own educations, and I decided that perhaps I'd gone as far as I could. I assumed that I'd been something of a trailblazer, the big sister whose job was to make in-roads for her siblings, but for whom professional success would always be elusive, just out of reach. I dropped out of college.

I did the only thing I could think to do. I got married and moved to Kansas with my new husband, a nice young man from South Dakota who'd become an engineer. After 18 months, the call of education became too strong to ignore, even if my shaken confidence took a bit longer to return. I enrolled at the University of Kansas, graduated with a degree in biology, and took the MCAT. I applied to medical school (only one school!) but wasn't accepted. Without a mentor to encourage me, I didn't know that it was common for students to reapply. Disappointed but not discouraged, I found work as a microbiologist and technical writer, but quickly became depressed again; the pressure was high, the staff introverted, and the laboratories stark.

Soon, my career began to redirect itself. In 1997, I began volunteering for a non-profit organization called Girls to Women, which provided mentoring in STEM fields—science, technology, engineering, and math—to middle school girls. The combination of science and mentoring was perfect for my social nature and my investigative interests. I felt connected and happy for the first time in years. Before long, I left the lab and went to work in the pharmaceutical industry as a medical writer. With only a Bachelor's degree, I realized that to become a leader—at least as a scientist—I would need more education. I began to think about a Ph.D. But—God!—the idea of being in a lab again was frightening to me.

Here's the thing, Mary. Psychology had always been a whisper in my ear—the first time the idea of becoming a psychologist occurred to me, I was standing in front of a statue of the blessed Virgin on the campus of the Catholic women's college I attended. At the time, I was hell-bent on ignoring any and all intuitive advice. By the time I was in my late 20s, although I liked science, I realized that I found microbiology, molecular biology, and even pharmaceutical research to be both stressful and generally unfulfilling. In my heart, I knew I was meant for greater things than working in a cubicle and writing reports that no one would ever read. But I had no real idea what that greater thing might be.

Then it happened. My marriage of seven years fell apart—in some ways, a great failure on my part. I was 30 and divorced. Almost at once I began a spiritual transformation, as well as an educational journey, that would last another full seven years. While I was in graduate school in psychology, I studied eastern philosophy, Native American spirituality, and optimal human development in addition to my courses in clinical psychology, research, and statistics. Somehow, as I found balance between science and spirit, between intellect and intuition, I found my place in the world.

Meeting Barbara during the third year of my Ph.D. program was the beginning of what I hope will be a lifelong collaboration—an ongoing exchange of thoughtful inquiry, sardonic banter, and at its core, a heartfelt friendship. I am lucky, Mary, because Barbara taught me the most important thing of all, which is to fall in love with an idea.

After I graduated from the University of Kansas and finished my post-doctoral residency at the University of Missouri, I moved to Arizona for love and work, which is what Freud says healthy life is all about, anyway. My work—to find, gather, guide, and empower talented girls and women—has developed into something far greater than I ever thought possible.

Mary, you asked for a book about this generation of smart girls, and I have some great stories for you. For the past eight years, I've done little else besides explore and understand the lives of talented 21st century girls and women, and I can't wait to tell you what we've discovered.

—Robyn McKay

Acknowledgments

I want to thank all the smart girls and women who have participated in the research projects that inform this book. I was inspired to write this new book by the girls, young women, and fellow project directors of the National Science Foundation gender equity projects, the young creative women of Project CLEOS, the Makers at the Lawrence Creates Makerspace, and of course, my classmates from the Southwest High School Class of 1969. Mary, Joanie, Debbie—you gave me the final push I needed to write about a new generation of smart girls. Robyn, dear co-author, our conversations on the porch swing at Captain's Creek will be forever in my heart, and this book will always remind me of that summer feeling. Thanks to Karen Multon for our many collaborations and for her faith in me; to my colleagues who brought me to the University of Kansas; and to the Del and Barbara Williamson whose Williamson Family endowment supported my academic position and my research. I am grateful to my school and university for the sabbatical fellowship that allowed me time to write during the spring of 2013. Thanks to Jim Webb, Janet Gore, and the whole staff of the Great Potential Press for bringing this book to fruition, prodding me when necessary, and always attending to making it the best it could be. Great Potential Press kept the three editions of *Smart Girls* on bookshelves for over 25 years, and for this I am very grateful. A completely new book on smart girls was long overdue!

My sisters, Cindy Kerr and Beverly Schaefer, are an inspiration to me through the ways they have lived their beliefs through healing and service to others, as is my 91-year-old Mom who loves her smart girls. The memory of my Dad, who taught me to love science, focuses me on the work of interpreting research so that others can benefit from it. My daughter Grace Claiborn, a film maker, and son Sam Claiborn, a video game executive, and my daughter-in-law Helene Grotans, music educator, are living their dreams. Their father Chuck and I tried to raise them to fall in love with ideas and

I believe they have each found their idea to love. They and my wonderful step-kids, Elizabeth, Nathan, and Sarah Billings, and their sweet Nora, have generously, and sometimes unwittingly, provided me with stories and anecdotes that enlivened this book! My deepest thanks go to Dee Ann and David Alvarez and Roseann Weiss, who pick me up when I fall down, whether from a horse or ridiculously high hopes. And finally, every day of writing and thinking here on the farm at Captain's Creek wouldn't be possible without the love and support of my husband, Barry Billings, man of the Western plains, front porch philosopher, and feminist. It was he, who through his lifetime of work with the powerless among us, fully awakened my understanding of how privilege, gender, and talent are inextricably interwoven.

—Barbara Kerr

Thank you to Barbara Kerr. My life changed the moment you walked into it. Also a fond thank you goes to Karen Multon for your match-making wisdom. To Tom Krieshok, my graduate school advisor, for your foresight to see what I needed in my own career development when I couldn't. To Joel Hutchinson for bringing me to Arizona State University and for saying *yes* to as many of my ideas as you possibly could. To my ASU Gifted Education family— Sanford Cohn, Kimberly Lansdowne, Gary and Jeannie Herberger, and Dina Brulles, thank you for the gift of co-creating the Herberger Academy. To the Herberger Academy smart girls and smart boys—I'm so proud of you and happy for whom you are becoming. A special thank you goes to Jim Webb and the team at Great Potential Press for publishing *Smart Girls in the 21st Century*. And finally, to my mom and dad, my sisters, Jennie and Kimmie, and my brother Jeremy—thank you for creating a positive, loving, happy family so that I could grow into myself.

—Robyn McKay

CHAPTER 1

Smart + Girl: A Beehive of Definitions of Intelligence

What does it mean to be smart? When you think of a smart person, what associations and images come to mind? For most of us, smartness is associated with words like giftedness, talent, genius, brilliance, high ability, and intelligence. Across most cultures today, when people are asked to imagine a smart person, a genius, or a brilliant individual, the image that comes to mind is most often an adult male—a scientist in a lab coat, a nerdy tech entrepreneur, a musician with frowzy hair, or a paint smattered artist throwing color upon a canvas. For most of the history of psychology, genius has meant men achieving the highest honors in activities that are highly valued by other men.

Clearly, the definition of high ability—giftedness—has been colored by ideas of gender, race, and culture. Early studies of genius were studies of eminent men, usually European or American white men, paralleling the appearance in literature of the stereotypes so well known to all of us.

From the beginning of the 20th century until the 1960s, there was one dominant paradigm of giftedness: giftedness equals high IQ. With the proper education, it was thought, all gifted men would have potential for eminence. But by the 1960s, it was clear that high intelligence alone was no guarantee of eminence, even for the most brilliant men. In addition, in the era of struggle for civil rights, the narrow definition of giftedness that seemed to favor white, wealthy, well-educated students was called into question. The need for a broader, "defensible" definition of giftedness led to the plethora of methods of identification in schools and eventually to the current situation, where the definition of *gifted* is so conflicted as to be almost meaningless. In his powerful book, *Ungifted, Intelligence Redefined,* Scott Barry Kaufman describes how the rigid definitions, labels, and conflicted meanings of gift-edness have real consequences in children's lives.[1] A reading disorder and auditory problems landed Kaufman himself in special education as a child, where his rapid learning ability and profound curiosity about the world went unnoticed. Only later, with good fortune, did he discover his own very substantial abilities.

We believe that, similarly, there are smart girls in every classroom whose capacity and desire to learn are overlooked and go unnoticed, simply because they don't fit their society's image—and their particular school's definition—of giftedness. This book will show how too many girls' abilities and passion for learning are ignored.

It will also show how even those privileged, smart girls who are lucky enough to be labeled gifted and given the challenges they need can be derailed from their dreams by their society's image of femininity and what a girl should be.

Let's review some of those conflicting ideas about what it means to be smart.

Smart is...

High Intelligence

Educators in the early 20th century wanted to know if there was a way of predicting which children might become the geniuses that move society forward. Scholars honed in on the idea of intelligence, defined as the ability to learn rapidly and to reason well, as the precursor to outstand-ing performance. In 1905 in Europe, Alfred Binet and Theodore Simon developed an intelligence test for identifying "mental defectives." In 1921, a professor at Stanford University named Lewis Terman decided to use the Stanford Revision of the Binet-Simon Scale as an intelligence test for iden-tifying genius, which he also called giftedness.[2] Terman made the decision, remarkable for its time, to study both boys and girls, and he even deliberately attempted to create a test that was not sex-biased by excluding items that differentiated between boys and girls. Not only did he develop an intelligence test on the assumption that both boys and girls could be intelligent, but he also asked mostly female teachers to nominate potential students to take the test and he hired female graduate students—like Florence Goodenough and Catharine Cox who later became psychologists—to administer those tests.[3]

Many social scientists have taken Terman to task for the fact that the original normative group for that test—and many other intelligence tests that followed—were primarily white, middle class, California children. Like most of the scholars of his day, Terman was influenced by eugenics, which held that white people were superior to all other races. Why is it that Terman decided to give the females in his sample a relatively fair opportunity to demonstrate their intellectual abilities in a time when females, like non-white people, were generally considered to have inferior mental ability? Was it the fact that he was surrounded by brilliant women colleagues in one of the first states to allow women to enroll in graduate education? Was it the increasing visibility of strong, achieving women in the American West? The answer will probably never be known. The result, however, was that from the beginning of the study of giftedness, with his sample of 1,528 California children, girls were included.

Without Terman's study that has followed these gifted children throughout their lives in the 20th century, we would know much less about the development of intelligence in girls. If his original study had been as fair to people of cultures that differed from his own—e.g. Hispanic, Native American, African American, Asian—we would have a more complete picture of the lives of girls who are smart but also distant from privilege and power. For that information, we have had to wait most of the rest of the 20th century.

Following Terman's study, however, intelligence became one of the most important ideas of the field of psychology, with thousands of scholars studying the concept, devising measures, and applying their findings to education, work, life satisfaction, and health.[4] Intelligence turned out to be a powerful notion, indeed, because it was able to predict school achievement, success at work, and even health outcomes for most people. Intelligence tests began to be used to select men and women for various military positions, for special educational opportunities, and for high-level positions in business and industry. Intelligence was powerful as a concept because it could be shown to be a single, general trait that affected all human achievement.

No matter how many tests and subtests were developed in different ability domains, such as verbal, mathematical, spatial-visual, the scores tended to correlate with one another; that is, people who are very quick to learn and able to reason well tend to achieve high scores across tests in different intellectual ability areas. In addition, it was shown that students selected by strong intelligence test scores benefited from academic acceleration and that gifted students were often capable of learning much higher level material than was previously thought, if they were allowed to proceed at a rapid pace.[5] Accelerated programs for gifted students proliferated throughout the U.S.

during the Sputnik-era of the late 50s and early 60s, as society raced to catch up in math and science with its Cold War rivals.

Throughout the 20th century, intelligence tests held the supreme position as the major identifier of giftedness, and few challenges were made to their effectiveness or generality. The earliest concerns were voiced by scholars who contended that intelligence could be considered as many different abilities rather than one. In the 1930s, the early psychologist Raymond Cattell made a case for both fluid intelligence—an ability to solve novel, open-ended problems—and crystallized intelligence—an ability to use knowledge and skills that one has already acquired; other psychologists subsequently used the statistical technique of factor analysis to demonstrate that there were specialized areas of intelligence, rather than simply a general one.

Creativity

The concept of creativity, promoted by E. Paul Torrance opened up the possibility that something else contributed to extraordinary achievement besides rapid learning and efficient problem-solving.[6] That something else was creativity—the ability to produce novel, original, and appropriate solutions to problems. Most people who achieve eminence in their field are both intelligent and creative, because they come up with new and very useful ideas. In society as well as in psychology, creativity has been the poor step-sister of intelligence. Although fascinating in its many faces from art to invention, creativity was considered to be too complex and unpredictable to be measured, and creative people have often been looked upon as too nonconforming and unusual to be productive members of society—that is, until they produce something of value.

Educator E. Paul Torrance changed this by not only championing creativity, but also by developing the first measure of what he termed *divergent thinking*, the intellectual cornerstone of creative ability.[7] Torrance claimed that creativity was a better predictor of eminence than intelligence, and he began a long term program similar to Terman's to track the lives of divergent thinkers. Eventually, it became clear that, although intelligence and creativity were not the same, they were overlapping abilities; some people were very intelligent but not particularly creative, and other people were both intelligent and creative. Like Terman, Torrance believed that both boys and girls had the potential for creative productivity, but he was also interested in creativity as it emerged in cultures other than the dominant, white culture. Torrance's work broadened the idea of giftedness to include those girls who were not necessarily high achievers in all academic areas, but whose achievement was in creative areas such as arts, design, writing, and music. He also opened the door to idea that giftedness could be found in all cultures.

Intelligence, Creativity, Task Commitment, and More

Torrance's work had a strong impact on gifted education because it was clear by the 1970s that gifted education programs based on intelligence testing alone were primarily serving white, privileged children. The criticism of intelligence testing and academic tracking reached a crescendo, and at the federal level the quest for equal opportunity led to a search for broader definitions of giftedness. The U.S. Office of Gifted Education, following the Marland Report of 1972, added creativity, leadership, and artistic ability to academic ability as important signs of giftedness.[8] The Marland Report definition of gifted was adopted by many states, and programs for gifted students sprung up across the country as schools tried to provide services for this group of students. What this meant for girls was that giftedness now included many abilities that girls receive encouragement in developing, such as aesthetic abilities and interpersonal skills.

The new emphasis on equity also encouraged research on "culture-fair" intelligence testing. And although the goal proved elusive, many new tests and adaptations of old tests appeared in the 1980s, such as the Raven Progressive Matrices, which claimed to measure fluid intelligence, or abstract reasoning, rather than crystallized intelligence, which was assumed to be based more on experience within one's culture.[9] The development of these new tests signaled a change in attitudes toward children of nonwhite, lower socioeconomic (SES) backgrounds so that educators were more aware and more motivated to search for talent among these populations. This, too, was a step forward for bright girls.

A new development in the 1980s and 1990s, however, had a negative impact on both smart boys and smart girls. Throughout the U.S., gifted education programs were de-funded and dismantled because of their association with tracking poor, nonwhite students into less challenging education programs. Educators and the general public were led to believe that *gifted* was a dirty word, with links to racism and the perpetuation of an underclass. Acceleration, the main educational intervention for gifted students, was also decried, even though critics were never able to show any negative results.[10]

It is extraordinary how pervasive the negative attitudes toward giftedness became, and along with the negativity came conflicts in every school district about what was to be done with children who demonstrated high intellectual ability. Often the response was to simply ignore smart children, to place them in the regular classroom, and to resist any calls for extra challenge or support by parents of bright children. Many educators tried to make the idea of giftedness more palatable to the public and defensible to policy-makers by broadening the definition and creating more flexible programs that involved *enrichment*—extending and expanding what was going on in the regular classroom—rather than acceleration. The range of students who could benefit from enrichment was much wider— nearly all of those students of above average intelligence who also showed creativity and "task commitment."

Joseph Renzulli and Sally Reis, the leading proponents of this model, created a school-wide enrichment model that soon spread throughout the U.S. and to many parts of the world.[11] (It should be noted that many countries, including England and Germany, however, retained some form of tracking.) Because these enrichment programs seldom involved acceleration of very rapid learners and often amounted to only a few hours a week with intellectual peers, both boys and girls with extremely high intelligence and academic abilities were left with little talent development.

By the mid-1980s, the only U.S. funding for gifted education, federal grants through the Jacob Javits Gifted and Talented Students Education Program, would provide support only for gifted education research and interventions that focused on underserved populations, and many other Western countries had similar restrictions on their funding. It is curious that despite three decades of focusing public funding on underserved populations, the image of giftedness and gifted education continued to be linked to privilege in the minds of most policy-makers, educators, and the general public. Nevertheless, these efforts to change the face of giftedness by showing that intelligence, creativity, and leadership emerge in all cultures and all strata of society may have improved the lives of many bright, less privileged children who might have been otherwise overlooked. Sadly, however, these were small waves in an ocean of resentment toward gifted children and gifted education, and even today gifted education programs that happen to enroll mostly white students receive scathing comments in the press.

What about the "other stuff"? Nobody really knew how to measure some of the other characteristics in the broader definition, like leadership and artistic ability; so checklists, portfolios, and a wide variety of procedures were used by schools attempting to identify smart kids according to the U.S. Department of Education definition. This resulted in such an astounding proliferation of methods that it was difficult to say what anybody meant by *gifted* without checking a particular school's approach. Many school administrators just threw up their hands and opted for the most minimal arrangements that they could get away with.

Precocious Math or Verbal Abilities

If the schools were ignoring bright children, the solution it seemed, at least to psychologist Julian Stanley at Johns Hopkins University, was to create university-based programs for gifted children. To return to the idea that intelligent children needed to be identified early and accelerated, Stanley and his colleagues developed the idea of *out-of-level* testing. They used the SAT, normally only given to high school students, to identify gifted students in seventh grade who could benefit from college-level courses. He and Camilla Benbow went on to establish programs for mathematically and verbally precocious youth that soon spread throughout the U.S. and eventually internationally.

The creation of university-based talent search programs, however, was somewhat of a mixed blessing for smart girls. These programs, which began at Johns Hopkins University and spread to seven other talent search regions, promoted the use of the SAT college admissions tests with seventh graders to identify youth who were already performing at the level of high school seniors. Although both the verbal and the mathematics tests were given, most of the emphasis was upon the high-scoring students in math, for whom the creation of linear, highly accelerated math curricula was simpler than the creation of accelerated verbal programs.

Sadly, for smart girls, the majority of the research publications, as well as the popular media, noted the predominance of males at the upper end of math scores and took this as evidence of a possible male superiority in mathematics. This is a finding which, to this day, has been misinterpreted and over-generalized to create barriers for females in math achievement. It took two decades of research and meta-analyses of mathematics achievement tests to overturn the belief among scholars of a hereditary superiority of males in mathematics, yet the notion of male superiority in math remains quite strong for the general public. As a result, the image of the gifted student, in the public's eye, still seems to be the mathematically talented boy.

Standardized achievement tests like the SAT claim to be tests of natural reasoning ability; however, the results have been clearly linked to the quality of schooling and home instruction, including opportunities for advanced courses. As a result, achievement test scores are strongly influenced by socioeconomic circumstances, so it is no mystery that most of the students served by these programs were white and Asian-American middle class students. Major efforts were made by all of the talent search sites to be more inclusive of poor and non-white students, with some success, particularly by programs at Northwestern in the Chicago area under the guidance of Paula Olszewski-Kubilius.[12] Even with additional funding to support scholarships and special programs, talent search programs have found it challenging to overcome the difficulties of students from poor and disadvantaged schools in demonstrating their potential.

Talent search programs, nevertheless, did open up a new method of identification of specific talents rather than the expensive and often-derided intelligence tests, and created matching programs during summers and after-school periods that helped thousands of students of very high ability. Many girls who otherwise might never have come to the attention of educators were provided with summer programs, camps, and out of school opportunities to enhance their academic abilities and to learn with intellectual peers.

The emphasis on specific abilities also linked giftedness with actual adult accomplishment because, although eminent people across professions indeed have high general intelligence, they also tend to have particular interests, passion, and motivation to develop their talents in just one, focused area of strength.

Multiple Intelligences

Howard Gardner's publication of *Frames of Mind: The Theory of Multiple Intelligences* in 1983 further expanded the possibilities of identification of talent, because, based on his studies of both people with brain impairments and of prodigies, he came to believe that human beings had many different intelligences.[13] He claimed intelligences were linked with specific areas of the brain, each with its own development, symbol system, and path toward expertise. He suggested seven intelligences (and later expanded further to eight and nine). The seven intelligences—linguistic, mathematical-logical, spatial-visual, interpersonal, intrapersonal, kinesthetic, and musical—were, he said, a better explanation of how talent actually emerges in societies than general intelligence. Gardner's ideas took the U.S. and the world by storm. In an era of democracy and egalitarianism, it seemed possible now to the public and educators that everybody could be gifted in some way—despite the fact that if all abilities are distributed according to the normal curve, a large group of people would still be average at everything. The multiple intelligences theory was immediately controversial in psychology because of its adamant opposition to the concept of general intelligence.

General and Specific Abilities

Intelligence researchers, turning to study specific abilities, still found over and over that most abilities were highly correlated and that most people of high ability were multipotential—that is, their intelligence could develop in many directions, across domains. Only when more sophisticated statistical techniques and access to large, diverse populations became possible did a new model emerge that encompassed both *G*, or general ability, and many specific abilities. The Cattell-Horn-Carroll theory, now the most accepted theory by intelligence researchers, holds that there is a hierarchy of abilities with three levels, from very specific to broad that all partake in G, general ability.[14] In addition to this well-researched theory of intelligence, other psychologists have shown the complexities of intelligence by demonstrating, for instance, that at the highest levels of ability—such as mathematical and musical genius—G breaks down. That explains why so many prodigies and extraordinarily eminent individuals have specific extraordinary talents, but may be only above average in other abilities.

Emotional Intelligence

Curiously, although feminist psychologists had long lamented the failure of psychology to recognize interpersonal skills as valuable enough to be considered an aspect of intelligence, it took male authors to provide the convincing argument. The advent of research on emotional intelligence by Reuven Bar-On and others, as well as its popularization by Daniel Goleman, opened the way for a discussion of those strengths that have long been considered the domains in which smart women express their giftedness.[15]

Most scholars now agree that although emotional intelligence overlaps intelligence, it adds to the explanation of why some people perform well in interpersonal careers. Although no differences have been found in men and women on tests of emotional intelligence, it is clear that females are more comfortable in school, home, and work using their emotional intelligence to solve problems. It does not matter whether this is because women truly think, reason, and express themselves with a "different voice," as cultural feminists such as Carol Gilligan claim, or because women, as lower status people in most societies, have had to cultivate emotional and social abilities in order to gain and preserve power.[16] What matters is that such capacities as understanding and managing the emotions of oneself and others (emotional intelligence) and understanding and using intuition to make decisions (social intelligence) are now part of the discussion about what makes it possible for smart girls to become accomplished women.

Specific Personality Characteristics

Next to intelligence, personality is the most important concept in psychology. Personality has taken its place beside intelligence because, like intelligence, personality is a very powerful predictor of behavior. That is, personality can help predict achievement, creativity, job performance, life satisfaction, and well-being. Also, like intelligence, personality has now been thoroughly researched across cultures, with thousands of personality scales. Throughout the 20th century, personality tests proliferated until the researchers Robert McCrae and Paul Costa gathered all major personality studies together and through factor analysis discovered what is now called the Big Five Personality Theory.[17]

From their research, five personality factors emerged that could be found universally among humans, had both genetic and environmental origins, and reflected brain structures found across humanity. According to the research, each of the five personality factors exists on a normal distribution curve with the majority of people falling within one standard deviation (SD) of the average score. As we discuss later, when we teach creative and talented girls about their personalities, we pay specific attention to the scores at either tail of the normal curve (that is, scores that are plus or minus one standard deviation from average) because these are the traits that help us understand what makes a smart girl unique.

The best-known personality trait, and one of the most powerful in determining behavior across different contexts, is *Extraversion/Introversion*. Extraverts tend to be positive, outgoing, social, assertive, and enthusiastic. They prefer being with people rather than being alone, and they feel energized by the company of others. In contrast, introverts tend to be more reserved and independent. They prefer to be alone, are less interested in people, tend to be quiet, and are less likely to lead.

Many descriptions and checklists of characteristics of gifted students include some reference to extraversion, because research is clear that teachers prefer students who are outgoing, enthusiastic leaders. Most scientists, however, tend to be more introverted than extraverted.[18] In school years, however, introverts might be overlooked and not considered gifted because of their unwillingness to speak up and be noticed. In extreme cases, introverted gifted girls hide away under tables and in other small spaces where they can spend hours reading fan fiction or writing story after story. The extraversion/introversion personality trait is only moderately correlated with intelligence, meaning that highly intelligent people can be either extraverted or introverted.[19]

Many people also have heard of the second personality trait, *Neuroticism/Emotional Stability*. People who are neurotic tend to be overly sensitive and to have difficulty regulating their emotions (especially anxiety). They tend to be self-conscious, sensitive to stress, and may experience frequent negative emotions such as depression, fear, embarrassment, sadness, and guilt. One of the strongest correlations between personality and intelligence is the *inverse* correlation of neuroticism with intelligence. That is, the majority of intelligent people are emotionally stable, well-adjusted, and non-defensive. Most people, including teachers, don't like to be around neurotic people, so it is no accident that most gifted checklists include good adjustment and stability. That said, we have encountered many smart girls—especially smart adolescents—who struggle with at least some features of neuroticism. The bad news? Maximizing one's potential is profoundly more difficult if one must also focus on regulating one's emotions. The good news is that with emotional self-regulation skills training, smart girls can learn how to manage their emotions so that they can better cope with the emotional ups-and-downs that accompany neuroticism.

The third characteristic is *Agreeableness/Disagreeableness*. Agreeableness is just what it sounds like—the tendency to be friendly, likeable, and willing to go along with others' ideas and directions. Disagreeableness is being prickly, unfriendly, competitive, and nonconforming. This personality characteristic is only moderately heritable and moderately related to intelligence. Teachers love agreeable students.[20] In fact, highly agreeable students are probably overrepresented in gifted programs because of the *halo effect*—nice kids just seem smarter.

However, we want to note that creative and innovative people tend to be fairly disagreeable, which turns out to be an asset when pursuing and implementing ideas that most people don't understand.[21] Disagreeable smart girls tend to tell you exactly what they think, and they won't have to be taught how to say no. Agreeable smart girls seem to have the opposite problem. Though there is nothing more pleasing to some teachers than an agreeable smart girl, as she matures she will have difficulty saying no, even when she's overwhelmed, because she doesn't want to disappoint anyone. What's the problem with the inability to say no sometimes? Her "can-do" attitude may give way to overcommitting herself and eventually dropping the ball on important tasks. Agreeability may also be related to a tendency to compromise one's goals and to put others' goals ahead of one's own—a tendency that could lead bright women to let go of their dreams.

The fourth aspect of personality is *Conscientiousness/Non-conscientiousness*, which seems to be mostly learned and only inherited to a small degree. Think about conscientiousness as work ethic. Conscientious people are industrious, orderly, and committed to finishing the tasks they begin; non-conscientious people are careless, impulsive, unreliable, and not interested in working hard—unless it is something that they really love. Teachers and supervisors love conscientious students because they're great at getting their work done and turned in on time. They're serious about work and unlikely to slack off when they lose interest.

Conscientiousness also plays a big role in being identified as gifted. In fact, no matter how intelligent a child might be, if she is not *task-committed*, she is unlikely to be selected for a gifted program. Many children who lack conscientiousness are labeled as having Attention Deficit Hyperactivity Disorder (ADHD). A great challenge for creative and talented girls who are not conscientious is to generate the self-discipline and internal motivation needed to complete tasks. As is the case with managing neuroticism, conscientiousness is something that girls can develop with the help of skilled counselors, teachers, and parents. For many creative women, the practice of what we call "selective consciousness" means being highly conscientious in one's chosen vocation, but less conscientious about things like housework, social events, and fashion.

Finally, *Openness to Experience/Closed* is the personality characteristic least known to the public, but it is possibly one of the most important to our society. Being open to experience means being curious, intellectual, ready for new experiences, and appreciative of beauty and sensory impressions. People who are open to experiences keenly experience both positive and negative emotions. Being closed to experience means being indifferent to new experiences and uninterested in new sensations. Closed individuals are conventional, conservative, emotionally restrained, and uninterested in intellectual pursuits.

Openness to Experience is moderately to highly heritable and moderately related to intelligence.[22] Some smart people are open to experiences, and others are closed. Sometimes we call openness to experience the "hallmark of the creative personality" because it is the personality variable most strongly associated with creativity. The research on teachers' reactions to openness to experience is mixed; most teachers do seem to enjoy creative children, but their constant curiosity and readiness to try new activities can make it difficult to keep them engaged in an ordinary classroom. Our society is also mixed in how it views of openness to experience. While we admire and lionize our great inventors, artists, performers, and writers, we often don't recognize or appreciate the characteristics of creativity during childhood. Creative personality characteristics, however, are an important aspect in checklists of characteristics of gifted children. In our experience, openness to experience is the personality characteristic that enables smart girls and women to say "yes" to (or take advantage of) opportunities for personal and professional growth and development.

A large number of articles and books about gifted children refer to *overexcitabilities*, which are considered to be psychobiological tendencies of gifted people to be highly responsive to stimuli in a number of different areas—psychomotor, sensual, emotional, imaginational, and intellectual.[23] Most of these overexcitabilities (OEs) seem to have a high degree of overlap with Big Five personality characteristics; some aspects of imaginational and intellectual OEs overlap with openness to experience, psychomotor OE reflects impulsive aspects of non-conscientiousness, and sensual OE reflects the overly sensitive aspects of neuroticism. What makes the overexcitabilities theory different from other theories of giftedness is the definition of giftedness as neurological characteristics that lead to advanced development (rather than to intelligence). It would be possible, therefore, for a child to be lacking in working memory or advanced problem-solving ability, but still to be considered gifted based on her sensitivity to stimuli, her intense emotional reactions, and her high activity level.

Because only psychologists generally have access to the research and the more sophisticated personality tests based on the Big Five Personality Theory, more teachers of gifted students know much more about overexcitabilities (OEs) than about Big Five Personality Theory. Unlike the Big Five Personality Theory, OE theory is based on small samples and case studies and does not have decades of research with tens of thousands of subjects; nor does it have supporting evidence of cross-cultural, genetic, and neurological validity. Although OE theory is known primarily within the gifted community, it remains a highly attractive metaphor and highly popular way of seeing giftedness as personal qualities, rather than being directly related to learning capacities.

Spiritual Intelligence

Since the great psychoanalyst Carl Jung broke from Sigmund Freud and developed his own theory of the self, thinkers and writers in many fields have noted that there is more to mental health than the absence of misery or pathology. That is, there may be optimal states of psychological development where people transcend the ordinary experiences of life—a state of integration of thought, emotion, and behavior that allows a person to see the "big picture" of connections between and among ourselves and the universe.

Abraham Maslow studied self-actualized people—those people who not only realized their full intellectual, emotional, and creative potential, but who also seemed to have reached their spiritual potential. He described self-actualized people as people who perceived reality efficiently, but with a spontaneity and freshness of appreciation for new experiences. Self-actualized people were quick-witted and funny, but with humor that was not cruel. They were comfortable with themselves and others, as well as with their place in nature. They had a sense of purpose, a mission, and cared about the fulfillment of an idea beyond themselves. They had little patience for authoritarians and were independent in their attitudes and behaviors. They had a few profound, satisfying friendships while having a sense of fellowship with all humanity, yet they were also perfectly happy savoring solitude. Finally, they had a capacity for a transcendent state that Maslow called "the peak experience"—a state of consciousness in which they were transfixed with awe, alive with wonder, and a sense of harmony and oneness with all being.[24]

When you consider all the other kinds of giftedness we have talked about, it seems as if spiritual intelligence encompasses general intelligence (efficient perception, quick humor), creativity (spontaneity, autonomy, freshness of appreciation, solitude), and emotional intelligence (acceptance of self, others, and nature; fellowship with humanity). That leaves peak experiences to be explained as frequent, deliberate entries into altered states of consciousness in order to feel connected, in harmony, and transformed.

Robert Emmons and Kathleen Noble call these abilities to enter transcendent states *spiritual intelligence*. When Howard Gardner proclaimed that spiritual intelligence was not an intelligence, he ignited a controversy. Robert Emmons retorted that there was good evidence for spirituality as a set of abilities that enable people to solve problems and attain goals.[25] He identified the components as:

- ❖ Capacity for transcendence

- ❖ Ability to enter into heightened spiritual states of consciousness

- ❖ Ability to invest everyday activities, events, and relationships with a sense of the sacred

- ❖ Ability to utilize spiritual resources to solve problems in living

❖ Capacity to engage in virtuous behavior—to show forgiveness, to express gratitude, to be humble, to display compassion.

Kathleen Noble added the ability to use spirituality in the service of one's own growth and that of others. [26]

People with spiritual intelligence, according to the researchers who have studied them, use spiritual skills such as mindfulness, meditation, prayer, trance, and ecstatic experiences. Howard Gardner claimed that the definitions and descriptions of spiritual intelligence were so broad as to mean "everything and nothing." After my immersion experiences in Native American spiritual traditions, as well as my study of healers across cultures, I defined spiritual intelligence as the "capacity to alter consciousness in the service of self and others," a definition that closely relates to anthropologists' definition of the major skill of traditional spiritual leaders.[27]

The Beehive of Smart Girls

The many conflicting definitions of giftedness made it very difficult to form generalizations about smart girls. We reflected on and discussed for many years all the research we could find on the many perspectives on intelligence, creativity, emotional intelligence, and spiritual intelligence. We developed the model you see here to help clarify what we mean as we talk about smart girls. Perhaps because the farm where we lived when we began this book had a lively beehive, the bee society became a way for us to talk about giftedness in girls.

The beehive is a good metaphor for the diversity of talents of smart girls, because it shows how particular abilities, when fully developed, lead to specific roles in society. In addition, a beehive has a broad foundation, as does this model of female giftedness. The model is based on the research that shows that high intelligence—the ability to catch on, make sense of things, and know what to do about it—is the foundation of giftedness. We built our Beehive model from the assessments and interviews of 500 gifted students, all nominated for their creativity in five domains.[28] Using statistical methods of factor analysis and cluster analysis, we discovered groups of students who shared common personalities and interests. We found that values—our sense of what is right, true, and important in life—added a little more information that was helpful in figuring out career paths.

Intelligence is measured by a wide variety of tests, most of them now based on the Cattell-Horn-Carroll theory of intelligence, and the range of intelligence test scores associated with giftedness is most commonly 95th percentile to the top of the 99th percentile, although many gifted programs accept bright students of "above average" ability, which is actually about the 90th percentile.[29] The intelligence tests that are used all provide many tasks in hopes of measuring diverse aspects, but most measure some aspect of working memory and speed of information processing.

We have already mentioned the problems with bias in intelligence testing and the fact that it is almost impossible to have a culture fair test when our very notion of intelligence is a modern, Western conception. Despite these problems, we think it is important to continue to recognize that speedy information processing and working memory, no matter how hard they are to measure, are the foundation of intelligence and therefore of giftedness. All of the other forms of giftedness we show here are combinations of intelligence with some other characteristic of that person that adds predictive power for forecasting the potential realization of ability. For example, creativity thinking and personality add to intelligence to predict that a person will thrive in a creative career. Emotional intelligence adds to intelligence to predict that a person will do well in careers requiring interpersonal skills. And spiritual intelligence may add to intelligence to predict that a person will thrive in a religious, spiritual, or philanthropic career. All of this adds to what we know—that intelligence predicts not only academic achievement, but also job performance. It is also one of the best predictors of health, psychological adjustment, and well-being.

So, here is our beehive. Figure 1.1 provides a summary of each of the bee types, along with their characteristics, the role that they play in our society, and their specific, work-related focus.

Figure 1.1. Beehive of Smart Girls

Type of Bee	Characteristics	Role in the Culture	Specific Focus
Queen Bee	Intelligence Creativity Emotional Intelligence Spiritual Intelligence	Transform	Visionary
Procreator Bee	Intelligence Creativity	Create	Innovator
Honey Bee	Intelligence Emotional Intelligence	Nourish & heal	Leader
Forager Bee	Intelligence Specific abilities	Gather/share knowledge	Scholars
Worker Bee	Intelligence Broad abilities	Maintain	Professionals

Worker Bees: The Professionals

Children who score above the 95th percentile on these tests are likely to do well in school, to graduate from high school and college, and to go on to become the professionals who maintain our society. As young girls, worker bees have multiple talents and interests; as teens, they may have a hard time choosing among their many options; and by adulthood, they have often gained degrees, honors, and awards in their field. These are the smart people we think of as our experts. These girls tend to combine conscientiousness with high abilities.

In the beehive, the problem-solvers figure out what to do to build the hive, keep it healthy and warm, and defend it. In our society, the expert/professionals (problem-solvers) are the lawyers, physicians, accountants, analysts, and engineers we turn to when we need highly trained individuals to advise us. Because of their capacity to learn quickly and reason well, the majority of gifted students grow up to be society's problem-solvers. Although professions were once dominated by men, more than 50% of entering classes in law and medicine today are women. Increasingly, smart women will fill these important roles by applying knowledge to the solution of practical, critical problems.

Forager Bees: The Scholars

The other kind of expert is the scholar. At higher levels of intelligence, we often see specialization of abilities. Seventh grade Talent Search students, who score at or above the average for high school seniors in one of the scales of the SAT or ACT, often become specialists in a particular field. These highly intelligent students may also grow up to be problem-solvers, but many will choose to be scholars. These gifted adults are professors and researchers, journalists, and high-level information technologists. Society's gatherers and sharers of knowledge are the forager bees of the hive. Many smart girls with high intelligence and very high specific abilities will become scholars in fields that match their high level abilities in math, verbal, spatial-visual, and musical areas. As girls, they are already finding one area of their vast general knowledge to be particularly interesting and beginning to hone their skills and learn rapidly in that area. As adolescents, they will excel in achievement tests in their domain and be very attracted to pre-professional programs. Later, as adults at colleges and universities, they will gather knowledge, whether it is in humanities, sciences, or arts, and share it through teaching and writing. As media and tech specialists, they will gather ideas and images to share throughout the world online, building human knowledge as they go along.

Honey Bees: Teachers, Leaders, Counselors

What happens when you add emotional intelligence to general intelligence? You get a very smart, caring, and persuasive person. Smart girls who combine intelligence with special skills in perceiving and managing emotions often become our society's leaders—in the family, the classroom, the community, and the boardroom. They also may become the people that others rely on for listening, help, and healing. We call this large group of smart girls the Honey Bees, because they sweeten and nourish the hive with their empathy and persuasion. Women have always been attracted to the helping and teaching professions; now they are also applying their emotional intelligence to leadership. The majority of teachers, nurses, counselors, social workers, and psychologists are female, and these roles are still preferred by smart women with emotional intelligence.

While the leaders of major corporations and governments are still overwhelmingly male, females are learning how to use their skills in persuasion and empathic communication to gain high-level positions in business, industry, and government. We should note that not all leaders have emotional intelligence; sometimes dominance and ambition alone take people to the top. Most of the current literature in management, however, shows that the most effective leaders are those who can listen as well as lead.[30]

Procreator Bees: Innovators

Although to be truly creative one must be at least above average in intelligence, it is possible to be very intelligent without being creative. Individual creativity in a wide variety of studies is predicted by a complex combination of personality factors, cognitive abilities, expertise, and motivation. The major personality characteristic is Openness to Experience. We call this group the Procreator Bees for good reasons. Although in a real hive, the only bees that can procreate with the Queen are the few males called drones. In the metaphorical Bee Hive, they are the women who fertilize the hive with their brilliant, original ideas. It is true that creative women tend to be a little more androgynous, having both traditional and feminine and masculine characteristics not in appearance, but in behavior. Highly creative women care little about gender roles, and they enjoy being both aggressive and nurturing, sensitive and yet hard-edged, or independent yet collaborative.

Creative women would be proud to be compared to the drones, even though it is a term with both reproductive and lazy connotations. That leads to the last reason that creative women could be compared to the procreating drones; most societies see creative people as slackers, bohemians, and outsiders—that is, until they produce something of great value to society. As kids, creative girls have a distressing tendency to get good grades in the subjects they like and to ignore the subjects they do not like. As teenagers, they are usually independent, nonconforming, and focused on learning everything about their own narrow interests, whether it be a genre of music, a style of graphic art, or a type of video game. As women, they may experience failure or success, depending on how ready society is for their ideas; they are unlikely, however, to abandon their own creative projects for higher pay or status. Procreators are not driven by external rewards or the approval of others.

The mental abilities long associated with creativity are fluency, flexibility, originality, and elaboration, as described by E. Paul Torrance. Fluency means the ability to produce a great quantity of ideas in a short period of time. Flexibility is the capacity to imagine a wide variety of functions for ordinary objects and a wide variety of applications for concepts and ideas. Originality is defined as the ability to generate rare but appropriate solutions to problems, and elaboration means the ease with which one can produce associations, implications, and elegant conclusions based upon an initial idea or concept.[31]

There are also core personality traits that all creative people seem to have. These traits include the characteristics of openness, such as independence of judgment, and autonomy. People who are high in openness to experience are creative in both artistic and scientific domains. On most studies of personality tests, creative individuals were found to be more self-accepting, self-confident, dominant, hostile, ambitious, and impulsive than their less creative peers.[32]

Mihaly Csikszentmihalyi identified several other core characteristics in both male and female creative people he interviewed.[33] He added to the above list of core qualities the ability to reconcile opposites and, most important, the ability to experience intense *flow consciousness*. Flow consciousness, which has been studied in depth mainly in the areas of sports psychology, and the performing arts, has been linked to creative productivity—an optimal state of intrinsic motivation where the person is fully immersed in what he or she is doing. The creative individual experiences great absorption, engagement, and challenge—and all other needs and sensory input are ignored.

Highly creative people who attain eminence are as rare as drones in the hive, but they are as necessary to society as male bees are to the hive. Without them, there is no procreation; without them, no new ideas, technology, or beauty. Creative women include inventors, entrepreneurs, artists, designers, musicians, writers, dancers, and actors.

The Queen Bees: Visionaries

Throughout history there have been extraordinary women like Joan of Arc, Mother Teresa, Jane Addams, and Buddhist teacher Pema Chodron, whose characteristics and abilities transcend intelligence, creativity, and emotional intelligence. These women seem to not only have these characteristics, but also the ability to see interconnections and possibilities that others cannot. They look beyond their own needs, beyond the status quo of their societies, and beyond our understanding of the way the universe works. We decided, therefore, to add spiritual intelligence to the characteristics that might define women whose integrative vision transforms societies. These are the Queen Bees, and they are aptly named, for it is the Queen Bee that has ingested a protein-rich secretion called royal jelly that makes her grow beyond the ordinary capacities of other bees. Not only personal characteristics, but powerful transcendent experiences lead women to become spiritually intelligent. These women don't just change their domain of art, science, or leadership; they change whole societies and the worldviews that guide them, just as the Queen Bee leads the swarm to make a whole new hive.

There are no measures of spiritual intelligence that would specifically predict that an individual would become a catalyst for societal or intellectual change. We would expect, perhaps, that these women would be intelligent, emotionally intelligent, creative, and able to engage in mental states such as mindfulness, prayer, or deep, solitary reflection. Of course, this is speculative. Until we better understand the nature of consciousness, self-actualization, and spirituality, it is unlikely that we could identify with any accuracy young girls who will become spiritual leaders. Is she the one that others turn to for wisdom? Is she the one who takes to religious activities with fervor? Is she the one with dreams and visions that nobody else understands? We don't know, but we must continue to look for, find, and learn about children who seem to have a spiritual or religious calling.

We will refer to the Beehive often as we talk about smart girls to represent which kind of smart we are talking about. We have left out a few popular ideas about definitions of giftedness that include sensitivities, intensities, or overexcitabilities because these ideas have not yet been linked by research to academic achievement, high performance at work, or life satisfaction, which are the predictions in which we are interested.[34] In addition, there is sufficient research in every area except spiritual intelligence that many of the popular notions of giftedness such as sensitivity or intensity can be subsumed under personality and self-regulation research. Finally, sometimes a focus on oversensitivity or extreme intensity can cause us to pathologize giftedness, to make it seem as if strong, even maladaptive, reactions are a sign of giftedness rather than the sign of a very frustrated, bored, or troubled child.[35] We will, of course, talk about sensitive and intense smart girls, but this is for a later chapter when we show how our current schools and societal attitudes make life difficult for very intelligent girls who also have personality traits that don't fit the norm for their peer group.

The Many Paths toward Fulfillment of Talent

What has become obvious to people who study the lifelong development of talent is that many other factors besides giftedness come into play in determining if smart girls will grow up to achieve their own dreams and goals. Mihaly Csikszentmihalyi, in a groundbreaking study of 100 eminent men and women, showed that intelligence, creativity, context, personality variables, and interpersonal relations all had an impact on the realization of talent.[36] He—and a new generation of psychologists such as Rena Subotnik who studied Hunter College gifted graduates and Westinghouse winners of scientific contests, Felice Kaufmann who studied Presidential Scholars, and Karen Arnold who studied valedictorians—showed convincingly that intelligence alone does not insure success in life, although it does lay the groundwork.[37] Even more important for women, these follow-up studies confirmed Terman's and Oden's observations that women often failed to fulfill their potential, not because of lesser abilities, but because of environmental factors, including less rigorous educations, less prestigious colleges, the absence of mentors, and the difficulties of combining family and career.

The first book, *Smart Girls, Gifted Women,* used these studies and many others to show how high intelligence in girls was often hampered by both internal and external barriers to achievement. In it, I showed how most barriers encountered by gifted young women remained similar to those encountered 50 years earlier by Terman's gifted women, and I lamented that gifted girls were too often expected to conform to society's image of femininity rather than to society's image of genius.

Smart Girls, Gifted Women was controversial when it came out because it so strongly supported encouraging smart girls toward the fullest realization of intellectual potential in the public arena of accomplishments, rather than in private and domestic pursuits. Even feminist psychologists critiqued the idea that women should be urged to pursue what they called a masculine model of achievement. The controversy continues today in the arguments of many gifted educators and others who emphasize the value of factors other than visible and quantifiable achievements in the lives of gifted individuals.

In the chapter on adult smart women, we review the work of one of the most influential current authors, Sheryl Sandberg, CEO of Facebook, on the fulfillment of feminine potential in our times. In her book, *Lean In*, she emphasizes that although women do indeed have more choice than ever in the kind of life they choose to pursue, they are still hampered by workplaces that offer no flex time for child care or other family responsibilities, or even discriminate against women for choosing to have children while pursuing a career goal.[38] In addition, constant messages from the media and vociferous politicians lead women to believe that reaching for their career goals while also pursuing their dreams of marriage and family might be undesirable and even impossible.

Bright, privileged women married to wealthy men, in fact, might be at higher risk for abandoning their career goals—because financially they can afford to, and because they receive unquestioning approval for their choices. Single moms, middle class women in dual-career relationships, and women who are the family breadwinners have no choice. One of the most important messages that we can communicate to smart women is that some portion of society will condemn you no matter what choice you make—so you might as well "lean in" to your most beloved vocation and demand support for your choice to work toward your full intellectual potential as well as toward your dream of family.

In all the history of the world, there has never been a generation of smart girls who are in a better position to "have it all." In most developed countries today, young women have the choice of when and how they will become pregnant and raise children. They have control over their own finances. This is definitely the time for smart young women to lean in. Despite worries of career women, a study drawing on 50 years of research found that infants and toddlers with working mothers were more likely to grow up well adjusted, more academically high achieving, and less likely to experience anxiety or depression in later life when compared to children of mothers who did not work when they were young.[39]

In addition, there is no group of young women more able to strategize, to use all of their personal and social resources, and to cleverly work around remaining areas of sexism than smart women. Being smart means more than being able to get good grades, do well on achievement tests, and enter prestigious programs of study; it also means being able to think on your feet, to compose a creative lifestyle, and to develop convincing arguments against those who would thwart your progress.

CHAPTER 2

Generations of Smart Girls and Women

One of the best ways to understand the social forces that shape smart girls' self-concepts, expectations, and aspirations is to learn about the generations of smart girls since the gifted education movement began. In addition, when we examine the lives of these women who went before, we can gain a better understanding of how, in our own families, great-grandmothers, grandmothers, mothers, and daughters differ. By understanding the different worlds in which smart girls grew, we can understand their attitudes toward their own and other women's potential.

The First Generation: Termites and Girl Geniuses

Who were the girls first identified as gifted? Every child in Terman's study took an individual intelligence test, the *Stanford Achievement Test*, a general information test, seven different character tests (measures of personal and social adjustment), and a test of interest in and knowledge of play. Besides all of these, 34 health measures were completed, along with medical exams, a home information questionnaire, a school information questionnaire, an interest survey, a two-month reading record, an assessment of socioeconomic status, and a case history. The sheer quantity of data gathered was unprecedented.

Some of the findings were to be expected, given that Terman had already prepared teachers for the idea that gifted students might be well adjusted rather than pitifully and strangely odd. Their social adjustment was not only better than average children, but it was even better than Terman had predicted. Terman and his colleague Melita Oden were to take this one finding and return to it again and again as solid evidence that the existing stereotype of the weak genius was false. With regard to gifted girls, they reported often how natural, happy, and friendly these young women were. Rather than strange, eccentric, or unfeminine girls, these were the kinds of girls who were admired by peers and liked by teachers.[40]

Even physically, gifted boys and gifted girls were superior; they were taller, stronger, and more athletic than their peers. In *Smart Boys*, Sanford Cohn and I suggested that this finding helped to dispel the taint of effeminacy that American notions of male genius included.[41] The impact of this finding for gifted girls was more complex. While promoting the idea that gifted girls were strong, healthy specimens of females, Terman carefully avoided any suggestion that these girls might be more masculine in appearance or activities than other girls. This, too, was important for the education of gifted girls, making it more likely that teachers would see athletic participation, physical strength, and aptitude as appropriate for women. At the same time in history, interest in women's physical education and women's sports was born, making it possible for bright, active girls to fulfill their athletic potential.

Although school achievement of these children was generally high, it was not as high as Terman had predicted. Good, but not perfect, grades were the norm. Terman implied that gifted children were too engaged in their lively interests and activities to be grade grubbers. Gifted girls were portrayed as serious students and voracious readers, but also as playful and adventurous. Terman noted that giftedness was much more important than sex in determining academic abilities and that the correlation in academic abilities was a very high (0.91 for girls and boys). That is, high intelligence scores predicted high academic achievement for both girls and boys when their grades were recorded over the course of their education.

In their play interests and dreams about the future, gifted girls were much more like gifted boys than like average girls. They spent a good part of their free time playing outdoors as well as reading; they liked adventure and novelty. They seemed to prefer the company of other bright girls and boys to the company of average girls or boys. Gifted girls had unusually high aspirations for females at the beginning of the 20th century and were less bound by tradition than average girls in their hopes for themselves. They dreamed of having careers that were as exciting, accomplished, and heroic as those that were desired by the gifted boys.[42]

Thanks to these Terman studies, teachers and scholars were given a new image of the gifted girl. She was confident and well-adjusted—an all-American girl who was healthy, tanned, muscular—and for the most part, a privileged girl who was white, middle-class, and from well-educated parents. A generation of educators was taught to expect gifted girls to be pleasant and well-rounded. Little did they know how much this rosy perception would create a generation of gifted girls who sometimes tried to be too well adjusted for their own good. Too often, the expectation that gifted girls would adjust easily to society's ideal of an American girl would conflict with, and thus perhaps lessen, these girls' motivation to achieve.

In actuality, that is what seemed to be the fate of Terman and Oden's gifted women. Though they were far more educated and had gathered far more academic awards than average women of their generation, most of them did not go on to distinguish themselves in careers. Like their average peers, they married, had children, and raised their children. They quit work, or worked in fits and starts, or did volunteer work. Fully half of this talented group were homemakers all their lives; and of the other half, most found themselves in traditionally feminine careers such as teaching and nursing. There were indeed a few authors and a very few scientists and leaders. For the most part, however, the group of gifted women at midlife was not very different from their average peers; they were quite cheerful about their roles as wives, mothers, and supporters of their husbands' careers.

Followed up in their elder years, however, the gifted women often regretted not having had the opportunity for paid employment and leadership positions. In fact, the group that had the largest proportion of dissatisfied women was made up of those who had been married and now were widowed or divorced, but without the financial independence that would have come from having a career of their own.[43] Given the conventional belief that a spinster is a pitiable thing, a surprising finding was that the happiest and most satisfied group was elderly, single, childless gifted women who had worked all their lives in income-producing careers. Apparently, being a brilliant girl and a cheerfully well-adjusted wife and mother did not predict that a gifted woman would look back upon her life without regret.

Leta Hollingworth

If Lewis Terman is considered the Father of gifted education, then Leta Stetter Hollingworth is the Mother of gifted education.[44] While Terman was doing his research on the West Coast, on the East Coast Hollingworth founded the first school for gifted children and established gifted education as a profession and a science. Like Terman, Hollingworth challenged both the popular stereotypes and scientific assumptions about gifted children. More important, however, she challenged the scientific establishment's certainty regarding the inferiority of women.

Leta Hollingworth was herself a precocious child who, as a Phi Beta Kappa college graduate in 1906, a dual-career psychologist with her husband, Harry Hollingworth, and a brilliant researcher, became a model and an advocate for generations of gifted girls and women. One of her first studies questioned the variability hypothesis. According to the variability hypothesis, men were thought to exhibit a wider range of physical and mental abilities than women. Men, therefore, were thought to be capable of both the greatest genius and the most profound retardation, while women, whose abilities clustered around the mean, were considered incapable of extraordinary accomplishment.

Leta Hollingworth learned that this widely accepted idea had little empirical support. She set about collecting data on the birth weight and length of 1,000 male and 1,000 female newborns and demonstrated that female babies were actually more variable than males. Hollingworth also collected data from the Clearing House for Mental Defectives on 1,000 clients, finding that while more men were institutionalized, just as many females of low intelligence existed, but were kept at home. In addition, the difference in ability between the two decreased with age. Hollingworth's argument was that the restricted domestic roles of women concealed both mental disabilities and extraordinary abilities. It was not females who were ordinary, but the activities to which they were assigned.

Leta Hollingworth attacked another common misperception through her doctoral dissertation titled "Functional periodicity: An experimental study of the mental and motor abilities of women during menstruation." During that time, it was widely accepted in the professional literature that women were periodically incapacitated by physical, cognitive, and emotional difficulties caused by their menstrual cycle. Leta Hollingworth measured the motor, memory, and learning capabilities of men and women over a period of one to three months. She found no evidence for variability tied to menstruation on these tasks, directly contradicting the prevailing assumptions of the scientific community. Interestingly, her advisor, the famous psychologist Edward L. Thorndike, supported her research despite being a proponent of many of the masculine-oriented theories that she debunked.

Hollingworth taught educational psychology at Columbia's Teachers College, attained the rank of full professor in 1929, and directed a child guidance clinic. Her interest in gifted education began with a child who was administered an intelligence test as part of a classroom demonstration in 1916. The child, referred to in publications as "Child E," was a 7-year-old boy who had been accelerated to the fifth grade and whose IQ was found to be over 180 on a new (and not often used) form of the Binet test that allowed for very high scores.

Hollingworth became one of the first scholars to study the psychological needs of gifted children and to develop ways of guiding them. In 1926, she published *Gifted Children: Their Nature and Nurture,* which became a guide to the special educational and guidance needs of highly gifted boys and girls.[45] In 1942, her longitudinal study tracking Child E and 11 other gifted children through adulthood was documented in *Children Above 180 IQ.*[46] By debunking the variability hypothesis and the periodicity hypothesis, and by carefully interviewing and guiding a group of extraordinary young girls and boys, Leta Hollingworth became the first great advocate for gifted girls.

While Terman in his works seemed to accept that eminence was simply too difficult for gifted women to achieve, given their household roles, Hollingworth showed both by her writings and her own life that extraordinary accomplishment was, and should be, possible for gifted girls. Sadly, Hollingworth died at midlife before she could complete her work, and her notable accomplishments were subsequently overlooked and neglected.

The decades of the 30s and 40s, so fertile for the growth of women's aspirations, were followed by two decades of strong pressure for bright women to get back to the business of keeping house and raising children—a pressure usually attributed to the end of WWII and the return of men to the workforce. Not only did women scholars disappear from academia, but many of their works also disappeared. Hollingworth's two major works went out of print, and her work was unknown to many educators until the rediscovery of Leta Hollingworth by a new generation of feminist scholars and gifted advocates of the 1980s.[47] Anyone reading about gifted education before then was unlikely to discover the truth that was hidden in descriptions of extraordinary girls who had to "suffer fools gladly" and who labored toward their goals, often without hope of recognition. Buried in Hollingworth's painstaking case studies was the realization that, despite Terman's praise of the perfectly adjusted gifted girl, it was the lonely, eccentric little girl genius who was more likely to fulfill her potential than all of her accommodating and better adjusted peers.

The Second Generation: From Rosie the Riveter to the Problem that Had No Name

With the Great Depression and World War II rapidly following, women in nearly all social classes found themselves thrust into the world of work. Black women and most other women of color had always worked, but this was the first time that large numbers of middle class white women worked of necessity.

During the Depression, not much work was available, even to college graduates, and women who were forced into work by their husband's unemployment or death were confined to teaching, nursing, farming, clerical, and domestic work for others. Women who worked in other fields were considered to be taking jobs away from men, the rightful breadwinners. It is little wonder that few educators concerned themselves with the failure of gifted women to achieve their full potential in a world swept with poverty and misery.

All of this changed with World War II when women in all warring countries, with the exception of Japan, took up the jobs of the men who had gone to battle. Women now served in academic, government, and industry leadership positions, in addition to the most commonly depicted "Rosie the Riveter" jobs. In munitions factories, research centers, and military commands, women worked alongside male scientists and leaders. This was not viewed as evidence of women's right to equitable status or pay; it was assumed that they were temporarily sacrificing for their nation until the crisis of war was over. Nor was it much noticed that women seemed to perform these high level jobs with alacrity and competence, against the earlier declarations from psychologists that women were biologically unsuited to positions of great responsibility.

When the war was over, these women were expected to give up their jobs and give them back to men. No matter how smart a woman might be, she was expected to do her duty, yield her position, and return to managing and maintaining her household. The media presented this as a triumph for the modern American way of life, and then, with televisions appearing in every household, a new vision of the American housewife as the ideal woman emerged in every drama and sitcom.

Backing up the notion that smart women should be happy in the home, Freudian psychoanalysts propounded the theory of "penis envy," warning that women who wanted men's work and male achievements were suffering from neurosis. Of course, penis envy was not thought to apply to poor working women; in fact, African-American women, who could only receive public assistance if they could prove they had no husband, were both stigmatized for not working and denounced for raising children in fatherless households.

Smart women seemed to pour all their intellectual energy and ambition into being perfect homemakers; they were supposed to be happy with the success of their sons and husbands. Despite the rosy picture of modern suburban life, not all bright women were happy with the loss of income and status they had experienced. Betty Friedan felt that loss, and a pervasive sense of malaise led her to contact and interview her fellow graduates of Smith College to learn about their current lives. These very bright women were now mostly homemakers—and they felt a growing dissatisfaction. Friedan's writing resulted in the groundbreaking book, *The Feminine Mystique*, in 1963.[48] In the first chapter, she described the "Problem That Has No Name":

> *The problem lay buried, unspoken, for many years in the minds of American women. It was a strange stirring, a sense of dissatisfaction, a yearning that women suffered in the middle of the 20th century in the United States. Each suburban wife struggled with it alone. As she made the beds, shopped for groceries...she was afraid to ask even of herself the silent question — 'Is this all?'[49]*

Change was everywhere in the 1960s—except in the classroom, where girls were expected to be pretty and popular, and boys to be accomplished and strong, where career education prepared the two groups for either "men's work" or "women's work."

Perhaps the most profound change came in the area of human sexuality where, for the first time in history, contraception was widely available. Most people are surprised now to learn that, less than a century ago and across the world, a woman had the potential to have 19 pregnancies during her life, of which only about half might come to term, and 20% of those children born would die during their first year. A woman could expect to spend most of her adult life either pregnant or nursing.[50]

Another surprise to contemporary, middle class women is that less than a century ago about one in 200 women in the maternity hospitals in Britain died in childbirth—about the current rate in Somalia.[51] But from the mid-60s onward in Western societies, women had access to effective contraception—making possible the continuance of their education, delay of marriage, opportunities to plan the number and spacing of children, and improved health. Unprecedented in history, these changes were mainly noted in the media as the time of "Sex and the Single Girl," as if the only importance of contraception was that girls and women were now free to have more fun.

It is interesting that even though a cultural revolution clearly had begun in the roles of women, it took many years for changes to filter down into all areas of society. It would be many more years before social scientists understood the full impact of the changes brought about by new ideas regarding women's roles and the development of their talents.

The Third Generation: Post-Sputnik Girls

The women who came of age in the late 1960s had the opportunities of good education and increased reproductive freedom, but equity in careers and in leadership were still decades away. The space race that began when Russia launched the first satellite, Sputnik, awakened Americans to the need to identify gifted children and to enhance their education. Every gifted child, it was thought, had the potential to become a scientist or leader in the great competition with Communism for world dominance. It was regarding this generation, the Post-Sputnik girls, that my first book, *Smart Girls, Gifted Women* was written.

The women interviewed for that book were a much more select group than Terman's sample. They had been not only identified as gifted girls, but they also had received the best education that America had to offer—an education designed to propel them to the top positions of leadership for their generation. They had come of age during a more auspicious epoch in American history, a time of idealism and high hopes, a time when anything seemed possible. They had entered college when the women's liberation movement was in full swing, and they had benefited from a new egalitarianism in work and in society. In many ways, even born 50 years after the Terman and Hollingworth's gifted children, these women nevertheless had met exactly the same fate as that earlier generation. They had compromised their dreams, pared down their visions of their possibilities and, at 30 years old, were perfectly happy with where their choices had led them. They had adjusted brilliantly to their circumstances.

Not long after the publication of my first book describing the follow-up study of this group of smart women, I (Barbara) stood before a chart of my findings at a professional conference. I pointed to the figures that represented the educational attainments, the career choices, the age of marriage, the number of children, and the occupations of the women's husbands—bankers, doctors, lawyers, and political leaders. My colleague, Camilla Benbow, raised her hand and wryly said, "Well, at least they married well."

It was not the end of the story for these smart women. I followed them further, writing 10- and then 20-year updates. Some who married well had divorced badly in the next 10 years, and some had husbands who lost their jobs. Of these, one group transformed their lives and rose to the challenge of becoming breadwinners and creative leaders. Others simply became overwhelmed. At 40, almost half of the women regretted having compromised their earlier dreams. At 50, regret had faded and, for most of the women, had been replaced by determination and drive. Their good adjustment had indeed derailed them for a decade or more from fulfilling the potential of their young girlhood; their resourcefulness had helped most of them to create rich and happy lives, whatever the compromises of their past. It was not so much the smart women who had lost out in the end, but society. They accomplished much despite the fact that most did not go on to higher educational degrees or high status occupations. We will never know what they could have contributed if they had been able to stay on track, complete their educational goals, and fulfill their career dreams.

The Fourth Generation: Generation X Smart Girls

Dear Mr. Vernon,

We accept the fact that we had to sacrifice a whole Saturday in detention for whatever it was we did wrong. What we did was wrong. But we think you're crazy to make us write an essay telling you who we think we are. What do you care? You see us as you want to see us—in the simplest terms, in the most convenient definitions. You see us as a brain, an athlete, a basket case, a princess, and a criminal. Correct? That's the way we saw each other at 7:00 this morning. We were brainwashed.

The Breakfast Club (John Hughes, 1985)

Smart girls from Generation X, born between 1965 and 1980, struggled to find themselves as leaders and attempted to find a place in the world, despite a feeling of having been born too late. As teenagers, they were known for their cynicism, rebelliousness, and independence. Adults called them slackers.

They would have loved to have something to protest, a cause to support, a boat to rock, but by the time Gen X smart girls came of age, there seemed to be nothing left to protest. The Vietnam War was over. Roe vs. Wade had given women reproductive freedom. Title IX had enabled them to play sports in greater numbers than ever before. Before they were old enough to vote, have sex, or join a basketball team, they were given open access to everything that earlier generations of women had fought for. Of course, there were new fears—the AIDS epidemic, the Cold War, the War on Drugs. But none of them seemed to evoke the passionate action of the 1960s.

Growing up as a member of Gen X without a cause to be passionate about was more than a little confusing for some. On one hand, they were the first cohort to be told "you can be whatever you want to be when you grow up," and actually have the realistic chance of accomplishing their career goals. No profession appeared to be off limits. Smart girls were studying biology, chemistry, physics, engineering, and mathematics. Many who attended college aimed for law school and medical school, and puzzled at the girls who were pursuing traditionally feminine careers in teaching and nursing. "Why would you settle for something less than law school or medical school?" they wondered. And they believed that they really *could* have it all—a great job, a husband, and a family. After all, isn't that what women's rights were all about?

On the other hand, the pressure to have it all—and to be perfect—was tremendous. Movie stars like Bo Derek, Jane Fonda, Olivia Newton John, and Farrah Fawcett sent a not-so-subtle message to Gen X girls: They should be thin, and beautiful, and smart. Is it any wonder that the great rise in eating disorders and body image issues was accompanied by the self-esteem plunge? In fact, the term *well-rounded* sometimes seems to be the code for *perfection*.

Fragile self-esteem notwithstanding, Gen X smart girls stepped into young adulthood armed with the belief that they really could have it all. But just because they were told they could do it was not a guarantee. Self-efficacy—the confidence one has in herself to accomplish her goals—is only part of the formula. The Gen X smart girls needed access to clear career pathways. For example, if a girl wanted to go to medical school, what were the milestones she needed to hit? They lacked access to mentors who understood the uncommon challenges of a girl breaking ground in a field where women had been previously underrepresented. They needed to develop the capacity to bounce back after failures and setbacks and to learn to seek new ways of accomplishing their goals. There was an overemphasis on positive thinking ("I can do anything I set my mind to!") and not enough emphasis on the practical steps necessary to make their career goals reality.

Unfortunately, most Gen X smart girls didn't know about the danger zones they would encounter as they entered adulthood. The culture of romance and the pressure to marry young would still cause many of them to compromise career goals, or worse still, give up their dreams altogether. Getting a C on an assignment would represent just enough of a failure that they would question their abilities, drop out of challenging classes, and change to easier majors. Dieting and over-exercise might help them look better on the outside, but it seldom fixed the uncertainty on the inside. They needed to be challenged, but they had to learn that to face challenge is a natural part of becoming a leader, that goals are not meant to be easy, and that perseverance requires a rise to the challenge. They needed to learn that how you respond to failure defines your character.

Today, Gen X smart girls are women in their 40s. They've been through breakups with college sweethearts, relationships, starter marriages, and divorces. Some of them have entered second marriages to true partners with whom they have passionate conversations, shared household and child-rearing responsibilities, and lots of fun. And some of them are single—focused on making a lasting contribution in their field of expertise.

As they watch their male colleagues surpass them professionally and financially, Gen X smart women may realize that they're hitting a glass ceiling or caught on a sticky floor that wasn't supposed to be there. In leadership roles, they may still be plagued by the *imposter syndrome*—the fear that someone is going to figure out that she's not really as good, as smart, or as talented as she led you to believe. Some smart Gen X women have opted out of their careers to stay home with their kids—perhaps because of their own experiences as latch-key kids whose moms and dads were both gone at work most of the day. They are raising their children with the enthusiasm and vigor that they themselves longed for as children. Still others have found a way to integrate their work and family lives through online businesses and entrepreneurship. They have much more in common with their daughters than previous generations; they naturally take into account their own childhood experiences as smart girls, which enables them to become their daughters' first mentors.

As their children grow and their careers change, Gen X smart women are picking up wherever they left off years before when they set aside their goals. They're seeking new ways to serve, contribute, and innovate, and ultimately to reclaim the parts of themselves that they thought were lost forever. As a generation, talented Gen X women are realizing that the depth to which they feel the loss of their dreams also represents the magnitude with which they will be able to pursue the promise of their potential.

These were the generations of smart girls that led up to the current generation which we call the Millennial smart girls. It has been a history both of rising hopes and diminished dreams. We have told you the story of our grandmothers' and mothers' generations, as well as of our own generations—the Post-Sputnik and the Gen X smart girls. Now, it is time to look at what is probably the most anticipated generation in history—the Smart Girls of a new millennium.

Chapter 3

Smart Girls, Millennial Girls

What Does It Mean to Be a Girl in the New Millennium?

The experience of a girl born between 1990 and 2010 is unlike that of a girl at any other time in history. Although there remain countries where girls lack independence, are still considered property to be bought and sold, or are denied education or the freedom to earn their own money, most girls in developed countries today have benefitted from vast improvements in women's health, economic status, and opportunities for education and work. Change has come about so rapidly, in fact, that even a young mother is likely to have a daughter already confronted with information, choices, and challenges that she never had. Smart girls across the world are impacted by changes in health variables, educational factors, and changes in the working conditions. In some cases, such as the increasing cost of elite educations, they are more affected than average girls. What are the major global and societal changes that have direct impact on smart girls today? As parents and teachers, how can we anticipate what is ahead for our smart girls?

Most of what we know about girls today comes from large national studies of the status of girls and women. The Shriver Report, the Pew Report, the annual Higher Education Research Institute's Annual Freshman Survey, our own NSF studies, and the AAUW series of studies on today's young women provide a glimpse into the present and future of girls.[52] Jean Twenge's focus on Millennials in college and traditional white-collar occupations was inclined toward upper middle class young adults, but her conclusion that this was the most individually focused group—"Generation Me"—struck a chord with both educators and policy-makers, and her findings were used in planning higher education and organizational changes.[53] For Millennial girls, there is much good news, but there are also some particular issues that appear to be potential problems for smart girls.

The Bad News

One of the most striking differences between girls today and their mothers and grandmothers of yesterday is the earlier onset of puberty.[54] Around the world today, puberty begins sooner for girls, with different onset in different cultures. Particularly in countries where obesity is a problem, puberty seems to be occurring earlier than in previous generations; other possible factors include family stress, experience of early sexual activity, better overall health, and hormones in animal food products. In the U.S., African-American girls are more likely to enter puberty earlier than white girls, possibly related to a difference in obesity, although both groups begin puberty earlier than their mothers. Whatever the causes might be, this means that mothers may be surprised to find that little girls of eight and nine years old are budding breasts. Girls who enter puberty ahead of their age peers are likely to be more at risk for early sexual activity, depression, low grades, and social difficulties. What are the implications of this for smart girls?

All of the literature on eminence and creativity agrees that the longer children delay sexual activity, the more likely they are to achieve their potential. Most of Csikszentmihalyi's creative adults acknowledged that although there were some drawbacks to being late bloomers, putting off intimate relationships until their training or post-secondary education was well under way was beneficial.[55] Eminent women tended to enter intimate relationships late and to marry late, according to many studies.[56] Finally, studies of women in science, technology, engineering, and math show that the largest single factor that contributes to their falling behind their male peers in salary, status, and rank is the timing of marriage and childbirth.[57]

In today's American society, however, there is increasing pressure on girls to be pretty and popular and to have boyfriends as early as possible.[58] Pre-teens are sexualized in fashion magazines, social media, and reality shows. The AAUW studies show that girls are much more likely than boys to be sexually harassed. If a smart girl begins puberty at nine and begins to look and act like a teenager, these pressures may be particularly dangerous. She is in added jeopardy because her advanced vocabulary and general knowledge already cause her to be perceived as older; the addition of physical maturity and fashionable clothes may now add to the asynchrony of her developmental levels. Asynchrony is one of the major features of all gifted children's lives—the tendency to be advanced in one developmental area, such as intellect, and simply average or even a little below average in one or more other areas. The smart girl who has reached puberty may be intellectually and physically a woman, but she may still be a child emotionally.

Food and eating likewise pose new challenges for Millennial Girls. The Shriver Report of 2011 shows that today's girls' and women's health is suffering.[59] Girls in all socioeconomic levels have higher rates of obesity than their mothers, and girls in poor communities (sometimes called "food deserts" because grocery stores with healthy choices are absent) have the highest rates of obesity. Lack of access to non-processed foods, fruits and vegetables, and low fat entrees is characteristic of many American communities, and school lunches often contain unhealthy sugar and fat content. Although Michelle Obama's leadership and strong attention in the media to the obesity epidemic have raised awareness and resulted in improvements, systemic changes have only just begun.

Perhaps related to this trend, eating disorders, including anorexia nervosa and bulimia, which were rare before the 1980s, are continuing to increase in the U.S. and in many cultures that are highly influenced by American media.[60] The girls who are most at risk are elite athletes such as gymnasts and dancers. In a study of talented at-risk girls, my colleagues and I found a high incidence of eating disorders even among math-science talented girls.[61] Although many researchers have sought links between perfectionism, giftedness, and eating disorders, it turns out that giftedness or perfectionism alone does not predispose girls to eating disorders.

Mood disorders, family history of dieting, and negative body image all contribute to eating disorders. It is nevertheless important to recognize that smart girls who already are depressed, perfectionistic, driven, and who are in performing arts and elite levels of athletics are particularly at risk. A family history of dieting is quite relevant. As one young smart girl said, "My mom diets and fails all the time. I think I developed a desire to be thin to show that I had better willpower than she does." Millennial smart girls, having grown up in an era of pressure to be thin and with the intellectual ability to research on the Internet and remember the caloric value of every food and exercise activity, may be more at risk than girls of previous generations. Because eating disorders pose such a threat to health, even leading to death in extreme cases, they must be taken very seriously by parents.

Another way in which Millennial girls' health is suffering is in terms of mental health. Millennial girls are much more likely than their mothers to be on medication and treatment for depression and anxiety, and in most societies girls and women are much more at risk for depression than boys and men.[62] Jean Twenge noticed the increases in anxiety and depression in this generation and blamed it on the culture of individualism:

> *Our growing tendency to put the self first leads to unparalleled freedom, but it also creates an enormous amount of pressure on us to stand alone. This is the downside of the focus on the self—when we are fiercely independent and self-sufficient, our disappointments loom large because we have nothing else to focus on. But it is not just us: Generation Me has been taught to expect more out of life at the very time when good jobs and nice houses are increasingly difficult to obtain. All too often the result is crippling anxiety and crushing depression.[63]*

Twenge also blames the self-esteem movement in the schools during the 70s and 80s for teaching children to believe that everyone is "special," that mere participation and effort, rather than excellence in academics and athletics, should be rewarded. This is controversial because it is clear that many children—those who are poor, who represent groups who are looked down upon, and who do not conform to gender stereotypes—do not feel special in any positive way. If her assessment is correct, it would have even greater implications for an increase in depression among smart girls because in a culture where everyone is rewarded equally, those girls who are outstanding in achievement are unlikely to be rewarded for their efforts. Smart girls who maintain high standards for their own achievement could easily become depressed when nothing they do receives any more recognition than the actions of any other student, when a teacher or parent rewards gold and garbage alike. In addition, those who have grown up in schools and communities where failure is impossible because all levels of achievement are praised are more likely to have difficulty dealing with criticism. When I asked a group of students at the elite School of the Art Institute of Chicago why such a high proportion of the student body drop out in their first year, they did not say it was due to finances or academic difficulty; instead, as one student said, "They couldn't handle criticism. If they had never had a portfolio critiqued as intensely as it is done here, they would just fall apart."

While depression and anxiety are the most common disorders among girls, diagnoses of attention deficit disorder (ADD), obsessive-compulsive disorder (OCD), and bipolar disorder are on the rise. James Webb and his colleagues in *Misdiagnosis and Dual Diagnoses of Gifted Children and Adults: ADHD, Bipolar, OCD, Asperger's, Depression, and Other Disorders* show myriad ways that giftedness can be mistaken for any of these disorders.[64] The heavy marketing of psychopharmaceuticals to doctors and the tendency toward overdiagnosis and misdiagnosis account for much of the rise in overall numbers of girls with these disorders.[65] Nevertheless, it is possible that the disproportionate funding of special education programs compared to gifted programs, along with other changes in the context of girls' lives, are influential factors as well.

One of the strongest findings of the 2011 Shriver report was that girls and women have greater responsibilities and pressures today than ever before. One quarter of girls are born to single mothers, and women in this generation are much more likely to be the primary breadwinners for their family. As a result, girls and women are working harder and longer hours. When a single mother works, the duties of childcare and housekeeping usually fall to an older girl sibling; by the teen years, most daughters of single mothers must work. In the NSF Talented At-Risk Girls study, we found that many of our girls were not only getting As in their classes; they were babysitting and fixing meals after school for little brothers and sisters, doing the laundry, preparing breakfasts, and often working at fast food jobs as well.[66]

What has suffered most in the lives of today's children, according to many social scientists, is play.[67] Overscheduled middle class children seldom have time to develop their own ways of playing and relaxing when they have to attend every possible athletic and performance event. Girls from low-income families often have no time for play because they are already working. Even in homes with two adults working, girls often find themselves overwhelmed with academic, family, and community responsibilities. In the current Freshman Year Study of the nation's newest cohort of college students, significantly more females than males said that they felt "overwhelmed."[68] For many young women in college, the stakes are higher than ever: they must choose their majors carefully with an eye toward repayment of college loans; they have greater social demands than their male peers in terms of membership in campus organizations and informal groups; and they often continue their family responsibilities.[69] Once they are out of college, stopping or dropping out of careers is not an option for most young women of the Millennial generation, not only because of loan repayments, but also because of the poor job market. Smart females, therefore, are likely to be just as pressured, stressed, and overwhelmed as other Millennials, for most of their lives, if current trends continue.

For smart girls, one of the greatest challenges is growing up in the era of the No Child Left Behind Act (NCLB) in the U.S. and similar policies that exist in countries like Australia and England. The movement for continuous academic testing, school report cards, and teacher accountability has resulted in most children in the U.S. receiving a one-size-fits-all education that focuses on basic minimal levels of competence, and which consequently lowers standards so that schools can meet their goals. Smart children have been left behind by No Child Left Behind, and there is increasing evidence that NCLB classrooms have lowered the achievement of the most gifted students. In 2004, in *A Nation Deceived*, Nicholas Colangelo, Susan Assouline, and Miraca Gross decried the state of education for gifted children under NCLB, showing how little programming exists, particularly the kind of acceleration that has been proven to be the most effective education for bright children.[70] What this means is that most gifted girls have been bored throughout their entire school careers prior to college. For the luckiest and wealthiest, there have been private schools, homeschooling, and online schooling; those families who could not manage these options had to try to enrich and accelerate their daughters' education outside of school by whatever means they could. Gifted girls not only missed out on academic challenge during the years of NCLB, but they missed opportunities to develop a strong body and a lively interest in the arts because schools made cuts to physical education, art, and music during these years.

In all this gloomy data from the Pew Report, the Shriver Report, the AAUW studies, and finally the NSF studies, is there any good news for millennial girls? Fortunately, yes. Plenty!

The Good News

The greatest good news is that the achievement gaps between males and females are closing. The gap in math and science achievement is closing as more and more girls take the advanced courses that are necessary—not only to gaining high scores on achievement tests, but also to promoting their understanding and comfort within the world of science, technology, engineering, and math.[71] More females than males now go on to higher education, and the gap is closing in their college achievements as well. In some majors, such as biology and law, women now outnumber men. Where once women did not aspire to even a college education, they now aspire to graduate school, professional school, and challenging careers. This generation of girls continues their superior performance in high school and carries that high achievement on to college.

The good news for parents is that the generation gap experienced by Baby Boomers, particularly regarding values and interests different from those of their parents, has also closed. Girls today are much closer to their parents than those of the previous generations, and they are particularly favorable of their mothers.[72] When asked who they admired most, the girls in our NSF Talented At-Risk Girls study—the majority of them children of single moms—most frequently named their mothers. Millennial girls trust their moms, share confidences with them, and often work side by side with their moms to nurture their families.[73] For mothers of smart girls, this means a great responsibility to understand that they are, in the most profound sense, the role models for their daughters. Fathers, too, need to recognize that, according to the studies referenced here, their smart girls may be less likely to rebel against their family rules and values than they once were. When U.S. college freshman, men and women, were asked what they wanted most out of life, a happy family life topped the list for the first time.[74] When we discuss Millennial smart girls, we need to be sensitive to the fact, that more than any other generation, they want to find a way to accomplish their dreams *and* have a happy family life.

Another great change for Millennials is the use of technology. It turns out that the fears and concerns parents and teachers have about girls sexting, solicitation, use of Internet, and social networking may be, for the most part, unjustified.[75] The Pew Foundation survey discovered that the young people of this generation are savvy users of the Internet and all the other technologies available. Most girls today not only know how to use Facebook, Twitter, texting, email, and a wide variety of social networking and gaming sites, but they are also well aware of the dangers of meeting strangers online.[76] The vast majority of girls name "keeping in touch with friends" as their primary use of texting, Internet, and social networking; only boys name "flirting" as one of their primary uses.[77] Some technology writers have recently said that the "Touchpad Generation" represents a whole new wave of changes in how children learn.[78] Little girls can follow their interests with ease, even long before they can work a keypad, and the tablet falls quickly into the bright toddler's hands as a gateway to knowledge, connection, and entertainment.

Studies show that Millennials are the most tolerant generation ever; those questioned by the Higher Education Research Institute's Annual Freshman Survey overwhelmingly endorse civil rights, equality for women, and gay rights.[79] They grew up in diverse classrooms and watched television shows that featured egalitarian couples and teams, families including almost every ethnic group, and positive presentations of gay people. Although most of them went to schools where kids ate lunch in separate ethnic clusters, many of them still have at least a few friends that are from dissimilar ethnic backgrounds. Most of them are religiously tolerant; even those from strong religious background understand the need for tolerance of others' religious and spiritual viewpoints. For smart girls, this is good news; many of them have known rejection because of their intellectual differences, and most of them empathize with others who have been rejected or bullied. Smart girls enter a world where equality of women is at least an ideal, although they know that they still may be paid less and rise more slowly than men in many occupations.

Millennials are the first global generation. They expect that at some point in their education they will travel far from home. They have ready access to news media from other countries and are aware of global issues such as climate change, hunger, and wars. Although most schools still do not offer language education at the elementary level, smart girls are eager to study various languages and cultures as soon as they receive the opportunity to do so. Smart girls in the Millennial generation often have international friends that they have met here or abroad and even have friends in other countries with whom they play online games. More than ever before, opportunities for education and work all over the world are open to these young girls.

Finally, although Twenge criticized this generation for its overconfidence, the positive side to this is that young people today have higher aspirations and greater idealism than any previous generation.[80] Despite all the challenges they encounter in a world that is "hot, flat, and crowded," they have hope.[81]

What does it mean to be a smart girl today?

- ❖ Her childhood is shorter because she enters puberty at an earlier age and the media she encounters sexualizes children and teens.

- ❖ She has been bored all her life in schools with little or no gifted programming.

- ❖ She is overstressed and overworked with little time for self-created play.

- ❖ She is more at risk for obesity or eating disorders than any other generation.

- ❖ She is at risk for misdiagnosis of psychiatric disorders.

- ❖ She may have difficulty with criticism and failure, yet also sees herself entitled to success.

- ❖ She has grown up in difficult economic times, so is more likely to have to work and to worry about financing her education.

On the other hand,

❖ She loves and trusts her parents, and she wants a happy family for herself one day.

❖ She is more confident and achieving in math and science than any of her predecessors.

❖ She has high aspirations.

❖ She uses the Internet wisely and has access to more knowledge and connectedness than any generation before.

❖ She is a citizen of the world, comfortable with diversity and ready for an international lifestyle.

❖ She is hardworking and willing to help her family, her school, and her community.

❖ She is open, tolerant, and able to work with and appreciate people who are different from her.

❖ She is hopeful, optimistic, and forward looking.

Smart Girl Profile | Alyssa, age 14

Alyssa is a 14-year-old African American girl who attends Arizona State University's Herberger Young Scholars Academy (HYSA)—an early college entrance program for highly able students.[82] During her second year, she served as the school's first student government president. That same year, she was awarded the Girls Rule Foundation's girl of the year leadership award. Her career goal is to become a veterinarian, and she wants to attend the University of California-Davis. Her career assessment characteristics include artistic, conventional, and enterprising interests, which suggest that she has the potential to pursue entrepreneurship or leadership in an artistic field. She is a competitive hip-hop dancer who has danced with a professional troupe from the U.S. Women's National Basketball Association (WNBA).

For two years, Alyssa took a university-level positive psychology course and regularly participated in Smart Girls workshops and in the Smart Girls Leadership Summit. She is strategic; that is, she is able to figure out several different approaches to meet her goals.

As an introvert, she is most comfortable by herself or with small groups, yet as a dancer and a leader, she has grown accustomed to performing and speaking in front of large audiences. She is a visionary; she has the ability to imagine her future and to create a multitude of ways of bringing her vision into reality.

Alyssa loves to learn; she absorbs knowledge rapidly and always desires more information and more experiences. Super-conscientious, she has an amazing work ethic. Her classmates and teachers can count on her to complete her work and to do her very best work as much as possible. She's courageous; she pushes herself, even though she feels reluctant, to try new things because she knows new experiences will help her grow as a person and provide new opportunities for learning and leadership. You never have to wonder what Alyssa thinks; she easily expresses her opinions even when they're unpopular. She doesn't hesitate to stand up for kids who need to be defended. Here is what Alyssa has to say about being a smart girl and her thoughts on issues that affect smart girls.

In Her Own Words by Alyssa

What's the hardest part about being you? *Being accepted for who I am. Staying true to who I am and reminding myself who I am. I have things that I need to work on, but I shouldn't have to do a 180 to fit how others want me to be.*

On her greatest strengths: *My greatest strengths are focus, work ethic, and having a vision and goals. I have the focus needed to accomplish a lot. I take the time to make sure that I am doing something to the best of my abilities by being alert and in the moment. In most of the things that I do, I need focus, whether it's in or out of school. My work ethic and focus keep me levelheaded. I need both of these qualities in my life and without them I imagine that I wouldn't be very successful in the tasks that I decide to take on. I'm not easily discouraged from the challenges that I'm given. I am capable of a lot of things; when I feel like I'm capable, I'm very confident.*

On being assertive: *I'm assertive, which can be both a strength and a weakness. It's a strength because I am able to get into a situation and get the job done even when it's high stress. I can be an effective leader even when it's tough to be a leader. Being assertive is a weakness because in friendships I'm sort of bossy. I get it when people tell me I'm being bossy. Then I'll stop being bossy in some situations. But if* *it's called for, I'll tone it down a bit, but I'll still be assertive enough in order to get things done. When it comes to stating facts, I don't say anything unless I know the answer for sure. But when it comes to giving my opinion on something, I'm willing to speak up.*

On being mature: *Because of my maturity, I'm more likely to tell my friends to knock it off when they're doing something stupid. I can see things from a teacher's perspective.*

On expressing anger: *Being pissed off is my way of expressing that I'm hurt. It's easier to express anger than to say I'm sad or to admit that my feelings are hurt.*

On qualities she would like to cultivate: *I wish to cultivate the qualities of openness to experience and positivity. I would like to be more open to experiences because I feel that it would allow me to leave my comfort zone more often, allowing me to explore options that I wouldn't normally explore. Cultivating more positivity would just allow me to be a better all-around person. I feel that now I am positive but not enough to where I would like to be. The change in my personality would be refreshing to others and to me. I don't want to be too positive, but I'd like to be a little more than I am now.*

On Being a Smart Girl: *When I first started at the program, I was feeling not smart. I wondered, 'Why am I trying to come here?' I questioned my smartness. I really felt so not smart. I'd like to be more confident when it comes to my intellect. I feel that sometimes I sell myself short by comparing myself to others who I see as smarter than myself. I am confident in myself when it comes to activities outside of school. I know I am a great dancer and cheerleader, but in class I feel that I am not the best or ideal student. I compare myself to everyone else. It seems that I look at how I don't add up to others, not how I do, which makes me sometimes question how I stack up against the rest of my classmates. Hopefully, my perception of myself will change with time.*

What's your advice for other smart girls? *Don't be afraid to ask for help. Asking for help doesn't make you weak. Also, stand up for yourself. Go for your dreams because they're possible. Just because you're a girl, it might make some things harder to do, but it's not impossible.*

What's your heart's desire right now? *Just be happy. It sounds kind of boring, but I want to be happy with the things that are going on in my life. To stay positive and to know that I can make it through.*

CHAPTER 4

Eminent Women

Throughout this book we encourage girls and women to challenge themselves, to get the best education and training possible, and to strive for excellence—but to what end? What is the goal of intense preparation that begins as early as elementary school? Is the goal to become financially successful? To attain personal excellence? To reach eminence? Eminence has typically been defined as a certain level of renown with biographies in major libraries or having many products or accomplishments cited or recognized in a domain. We will use this definition, but with caution because, as will be seen, in many fields of endeavor women's contributions have not been recognized.[83]

We believe that smart girls should be prepared to optimize their chances for innovative contributions that transform their fields of expertise. During the preparation period, the smart woman's goal should be to develop eminence in a field of study that most closely aligns with her creative flow as well as her interests, needs, and values. Financial success, status, and even eminence are less important in our opinion than finding one's true vocation and calling in life.

However, we also believe that *optimal development* should be a smart woman's goal that spans her lifetime. Optimal development is not only the realization of one's talents, but also includes the fulfillment of one's most deeply held values. In Western societies, self-actualization has been a synonym for optimal development. Self-actualizing people lead a life that incorporates daily challenge and frequent experiences of flow, which allows for the possibility of transcendent, peak experiences.

Eminence for women is a controversial topic. As we noted earlier, from the first studies of eminent women, scholars have objected to using judgments of eminence as a measure of realization of women's potential.

49

When it came time to follow up the achievements of Terman's gifted youth 40 years after identification, Oden was not able to include women in the measures of eminence.[84] She said, "The study was limited to men because of the lack of a yardstick by which to estimate the success of women...no one has yet identified the best measure for identifying the success of housewives and mothers."[85]

It is easy to guess what the big problem is with using eminence as a measure of achievement of potential. Eminence has always been determined by men. Not just in the past, but in the present too. The people who decide such things as the Nobel Prizes, the Fortune 500 CEOs, the conductors of leading orchestras, and the exhibits for the Museum of Modern Art are primarily men. Even though women have achieved great gains in all fields of endeavor, the leaders of their fields—the people who decide who will achieve the greatest status—remain men. Even when both women and men are involved in selection, such as election to the highest political offices, there is a tendency to vote for men over women. There are many reasons for this, which range from actual bias of male leaders, to lack of societal support, to women's own choices not to compete for the highest positions in a discipline. The result, however, is that in almost every occupation and discipline, there are far fewer eminent women than men. In addition, many of the fields where women have done their most extraordinary work, such as teaching and social action, are less valued in both prestige and financial reward by society than leadership in sciences, business, or politics.

Some have argued that eminence as the goal of gifted education is unrealistic, given the scarcity of high positions. Others have claimed that eminence as a goal of education leaves out the development of emotional intelligence, character, and spirituality. Still others point to education for eminence as perpetuating elitism and class differences because eminence comes more easily to people who have both financial and social resources. Many of these arguments were presented in a special issue of the journal, *Gifted Child Quarterly*, devoted to an eminence model of talent development. The major article, by Rena Subotnik, Paula Olszewski-Kubilius, and Frank Worrell, concluded:

> *Finally, outstanding achievement or eminence ought to be the chief goal of gifted education. We assert that aspiring to fulfill one's talents and abilities in the form of transcendent creative contributions will lead to high levels of personal satisfaction and self-actualization as well as produce yet unimaginable scientific, aesthetic, and practical benefits to society.[86]*

We agree with those leaders in gifted education that eminence should be the goal of gifted education—because only the most rigorous, sustained, and focused education will provide a young woman with the most options for her future. Smart girls need the best possible education, targeted toward the development of advanced levels of language, mathematics, science, computer skills, and social sciences. Those with specific, extraordinary abilities need coaching toward the mastery of a musical instrument, vocal music, fine or dramatic art, technology, or athletic ability. Anticipating eminence by providing high-quality education and training means that the smart girl will have choices as she reaches adulthood—choices she would not have had if she opted out of the pursuit of the highest level of accomplishment too early.

Trying to fit women into traditional models of academic and career development, however, usually means that girls are encouraged to be more like boys are expected to be—more assertive, less emotional, more competitive, less relationship-oriented. Too many career development programs for young women in business and in Science, Technology, Engineering, and Mathematical (STEM) fields simply provide remedial masculinity lessons. Young women are encouraged to think about careers as if one's occupational life existed in a vacuum, completely isolated from one's relationships and emotional life. This isn't good for boys *or* girls because a satisfying and successful adult life for most people is as rich in relationships as it is in work. For women particularly, eminence as the goal of education seems to ignore the very real facts of women's childbearing and their continued high investment in childrearing. Most examples of eminence have been men who not only had little responsibility for childcare, but also who had wives whose main activity was support for their husband's career. Even in today's world of dual-career professional couples and great opportunities for women, those individuals who attain the highest levels of productivity and eminence in most fields are married men, while married women trail behind both single men and single women.

Kate Noble, Rena Subotnik, and Karen Arnold made a convincing case for their model of talent development for gifted girls and women; their model takes into account more than simply ability and education, but also the context of women's lives. By the end of this book, we hope to have expanded their model, based on new research, into one that takes into account all the foundations and filters in a woman's life—and all the paths to optimal development.[87]

Even though the number of women attaining eminence in all fields has grown steadily in the last three decades, many authors who studied eminence continued to focus initially on how men attained eminence. For example, Simonton's first study of genius in 1988 and Gardner's many popular books about creative people and leaders have little to say about eminent women.[88] Mihaly Csikszentmihalyi's book *Creativity*, in 1996, described one of the first major studies that carefully included a proportionate representation of women.

There are, however, some findings about eminent people that are so robust across studies of both men and women that they should be considered in determining the strengths of eminent women. The lives of eminent women today who are now achieving acclaim in their domains of talent provide examples of how those research findings play out in women's development of eminence, and the next section provides short biographies of eminent women of the 21st century. First though, let's explore what conditions predict eminence in women.

Conditions of Eminence for Women

What are the characteristics of smart girls that predict significant accomplishment during adulthood?

In the first edition of *Smart Girls*, several key themes emerged in the analysis of the lives of eminent women: voracious reading and learning; ability to be alone; willingness to be different and a corresponding acceptance of being special; and high aspirations. These traits set smart girls with potential for eminence apart. In preparation for their work, they often had experienced single-sex education or intensive, individualized education and excellent mentoring. The women had a sense of individuality and separateness in their lifestyles; they chose partners who valued the women's goals; they combined career and family in creative ways; and they had all fallen in love with an idea.[89]

Mihaly Csikszentmihalyi studied both eminent women and men with significant creative achievements.[90] However, he was careful to delineate some of the specific characteristics of eminent women, such as having delayed or carefully planned and integrated marriage and childbirth into their careers. In addition, he found that these women experienced flow consciousness in their work—a state of mind in which they felt fully engaged, challenged, at one with their work, and free of the constraints of time.

Carolyn Yewchuk's studies of Canadian and Finnish eminent women placed a strong emphasis on the role of "being special" and showed how supportive, loving parents (particularly fathers) who encouraged girls' identities as brainy, smart, and capable were vital to the origins of eminence.[91]

Yewchuk's studies, however, found that the eminent women gave primary importance to their own abilities and personal characteristics in childhood, rather than their family's support, as the source of their accomplishments.

In Leonie Kronborg's studies of Australian eminent women, family members provided strong support for their daughters' interests and talents.[92] Personal characteristics and individual abilities contributed to the women's success as well. These included developing a strong belief in self due to particular educational and work experiences, perseverant effort, resilience, independence, courage, passion, risk-taking ability, and self-determination. Additionally, these women demonstrated high abilities in their talent domains. Kronborg suggested that one of the strongest themes in her findings was the women's passionate engagement in a talent domain. The women were intrinsically motivated to engage in their talent domain; they had frequent flow experiences along the way. She said, "Most of these women who fell in love with an idea and through their passion, emotional intensity, excitability, and high energy levels were able to succeed at what they loved to do while enduring adversity and overcoming obstacles set in their path."[93]

Ability and personal characteristics, such as self-esteem and self-efficacy might be necessary, but these traits alone are not sufficient for the development of talent, according to the National Science Foundation Gender Equity Study of Talented At-Risk Girls.[94] These authors found that the childhoods of most eminent women were marked by loss, stress, and adversities that had to be endured or overcome. In their NSF studies of girls gifted in math and science, they tested the idea that being an at-risk gifted girl might actually build the resilience that would be necessary to deal with difficult challenges in adolescence and adulthood. Their samples of talented, at-risk girls did indeed match the profiles of scientific interest and curiosity, self-efficacy, and resilience that are characteristic of accomplished women scientists.

Karen Freeman and Herbert Walberg studied eminent African-American women and found that they shared psychological traits and conditions generally similar to those that benefit other eminent men and women.[95] However, they were significantly more likely than other eminent people to show independence, perseverance, single-mindedness, and alertness to novelty.

David Lubinski and Camilla Benbow's 35-year follow-up of mathematically precocious youth provided additional insights into women's preferred career paths.[96] They found that even women who were at the highest levels of achievement in mathematics often still preferred fields that matched their social and personal values, often in the humanities or social sciences.

Finally, Diane Halpern and Fanny Cheung interviewed women who were international leaders in both politics and business, asking primarily how they combined career and family.[97] They found these eminent women were extremely organized, insisted on their identity as excellent mothers as well as excellent and high achieving in their domain, planned for motherhood with careful timing, and married a partner who shared equitably in family responsibilities.

Do eminent women today differ from those in previous generations?

The individual lives of eminent women representing three generations illustrate and illuminate the research findings. In the first *Smart Girls*, published in 1985, it was much easier to choose representative women because so few biographies and autobiographies of eminent women were available. Those chosen were the obvious ones, like Marie Curie, Georgia O'Keeffe, and Eleanor Roosevelt, because only about 50 biographical books that pertained to women could be found in a major university library. The explosion of women's achievement since 1985 and the vast opportunities for exploring eminent women's lives not only in biographies but also through interviews and videos on the Internet made the current selection a far more daunting task.

We chose to limit our selection to women whose families, schooling, and career paths reflected today's world. Diversity was important, too, including not just various cultural groups but also women from many talent domains. Our biographies begin with Generation X women and one special Millennial girl, all of whom have broken new ground in their respective fields. We begin with novelist J. K. Rowling, actress Tina Fey, activist Malala Yousafzai, vocalist Jennifer Hudson, and businesswoman Sheryl Sandberg. Then we focus on earlier generations of women, trailblazers who are paving the way for today's talented women, including the first Latina U.S. Supreme Court Justice Sonia Sotomayor. From the scarcity of autobiographies or biographies of physicists or engineers, it appears that women in the physical sciences and engineering apparently are less likely to share the story of their lives despite the many eminent women scientists. Fortunately, we found a distinguished animal scientist and anthropologist, Jane Goodall, and a remarkable health scientist who is also a U.S. Military leader and gay rights activist, Margarethe (Grethe) Cammermeyer.

J. K. Rowling | Writer[98]

No list of eminent women would be complete without J. K. Rowling, the creator of the most popular fictional smart girl in the world—Hermione Granger. As the author of the Harry Potter books and the inventor of Hermione Granger, J. K. Rowling has been credited with being the first planet-wide phenomenon in children's literature and with introducing an entire young generation to the pleasures of reading. Although a very private person, J. K. Rowling's own story has taken on the elements of legend; for our purposes, her life illustrates many of the qualities and conditions of eminence for creatively gifted young people.

She was born Jo Rowling in the small town of Yate, England, to working class parents in 1965 at the beginning of a turbulent era in history. From the time she was two years old until the age of nine, she lived in Winterbourne—a beautiful, natural part of England near a town with all the resources of modern life. Her sister was born two years later, and the two girls would grow up in a household of books and imaginary play with little television or other media to distract them. Her mother, Anne, cared for the girls full time; both Anne and Jo's father, Peter, read to the children often. Even as a very young girl, Jo loved to write as well as read, and she wrote her first story about a rabbit when she was about five years old. She and her sister played with their best friends, the Potter children, as wizards and witches around the family homes, riding broomsticks and creating adventures. Not only did she develop a fondness for the name Potter and wizards, but she also grew up to look and act very much like Hermione Granger, the smart, young heroine of the Harry Potter books. She described herself as a child as plain, red-haired, and bookish.

Jo was the youngest child in her class in the small school in a beautiful old building near her home. It was an open-plan school that provided a safe and happy learning environment in which she was able to continue reading voraciously. She went to school with the Potter children and then followed school with more imaginative play.

When she was nine years old, the family moved to a home near the Forest Dean, a magical area that included the ruins of old castles and churches like Tintern Abbey, made famous in the poem of the same name by Wordsworth. Even though her parents believed that their new home was a better place to raise their children, it was a difficult move for nine-year-old Jo. The new school she attended at Tutshill was a strict place that she says was like something out of Dickens—implying a very mean-spirited environment. Without her old friends, it seems that she turned to academics, attempting to prove herself to her teachers.

By the time she was 11 in secondary school, she had soured a bit on school, but not on reading. She read Jane Austen and fell in love with the character of Emma; she was so impressed with Jessica Mitford's book, *Hons and Rebels*, that she would later name her daughter Jessica. The story of an independent, intellectual girl rebelling against a society of rigid class structures seemed to bring clarity to her own discomfort with the inequalities she saw at her own school.

In secondary school, she hated shop class and found chemistry difficult, but loved English. Her teachers noticed her as a talented writer, and one particular teacher, Lucy Shepherd, became a mentor who had a great effect on her. Lucy was a demanding instructor who taught Jo how to structure her writing and how to edit and shape a piece until it was nearly perfect. She was also a supporter of women's rights and women's goals, and encouraged girls to have their own dreams beyond marriage and family.

At age 12, Jo wrote *The Seven Cursed Diamonds*, a fantasy tale, and entertained friends with her stories. Bored living in her small town, she wrote and read and learned to love reading Shakespeare. She also loved art and created images to go with her stories. She played guitar with her mother. Soon, however, her world changed when her mother was diagnosed with multiple sclerosis. The prospect of her beloved mother's health deteriorating under the ravages of a very harsh form of the disease was terrifying to Jo, and this unfortunate situation loomed over much of her adolescence as a source of anxiety and sadness.

She turned to alternative culture and the punk rock scene with her friend Sean Smith to escape the sadness of her home life and dull village. They went to concerts and shows in his car and spent hours in each other's company, feeling like outsiders but loyal to one another.

Although she had excellent grades and the praise and recommendations of her teachers, Jo was not admitted to Oxford, her first choice for university. Although her parents were proud that she was going to college, the rejection was a huge disappointment to her. She went to Exeter, her second choice school, but found it very different from what she expected of college. She didn't perceive the other students as particularly intellectually oriented, and she wasn't inspired by her classes or teachers. Although she dreamed of being a creative writer, she chose a practical major in languages. Perhaps it was her lack of enthusiasm for this major that led her to often skip classes, which made for a mediocre academic career. Her only positive academic experience seems to have been her time abroad in France, where she taught English and lived with a multicultural set of roommates.

In her early career, as with her college education, Jo chose to be practical and took secretarial courses and jobs. One can wonder how much she was influenced by her working-class parents and by the career advice that girls in the 1970s and 1980s typically received. Regardless, she learned to type fast and to camouflage her own creative writing as work projects, which became the major positive outcome of such mundane, noncreative work. In fact, she worked on a novel for adults much of the time she was working as a secretary.

She lived in London and travelled frequently to Manchester to visit her boyfriend. It was on one of these trips that something happened to her that became the stuff of legend and many retellings. On one long trip, with the train delayed for four hours, Jo began daydreaming out of boredom. She says that the character of Harry Potter just came to her, fully formed, right there on the train. From that moment on, she jotted down notes whenever names, places, and events emerged in her mind. She wrote notes in longhand and typed them later. She had found her story, and the passion for creative writing she had nourished for so long burst forth in her first full novel manuscript.

Despite the joy of discovering Harry, the next years were filled with sorrow and difficulty. After a long illness, her mother died. Jo was bereft. Her grief was intense, and the loss led to a time of intense introspection and much writing. As she created the story of Hogwarts School of Wizardry and Witchcraft and young wizards, she found respite from her sadness. Around the same time, she also broke up with her boyfriend. With her mother gone, and her father and sister living far away, there was nothing to hold her to England, so she went to Portugal to teach English and to write. She fell in love with a Portuguese man, Jorge Arantes, and married him in 1992. She became pregnant soon after, but the marriage was not a happy one, and she and her husband began to quarrel intensely shortly after the birth of her daughter, Jessica. Eventually, she divorced him, returned to the United Kingdom with her baby, and settled in Edinburgh, Scotland where she lived in poverty while she wrote.

This period in her life also became a much-told story, because she lived in a shabby, tiny apartment with her baby, survived with government assistance, and tried to find a way to support herself and her child. She studied for and earned a teaching certificate. During this whole time, she lived not only in the world of struggle and sadness, but also in the magical world of wizards, for she remained hard at work on her novel. Every day she walked her baby in the stroller until she slept and then went to a café owned by her brother-in-law to write. It was a difficult time, but she was doing two things she loved: raising her daughter and writing. Eventually, she began teaching as well, and her economic burdens lifted a bit.

At last the book was finished, and she sent a professionally written query letter along with three chapters to a literary agent. After reading the rest of the manuscript, he agreed to take her on and began shopping the manuscript to publishers. Jo received 12 rejections before Bloomsbury Press in England finally purchased the first book, *Harry Potter and the Philosopher's Stone*. Although only 500 copies were printed initially, readers loved the book, and it began to win awards. She received a cultural grant from the government that made it possible for her to take time off from teaching to write. She didn't know it yet, but her world had changed forever.

This first book was quickly sold at auction to Scholastic Books in the U.S. for what was, to Jo, an unbelievably large amount of money. And that was just the beginning. During the time her first book was being prepared for publication and then distribution, she was already working on her second, *Harry Potter and the Chamber of Secrets*. It sold immediately, allowing her to move to a pleasant apartment and enroll her daughter in an excellent school.

Even though the worldwide Harry Potter craze would be like a fairy tale come true to many people, for Jo there was a downside. The huge crowds, the deluge of fan mail, and the demands on her time and privacy were stunning for her. As an introvert and an independent woman, the stresses of being a public figure were immense. By 1999 and publication of the *Harry Potter and the Prisoner of Azkaban*, she was so popular in the U.S. that she was practically mobbed in Boston and was badly frightened.

The story of Harry Potter became more complex and darker as it grew, but Jo's audience was growing up alongside Harry and his friends. Many Millennial gifted children led two lives, one in the real "Muggle" world and one in the imaginative world of Harry Potter created by J. K. Rowling. All seven books sold 450 million copies, making it the best-selling series in history. The books were translated into 67 languages. Each book was made into a film, and the films became blockbusters. Even theme parks arose around the world of wizards. All of this made J. K. Rowling the first and only author to become a billionaire.

The extraordinary success of the Harry Potter series did not mean the end of writing for J. K. Rowling. She had wanted to write a novel for adults for a long time and in 2012 published *A Casual Vacancy* about a highly contested and controversial parish election in a divided village. Although much of the story is told through the eyes of the adolescent children of the contenders for the election, there is much adult material including sex, alcohol, and violence. Some have criticized Rowling for publishing this book, given that children might not be able to resist a book written by her. Defenders repeat that an author is not responsible for who reads her books. She has also now published two mystery novels for adults under the penname Robert Galbraith, for her own reasons. Rowling continues to defy anyone's attempts to pin her down or categorize her.

Tina Fey | Award-Winning Actress, Writer, Producer, Comedienne[99]

Tina Fey is, without a doubt, talented and smart. Whether she performs in comedy skits on Saturday Night Live or as the lead actress in feature films, she possesses a sharp wit, wonderful spontaneity, linguistic brilliance, and self-confidence. Her writing is impeccable; she is a funny, ironic, and unselfconscious storyteller. Yet ability and intellect alone cannot explain Tina's prolific accomplishments. Over the course of her career, Tina has received seven Emmy Awards, three Golden Globes, and four Writers Guild of America Awards.

In 2010, she became the youngest-ever recipient of the Mark Twain Prize for American Humor. Twice, she has been named to *Time Magazine's* list of the 100 most influential people. Her memoir, *Bossypants,* sold over 2 million copies and was at the top of the *New York Times* Bestseller list for five weeks.

Tina possesses the unique combination of openness to experiences, extraversion, and conscientiousness that has enabled her to rise to eminence as a comedic actor. She's playful, funny, and outspoken. She's conscientious—a high achiever who has the self-discipline necessary to persist beyond what ordinary people would consider extreme. She's spontaneous and flexible, but also possesses excellent boundaries; she avoids personal drama in her own life and in the lives of her colleagues. She says she has never used drugs and drinks alcohol sparingly.

Clearly the powerful combination of personality traits, intelligence, and creativity has contributed to her notable career. But one aspect in particular makes Tina's story special: Her parents never once asked her to change her career path away from entertainment to something more sensible, like science, law, or medicine. Instead, they provided what we wish all parents would—the essential elements for nurturing a creative person, including exposure to arts and culture, acceptance of Tina's adolescent friendships, and the freedom to explore and develop her talents.

A member of Generation X, Tina was born in 1970. She grew up with her brother—eight years older than she—and her parents in Upper Darby, Pennsylvania, a working-class suburb of Philadelphia. Tina's mother, Jeanne Fey, the eldest child in a Greek immigrant family, was 39 when Tina was born. Her colleagues at the brokerage firm where she worked referred to her unexpected pregnancy as "Mrs. Fey and her change-of-life baby."

Long before Tina's birth, her mother had dreamed of going to college. She had grown up watching a generation of adult women take up the slack in the U.S. work force left by men fighting in World War II. But by the time Jeanne was old enough to go to college, the days of Rosie the Riveter were over; the war had ended, it was 1948, and women were expected to return home so that the boys who had been in the war could get back to work or go to college. In hindsight, it is probably not surprising that, at 17, Jeanne's dream of college was dashed. Not only was she not going to go to college, but the money that would have paid for her education was sent back to the village in Greece to help family there. When it came time for each of Jeanne's younger brothers to attend college, they were each allowed to go.

Tina was in her 30s when she learned this part of her mother's story. She says that she was shocked: "This was one generation ago. She's not my grandmother..." So when Tina was ready to go to college, her mother had a list of schools for Tina to apply to, including Princeton and all of the other colleges that she herself wasn't allowed to attend. Is it any wonder that Tina's mother supported her daughter's educational opportunities?

Tina's father, Don Fey, was a gifted linguist—he was a code breaker during the Korean War and speaks self-taught, flawless Greek—and artistically talented as well. Tina says that he's a "skilled water colorist." He's also an immensely practical man; he worked as a fireman in Philadelphia and later as grant writer at the University of Pennsylvania. Tina succinctly summarizes his intense, intimidating presence in this way: "He's just a badass." Don Fey was a big influence on his daughter; he provided her with structure and freedom, reasonableness and ingenuity. Because of his own passion for the arts, he introduced Tina to painting, art museums, and other creative endeavors. In the mid-1970s after Title IX made gender equality in sports the law, her father taught her how to play baseball and not to "throw like a girl." Throughout her childhood, Tina did everything she could to make sure that she didn't get into trouble with her father. In summary, Tina says that her father gave her "the knowledge that while you are loved, you are not above the law."

When she was in kindergarten, a stranger with a knife attacked Tina and slashed her face. In spite of this traumatic event, Tina says that she went through her childhood quite unaware of the scar. It is interesting, in terms of resilience, how little attention she gives to this event. She was an inventive, self-confident little kid; her active imagination allowed for hours of solitary play. She was strongly influenced by the 1976 U.S. Bicentennial celebrations; in an NPR interview, she recalled that she was often "off by [her]self, playing dress-up in colonial garb." She watched the *Love Boat* on television, Gene Kelly movies, and played the flute in middle school. In the eighth grade, she completed an independent study of comedy while a schoolmate simultaneously studied communism. Though she wasn't especially athletically talented, Tina went on to compete in tennis and reflects that team sports produce "a different kind of woman" with a "game-on, let's-do-it work ethic." The positive experiences Tina had with her father playing baseball and her experience on the tennis team most likely contributed to her self-confidence as well as her sense of body awareness, which are critical to comedic actors' success.

In high school, Tina rarely dated. Instead, she focused on choir and theater performance. As verbally talented girls are apt to do, she wrote a "tart" anonymous column for the school newspaper under the byline "The Colonel." She calls herself a super-nerd. In her junior year, Tina joined a theatre group called *Summer Showtime* because her boyfriend wanted to join. He then quickly ended their relationship, leaving Tina for one of the show's blonde dancers. As Tina recovered from this heartbreak, her social life blossomed. She became friends with the gay boys who weren't out yet, which in the late 1980s was not unusual. Her social circle expanded to include other creative young people, but her closest friends were two women in their mid-20s—a lesbian couple—Karen, an improv teacher, and her partner Sharon, a scene painter. We should note here that it is a huge thing for parents to tolerate a bright girl's outlandish friends, particularly when she's involved in the theatre, but Tina's parents went beyond tolerance and enthusiastically accepted all of her creative friends regardless of their sexual orientation. She remembers that her parents "never reacted negatively to the four-year-long pride parade that marched through their house." Her parents' acceptance sent a subtle, yet empowering, message to Tina that they trusted her judgment and choices.

After high school, Tina attended the University of Virginia where she majored in drama. When she graduated in 1992, she decided that she wanted to work in comedy. She moved to Chicago and began training with the famous improv comedy troupe, *Second City*. While studying improv, she worked at a local YMCA to make enough money to pay her bills. Her parents reinforced her confidence; she says that they never worried that she would return home having failed in her work.

Tina's romantic life naturally intertwined with her career; she met her husband, Jeff Richmond, who is 10 years her senior, at *Second City* in 1994. The couple dated for seven years, working alongside each other for most of it. While at *Second City*, Tina was invited to submit scripts to *Saturday Night Live* (*SNL*) and was subsequently hired as a writer for *SNL* in 1997. In 1999 at age 29, she set a precedent as the first female head writer at *Saturday Night Live*. Tina and Jeff continued their professional collaboration during her tenure at *SNL*.

Since childhood, Tina was reasonable and self-confident about her appearance, though she humorously recalls her hope to someday become good-looking enough for radio—"NPR pretty." The entertainment industry holds a high bar for a woman's appearance, and much has been written about Tina's weight loss and makeover, which she undertook while a writer. After the physical transformation, she received the onscreen role as one of the anchors on *SNL's Weekend Update*, which Tina refers to as a career upgrade.

Tina and Jeff married in 2001 when she was in her early 30s. Jeff describes their marriage as "borderline boring—in a good way" and reveals that the couple has strong boundaries around their relationship. They had their first daughter in 2005 when Tina was 35, at which point she was well established in her flourishing career.

Tina's successes have been widespread. In addition to her work on television, she wrote the screenplay for and co-starred in the feature film *Mean Girls* and went on to write, direct, and produce several other acclaimed comedies. In 2006, Tina left *SNL* to create *30 Rock*, a comedy that in many ways mirrored her life; the show's protagonist, a variety show producer named Liz Lemon, was very much Tina's alter ego. Tina continued to work with her husband Jeff, who became the show's music composer-producer. The show got off to a slow start, but after the first few seasons, *30 Rock* eventually became an award-winning series.

When American political satirists focused on candidates for the 2008 U.S. Presidential elections, a colleague noticed Tina's uncanny likeness to the female Republican vice-presidential candidate, Sarah Palin. Tina returned to the *SNL* stage to play the role she is now probably best known for—her flawless impersonation of Sarah Palin.

Tina's show *30 Rock* ended its 7-year run in early 2013. She says she's not certain what she'll do next. In the meantime, she remains pragmatic about a 40-something woman's longevity in the entertainment industry. As she notes in her memoir, "I have observed that women, at least in comedy, are labeled 'crazy' after a certain age," though the term *crazy* is most likely a euphemism for older women's diminished sex appeal in Hollywood.

There is a steadiness in Tina, a kind of responsibility and seriousness that both belies and informs her comedic timing. Only a woman with a swift intellect and a profound mastery of her craft can make comedy look effortless. Whatever Tina does, there is little doubt she will continue to surprise us and make us snort with laughter when she says the next provocative thing. The very thing that when combined with proper timing, cadence, and tone sets the world right again after an insult, a rejection, or even worse. We can be sure that Tina will say the thing that other smart girls play over and over again in our heads because the perfect moment to say it aloud has long since passed. It speaks profoundly to those who didn't have the courage to say it out loud in the first place.

Jennifer Hudson | Award-Winning Vocalist and Actress[100]

The first time many people noticed Jennifer Hudson—really noticed her—was probably in her role as Louise from St. Louis, Carrie Bradshaw's assistant in the feature film *Sex in the City*. As Louise, Jennifer was radiant; her character's confidence, hope, and future-mindedness played in stark contrast to Carrie's cynicism and sadness. Jennifer's performance was captivating.

The evolution of Jennifer's professional career has been a remarkable, straight-shot to the top. First, she was a finalist on the popular television show *American Idol*. Though she was eliminated midway through the competition, she caught the eye of filmmakers in search of a buxom African-American female vocalist for a supporting role in a feature film. Though relatively unknown and with little acting experience, she was nonetheless selected for the role in *Dream Girls*. She went on to win an Academy Award for her performance as Effie White in the film *Dream Girls*; soon after she was featured on the cover of *Vogue* magazine, and she was subsequently selected for her supporting role in *Sex in the City*. Just a few years later, she became only one of eight women in history to win both an Oscar and a Grammy, joining Whoopi Goldberg, Barbra Streisand, Julie Andrews, and Audrey Hepburn.

But where did she come from? How did she emerge as the bright light of Louise from St. Louis? "My family always says my voice is a gift—a precious jewel I inherited from my maternal grand-mother," Jennifer Hudson has said. But even from the beginning, Jennifer had economic, cultural, and personal barriers to overcome. Despite the odds, her talent and personality, her willingness to seize opportunities, and the support of her family and community, along with some serendipity, all contributed to her success.

Raised by her single mother and maternal grandmother on Chicago's South Side, a historically poor, predominantly African-American part of Chicago, Jennifer was a funny, creative, playful little girl who sang like an angel. Her vocal training began naturally in her church, and soon people from all around Chicago came just to hear her sing. Her passion for music was spurred by her inherent talent as a vocalist combined with the relationship she was able to create with her audience.

In much the same way that sports are a vehicle for exceptional athletes to emerge from economically difficult circumstances, music was Jennifer's way out. She didn't have the advantage of attending high school in a high income, privileged part of Chicago, which would have made her journey easier; instead, her academic environment was less than exceptional, with a 60% high school graduation rate.[101] Unlike many of her schoolmates who succumbed to the risks inherent to growing up in an economically and socially underprivileged community—teenage pregnancy, crime, and violence—Jennifer developed her talents by depending upon the expertise of teachers in her high school's music department. She sang in the high school chorus and distinguished herself as a top performer. She was not only committed to her goals but also possessed the self-discipline and internal drive necessary to persevere. Social life was not a priority; she rarely attended parties or spent time with friends outside of school. Her dedication and focus helped her to persist in an academic environment where many of her schoolmates failed. Like most of her peer group, she worked briefly in a fast food restaurant, but a conflict with a manager strengthened her determination to succeed as a vocalist.

Soon, Jennifer partnered with an enterprising high school friend who booked singing gigs for her at local churches, funerals, and weddings. He encouraged her to compete in talent shows and even purchased her evening gowns with his personal credit card. Jennifer recalls that after each performance, they returned the dresses for a full refund. Later, her friend would encourage her to audition for a singing role on the Disney cruise line, which she won, and *American Idol,* which gave her international visibility. After high school graduation, she saved money and worked to be able to get advanced training on vocals, performance, and stage presentation.

Creative teenagers often announce their need for self-expression through their clothing choices. Jennifer was no exception. In high school, she developed her own style that accentuated her shape and size, but rather than serving as a connection with others who could help her succeed, she was still discriminated against for her weight early in her career. Beyond the high school experimentation phase, personal flair is often misunderstood and therefore not accepted by the gatekeepers, the entertainment industry leaders in Jennifer's case. She lost opportunities—not because of her talent, which critics agreed, was extraordinary—but because of her appearance. She soon discovered that her talent alone was not enough to help her achieve her goals, and she came to realize that talent and public image go hand in hand. As she slowly transformed her physical appearance, she became increasingly sought after in television and film. Still, it is notable that early in her career, Jennifer won an Academy Award for her portrayal of a curvaceous African-American woman.

Jennifer's life has been infused with tragedy and loss. She was 16 when her grandmother died, and it was then she decided to pursue her music seriously. In her memoir, Jennifer describes her own resilience and strength: "Instead of wallowing in my sadness, I vowed that I would go on with my life, follow my dream, and make good decisions along the way so I would make her proud." Then less than a month after her debut album was released in 2008, Jennifer's life took a devastating turn: Three of her family members—her mother, brother, and nephew—were murdered by her sister's estranged husband. Jennifer removed herself from the spotlight to mourn privately. In much the same way that she dealt with her grandmother's death, she found positive ways of coping with the tragedy.

Of all of her performances, one of the most poignant moments of Jennifer's career came during the 2013 Super Bowl pre-game show where, five years after losing her own family to gun-related violence, she joined the children from Newton, Connecticut, who were survivors of the shootings at Sandy Hook Elementary School. Together they sang *America the Beautiful*, offering evidence of the healing power of solidarity and song.

The pathway to eminence for Jennifer required her unstoppable spirit, the emotional support of her mother and grandmother, and further support from a church community that encouraged and celebrated her talent. She actively made decisions early in her life to focus on her music; she seized opportunities to audition and perform and she persisted in spite of great tragedy to find her way back into the spotlight to thrive once again.

Malala Yousafzai | Pakistani Schoolgirl, Education Activist for Girls

It is not often that someone so young rises so quickly to eminence. Yet Pakistani schoolgirl Malala Yousafzai at age 14 has already done much in her young life to raise global awareness of the problem and the importance of girls' education. Unfortunately, her activism came with a great personal price.

Just three days before the United Nations' first International Day of the Girl—a global campaign in 2012 to raise awareness about the importance of educating girls around the world—gunmen boarded Malala's school bus and shot her in the head at point blank range. Her injuries were severe. In the days that followed, she remained in critical condition after surgeons removed a bullet lodged in her neck. Within days of the shooting, she was transported from a military hospital in the Swat Valley of Pakistan to the United Kingdom, where she underwent rehabilitation, including skull reconstruction and cochlear implants. She was released from the hospital in early 2013.

When the Taliban claimed responsibility, their spokesman justified the attack in this way: "She was pro-West, she was speaking against Taliban, and she was calling President Obama her ideal leader. She was young, but she was promoting Western culture in Pashtun areas." The spokesman promised that if she recovered, they would make another attempt on her life. One might wonder why a 14-year-old girl was viewed as a threat worthy of assassination.

Malala's story begins long before she was born. Before the Swat Valley became a stronghold of the Taliban and even before it was a Pakistani province, Swat was a British holding. The regent of the area brought Western ideas to his people—even to the peasants. A university was built, and a young man, a member of the rural underclass, pursued his education. He learned English and studied poetry and Urdu. He became a social activist with a radical idea for that time—opening a school for girls, a goal which he achieved. Soon after, he became the father of a little girl with bright, shining eyes: Malala.

She was named for the Afghan Joan of Arc who died helping the freedom fighters at war with the British in 1880.[102] Like her namesake, Malala found herself at war. In the 21st century, atrocities in Pakistan are committed by extremists who go to great lengths to maintain the traditionally conservative beliefs and practices, including prohibiting girls' education. Despite the threat, her father read the poetry of Rumi to her and "encouraged Malala to speak freely and learn everything she could." He had created her school, which Marie Brenner describes as "an oasis of enlightenment, a tiny dot in a surrounding theatre of war..." which in turn cultivated her love of learning and her passion for education.

When watching Malala in video interviews, it is easy to forget that she is so young; she is courageous, curious, well-spoken, and self-assured. Along with her classmates, she studied English, Pashto, Urdu, physics, biology, math, and Islamic studies. She has a magnetic and passionate personality, and the principal of the school remembers her this way: "She would sit in the classes when she was only three, listening, her eyes sparkling...a little girl taking in the lessons of the older children."

When BBC journalists decided to create a documentary to investigate the Taliban's actions against women's education in Pakistan, they wanted to focus on a girl who would bring their story to life. The journalists spoke to Malala's father. Initially, an older girl had been chosen as the subject of the story but she backed out; her family was frightened for their daughter's safety—and rightfully so. When the opportunity arose for someone else to become the face of the documentary, her father chose Malala, then only 11 years old.

Producers decided Malala's story would take the form of narrative journalism, a blog for BBC-Urdu. *The Diary of a Pakistani School Girl* was to have been anonymous, but it did not stay that way.[103] According to Marie Brennen, within months of writing her blog posts, Malala became the symbol for everything that was wrong in Pakistan and ultimately a danger to Pakistan's conservative ideologies. Still, no one could have imagined the jeopardy that her simple narratives would put her in.

Her BBC blog entries began just days before the Taliban edict went into effect in 2009. She handwrote her posts, which were secreted to a contact at the BBC, translated from Urdu into English, and posted on the site. Her posts are the simple and thoughtful contemplations of an 11-year-old school girl. Yet she writes about experiences that no parent would wish his child to endure, as illustrated by her entry posted the day before the Taliban's order was to begin:

> *15, January 2009. The night was filled with the noise of artillery fire and I woke up three times. But since there was no school, I got up later at 10 a.m. Afterwards, my friend came over and we discussed our homework. Today is the last day before the Taliban's edict comes into effect, and my friend was discussing homework as if nothing out of the ordinary had happened.*[104]

In an interview with the BBC just a few months after the 2012 shooting, her father reflects on his decision to allow his daughter to write the blog. "Of course," he said, "it was a risk. But I think that not talking was a greater risk than that because then ultimately we would have given in to the slavery and the subjugation of ruthless terrorism and extremism." [105] Her father's determination seemed to defy the prevailing notion in that region that girls are the property of men, with limited choices as a result; many girls are forced to leave school after their primary education, to stay at home and marry young.

Early in her life, Malala thought she wanted to become a doctor. But her father seems to have seen a different promise in his daughter that couldn't be ignored. In the 2009 *New York Times* documentary, he said that he wanted her to become a politician because he could see that she had the power to change a system of oppression.[106] One can understand why; Malala seems to understand her role in the politics of educating girls. Before her shooting, she visited with Richard Holbrooke, U.S. President Obama's special representative to Afghanistan and Pakistan, and ardently requested, "Respected ambassador, if you can help us in our education, so please help us."

What might cause a girl living under Taliban rule to be so consistently defiant, so frankly disagreeable in the face of such danger? Like her father, she is fearless, if a bit reckless. In a 2011 interview, Malala told CNN reporters, "I was scared of being beheaded by the Taliban because of my passion for education. During their rule, the Taliban used to march into our houses to check whether we were studying or watching television."[107] Her tenacity seems not to have been shaken by the shooting.

The relationship between Malala and her father is situated at the center of her story. But what role did Malala's mother play in her daughter's life? Other than brief allusions to her support of Malala, little has been written about her mother. Documentary director Adam Ellick comments on this fact in a blog post on the day of Malala's shooting saying, "Her father was a bit traditional, and as a result, I was unable to interact with her mother. I used to chide Ziauddin about these restrictions, especially in front of Malala. Her father would laugh dismissively and joke that Malala should not be listening. Malala beamed as I pressed her father to treat his wife as an equal. Sometimes I felt like her de-facto uncle. I could tell her father the things she couldn't."[108]

Members of the Western media have described Malala as a little girl who leveraged the power of the social media. She was, after all, a girl whose timely message captivated the West. Yet Malala's story is not simply about a girl who wanted an education. Social, political, and economic issues that surpass the educational needs of a 14-year-old girl are also at work. The Taliban, Western journalists, and Malala's own father each play a significant part in her rise to international prominence. Malala was selected, groomed, coached, and filmed by people whose agenda seemed to be to expose the world to the situation in Swat. There is cause to wonder: Was she also exploited? Her father was a business owner. His schools were being shut down, which meant the loss of his livelihood. Though her father has not expressed regret, members of the media express both guilt and remorse about her shooting, and one member of the media even wondered if their efforts made a commodity out of this small, graceful, shining, little girl. The facts suggest that perhaps yes, she was.

Yet there are things about Malala's journey that even her own father could not predict or control. In Pakistan, the literacy rate is just 13% for women over age 15.[109] Malala is one of few Pakistani women who have been empowered through education to use her voice. Her ongoing collaboration with Western media gives her a powerful platform from which to communicate her message. The actions that made her an icon in the West have put her life in danger in Pakistan. Her father's willingness to seize opportunities on Malala's behalf and to permit media access to her was the catalyst for both her shooting as well as her international visibility. In 2011, she was nominated for the International Children's Peace Prize. That same year, she was awarded the first Pakistan Peace Award.

Malala's story continues, as does the plight of girls' education in Pakistan, but there is promise of change. In February of 2013, Malala was nominated for the Nobel Peace Prize, the youngest person ever to receive a nomination.[110] As she recovered from her injuries in the U.K., she continued to gain the support of powerful advocates in the West who have started the Malala Fund, which she will use to promote the education of girls around the world.

Malala returned to school in the spring of 2013, this time in the U.K. where her father secured a position as a diplomat at the U.K. consulate. About her return to school, Malala said, "I think it is the happiest moment that I am going back to my school. Today I will have my books, my bag, and I will learn…. I want to learn about politics, about social rights, and about the law. I want to learn how to bring change in this world."[111]

In the meantime, Malala continues her work. At the 2013 Women of the World Summit in New York City, she announced a $45,000 grant from the Malala Fund that would be used to educate 40 girls in her native Swat Valley. Ever an activist, she sparked others to join her movement: "Let us turn the education of 40 girls into 40 million girls."[112] In 2014, she became the youngest recipient of the Nobel Peace Prize, which she shares with Kailash Satyarthi.

Sheryl Sandberg | American Business Woman & Leader[113]

The very first edition of *Smart Girls* was published when Sheryl Sandberg was in high school, and it suggested that gifted girls are sometimes too well-adjusted for their own good. As an adolescent, Sheryl Sandberg was at risk of becoming just that—extraordinarily ordinary. She was all that Gen X girls were encouraged to be: pretty, likeable, smart, and *well-adjusted*. In fact, what strikes us about Sheryl Sandberg is how *nice* she seems. Despite that, doormats—the idiom sometimes used for overly-agreeable women who can't say *no*— are not ranked #5 on the *Forbes* Most Powerful Women list. And they certainly don't become the Chief Operations Officer of Facebook or the first female member of the Facebook Board of Directors. How did Sheryl get there?

Sheryl, born in 1969, grew up in North Miami Beach, Florida, as the oldest of three children. She was a smart little girl—bossy, independent, spirited, and always picked last on sports teams—which may explain why she rarely played childhood games, but instead organized other children's (and adult's) activities. As she grew, she learned to temper her opinions by becoming chameleon-esque—our term for a bright girl who hides her opinions, creativity, and intellect behind an ordinary, well-adjusted facade. Sheryl reflects, "I spent more time in high school worrying about getting a date to the prom than I spent worrying about math. And I was a smart girl."[114]

Even as an adult she sometimes expresses embarrassment about her childhood assertiveness. As a teen, she masked her assertiveness and her drive, perhaps to fit in to the social scene of her large public high school. When she discovered that she had been voted most likely to succeed, she made the yearbook editor give the award to someone else.

Despite her reticence to be acknowledged for her high school achievements, Sheryl clearly had ambitions. She applied to Harvard University; upon learning of her acceptance to the prestigious institution, mystified high school friends asked her why she wanted to go to school with all of the nerds. Her guise as a well-adjusted girl was reinforced during her freshman year at Harvard when she received a C on the first 5-page paper that she'd ever written in college. When she went to an academic advisor for help and support, Sheryl was told that she was accepted to Harvard based on her personality, not on her academic abilities.

It is unfortunate that we need to talk about Sheryl Sandberg's personality at all. Her work and life should stand as the marker of her contributions. Yet clearly something inherent to her personality—besides her likeability—has enabled her to become one of the most influential leaders in the 21st century. We believe that her quiet ambition, assertiveness, self-discipline, and her warm, gregarious personal style enable her to be both liked and respected—a combination that is difficult, yet essential for female leaders to master. In her highly popular book *Lean In: Women, Work, and the Will to Lead*, Sheryl provides clues concerning why the mastery of both respect and amiability is considered a leadership "sweet spot" for women. She describes research on the *success penalty*, which reveals gender differences regarding how others perceive successful men and women. That is, as men become more successful, they become more likeable; when women become successful, they are less well-liked by both men and women.

In fact, after Sheryl was named to the *Forbes* Most Powerful Women list, she worried about just such a reaction—until a colleague encouraged her to accept the recognition gracefully and use the platform it provided to further her purpose. She reflects, "If more women are in leadership roles, we'll stop assuming they shouldn't be."

Bright girls who are taught to focus on personality and appearance over the substance of their work will need to learn that, in order for others to take them seriously, they must first take their own work seriously. Until then, they will likely suffer from the *Imposter Syndrome*, and Sheryl had a severe case of it throughout college. She was plagued by self-doubt and says, "No matter how well I did academically, I was always afraid that I was going to get caught for not really knowing anything." She describes the syndrome's symptoms perfectly: "Every time I was called on in class, I was sure I was about to embarrass myself. Every time I took a test, I was sure that it had gone badly. And every time I didn't embarrass myself—or even excelled—I believed that I had fooled everyone yet again. One day soon, the jig would be up." Regardless of her internal conflict, on a deeper level she did take herself and her ambition seriously: She majored in Economics, not a major for the meek.

At home, her parents took their own work seriously and expected her to be successful. Her great-grandparents were poor Jewish immigrants who valued education. Her father, a physician, was ambitious and focused. With a degree in French Literature, her mother had begun to pursue a Ph.D., but dropped out to raise Sheryl and her two younger siblings. As their children became self-sufficient, Sheryl's parents started a non-profit program to help religious and political prisoners in the former Soviet Union.

Her parents' dedication to social causes inspired Sheryl, who expected that she herself would lead a social movement. "I hoped to change the world," she said. Her vague career vision began to change during her junior year at Harvard, when she and her female class-mates formed a student organization to encourage more women to pursue careers in economics and government. Her professor, Larry Summers, encouraged their efforts and ultimately became Sheryl's thesis advisor. Ironically, years later Summers sparked controversy by suggesting that the reason there are so few women at the top of their fields in science may be due to "issues of intrinsic aptitude," (an issue which we discuss later in Chapter 10).[115] Regardless of this ridiculous suggestion, Summers was a key sponsor in Sheryl's career.

In 1991, Sheryl graduated *summa cum laude* from Harvard with a B.A. in Economics. After graduation, she accepted her first job as a research assistant to Larry Summers who, at that point, was Chief Economist at World Bank. She turned down an opportunity to study abroad and instead moved to Washington, DC, where she said there were plenty of eligible men.

Why would an ambitious, intelligent young woman consider marriage so soon after college? It turns out that Sheryl, like many gifted Gen X girls, received many conflicting messages about work and marriage. Though her parents encouraged her to be academ-ically successful, they also wanted her to marry young, "before all the good ones were taken." According to their wishes, she married quickly, but soon realized it was the wrong marriage for her. Though the breakup was painful and Sheryl viewed her divorce as a failure, she eventually learned to worry less about what other people think.

Meanwhile, she returned to Harvard Business School and earned an M.B.A. in 1995, then worked at a global management consulting firm, McKinsey and Company, from 1995 to 1996. In 1996, she was tapped to be Larry Summers' Chief of Staff for the U. S. Treasury Department for the Clinton Administration. During her tenure, she realized that the technology sector held the most promise for bettering the human condition and decided to pursue work in that area when her term at the Treasury Department ended in 2000.

Sheryl deliberately made a transition into the technology sector and joined the global technology company Google as Vice

President of Global Online Sales and Operations. She debated taking the position until a mentor told her, "When you're offered a position on a rocket ship, you don't ask which seat...you get on the ride." In 2004, Sheryl married her second husband, a successful entrepreneur, and together they are raising their two children. With the success of her second marriage, she tells women, "The most important career choice you'll make is who you marry." She advised women that they should marry a man who's willing to do half the work or to marry a woman because women tend to share responsibilities at home equally.

In 2008, Sheryl accepted Mark Zuckerberg's offer to leave Google and become the Chief Operations Officer at Facebook, and in 2012 she became the first woman to be appointed to the Facebook Board of Directors. Her partnership with Zuckerberg sets the tone for the next generation of leaders; this was the model for her vision of empowered, intelligent men and women working shoulder to shoulder with each other. It is worth noting that Mark Zuckerberg is from a generation of men raised by mothers who came of age at the height of the feminist movement; Mark's mother, Karen, attended medical school and became a licensed psychiatrist. Could it be that the first generation of men who are truly comfortable with egalitarian relationships are those whose mothers are from the Post-Sputnik generation?

Now in her early 40s, Sheryl has focused on raising awareness about the importance of men and women working collaboratively both in the workplace and at home. Her book, *Lean In*, provides an in-depth look at her philosophy and the inherent challenges that successful women encounter when combining work and marriage.[116] She writes from first-hand experience and holds herself up as a role model for what is possible for young women. Sheryl has been willing to start a conversation about changing the face of leadership at the highest levels of business and politics. Since becoming an advocate for women in leadership, she is intent on changing the perception that women cannot be leaders and that men can't be equal partners in the home. She addresses the stereotypes of women in leadership head-on, saying:

> *Leadership is not a gendered characteristic. Leadership is for both men and women ...[but] our stereotypes run deep. Men should lead. Men should speak up. Men should have opinions.*

Women should nurture, help others, sit back ...I think we can change that. Now is our moment to change that. If we understand the stereotypes and how they are holding us back ...if we start applauding girls for leading, applauding women for reaching for ambitious posts, we can change this. ...If we draw on the talents of women in the workforce and men at home—our companies will be more efficient and more effective, and our kids better off because they have involved fathers in happier marriages. ...[I] believe in women and men having both a successful career and family. The more women we get into positions of power, the more likely we'll get that.[117]

Turning from the Generation X and Millennial women who will continue to evolve as leaders, we now examine the lives of women in their 50s, 60s, and beyond who pushed the boundaries of their fields and became trailblazers whose lives continue to inspire generations of gifted women by demonstrating what is possible.

Sonia Sotomayor | First Latina
U.S. Supreme Court Justice[118]

Born in a poor Puerto Rican neighborhood of New York, Sonia Sotomayor seems to have been shaped by two great forces in her life: the challenges of having Type 1 diabetes and a severely alcoholic father on the one hand, and on the other, the support of her mother, who believed in education, and her grandmother, who provided shelter from the storms of life.

Sonia grew up surrounded by poverty. Her father was crippled by his alcoholism; after work as a tool- and die-maker, he locked himself in his room and drank. Her mother, who seemed distant and distracted to Sonia, worked as a practical nurse nights and weekends so that she could send Sonia to a parochial school that provided a better education than the public school. Diagnosed with diabetes at eight years old, Sonia at first needed to depend on the adults in her life to give her the daily insulin shot that would keep her alive. When she saw that her mother might not be there and her father's hands shook too much, she made a decision to do it herself. It was her first great act of independence and courage. Her joys in life came in the time she spent with books that she read and with her grandmother, her Abuelita, who gave her the belief that all people have a purpose. She learned to read early, taught herself English, and spent all her time one summer immersed in reading books. Her favorite books were the *Nancy Drew* mysteries that captivated her with the stories of a young detective who always solved the mystery and brought justice to wrongdoers.

Despite dreams of being a detective, she was aware of her limitations. How could a girl with a life-threatening disease live a life of action and intensity? She was determined to find a career that would allow her to use her gifts of problem-solving and debating, and by the time she was 10 years old, she knew that she wanted to be an attorney. The idea of learning everything she could in order to fight for justice fired her with passion. Her brilliant, troubled cousin Nelson saw her growing sense of purpose. In her memoir, Sonia writes, "What Nelson saw driving me arises from a different kind of aspiration: the desire to do for others, to help make things right for them. Strange ambition for a child? Some might say so, but I've been aware of it for as long as I can remember."

Her school, Blessed Sacrament, was a strict, sometimes terrifying place where the nuns ruled with an iron hand; nevertheless, a few teachers recognized the young girl's talent and encouraged her in her writing and reading. When her mother purchased a set of *Encyclopedia Britannica* books, Sonia's world opened up.

The large and lively extended Puerto Rican family and community had a profound influence on Sonia's life. Family gatherings in times of celebration and sorrow filled her with respect for the struggle of all Puerto Ricans who make a new life in New York City. Her family returned to Puerto Rico for visits often, and she was able to grow up both bilingual and bi-cultural, feeling fully American and fully engaged in the culture of her origin.

The death of her father was a time of hardship and despair because her mother became paralyzed by her grief, refusing to reach out to Sonia and her brother. Once again, Sonia seized responsibility, doing everything she could in the household, but one day she simply insisted that her mother get up and get well. This was the beginning of her attempts not only to understand her family's past and present dynamics, but to change her own conditions through forceful influence on those around her.

At Blessed Sacrament, she was so successful as a student that she graduated as valedictorian. Her teachers encouraged her to apply for a competitive high school, and she was admitted to an outstanding Catholic school, Cardinal Spellman, where her talent for argument and debate blossomed. It was also there that she met one of the most important teachers of her life: Miss Katz. Miss Katz was a Jewish progressive working in a Catholic school; she told Sonia she was there because she admired the many priests working for human rights and freedom in South America. Not only was Miss Katz Sonia's first broad-minded mentor, but she was also the first teacher to instruct her students in critical thinking and the art of the persuasive essay. Through this teacher and others who recognized her talent, Sonia bloomed academically, and worked harder than ever to prove herself. In debate, she found that she had a powerful talent for putting together an argument and telling it like a story. She loved the idea of arguing a point from opposite perspectives; it built in her the capacity to see an issue from many viewpoints and to appreciate the complexities of any controversial issue. Kenny Moy, a Chinese student growing up in an African-American ghetto, was her student coach. His brilliance in dissecting an argument, his intense criticality, and his insistence on perfection in presentation were to be the training that she needed to win one debate after another.

Few people in Sonia's life knew anything about college or college culture; it was Kenny Moy, who went to Princeton, who called her and told her that she must apply to Ivy League colleges. She didn't even know what that meant, but she had seen the film *Love Story*, supposedly set at Harvard, and she fell in love with the vision of academic life in one of these bastions of learning. She got little encouragement from her guidance counselor who simply attempted to steer her to Fordham, a nearby Catholic university, but she persisted nevertheless, and her high SAT scores and high GPA won her visits and interviews at major colleges. Her visits taught her that Ivy League colleges were dominated by highly privileged, white people who were very different from her.

"I don't belong here!" she thought at Radcliffe. At Yale, she found many more students of color, but she was put off by the "Down with Whitey!" attitudes. It was at Princeton where her longtime friend Kenny Moy led her to a comfortable group of intelligent students and she met casual, interested faculty. She had found her academic home.

At Princeton, she became involved with the Puerto Rican Student Association and for the first time truly delved into the history of her culture. She revived a course in Puerto Rican history that had not been taught in several years and used her travel to Puerto Rico to compare her own observations with what she read in the literature and history of the island. She learned that there were Hispanic chronic patients in hospitals who had no access to bilingual speakers, so she organized a group of campus students to be volunteer helpers and visitors to these lonely people. Finally, she did her senior thesis on the history of the first governor of Puerto Rico. In all these ways, she claimed her ethnic identity and learned to understand the problems and appreciate the riches of her culture. She graduated with a Phi Beta Kappa induction and *summa cum laude*—both honors that she had previously been unaware of.

Throughout college, Sonia dated her boyfriend, Kevin, and after college, they married. In her memoir, she reflects, "If our decision to get married was essentially unexamined— it was what couples like us were expected to do— we were hardly more reflective about the marriage once inside it. We simply set about playing house, which seemed a natural enough extension of our companionable coexistence before exchanging vows." They had an egalitarian marriage, and that meant not only sharing household tasks, but also mutual consideration of each other's career goals. Because Sonia had more clarity about her goals and had been admitted to Yale law school, they moved to New Haven, while Kevin took a laboratory assistant job and applied to medical schools.

Yale law school provided an extremely challenging education taught by giants in the field; it also provided the support that Sonia needed to learn a whole new way of thinking and argumentation. She was required to learn how to think on her feet and to argue aggressively for her point. José Cabranes, who had served as special counsel to the governor of Puerto Rico and was Yale's general counsel, was Sonia's first true mentor. She said, "When a young person, even a gifted one, grows up without proximate living examples of what she may aspire to become— whether lawyer, scientist, artist, or leader in any realm—her goal remains abstract. Such models as appear in books or on the news, however inspiring or revered, are ultimately too remote to be real, let alone influential. But a role model in the flesh provides more than an inspiration; his or her very existence is confirmation of possibilities one may have every reason to doubt, saying, 'Yes, someone like me can do this.'" She worked for him, joined the many causes in which he was involved and was introduced to the many extraordinary attorney friends. She published her first article on the legal issues surrounding Puerto Rican statehood and went on to work for the *Yale Law Journal*.

Throughout her academic life, Sonia received feedback that seemed strange to her, like "You argue like a man," or "I've never liked brassy Jewish women." In terms of her argumentative style, it is true that she never hedges or qualifies her statements the way many women do, but these perceptions of her aggressiveness seemed odd, given that her greatest gift, in her opinion, is perceptive listening. Perhaps much of this feedback was related to the fact that in her time, few people had ever seen a Latina who argued with such precision, clarity, and impassioned strength. An example of this was when a partner in a firm at a recruiting dinner asked her rudely if she thought that she got into law school because she was Puerto Rican. She replied, "Perhaps, but membership in Phi Beta Kappa and graduating *summa cum laude* from Princeton didn't hurt." He went on to talk about how affirmative action candidates were unqualified, and Sonia was thoroughly insulted that he stereotyped her as an unqualified, affirmative action candidate. She actually brought formal action against the recruiter, and won her case.

Although she had assumed she would go to work in corporate law like so many other graduates, an accidental meeting with recruiters who were talking about public service career paths changed her life forever. She went to work for the New York District Attorney's Office and never looked back. This was her chance to fulfill her lifelong "Perry Mason" vision of actually seeking justice in a courtroom, rather than writing briefs in a corporate office. She commuted from Princeton, where her husband now attended graduate school in biochemistry, to her new, cluttered, under-resourced, but lively office in New York.

Sonia was known by her colleagues both in prosecution and defense as a person with a truly merciful nature; even when she won a case against an offender she would often seek ways to be sure that the sentencing was not too harsh if the offender seemed to be repentant and making a strong effort to change. On the other hand, she began accumulating an extraordinary number of convictions and even more when she later moved into prosecuting felonies, the kind of heinous crimes rampant in New York at that time. Moreover, she was on the board of the Puerto Rican Legal Defense and Education Fund, providing *pro bono* help with litigation in important cases of voting rights, civil rights, and discrimination. She also joined the Campaign Finance Board for New York City and enjoyed working out structural organizational issues.

Sonia and her husband had by now grown apart in their two different worlds. Besides, he said he could never catch up to her in accomplishment, and she would never need him. She realized that her independence, born of the unreliability of the adults around her in childhood, had led her to never even attempt to rely on another person for financial or emotional support. She knew she needed to accept help, particularly from intellectual mentors, but on the whole she believed her independence had been critical to her survival. She and Kevin separated, eventually divorced amicably, and Sonia moved back in with her mother until she found her own apartment. She realized at this time that she might never have a family of her own; the demands of her work made balance difficult, and her diabetes made the choice to have a child a life-threatening one. So instead she built a family of friends and relations, including children she could love and support.

Her success in several extraordinary cases—including a notorious murder and a child pornography ring—made it clear that she was a first-rate prosecuting attorney. She had her eyes set on the federal bench and realized she needed more experience with other kinds of law, especially commercial law. She landed a job with a firm, Pavia and Harcourt, where she was able to engage in civil litigation. Because of her successes, she was made a partner in a short time, all the more extraordinary given that her partners knew that she hoped someday to be a judge.

The great moment came when Senator Patrick Moynihan arranged for her to apply for a federal judicial position; it was a grueling vetting process, but people like Sonia with her diverse experiences, her Latina cultural knowledge, and her sheer legal brilliance were desperately needed on the bench. She was selected by the Bush administration as a federal district court judge for New York—a stunning achievement, given that she had been nominated by a Democrat. She was glad that she had always refused to declare a political affiliation and remained an Independent.

She went on to the Second Court of Appeals, where she heard over 3,000 cases and wrote hundreds of opinions. She had proven not only that she could handle the pressure of the judicial position, but also that she could work 24/7 without ceasing. Her great moment came in 2011 when she was nominated by President Obama to join the Supreme Court, replacing Justice David Souter. Her nomination battle was long, partisan, and difficult, but at last she was affirmed by a majority and went on to become the first Latina on the U.S. Supreme Court. About her fulfillment of her lifelong dream, she said, "I was under no illusion of having been singled out, chosen for some particular destiny. But I did come to recognize in my good fortune the work of a blessing, a gift that made my life not entirely my own: I was not free to squander it if I chose. Gifts, Abuelita showed us, were for sharing with others."

Margarethe Cammermeyer | Expert on Women's and LGBT Issues in the Military [119]

The tradition of concern for human rights was the cornerstone of Margarethe Cammermeyer's family life. Growing up in Norway during World War II right across from Nazi headquarters meant engaging in her family's actions in the Norwegian Resistance even as a little girl. Her parents sheltered, fed, and distributed arms to Resistance fighters, often hiding the items in her baby carriage as they walked her. Another family tradition was healthcare; her father was a physician who had served in the Belgian Congo, and her mother was the daughter of a director of a psychiatric hospital. Her earliest memories were of the struggle to survive Nazi occupation and the joy of being liberated by American soldiers. After this, she loved the U.S. and the military that had freed her country from the Nazis.

After the war, her father worked at the University of Oslo as a neuroanatomist and pathologist. She was convinced that a laboratory with its papers, equipment, and mice running around in cages was a place where "things were happening" and said, "I love the smell of formaldehyde…it always reminds me of my visits to my father's lab."(p. 31). Her father received a Rockefeller Fellowship and the family visited the U.S. for a year; then in 1950, her father was offered a position in the U.S. Armed Forces Institute of Pathology.

A few years later, when she was 10 years old, they had all become American citizens.

It was a difficult transition for Margarethe because she didn't speak English and everything in the U.S. was very different from things at home in Norway. They moved frequently, and to more comfortable homes, but she was never in one place long enough to make friendships that lasted. In addition, her height and her ability with mathematics meant that she ended up skipping fourth grade into fifth, where she felt awkward and alone. She struggled for several years until she became comfortable with bilingualism; until then, her primary social life was with her siblings. As the oldest, she felt concern for their difficult adjustment as well and did everything she could to make life better for them, including playing lots of tomboy games with her younger brothers.

In athletics, Margarethe found herself taking pleasure in the teamwork and excitement of competition. Her best friend, who used a wheelchair, invited her to watch her sister's fast-pitch softball team, and she was later delighted when asked to join the team. The next years were full of fun out-of-town games, travel, and teamwork.

She also loved science and spent a great deal of time dissecting, categorizing, and organizing specimens of tissues that she brought home from her father's lab. Fascinated by the methods of science, she took to the work spontaneously and with passion. Although she was successful in both softball and in the science laboratory, she felt like a failure as a girl because she wasn't interested in dating or being like other girls. A gym teacher, who demanded excellence and yet provided support and understanding to the girls that she mentored, proved to be an important influence in her life.

It was only decades later that Margarethe had an *Aha!* experience: her first crush on a woman. At this point in high school, however, she knew nothing about romance or sexuality; she dreamed of becoming a doctor, not of being married. Any realization of her own sexual orientation came much later in life.

Margarethe was certain she would be a doctor. She enrolled in the University of Maryland and took the most rigorous classes in math and science that she could find in a grueling double-course schedule. Unfortunately, she also discovered college social life and the pubs, and she went overboard, doing so poorly her first year that she was put on academic probation. All she had ever wanted was to be a doctor, like her father, but oddly, he was indifferent to her dreams, believing that only boys should be supported in career goals. He would not help her with tuition, and her vision of her future began collapsing. The only way she could continue in the medical field and afford her schooling was to go to nursing school, something she regarded scornfully as a lowered aspiration and a "woman's job."

Training in nursing, however, was a transformational experience for her. The constant, dirty, difficult tasks, the contempt of doctors, and the long hours were all a way of re-training herself to focus on the patients rather than the job. She believes she learned compassion for the first time, saying, "It occurs for some in a flash. For others, like me, it is a slower transformation. As you bathe, monitor, and inject each patient, you come to realize that you are also a healer—the hope that begins to surface, the touch that gives comfort, the voice that says, 'You matter'—and when healing is no longer possible, you're the eyes that say goodbye."

She liked the work, but hated giving up her dreams and working in a subservient role. She had a long period of depression, even cutting herself to ease the pain, but she was either frightened out of her symptoms or let them go because of her fear of failing again due to her emotional state.

The U.S. military saved her again, this time with a place where she would not be diminished as a nurse serving soldiers. She became an Army Student Nurse, and there she found herself in a job that fit her true calling—applying medical science, healing, and serving the country she loved.

She graduated in 1963 with a nursing degree from the University of Maryland and went from there to active duty. After basic training, she went to the Martin Army Hospital at Ft. Benning, Georgia and later transferred to Nuremberg, Germany. She was quite comfortable in the European environment—after all, she was a bicultural person. Although she had had little romance in her life, she met a man she liked and was comfortable being with. Harvey Hawken was, in her words, "tall, an officer, and educated." They dated for a year and married in 1965. Together, they were assigned to go to Viet Nam during the most intense battles of the war—the Tet Offensive. They were, however, often stationed in different locations. As military persons, they both accepted this as a fact of life. Nursing during wartime meant attempting to save lives under the most trying of circumstances. At the 24th Evacuation Hospital of Long Binh, Vietnam, Margarethe became head nurse of a medical unit and then head nurse of the neurosurgical intensive care unit. Few women in the military had ever had an opportunity to have so much responsibility for the lives of others; she worked 12-hour days treating men with blown-off limbs, damaged brains, and tropical diseases. Her husband, serving in Cambodia, was enduring similar intense battle scenes. Both were awarded the Bronze Star. She noted that they seemed the ideal military couple.

After their service in Viet Nam, the couple moved to Seattle, Washington, where they farmed, lived self-sufficiently, and began a family. On becoming pregnant, Margarethe was discharged from the military because at that time pregnancy was considered a disability that was unacceptable; women could not have dependents. She returned to school to earn her Ph.D. in Nursing and raised her family in strict, military fashion.

Throughout these years, she became increasingly unhappy. Nothing had prepared her for a life outside the military, a role as a wife, or the tasks of being a mother. She felt like she was being somebody else. The feelings she had often had in the past, the sense of not living her true self, became stronger and stronger, but she had no name for the identity crisis she was enduring. She was innocent of the idea that these feelings came from living with an incompatible sexual orientation; she continued to hear her husband's disparagements of homosexuals and thought nothing of it. In an interview later she noted, "My personal life was falling apart…Things weren't right. Something about my life was wrong. No matter what I did, it wasn't sufficient. I was feeling very desperate."

When the pregnancy regulation changed in 1985, Margarethe was able to rejoin the military in the army reserves. By 1987, she was a Colonel in the Army Reserves. She threw herself into her work achievements, rising higher and higher, and yet the unhappiness remained. She feared that her misery and constant inner pain was bad for the children and that she could not be a good mother. So one day, while the children were in camp and summer activities, she left her family. It was a heart-rending decision and was to have a lasting impact on both the children, who felt abandoned, and her husband, who felt angry and betrayed.

She finally faced up to a fact she had ignored throughout her entire life—that she was a lesbian. There had been many signs for her, but she had denied the possibility. In 1988, she met Diane Divelbess, an artist and retired professor, and fell in love. At last, reflecting upon her life, she knew and accepted the truth. In characteristic boldness, she not only accepted the fact but also refused to hide it from others. During her interview for security clearance in 1989, she spoke the truth, telling the military she was a lesbian. Even though she had an exemplary military record and extraordinary personal accomplishments, she was discharged. There would be several years of conflict with the military over the decision to discharge her. Her attorneys filed suit in the Federal District Court of Seattle to challenge the ban on homosexuals in the military and to demand reinstatement. In this way, Margarethe Cammermeyer was to become the face of change, not only in the policies of the military but also in the attitudes of a nation.

The long court battle was like every other battle she had experienced—it had to be endured. Finally, the judge ruled that the military policy against homosexuals was unconstitutional. Margarethe was reinstated in the National Guard as head nurse once again. She had by this time earned her Ph.D. at the University of Washington and had developed a neurological specialty, particularly in sleep disorders. She could have continued as a researcher, but there was work to do as an advocate.

She never imagined that she would become a spokesperson for gay and lesbian people; however, she realized that because 17,000 gays and lesbians were discharged from the U.S. military between 1980 and 1990, she needed to become their advocate. The Clinton Administration had implemented *Don't Ask, Don't Tell*, a policy whereby homosexuals could serve in the military as long as they were not open about their sexual orientation. This, she realized, was an incomplete liberation. She had been working steadily on her autobiography, *Serving in Silence*, and with the help of writer Chris Fisher, she published this book in 1994. It was recognized by the National Education Association as an outstanding book on human rights and, to her surprise, was made into a movie. In the movie, she was portrayed by Glenn Close; the film won many awards, including a Peabody Award and Emmys for best screenwriting and best actress.

By 1997, Margarethe had retired from the military and entered a new life work in advocacy, politics, and public service. She was constantly in demand as a speaker on LGBT rights. Though she ran for Congress as a Democratic candidate and lost, she believed she learned from the experience. While she had become an accomplished speaker, her love for nursing was too great to abandon. Since she had retired from her successful career in military nursing, she pursued her nursing interest through home care for the elderly. As an expert in neuroscience, she had a profound understanding of the aging brain and knew that she had much to give in this area as well, and so she served in various public health positions, focusing on aging. In 2006, she opened an Adult Family Home where elderly people could be cared for using the most up-to-date medical and psychological strategies.

Her private life continued to be public as the struggle of gay and lesbian people for equality in all aspects of life, including marriage, continued. She hosted an Internet radio talk show where thousands of LGBT people called in with their concerns, their dreams, and their anguish. In the next decade, massive changes would occur in societal attitudes toward homosexuality. Even as society changed, her own children, alienated from her for eight years, came to understand and accept her. Eventually, she and her partner Diane were able to become a blended family, raising her teenage son, enjoying many grandchildren, and pursuing their dual careers.

As an expert on women's and LGBT issues in the military, she was called on to advise the Obama administration on policy, and she was able to celebrate a great victory when the vestiges of *Don't Ask, Don't Tell* disappeared. Gays and lesbians could now serve openly in the military, but they still did not have the same rights and benefits as straight married people. Margarethe continued to speak out against these bans. She and Diane had a civil ceremony in Oregon in 2004; she felt betrayed when her own state of Washington nullified gay marriages. It was, therefore, one of the happiest days of her life when she and her partner of 15 years were married after the state of Washington later approved gay marriage. In a celebration that was spread throughout the world as a victory for human rights, Margarethe and Diane were the first to get a marriage license in 2012 in their home state of Washington.

Jane Goodall | Anthropologist[120]

Jane Goodall believes that the experiences she had as a child not only shaped her future, but also were almost prophetic. Born in 1934 in England, she spent most of her childhood with her mother, aunt, and grandmother in a large, old house surrounded by gardens that they named "The Birches" because of the three beautiful silver birch trees that grew there. She remembers that the stuffed chimpanzee, which she still has today, was her first and most important gift. Jubilee, as she called the stuffed toy, was a symbol of an animal she had never met but had already learned to love. Most of all, she loved real animals, free in nature. When she still lived in an urban area, it meant that she observed and interacted with any creature that was available: her beloved dog, Rusty; the pigeons, sparrows, and urban birds; and the occasional rabbit or squirrel. At an early age, she showed a gift for intense, concentrated observation. She followed her dog around to understand his habits and his view of the world. Once she waited for hours in a chicken coop to be there at the moment a hen laid an egg.

Unlike many parents at that time, Jane's mother encouraged her in her fascinations, even during her long wait in the chicken coop when everyone feared she was lost. She learned to read early and tried to learn as much as possible about the world around her. Fortunately, the house had many books, and she was introduced to the wonders of the library. Her favorite books were *The Story of Dr. Doolittle*, *The Jungle Book*, and *The Wind in the Willows*. Stories of animals who could talk and people who could talk to animals had an almost mystic quality for her. In her books, she discovered the continent of Africa and decided as a child that she would find a way to get to Africa and live there with the animals.

Despite her great intellect and curiosity, she did not like school at first; it took her away from what she wanted to learn and her adventures with her dog, Rusty. As time went by, she found ways to enjoy it and learned as much as she could in the courses she most enjoyed. She received high marks, but her focus was always on learning rather than achieving high grades. She had friends at school and at the riding stable where she cared for horses in return for riding lessons. She loved developing relationships with the horses and the lessons that brought her closer to an understanding of them.

Her first fox hunt filled her with disgust at the cruelty of killing an animal for sport. A lifelong theme for her would be sadness and anger at the cruelty of people toward animals.

Growing up during World War II would also make her deeply aware of human cruelty to other humans. As news poured in about the horrors in Nazi Germany, Jane found herself turning toward religion as a way of understanding the problem of evil. Fortunately during her adolescence, she found a mentor in her pastor who could guide her not only toward Biblical writings but also toward the writings of great philosophers and poets who had considered the same moral questions with which she struggled.

When Jane was 12, her mother and father divorced. Because he had been gone so long in the war and was often absent from home even before that, she says she did not suffer much from the split; life went on as usual at The Birches. The family was not poor, but did not have money for a university education. Jane enrolled in a secretarial school in London, and when she wasn't taking classes, she thoroughly enjoyed the museums, libraries, and concert halls. She dated a number of young men and had a pleasant group of friends. She took a job in her aunt's physiotherapy practice as a secretary and assistant, and here she learned compassion for people who were ill, in pain, and struggling with disabilities.

Although she would have liked to attend Oxford, she was unable to do so. She did what seemed to her the next best thing; she found a secretarial job on campus there. You could say she was a pioneer in creating her own education because she took full advantage of the intellectual life of the campus by keeping up with what other young people were reading and thinking. It was during another secretarial job, however, that she received a life-changing letter from an old friend, inviting her to visit her in Kenya. She knew she simply had to go. With the full encouragement of her family, she saved every coin she could until the day came that she had enough money for a round trip ticket to Africa.

She called it her glorious voyage, the voyage where she would glory in the discovery of the ocean life, the excitement of independence, and a growing sense of her inner self. It was on board the ship, not far off the coast of Africa, where she says she made her commitment to Africa. She knew she must find a way to live there rather than return home. In Kenya, she enjoyed her time with her friend's family but wanted to make her own way, so she took a job in Nairobi as a secretary for an English company. There an acquaintance suggested that she meet Louis B. Leakey, the great anthropologist who was studying the origins of the human species in the fossils of the Olduvai Gorge. She described him as a giant and a genius—and they were both entranced by each other's enthusiasm for Africa and for learning. He hired her as his personal secretary, and her new life began.

In this roadless area of Africa, she went on digs with Louis and Mary Leakey, living in a small camp, digging by day, and talking by night in the lamplight surrounded by the sounds of the animals. Of this wonderful time, she wrote, "Suddenly I woke up one morning and I was living in my dream. The dream had become my reality, for the animals were all there." Leakey not only taught her his methods, but also his philosophy of life. Like her, he did not believe that science and religion were incompatible and, like her, he was most distressed by the cruelty of humans toward one another, bigotry, and carelessness toward nature. Leakey was profoundly interested in the behavior of humans, but unlike bones and stones, he said, behaviors do not fossilize. He believed that by studying the behavior of primates in a natural setting, it was possible to learn about the behavior of the earliest groups of humans. He knew there was a nearby colony of chimpanzees, but he waited until Jane suggested the idea of studying them to enthusiastically affirm her desire to study the chimpanzees. He went to raise money for the research, and she went back to England to learn everything she could about chimpanzees. She found there was little known about this group of primates that fled at human presence and had never been observed for any length of time in their native habitat. She prepared herself as best as she could, and returned to Africa, not as a secretary this time but as an ethnologist ready to apply the methods of keen observation to the behavior of nonhuman animals.

Because the authorities were reluctant to allow a woman into the forest alone, her undaunted mother agreed to accompany her, and with a few local helpers they went off to live in Gombe National Park at the preserve where the chimpanzees lived. It was a time of great adventure; there were rhinos, buffalos, lions, snakes, malaria, hot weather, and little food. She had never been happier, for on her peak of rock she could watch, in all directions, the chimpanzees below. They were very far away, and it was months before she could get close enough to observe the groups and a year before they allowed her close enough to observe their most intimate behaviors. This is when she made the discoveries that were to forever change the views of scientists—and the public—about primates. One day, for example, the chimpanzee she named David Greybeard took several stems of grass and used them to fish termites out of a hole. She had witnessed an animal using a tool, which was once thought to be an ability unique to humans. In addition, she was learning about family groupings, infant rearing, and social activities—all behaviors that had never been seen. She began to publish her findings, although many scientists were very reluctant to accept them. The idea of humans as the only truly collaborative, tool-using animal died hard. Leakey sent her to Oxford to earn her Ph.D., and Jane became one of the few people in that university's long history to earn a Ph.D. without an undergraduate degree.

What followed were many years in the forest. She loved the solitude; she believed that here in nature she felt closest to a spiritual presence. Here, she believed she could perceive a greater reality than the narrow worldview that we have among humans. It was indeed a very strange thing to Africans, and to most people in the world, that a woman would go alone into the forest to live among the chimpanzees. She was not truly alone because she had been accepted as a member of the group. She remembers vividly the moment she gazed into David Greybeard's eyes and he into hers; he touched her hand gently, and she says she knew a form of loving communication that reached back before language.

She met Baron Hugo van Lawick when he came to film her work and fell in love with this man who understood so well the life she was living. They married in 1965, and two years later they had a son, born when lions were roaming the area. Their nickname for their baby, Grub, became the name he was known best by. Jane had learned a great deal not only from her own mother, but also from the chimpanzee mothers she had watched. She was determined to keep her baby close to her, so he rode along in the backseat of the car as she drove over the African roads, stayed with his mother and father in the tent, and played out of doors just as she had loved to do. He also accompanied her on her lecture tours; she disliked these long trips to America to speak, but it was how she gained support for the research center that she and Hugo were building. Soon graduate students from all over the world came to study at Gombe with the famous Jane Goodall.

Her first books, *My Friends the Wild Chimpanzees* and *In the Shadow of Man* were sensations, winning her awards not only for their contributions to scientific progress but also for their graceful, persuasive writing.

Although there was much joy and uplift in her work, there were also times of sadness. Her marriage ended in divorce after 10 years; she believes all the years they spent apart led to many misunderstandings. She wishes it could have ended differently, but she and Hugo did find a way to continue to help their son to learn and grow; when he was old enough, he chose to go to boarding school in England. She remarried the next year to Derek Bryceson, who was the director of the national parks, including the preserve where she worked. They had only six years together before he died a lingering, painful death of cancer in 1980.

There was another reason the second decade of Jane Goodall's work was a painful one, and that was her discovery of aggression and war among the chimpanzees. The Four Year War, as she called it, would have been unthinkable to her and scholars if she had not witnessed the division of the large group of chimpanzees into two competing factions taking part in boundary wars and terrible raids that left chimps tortured and dying. In addition, she witnessed a female chimp stealing the newborn infant of another, weaker mother, and then killing and eating it ruthlessly. Not only was the mother chimp heartbroken, so was Jane. It was a true spiritual crisis, in which she asked, "Is there hope for humans? Is war inevitable? Is cruelty in our genes?" She concluded that though we do indeed inherit from our ancestors a tendency for aggression, there is "reason to hope," as she titled her book in which this story is told. Not only do we inherit aggression, but also cooperation, hopefulness, and the ability to think about a better future.

Jane Goodall's influence around the world grew as she won many awards and as she continued to tell her own story in autobiographies and narratives such as *Thirty Years at Gombe* and *Forty Years at Gombe*. She was not only a scientist but also an advocate because she believed that she had to do something about what she was seeing in Africa. Her causes have included: work against cruelty to animals, especially those used in scientific laboratories; preservation of habitat for primates; the creation of ecotourism jobs for the subsistence farmers who must destroy habitat to farm; and preservation of native plants and seeds. One of her most precious organizations is Roots and Shoots, a children's organization to promote a love of nature and animals. One of the unique aspects of her work and writing has been its spiritual quality; she has lived a life in which science and spirit were not separated and seeks to share that experience with other people. Only by recognizing the interconnectedness of all beings, she says, can we hope to save the planet from our own destructive habits.

CHAPTER 5

What We Can Learn from Eminent Women's Lives

In the lives of eminent women across the generations, several themes run across their experiences. These include: the loss of a parent or loved one, early interest in and time spent learning, connection to a master teacher, a love of solitude, developed identity, boundaries, resistance to stereotype threat, resistance to the culture of romance, financial independence, egalitarian relationships, flexible childrearing, and falling in love with an idea. All of these themes seem to involve some degree of conscious separation from socially prescribed paths for girls and women. Even the loss of a parent led to a feeling of "differentness" that led to emotional independence. Despite the constant messages that girls receive to conform to expectations, to depend on others' opinions, and to define themselves in terms of their relationships, these women chose a different path, a path that would lead them away from an ordinary life into an extraordinary one.

Loss of a Parent or Loved One

The loss of a parent as a commonality was not surprising; many studies of eminent individuals have also noted early parent loss. Among our eminent women, only Sheryl Sandberg and Tina Fey did not suffer a great loss in their early life. The strange and disturbing fact of early grief has led to much speculation about how parental loss can engender creativity, drive, and achievement. For eminent males, the loss of a father seems more common than loss of a mother; for females, it is unclear whether it is the loss of a father or mother that is most significant. Yewchuk's work would suggest that the presence of a strong father figure is very important to the development of eminence for women.[121] Perhaps psychological or physical separation from a mother might allow girls to diverge from traditional paths of marriage and motherhood. The loss of a parent may promote early emotional and financial independence, according to Csikszentmihalyi.[122] In addition, losing a parent might lead to a more creative, less linear approach to career development. For many of the talented, at-risk girls in the NSF Gender Equity studies, the absence of a father meant that they took additional responsibility for themselves as well as for siblings.[123] Many of the girls spoke proudly of their role as their mother's ally and of their desire to achieve their career goals for the sake of their mother and siblings. The absence of a mother can lead to a strong and independent identity if a daughter is not required to take on too many of her mother's responsibilities.

In sum, the loss of a parent, although devastating for any child, may actually lead to greater creativity and autonomy in the long run for girls who transcend their grief through learning and achievement. The strengths of eminent women that can be related to early loss include resilience in the face of setbacks, individuation and independent identity formation, and early assumption of adult responsibilities with the associated life skills.

Early Interest in and Time Spent Learning

Across studies of eminent individuals is the finding of early engagement with a specific domain of talent. All of our eminent women began their path toward eminence by the time they were adolescents. Most creatively eminent individuals show an early passion for a specific intellectual activity. Future artists spend many hours as children perfecting their drawing, copying cartoons, and experimenting with designs. Future scientists develop science projects at home and read about science. Future writers read voraciously, write journals and stories, and are fascinated by language at an early age.[124] The specific, powerful interests of these girls can get in the way of general school achievement because many young people destined for eminence show little interest in being well-rounded or in stellar achievement outside of their areas of interest. Nevertheless, early engagement is critical in some fields such as music, where few achieve eminence that have not begun their career as young children, and other, later-developing talents such as writing.

In addition, great accomplishment in any field is directly related to the number of hours spent working toward expertise and the number of hours spent while on the job. Although most females are socialized to be "well-rounded" and to give equal energy to all roles expected of them, it is clear that part-time commitment to a passion will not result in great achievement in a field. Therefore, early engagement with a domain of talent, including working toward excellence and expertise, gives smart girls a head start in gathering the sheer amount of knowledge and skills needed to make a difference.

Therefore, it is likely that preoccupation with a specific talent domain is a strength for smart girls that can translate to adult accomplishment. For girls, an early passion not only builds important skills, but also may provide resilience in the face of societal pressures to redirect interests to prettiness and popularity.

Connection to a Master Teacher

Although proximity to a master teacher is characteristic of the eminent person's environment, the capacity to make a connection with a master teacher is a psychological strength. All people who achieve eminence in their fields have come in contact with at least one teacher who challenged the student to achieve his or her full potential, held extremely high expectations, developed the student's technical skills and knowledge base, and provided access to the student's future profession. All of our eminent women had master teachers, ranging from an inspiring gym teacher to the leading paleontologist of his generation. Benjamin Bloom, in his classic study of the talent development of people at the top of their fields, gave a great deal of attention to describing their master teachers.[125] Master teachers can be difficult and demanding, and it takes a special set of strengths to be able to profit from their instruction. Students who can persist with only minimal reinforcement and who can weather intense criticism are those who respond best to master teachers. These students are primarily interested in gaining skills and knowledge rather than in garnering approval from their teachers.

In most studies of eminent individuals, the future artist, musician, scientist, or inventor went to great lengths to find the right teacher, to find the resources to pay for instruction, and to engage the teacher in mentoring and guidance beyond the usual expectations.

The strengths that are necessary for the smart girl to obtain such rigorous instruction and mentoring are persistence and resourcefulness. The strengths necessary for a continuing bond with the master teacher are a "thick skin," a desire to prove oneself worthy, and a willingness to show consistent and sustained effort.

A Love of Solitude

Eminent women remember girlhoods full of exploration, adventure, and voracious reading. Although both eminent women and men spent a great deal of time in solitary activities as children, solitariness is considered more unusual in girls, who are expected to be more sociable. All of our eminent women had alone time as children, by choice or chance. Some chose solitary exploration, like Jane Goodall. Others were isolated by circumstances beyond their control. Alone time seems critical to the development of girls' talents.[126]

Why is aloneness so much more important to the achievement of goals for women? Perhaps it is because society places so much more emphasis on social achievement for girls and women than for boys or men. Girls are expected to participate in extracurricular activities, informal social groups, and a wide network of friendships. From a human capital perspective, girls have less time available for intellectual pursuits because of their investment in social activities, particularly following adolescence. Therefore, girls who spend time alone in childhood, by choice or chance, are likely to have more time for reading, reflection, and skill building. It is also possible that aloneness in childhood develops the habit of solitude, a condition that is critical to adult productivity. People who have difficulty spending time alone may never develop the capacity to spend long hours solving a problem or experimenting with a new design. Girls who are able to be alone are less likely to be caught up in the culture of romance that persuades them that their career goals are less important than their relationships with men. Solitude to these girls becomes not a source of social embarrassment, but a source of strength.

Highly Developed Career Identity

Eminent women differ from other bright women in their early and highly developed career identity. Even as teens and very young women, our eminent women thought of themselves as a scientist, a writer, a comedian, or a singer.

In contrast to our eminent women, it seems that many talented females are slower, or perhaps less willing, to claim an identity in their chosen vocation. For example, in one study of sex differences in artistic creativity, male students at the School of the Art Institute of Chicago claimed the identity of *artist*, while female students were more likely to say that they were *students*. Similarly, in Holland and Eisenhart's study of the "culture of romance" on college campuses, the authors observed that bright women subverted their career identities to the development of their romantic relationships.[127] They found that smart women were encouraged by their peers to define themselves in terms of their romantic partners, and that college women were much more likely to identify fellow female friends by their boyfriends rather than the careers they aspired to.

In general, there may be gender differences in how men and women form their identity, but the early research showing sex differences has yielded to studies that showed similarities. The current consensus is that women and men differ in how they develop their identities in particular domains, such as occupational and sex role domains, but also that they are similar to one another overall. Women seem to develop their relationship and career identities simultaneously, while men may delay exploration of their relationship identity until after achieving their career identity. Nevertheless, it is clear from the studies of lives of eminent women that the development of a strong, clear vocational identity is essential to adult accomplishment in all domains. The identity of the smart girl must be as a confident member of her field, seeing herself as a musician or scientist for example, to advance towards eminence.

Boundaries

For many eminent women, childhood isolation protected them from pressures to conform to feminine norms. Many smart girls today experience social isolation in a slightly different way; they have social isolation because they don't fill the traditional mold, even though they may also try to hide or deny their abilities as a way to become socially accepted. As a result of negative reactions to their talents, smart girls often develop "thorns and shells" in their personalities as boundaries to protect themselves from social scrutiny. Thorns can manifest themselves by way of sarcasm, intolerance, self-righteousness, brusqueness, or simply having a sharp tongue. On the other hand, a smart girl can form shells by wrapping herself in shyness, timidity, and modesty. In this way, girls can protect themselves from the social persecution they otherwise might experience. In one key study, it was found that the strongest need and characteristic of talented, at-risk girls with career goals in science was defensiveness—the need to defend oneself from interpersonal attacks and threats. Defensiveness was also one of the strongest needs of creatively smart girls.[128] Although defensiveness is often seen as a negative personality trait by psychologists, it may be a necessary protective factor for smart girls who are focused on accomplishment.

Another trait seen among eminent women is their resistance to confluence—that is, identifying and merging with someone else's identity. Many females tend to view themselves as part of someone else; they may have borrowed values and interests from their romantic partners and friends, and tend to say *we* instead of *I*. For example, a woman may say, "We have been promoted (or transferred or accepted) into a new program," when what she really means is that she or her partner received a promotion as though their two identities are locked together. Although the capacity to connect to another in intimacy is a basic human need, the tendency to over-identify with another's needs can cause women to lose their identities. However, eminent women have the ability to still feel connected with others without relinquishing their sense of self, which is likely a testament to their strong personalities.

Resistance to Stereotype Threat

Stereotype threat works by lowering expectations for women in the areas of achievement where people have come to believe that boys are superior to girls—math or science, for example. Not only does society disadvantage women by expecting mediocrity in these areas, but it also harms them by making them believe that they simply cannot do certain things on the basis of being female. Our eminent women seemed to ignore stereotypes or deliberately challenge them.

How then, do young women protect themselves from stereotype threat? In order for women gifted in areas of math and science to achieve, they must be educated about the existence of these stereotypes and how that relates to the widespread belief that boys are better than girls in some areas. Our eminent women were extraordinary in their resistance to stereotype threat. They had heard all the myths of sex differences, but they either sought out the truth or just ignored the media telling them that they were inferior. They simply refused to believe that their talents were not equal to those of men.

Resistance to the Culture of Romance

Young women, particularly upon entering college, are at risk of becoming entangled in the culture of romance, which revolves around the pressure for young women to become heavily involved in the romantic world. Rather than focusing on academic goals and career development, women often find themselves being pressured to make themselves attractive, participate in parties and dances, and go to places like bars and clubs, all with the sole purpose of meeting eligible men. These female students are pressured, both subtly and overtly, to participate in romantic pursuits, which require them to devote much of their time and energy into beautification and finding men to date who will boost their societal position. By dating men of high status, such as athletes or other "big men on campus," women think they prove how highly attractive they are and thereby boost their prestige among their peers. A strong personality and a resistance to confluence may protect talented young women from becoming enmeshed in the culture of romance. All of our eminent women resisted the culture of romance, for a wide variety of reasons, ranging from intense commitment to their studies to the need to hide a romantic attraction to the opposite sex.

Financial Independence

Being without sufficient financial resources is a great handicap to self-actualization and eminence. Smart girls who have experienced poverty—or even a lack of funding for a single semester—recognize that money affects every aspect of life, particularly when there never seems to be enough of it. Having the ability to fund one's educational aspirations, to travel and expand one's understanding of the world, and even to simply pay one's rent is essential for a smart woman to fulfill her potential.

Although most eminent women in the last chapter were born into families who were not privileged, they found a way to manage their financial resources independently. Of course, some of them, like J. K. Rowling, found themselves flat on their faces financially at some point, but throughout their lives they seemed to understand that nobody would take care of them except themselves. Each of these women, even young Malala, expected to have to make their own way—and wanted to be financially independent. Some, like Sonia Sotomayor, found scholarships; others started their own enterprise of writing books or performing; and some, like Sheryl Sandberg, became financial wizards. It was not that eminent women all became wealthy, but all of them were intentionally economically responsible for themselves.

Egalitarian Relationships and Flexible Childrearing

There is increasing evidence that accomplished women create their own models of marriage, family, and mothering that are independent of societal ideals and stereotypes. The first *Smart Girls* emphasized how eminent women found their love through their work, that they chose partners who either shared the same career interests or respected their partners' chosen work and equally devoted themselves to their own cause or purpose. Recent studies show that women scholars are more satisfied with their positions and more likely to persist in their fields when they are in dual-career relationships rather than more conventional marriages.[129] Eminent women tend to find ways to have children on their own terms, taking their children with them to work and in the field, making creative use of extended family and friendship networks for childcare, and aim for high quality childcare. They refuse to participate in the Mommy Wars, or when drawn into them, like Sheryl Sandberg, insist on the importance of finding one's own way to compose a balanced life.

Falling in Love with an Idea

Of all of the characteristics of eminent women, the capacity to fall in love with an idea may be the most powerful determinant of success. Every biography we read had a beautiful passage in which the eminent woman came to understand that she had found an idea worth living for. In the cases of Malala, a terrorist target; Jane, a lone researcher in the jungle; or Margarethe, a servant to her country in peace and war, they had found an idea for which they would happily risk death. What is it that causes a person to fall in love with an idea? What special experience allows them to follow that idea throughout their lives? It may be that the flow experience guides these women's choices.

Csikszentmihalyi described the sense of flow that was experienced by eminent individuals while participating in their chosen domain. This is a special state of consciousness that seems to be felt when one is doing the work that seems closest to one's heart. Whether art, science, or leadership, these creative people felt at one with their work, discovered a sense of challenge and mastery, and experienced a timelessness and joy in the practice of their discipline.[130] Falling in love with an idea strengthens a smart young women's resolve in almost every other area of her life, giving her the courage to overcome obstacles, to ignore gender barriers and stereotypes, and to spend intensive time alone in pursuit of mastery in her field. In addition, falling in love with an idea may encourage even a shy, isolated smart girl to seek master teachers and mentors and to insist on the educational opportunities she needs to fulfill her potential. Every study of eminent women stressed their passionate engagement, their love of their work, and the intensity with which they lived out their deepest values. Later in this book, we will show the way that the love of an idea becomes the fire that energizes a woman's passion for her life's calling.

CHAPTER 6

Smart Young Girls

From a parent of a four-year-old smart girl:
> *Sara comes into the kitchen after being in bed for 30 minutes.*
> *Sara: Dad, I'm not tired.*
> *Me: Why not?*
> *Sara: It's because I'm nocturnal.*

Early Signs

Most parents of bright girls, even if they are uncomfortable with the label *gifted*, will tell you that they saw the signs of high intelligence in their girls in infancy.

"Her eyes were so bright, moving constantly, watching and taking in everything," one mom said of her daughter at three months old. "She seemed so alive."

Bright little girls not only are often curious, even before they can reach out and affect the world around them, but they also seem to learn more quickly than other infants. A daycare teacher described the smart little girls she had cared for: "They just pick up on everything so fast! I had a five-month-old who would go on a hunger strike if you picked up the jar of peas instead of bananas even before she tasted it, as if she had figured out the color and shape of the stuff she didn't like!"

Observations like these, affirmed by infant research, consistently show that these early signs of speedy processing, working memory, and shifting attention are indeed linked to later intelligence.[131] Easily fascinated and ready to learn, bright girl infants may not sleep as much as other babies because they don't want to miss any of the exciting sights and sounds around them.

If the girl is a first-born, and parents don't have much experience with other babies, the parents may not recognize that their baby is more curious and quick to learn than others; they may simply assume that all babies are like this. If they should notice some precocious behavior like naming Mom, Dad, and pets while six months old, their friends and family may simply attribute their claims to wishful thinking, and effectively shut down any other observations the parents may make.[132] Well-meaning parents then may begin to discount their daughter's abilities, even as they search for answers. When parents find themselves saying things about their daughter such as, "Oh, I'm just making this up," or "Maybe I'm just biased," they perhaps should consider that their baby girl is, in fact, gifted.[133]

Even when parents are unaware of their daughter's precocity, giftedness will have its way. Sandra Scarr, a developmental psychologist, was the first to point out that not only do parents shape their infants' behavior, but infants also train their parents.[134] Smart baby girls are likely to begin shaping their parents' behavior quickly, by demanding new experiences and information and rewarding their parents for providing these stimuli. According to many studies, girls outperform boys in the acquisition and use of verbal information, and this begins even in the early years as smart girls pick up the meaning of words and try to use them appropriately.[135]

If parents suspect that their little girl learns quickly and reaches out for more information, it is important that they provide as much stimulation as she requires. Parents are always told to hold their little ones, read to them long before they can read, and engage them in words, song, and physical play; with little ones who seem to be smart, such advice is all the more important.

Asynchrony

Even in the earliest years, parents may become aware of one of the important characteristics of most smart children—asynchrony. Asynchrony is the term used when a child's development in one area is at a different level than in other areas.[136] For smart infants, a young child's comprehension and desire to verbalize may outstrip her physical ability to form the sounds and words that she wants, leading to frustration and tears. Just like an elderly person knowing what she wants to say, yet being unable to retrieve the words, the little girl who knows what she wants but can't articulate it can be very impatient and frustrated.[137]

It is clear that intellectual development and physical development are different for smart girls than for other girls; in addition, emotional development may not be synchronous with verbal ability. Listening patiently, reflecting on what your bright young child is trying to tell you rather than interrupting or making assumptions about what she is trying to say, can prevent much uproar.

At times, you may forget that she's a little girl because her wisdom so often outstrips both her height and age. You'll forget, until she has an epic tantrum in, say, the middle of Disneyland over something so inconceivably simple, like not wearing the proper shoes to meet her favorite Disney character. In those truly out-of-control moments, it is important to remember that her brain is on overload and that she is likely overstimulated, tired, or overwhelmed. These are not moments to try to reason with her. Whatever rationality she does possess has gone off-line. Instead, soothe her (and yourself) with deep breaths, rocking, and other loving gestures that help her feel safe and secure. And remember in those moments that she really is just a little girl.

Early Reading

By preschool years, from ages three to six, another major event happens in the lives of smart girls—they begin to read. Smart girls are more likely to read early (between 3 and 5) rather than at the average age (between 5 and 7), and intellectually gifted girls are even more likely to read precociously.[138] These preschool girls like to seek reading opportunities, to match letters to sounds, to sound out words, and to spontaneously pick up reading without instruction. Large studies of precocious readers have found that very little of what could be called *teaching* of reading takes place for these children.[139] Rather, reading begins within a warm, playful relationship with a parent or caregiver who engages in storytelling, reading aloud, and word play. In many cases, parents of smart girls cannot tell you what they might have done that specifically led their daughter to reading, and they have often been surprised to see her reading so spontaneously and fluently.

The onset of reading ought to be one of celebration; a whole new world has opened up to the little girl now that she can read the voices of so many other people, learn about new places, and see all kinds of new things to do. Sadly, precocious reading is seen by educators as a problem rather than a gift in many countries where precocious reading has been studied. For parents, this can come as an awkward surprise. Upon sharing with a preschool teacher, kindergarten teacher, or school principal that their daughter is reading independently, parents are often met with the following untrue statements:

- ❖ Precocious reading doesn't mean anything and isn't a sign of giftedness.

- ❖ She's just decoding, not comprehending.

- ❖ She may have hyperlexia, compulsive reading often found with autistic children.

❖ She's just memorized stories you have read to her

❖ You probably pushed her to read before she was ready.

❖ Why don't you just let her be a child and play, rather than making her read?

All of these statements are based on myths or misunderstandings. What is the truth about precocious reading? First, not all precocious readers are gifted; however, many smart children, especially girls, are early readers. Precocious reading does often indicate giftedness. It is wrong to assume that any child who is reading at age three or four is just memorizing or decoding words without comprehension.[140] It is even worse to label enthusiastic reading as a disorder like hyperlexia.

Second, it is simply not true that precocious reading is a sort of accidental early start in a race where everyone else will eventually catch up. Follow-up studies of early readers have shown that, even by age 11, they maintain their advantage in reading skill and vocabulary. Third, even though reading to children and easygoing reading instruction does indeed contribute to precocious reading, it is not "pushing" children to produce this kind of gifted performance. Many smart girls have superior ability to pick up the skills of reading and to read independently, as long as they simply have access to the sounds of the alphabet and phonemes. This is why so many parents of smart girls say that they seemed to pick up reading from watching television shows like Sesame Street and learning the sounds of letters.

Finally, many parents and teachers are unsure about what kinds of reading activities and books are needed for precocious readers. Judith Halsted provides guidance in her book *Some of My Best Friends Are Books: Guiding Gifted Readers from Preschool to High School, 3rd edition.*[141] The Junior Great Books Foundation provides reading lists even for very young readers at www.greatbooks.org/programs-for-all-ages/junior/. Many public libraries also have children's librarians who can offer guidance and can share lists of recommended books for different ages and reading levels.

Smart Girl Profile | CJ, age 2

By age two, CJ would accurately repeat multisyllabic words that she heard from her parents and other adults. For example, CJ overheard her mom, a physician, use the phrase "biliary atresia" while discussing a case involving a liver disorder. CJ repeated the phrase perfectly. Yet her parents wondered if CJ was autistic because her eye contact was limited and she could spend hours playing alone with her toys. One of her favorite playmates was Mater, the tow truck from the Pixar film *Cars*. Her mom noted, "CJ just stands in front of the Cars poster that hangs in her playroom and talks to Mater like he's a real person. She was thrilled to get a plush toy version of Mater for Christmas."

Since then, CJ has become very engaged with other people. Her early verbal abilities, which have always been excellent, are now coupled with sustained eye contact and a marked sensitivity of other people's well-being. Her mom says, "CJ gets really concerned if I'm upset, and she tries to soothe me."

At age three, CJ announced to her aunt, an obstetrician/gynecologist: "I am *never* going to have a baby." When asked why not, she said, "Because it looks like it hurts a lot!" As it turned out, CJ had been reading the finely illustrated anatomy text, *Grey's Anatomy*, a beloved volume from her aunt's days in medical school. At that point, she didn't know how a baby was conceived, but she had quickly figured out how and where a baby emerged from a woman's body.

When to Start School and Special Lessons

Case studies like CJ's raise questions for parents and educators. How important is early reading? Should bright girls start school early? Noted educator James Borland summarizes the conundrum as follows: "Acceleration is one of the most curious phenomena in the field of education. I can think of no other issue in which there is such a gulf between what research has revealed and what most practitioners believe."[142] Similar statements abound in the gifted education literature.

Parents need to be armed with information about the myths and misunderstandings about early reading, particularly when they meet with educators about their daughters' reading development. In the best case scenario, it may mean that their daughter can take the tests and interviews required by the school to be admitted to pre-kindergarten and kindergarten gifted programs as an early entrance student. When gifted programs are not available, early admittance to kindergarten may be the best option, although there is great resistance to this in many school districts. In some places, laws or school district policies prevent four-year-olds from entering kindergarten, despite the fact that it is often the best choice for smart girls who are functioning well in emotional and social development.[143] In schools that have no opportunities at all for acceleration, early admission may be the only guarantee that a smart girl will not spend her first years in school simply marking time and waiting for other children to catch up with her reading (or other) abilities. Parents, therefore, need to advocate for their daughters' right to start school when she is truly ready. This may mean getting private intelligence testing and developmental assessment of social and emotional skills from a licensed psychologist—unfortunately, the parents usually need to pay the fee. (Only when the parents are concerned about developmental disabilities, such as Autism Spectrum Disorders, can they qualify for financial assistance from schools in getting individual testing, and even this may not be available until second or third grade.)

Many schools require intelligence testing by a psychologist, but intelligence testing before the age of nine can be problematic. Despite great advances in our understanding of giftedness in early childhood, most intelligence tests cannot reliably identify giftedness in the preschool years. This is because of the variability in intellectual development, with vast leaps in ability in short periods, and the difficulty of testing young children when they are not accustomed to long periods of attentiveness in the presence of a stranger.[144] As a result, a child who tests as 130 at age five may score 110 two years later—or may score 150. Parents are understandably upset when told by a fourth grade teacher that their daughter isn't gifted anymore. Or that she is more intellectually able than previously thought, but it is too late to get into a program for highly gifted. There simply is no way that one test at one particular time can deliver an answer with certainty to parents and teachers of a young girl about intellectual giftedness. Instead, schools should use a variety of interviews, samples of work, assessments, and checklists, and even then with caution. If parents do seek intelligence testing before nine years old, it should be with the understanding that all of the tests may not agree, and that scores may later change. It is important to use resources like the Institute for Research and Policy on Acceleration and the very useful *Iowa Acceleration Scale* in order to assess the readiness the child has for kindergarten, a whole-grade skip, or other accommodation such as single subject acceleration.

Parents also need to have a thorough understanding of the policy on early admission, which varies from state to state, in order to be ready to take advantage of possible exceptions or gateways. For example, in Arizona if a child has already completed first grade in a private school, she can be admitted to second grade in a public school no matter her age. Parents who did this enrolled their daughter in a private kindergarten a year early and kept her there through first grade. Sometimes such a transition can be a difficult one if the teachers are opposed to having such a young child in the classroom. Sometimes, teachers hold grade-skipped students to a higher standard for their social and emotional development as well as intellectual development, refusing to acknowledge asynchrony as a normal reality for smart children. If any problems in self-regulation or social skills emerge, teachers may immediately put the blame on the grade skip, rather than asynchrony, bullying, or even the appearance of ADHD as factors impeding learning or interfering with social skills.

The question of whether to implement a full grade skip is a dilemma for parents who must weigh the economical, psychological, and social costs and benefits. In general, early admission is the best choice, especially if the girl is within just a few months of the required age, and parents should seek advice from psychologists familiar with giftedness before making a decision. For parents of limited means, think of the cost of a professional psychological assessment as the first, critical investment in your child's education. It may be expensive to get such testing, but it will probably be cheaper than getting braces for her teeth—and is certainly as important to her future well-being. And neither is likely to be covered by insurance.

Preschool and kindergarten teachers who want to provide the best opportunities for smart girls should include flexible reading activities in the curriculum and plenty of books that appeal to a wide range of reading abilities. Smart girls need a variety of books—from picture books to third grade reading level books in their classrooms—if they are to be challenged and actively learning. One of the simplest ways that preschool teachers can acknowledge a girls' giftedness is to allow them to read during nap time if they are not sleepy, since many smart girls give up napping before their peers. Parents should ask about this option when choosing a preschool.

Though many smart girls are early and avid readers, others may show signs at an early age of extreme precocity or talent in a specific area, like math or music. In fact, these are two domains of talent where precocity is often observed at very early ages. Research is quite clear about the importance of early nurturance of musical talent; it *must* be developed before age seven if a child is to achieve her full potential.[145] Julie Wosjik, in her summary of the research, says:

> Children who are musically gifted show early developmental signs of musical precocity, which may include noticing off-key music, remembering melodies, singing in tune, fondness for playing instruments in preschool, rhythmic ways of moving and speaking, humming to themselves, tapping rhythmically while working, and

sensitivity to environmental sounds (waterfalls, rain on the roof,
etc.). Researchers recognize such indicators of precocious musical
talent as an innate ability to identify pitch (i.e., to imitate pitch
with precision), precise rhythmic ability, intense interest in a variety
of music, and an ability to learn and express music through rote
methods (recognition and imitation) ...in the inner city, where
resources may not be readily available, they are often identified in
religious organizations, where they participate regularly in choirs
and are encouraged to express themselves musically. Although
early intervention and instruction are not necessary for developing
musical talent, they appear to be significant factors in determining
a child's full realization of a musical gift.[146]

It is important that parents make every effort to get some kind of musical training for their children when the behaviors of musical precocity seem to be present. Expensive master teachers are probably not needed this early; lively, engaging teachers can expose children to the sounds of instruments and the joy of singing.

One of the most neglected domains of talent in the U.S. and other English speaking countries is linguistic ability. One of the major ways that dominant cultures assert their superiority is by insisting that everyone speak their language; for example, in the U.S., children who speak Native American languages or Spanish have historically been shamed for the use of their own home language. Sadly, this attempt to make kids "unlearn" their native language interferes with one of the greatest gifts they have—the gift of bilingualism.

Many myths have been perpetuated about the early learning of more than one language. Teachers and speech therapists may insist that learning a second language will interfere in language learning, citing the fact that young children may sometimes use two languages in the same sentence. Not only is this *not* a sign of confusion (bilingual children only do this rarely, when speaking to someone they know also understands both languages), but also it more likely may be a sign of linguistic giftedness.[147] It is true that nearly all children learn to speak a second and third language in an unaccented way by age four if they begin hearing and speaking in all of the languages; millions of children in bi- and tri-lingual countries are living proof. Often, however, one of the earliest signs of linguistic giftedness is a child's fascination with language and insistence on trying other languages. Just as smart girls are early readers, they are also more likely than any other group to show signs of linguistic giftedness. When a parent notices this, it is a wonderful investment in the child's future as a communicator to begin informal language instruction at home, online, or even through early immersion classes. It is important that parents do not abruptly switch languages at home because this can be emotionally confusing and frightening to preschool children. For more information on language learning, explore the website of Center for Applied Linguistics.[148]

Fortunately for parents of smart young people who show an early interest and ability in mathematics, there is much written about this critical ability. Jennifer Rotigel explains:

> *Many of these students' gifted characteristics emerge during the preschool years. Parents of preschoolers may report that their child demonstrates an unusual interest in mathematical concepts and particularly enjoys games involving numbers. At an early age, some gifted students note relationships between products and prices in the grocery store, the passage of time, changes in weather temperatures, and measurements of distances. Parents of these "number sense gurus" are fascinated by their children's precociousness but are often unaware of the significance or relevance of these early mathematical discoveries. By the time these emergent mathematical geniuses arrive for their first formal math lessons in kindergarten, they may have already established their own unique theories of number sense, sequences and patterns, problem solving, and computational strategies.[149]*

Unfortunately for smart girls, math ability may be less noticed by parents and teachers because of common stereotypes and myths about sex differences favoring boys. A smart girl will spend a lifetime hearing others say that boys are better at math; it is all the more important, therefore, that parents counter these myths early and help build a strong identity in a smart girl as a mathematically competent and achieving person.

Although most schools have little to offer very young mathematically gifted girls, enormous progress in understanding and providing for the needs of these children has been made in gifted education. From Ann Lupkowski and Susan Assouline's many writings on children who love mathematics (*Jane and Johnny Love Math*) to online resources for parents who want to provide extra challenge for mathematically precocious little girls, there are now ways of identifying and teaching accelerated mathematics to young children.[150] The Hoagies website for gifted children provides a comprehensive

list of online math challenges for gifted children at www.hoagiesgifted.org/
math_gifted.htm.

Like mathematical ability, there is now a tendency for scholars to
emphasize sex differences in spatial ability favoring males.[151] These differences are seen most often in tests that emphasize tasks that are particularly
interesting to boys, such as imagining what something looks like when it is
taken apart or how something mechanical works. If artwork is used instead
as the criterion of spatial visual ability, we see many young precocious
female artists.

One study that examined the lives of famous inventors asked about
early experiences with spatial-visual problems.[152] One of the inventor's
wives, Mrs. Skromme, said, "I was an early inventor, too! But the things we
girls invented all got eaten or worn out." She was pointing to the fact that so
many of the spatial-visual tasks that little girls learn are in cooking, sewing,
drawing, crafts, and doll play—all of the activities that might easily be
ignored as signs of early spatial abilities. Little girls need lots of opportunities
not only for these traditionally "feminine" activities but also traditionally
"masculine" activities, such as Legos (not just the pink ones), early chess
activities, and video games like Tetris that emphasize spatial-visual skills.
For more resources on spatial visual giftedness and artistic ability, see www.
hoagiesgifted.org/visual-spatial.htm, and for excellent online art activities
for young children see www.dpeasley.com/Peasleburg_Academy/Preschool/
pa_art_for_young_preschoolers.htm. Many art museums offer preschool
art classes, and these can spark the visual genius of the creative young girl.

First Friends

All children pass through developmental stages in their understanding
of friendship, and girls are consistently more advanced than boys in their
choices and expectations for friendships. Most children before age five want a
play partner—someone to share toys and experiences—but they don't expect
much in terms of conversation or reciprocal loyalty. The need for loyalty,
intimacy, and recognition of mutual responsibilities to each other is the last,
mature stage of friendship. Historically, most educators have thought that
gifted children's social needs were mainly for intellectual equals who could
discuss ideas on the same level. However, Miraca Gross, in her study on
the friendships of 700 children of average, moderate, and high intellectual
ability, found that gifted children also needed friends who had developed
to higher levels of understanding in friendship. Gifted children, she found,
passed rapidly through the earlier stages of friendship. Highly gifted, young

children already wanted a "sure shelter" in a friend, someone who provided and received trust, fidelity, and compassion. Even moderately gifted girls matured more rapidly than other girls in their friendship needs and sought the company of other gifted children or older children.

For smart little girls, the whole matter of friendship is puzzling. The five-year-old smart girl would love to share her excitement about the story she just read—but the other kids her age aren't reading at her level. She would like to follow the older kids as they run off to play somewhere new—but she knows she is not allowed to leave her front yard. When girls her age are invited over to play, they don't seem to understand the rules of even simple games like hide and seek. They don't want to act out a play she has thought up. They get tired of her strenuous efforts to teach them how to have fun.

And when a smart little girl does find a friend—especially if she's another little girl—the drama often begins. Six-year-old Lily and her friend Meredith were inseparable. They played together at recess, sat together at lunch, and took turns spending the night at each other's houses. Then one day during recess, Meredith announced that was mad at Lily and no longer wanted to be her friend. Lily was confused. She didn't know what she had done wrong. Rather than accepting Meredith's attempt to bully, Lily responded, "Well, Meredith, we *are* friends. And friends don't treat each other this way." Yet after that day something did change in their friendship. Lily talked it over with her mom and realized that there were other girls in the grade ahead of her that were nice and didn't seem to attract drama and fighting in the same way that Meredith did.

For reasons like this, a smart girl's first friend is likely to be an older girl or boy. In a time when children are locked into same-age classrooms, sports, and activities, it is increasingly difficult for gifted children to find friends and playgroups that are right for them.[153] Forced to learn, play, and socialize with children of exactly the same age, the smart girl will often be the odd girl out, because neither she nor they understand why she is different. On the other hand, when a smart girl is lucky enough to go to a school that combines age groups or to have a family with multi-age social gatherings, she will gravitate toward the girls or boys who are right for her. Her first friend might seem an unusual choice to adults, but she knows when she has found someone with whom she can talk without fear of being misunderstood or abandoned.

Smart Girl Profile | Sidney, age 5

Sidney is a bright, sensitive young girl, whose intellect and interests far exceed most others her age. Her ability to engage in conversation is more characteristic of a mature young woman, with topics ranging from synonyms and penmanship (which she excelled in) to her family's trip in Europe to the plants in a desert botanicals magazine. She correctly identified a fleshy, blue succulent, saying, "Agave is dangerous," and relating a moment when she pricked her finger on the plant's sharp tip. Despite her breadth of knowledge, Sidney doesn't yet understand the concept of time in hours and minutes; instead, she tells time by the length of Sponge Bob Square Pants episodes. Sidney's sensitivity was also notable when she mentioned, "It hurts my heart when my friends are mean to me."

Is it any wonder that so many smart girls prefer to be alone? Parents and teachers tend to worry about girls who want to be alone, but a smart girl's solitude is not necessarily a sign of loneliness or rejection. She may have found voices in books far more interesting than her age peers. She may have discovered interest groups on children's websites where kids of all ages are discussing a film or game. She may have all of her needs for companionship met by a pet she trains and lavishes attention upon. Finally, the bright little girl may have discovered early the joy of solitude, where she is free to roam about out of doors or gaze at pictures and listen to music she loves while lost in thought and fantasy.

In preschool and early school years, the day when she can play with children who are both her intellectual and emotional peers is often years away. Schools for gifted children are few and far between, and most camps and summer programs for gifted kids begin at age nine or 10, when most kids are ready to be away from home for extended periods. Even one after-school or Saturday morning gifted program that allows her to meet kids like herself can lead to joyful recognition and long lasting friendships.

The Princess Industrial Complex

From a mom of a smart little girl:

> *At the Children's Place*
>
> *Store person: "Can we help you find anything?"*
>
> *Me: "Yes. Do you have any super hero T-shirts for little girls?"*

Store person: "Oh, no we don't. Sorry."

Me: "Anything with horses?"

Store person: "Um, not sure. Doubt it."

Yeah, so, pink, purple, hearts, and butterflies...because little girls couldn't possibly like anything else. This will be my experience in every flippin child's store or section.

"The 'princess phase.' So inevitable is this period in the maturation of girls today that it should qualify as an official developmental stage, worthy of an entry in Leach or Brazelton: first crawling, then walking, then the urgent desire to wear something pink and sparkly," wrote Annie Murphy Paul in the *New York Times.*[154]

Three decades ago, boys' and girls' books, toys, clothes, and games were much less segregated. Now, the girls' aisles of stores are a blaze of pink and shiny beads or sequins, while boys' aisles are unadorned, though multicolored—except for shades of pink. What happened in the 1990s to create a billion dollar industry of princess items? Peggy Orenstein tells the story of Disney's discovery of the marketing power of princesses and the explosion of Disney princess films, clothing, toys, and decorations.[155] Disney's marketing, and soon the marketing of every other child-oriented company, resulted in burgeoning demand for everything princess by girls and their mothers. Most puzzling was that the princess explosion happened at the same time that the "girl power" movement began, including the popularity of the first *Smart Girls* book.

Girls were being told for the first time that they were strong and brave, that they could be anything they wanted to be, and that there were no differences between them and boys in abilities, achievement, or possible careers. Girls seemed to get both messages—they should be pretty *and* smart, sweet *and* aggressive. Given the demand of little girls for pink, glittery princess items, however, it is clear that for most little girls, pretty and sweet is best.

Developmental psychologists help us to understand the powerful urge of little girls to participate in all things princess. From two to four years old, children have very rigid, concrete notions about categories, and gender is the most powerful category of all. They form their ideas about categories through superficial cues. Most little children believe that it is the clothes and toys that make them boys or girls, and they are eager to show that they understand their category and anxious about any change in the cues that make their gender less obvious. Take away her pink tutu and put her in overalls, and the little girl believes that she might not be a girl anymore.

One of my most vivid memories of raising my daughter Gracie was the Tutu Wars. At three years old, Gracie began to insist on wearing her pink tutu every day to preschool. I objected, anxious in no small part because I believed that one should "dress your girls in clothes with bright colors, suitable for outdoor play," as I had written in the first Smart Girls book.

"You can't wear that tutu every day! It's so frilly you can't play in it!"

"Yes, I can, I can just pull it up high when I jump, see?"

"People won't know how strong you are if you wear clothes like that."

"I'll just show them my muscles! Look at my muscles! Ballerinas have really strong muscles!"

"It's boring to wear the same thing every day! Try something new."

"I want to wear my tutu!"

"No, not today."

"Mommy, you are being ridiculous! I want to wear my tutu!"

At this point, my husband Chuck peeked around the doorway. "Um…if the point is that she needs to be assertive and bold and stand up for her point of view…I kinda think she's got that."
—Barbara

It is likely that your smart little girl may go through the princess stage—not because she is "biologically programmed" to do so as a female but because she is developmentally wired to defend what she perceives as her gender. Go ahead and provide some princess clothes and toys because denying them and insistently rejecting them is the sure way to increase her desire for them. Help her to see the distinction between princess as a play identity and princess as the end goal in life. There is a wonderful Sesame Street episode where Sonia Sotomayor asks Abby what she wants to be when she grows up. She says, "A princess!" Justice Sotomayor maintains that playing princess is fun, but "Princess is not a career."

Go ahead and enjoy the movies you loved along with her, help her with dress up, and engage her imagination in making up her own stories. Do emphasize Belle's bravery, and Ariel's assertiveness, and Jasmine's adventurous nature—but gently, without a lot of editorializing. Simply mention, "No girl should ever let somebody yell at her like the Beast does," and "Ariel shouldn't have given up her voice just to be with her boyfriend; now she'll have to work hard to get it back from Ursula." Be clear that she can be beautiful and strong at the same time, but that when she has to make a choice, strong is better.

One of the saddest things we see is moms, and sometimes dads, anxiously pressuring their little girls into princess culture when the little girl would rather wear baseball caps and play at "boys" games. For the little girl who doesn't want to participate in the princess scene, support her mightily and defend her right not to buy pink and not to play princess. Smart little girls have often intuited for themselves the downside of being a princess—long hours sitting still, having to be nice all the time, and hanging out with nobody except other princess clones. For a hilarious video of a four-year-old girl's protest you can play for your daughter, see "Why do girls have to buy pink toys and princesses?" at www.youtube.com/watch?v=7OrMT8Wv9mI. She pounds her fist, stamps her feet, and shows that she can assert her own tastes in toys and clothes—a valuable lesson indeed.

Preschool Years: What Little Bees Need

Certainly, preschool is too early for career planning. However, it is a time when the basic temperaments show themselves in the preferences of young girls and will likely have career consequences later on. Here are some things we know about the different bees and what helped them to thrive as little girls.

Worker Bees and Forager Bees who are academically talented are already showing broad interests and curiosity and need access to media and books that will allow them to pursue all those interests. The "Touch Pad" generation needs touch pads—and grown-ups to guide them in their use, e.g., "Do you want to learn about kitties? Let's Google kitties!" Let us not forget, however, that books have always played an important role in sustaining continuous attention. When a picture-story is going slowly, it is too easy to just touch a screen and leap to another one. Real books can help teach girls to maintain attention on a story. Let little girls grow in the recognition of the treasure that books are—something solid they can hold and keep, along with their stuffed animals, as the symbols of their identity.

Honey bees—those girls with emotional intelligence—are probably already showing the signs of being helpers, teachers, and leaders. They may hold their dolls and toys tenderly, cooing and attending to their baby's needs. They may organize their animals around them to teach them or lead them in songs. Honeybees often try to organize other kids, and they become mightily frustrated when their playmates run off to do something else. Support your smart girl's attempts to nurture, heal, and lead by praising her skills and asking her lots of questions about her toys' needs and how she is meeting them. When she leads, encourage her and let her know that other kids might be too little to understand what she wants. Perhaps you can teach her some skills for sustaining younger children's interest in being helped, taught, or led, e.g., "Don't forget to ask them what they want to learn," or "Don't make too many rules, because other kids don't like that. Just help them have fun playing. Like this..." and then model the behavior of encouraging fun rather than making rules.

Procreator Bees—the most creative girls—want to draw, tell stories, build things, and make toys work the way they want them to. Try not to be too shocked when the dolls end up in surgery. Provide lots of stuff to make things—not just crayons but spools, strings, fabric, sticks, clay, cans, bottles, jars, and of course, mud. Then make time for her to play alone. Listen to her long stories, delight in her inventions, and show off her creations to the family. Most of all, try not to reign in her nonconformity when it is merely inconvenient or mildly off-putting to other kids.

What about the Queens, the spiritually intelligent? In our culture, we don't understand much about the early childhood of people with spiritual leanings. Native American families often encourage their children to talk about their dreams, and they take their kids' fantasies seriously. Respecting rather than fearing the unusual psychological experiences that your pre-school girl relates, often in symbolic language, is the first step toward helping her to understand her own intuitive mind. I remember very vividly telling my grandmother that the stars seemed to be talking to me. In a hushed, respectful whisper, she said, "What do they say?"

CHAPTER 7

Smart Girls: The Flowers That Bloom in the Spring

Prior to entering school, smart girls generally thrive in their development, yet the schools that should become a treasured haven for them fail to live up to their hopes. Like flowers that bloom in the spring, a smart girl will never again be as radiant and rapid in her development as during her childhood years. At seven, she might already be a passionate reader, an adventurer, a part-time drama queen, and a comedian. From the earliest gifted studies, psychologists have emphasized the social skills, emotional balance, and healthy psychological adjustment of gifted girls. Although gifted boys share some of these same characteristics, gifted girls are usually remarkably expressive, imaginative, and verbally precocious.

The smart girl's desire to learn is insatiable. If she is intellectually challenged in school, she rises to the challenge, often asking for more reading and more projects. If she is unchallenged and a little bored, she will do what she can to make life more interesting for herself; she is often too young to know that this may be a life-long experience. She does this in her characteristically resourceful way, by finding things to read, things to think about, and games to play in her head. Even when the school doesn't respond to her needs, she is ever hopeful that the next teacher or maybe the next school will hold the keys to the knowledge she craves.

At home, she goes through new projects rapidly and does not always value finishing them. Once she has experienced the excitement of the miniature village, her butterfly collection, or her horse paintings, she seems unconcerned about perfecting it or putting away her materials. She is happy to read, explore online, or play in her imaginary world for long hours.

Like gifted girls in previous generations, her interests, aspirations, and play activities are more like those of gifted boys than they are like those of average girls. Gifted children of both genders tend to be androgynous in their interests and activities, or in other words, girls like typically boyish things in addition to girly things and vice versa. That means she loves to explore her world—she imagines herself talking to dolphins in her swimming pool, jumping on a spaceship to Mars while she sits on the lawn gazing at the stars, or maybe finding dinosaur eggs in her backyard. She has a strong voice and she is not afraid to use it by vigorously stating her opinions and engaging in debate with anyone who disputes her point of view. She is just as competitive on the soccer field as the boys, and she is confident in her strength, smarts, and courage. Although friendly with groups of girls, she finds many of the activities of her age peers a little boring or babyish and prefers the company of older kids or other smart kids. Sometimes, though, she is so highly gifted that she can't hide her boredom and impatience, or she's so imaginative that she seems a little weird to others. Highly gifted and creative girls sometimes face rejection from other kids—and if that happens, she seeks out an adult to befriend, buries herself in her reading, or finds company in nature or with her pets.

In Schools

What is it like to be a smart girl in today's schools? Bright girls' experience with schools ranges from Malala Yousafzai's impoverished school in Pakistan, which was shut down multiple times by the Taliban, to average public schools in the U.S. where children are grouped by age and teachers try to improve standardized test scores for all students so as to leave no child behind. Then there are beautifully appointed private schools in large metropolitan areas that individualize learning based on student interests and ability, and which offer art, music, and drama as well. In addition to the brick and mortar schools, thousands of smart girls now receive their education online or through home-schooling. What follows is the description of smart girls' education in settings ranging from the worst schools to the best schools, along with suggestions for parents and teachers who are hoping to provide the best education possible for their smart girls.

The Worst Schools: Poverty, Violence, Despair

Bright girls in poor communities throughout the world go to schools with very few resources, and they are often the worst kind of schools for smart girls. Although most people think of Africa when they think of poor schools, it is important to know that in the U.S., many children are going to school in conditions that are similar to those in third world countries. We have visited schools on Indian reservations, in decaying urban areas, and in poor rural communities where even basic needs—such as clean bathrooms and eating areas—are not met, and essential resources like books, computers, and desks are lacking. In one combined elementary and middle school in rural western Nebraska, ceilings were cracked, floors were wet from flooding bathrooms, the air was swampy with the windows sealed and no fans, and there was a basketball gym in back that couldn't be used by classes because of possibly dangerous damage to the floor! We have seen computer classes with a few, old Apple IIe computers (circa 1985) in windowless, cement block rooms with flickering, fluorescent lighting, and schoolyards that were nothing more than patches of concrete surrounded by walls and wire, almost like a prison. In schools like these, students often suffer from multiple problems: homelessness, poverty, low achievement, learning disabilities, and health issues like obesity, diabetes, and asthma. Teachers in these schools are often overwhelmed with their large classes of needy students and the pressure to either raise performance or lose their jobs, as well as a constant, underlying fear of violence.

Those Who Survive

Can a smart girl emerge successfully from a school like this? Although the odds are certainly against it, some bright girls are able to survive these conditions, and some go on to high achievement. They are usually very smart, resilient, and emotionally stable, and they usually have a support system that is unusual for the community in which they live. One study of these kinds of students, most of them minorities, found that they not only survived but also eventually scored in the 95th percentile on the ACT.[156] What made these gifted girls different? They usually had constant adult presence and support in their lives through large and extended families; they were kept safe (many were literally kept indoors when not in school or in supervised activities); they had one important teacher who made them feel special and provided challenge; and they were involved in activities—religious, musical, academic, or athletic—that took up a great deal of their free time. They also spent an enormous amount of time reading on their own or at the library and on the computer. They also usually had many home responsibilities like housekeeping, cooking, and childcare, but they were not expected to be full-time parents when they were not in school.[157]

Earlier, we wrote about Sonia Sotomayor and Malala Yousafzai— smart girls who lived in poverty but had many of the individual, family, and community supports and sources of resilience needed to become high achievers. It may seems like extreme advice, but to parents of smart girls living in extreme poverty, we suggest first that you keep your daughter safe with reliable adults in a secure place, and second, that you provide supplementary education to counter the low expectations at her school. If possible, get involved in improving the school and provide a rich community centering on multi-age activities with lots of adult role models, or even try to move to another school.

It is not always the teacher's fault. Often, teachers in these poorer schools are new college graduates who feel frightened, overwhelmed, and alone; they may need some friendly support and encouragement. Build an alliance with the teacher who is the least despairing. Your smart little girl can be a bright spot in a teacher's difficult day; you can make that possible by knowing what will be happening in school each week and doing your best to support the teacher's plans. If you are not working, you can volunteer as a teacher aid in the classroom.

Average Schools

Today's schools are far different from the schools you attended; if you were in school more than 15 years ago, your daughter's school is quite different. Everywhere, schools are more reliant on technology than ever before. In most average schools, your children will be more involved in learning keyboard skills than in penmanship. Teachers today use more visual aids, videos, and varying teaching strategies than the ones you experienced. Classes are much larger—so large, in fact, that you will wonder how the teacher can possibly manage so many children, sometimes as many as 40 children. Classes are also increasingly diverse with children of differing ethnic backgrounds, often speaking several different languages. For example, in the Los Angeles Unified School District, more than 123 different languages are spoken by students.

The school buildings themselves are probably in some state of disrepair because budgets are tight and few new schools have been built in the last decade. You are most likely to find that children of all ability levels are included in the same classrooms, and several children likely will have special needs. There may be classmates with physical disabilities: a child who uses a wheelchair or wears a hearing aid; a child with a behavior or emotional disorder such as oppositional-defiant disorder; and very likely, one or two children with ADHD, Autism Spectrum Disorder, or specific learning disabilities. If your daughter is twice-exceptional—gifted in addition to a disability or special need—there may be a resource teacher to help with disabilities but no specialist to address the needs of gifted students; it is quite rare to find an understanding teacher with training in both areas. Services for children with learning or physical disabilities are mandated by federal and state laws; services for gifted children are usually not required by law, or if they are, there is no funding to help pay for them. The only federal law providing minimal funding for gifted education, the Jacob K. Javits Gifted and Talented Students Education Program, was "zero-funded" in 2011 through 2013; funding has continued in 2014 but with the lowest dollar amount seen in the history of the program (excluding the three year hiatus).[158]

Probably the most sweeping changes to public education in the U.S. have occurred because of the *No Child Left Behind* legislation (2001) and its requirements for frequent testing with state-developed assessments showing adequate yearly progress in raising scores on tests.[159] With this law, the burden falls on the teachers to raise test scores of their classes, no matter how large or diverse the learning needs of their class. As a result, teachers must spend most of their time with learners who struggle and are therefore "behind." Not only are teachers under pressure in the classroom, but they also perceive themselves to be under attack by their communities and state legislatures for not "measuring up." Their schools are judged by comparing their test scores with other schools' test scores, even though it is unreasonable for an urban, high-poverty school to compete favorably with schools in upper middle-class neighborhoods. A recent report by the Thomas B. Fordham Institute describes in detail the ways in which NCLB has been implemented and the impact it has had. The findings are damning, particularly for gifted children. Chester Finn of the Fordham Institute says in an article, *Young, Gifted, and Neglected:*

> *They depend on public education to prepare them for life. Yet that system is failing to create enough opportunities for hundreds of thousands of these high-potential girls and boys. Mostly, the system ignores them, with policies and budget priorities that concentrate on raising the floor under low-achieving students. A good and necessary thing to do, yes, but we've failed to raise the ceiling for those already well above the floor. Public education's neglect of high-ability students doesn't just deny individuals opportunities they deserve. It also imperils the country's future supply of scientists, inventors, and entrepreneurs.[160]*

A worst-case scenario, not all that uncommon in an average public school, is that the smart girl is not only neglected in the classroom but also seen as a liability. Although most teachers do not hold negative attitudes toward gifted girls, some teachers in regular classrooms regard gifted girls as conceited or disruptive to their lesson plans. A substantial number of teachers view parents of gifted children as pushy and elitist, particularly when they ask for some form of acceleration, which is viewed negatively by about half of all teachers, according to a national survey.[161] In cases like this, the smart girl is ignored or criticized by the teacher; her curiosity, restiveness, or boredom is punished rather than remediated; and she is expected to simply wait quietly while other children catch up with the lesson. When her parents request assistance, they are usually lectured about their daughter's need to "fit in" and to "learn to be more patient."

Smart girls are often invisible in the classroom. In neutral conditions, the smart girl is neither blamed nor praised but somehow goes unnoticed. Smart girls are likely to sit quietly without complaining, indulging in fantasy or discreetly reading a book hidden behind the covers of her binder. In contrast, smart boys' greater need for action often leads them to act out when bored.[162] Some smart girls have learned to camouflage their abilities by reducing the number of times they raise their hands, by purposely giving a few wrong answers so as not to get too many perfect scores on tests, and by pleasantly joining in girls' conversations no matter how far they may be from her own interests. Girls who use these coping skills are able to blend into the classroom so well that their teachers are often surprised when high scores on intelligence or achievement tests show these girls' true abilities.[163]

What are the optimal conditions for smart children in a public elementary school? The research is clear about this: Teachers who have had some training in gifted education are much more positive about gifted children and actively try to use the information they have to help make their teaching of smart kids more effective.[164] The teacher with training not only notices the gifted girl but can also see her even if she has gone "underground."

The smart girl lucky enough to be in a school where there is a gifted specialist is likely to have some special accommodations for her ability. The school may have *cluster grouping*, which makes it possible for her to be grouped with children of a similar ability level in one or more subject areas. In math, perhaps, she is in the group that is moving more rapidly and with greater depth through the math curriculum. The teacher may have also observed, for example, that the smart girl is a passionate, very advanced reader and that even the cluster grouping for reading may not meet her needs. She then meets with the girl and her parents to discover the girl's favorite books and devises an individualized plan of reading projects that will take her even further into literature that she enjoys. For example, she may use curriculum from Joyce Van Tassel-Baska's research-based strategy for *differentiation* in language arts or other curriculum designed for higher level thinking for gifted students.[165] The teacher has knowledge of the many models of gifted education and chooses those strategies that fit the individual child.[166]

Parents wanting to advocate for their smart girls should learn as much as they can about gifted education options before going to the school with requests. If parents search the Internet for gifted child information, they will find web sites and both state and national associations that advocate for gifted children and offer information. Many books for parents likewise exist to help them understand various options and curricula for gifted students. Parents can find information about in-school and afterschool programs, special schools, and summer opportunities. There are books that offer valuable parenting advice; there are also publishers who specialize in information about all things related to gifted children.[167]

In the average public school, the best that parents can expect is probably some combination of cluster grouping, curriculum differentiation, and special programming for gifted children. Parents need to be aware that even these strategies usually stretch the school resources and challenge an already overwhelmed teaching staff. Expecting more—such as individualization in every subject or daily individual time with a gifted resource teacher—is not fair to the school. Parents who want more will need to be activists in support of gifted education, advocating not only for their own children but also for other smart children and the teachers who want to serve them.[168]

The Best of the Best: Special Schools for Gifted Children

One word describes how most smart children see their special school—paradise. An excellent example is the Nueva School in California, where a day at that school is a joyful experience even for a grown-up. Instead of manicured lawns, lush woods surround the school. If you venture into the woods, you are in for a surprise—it looks like an Ewok village! This is the Forts program, an ongoing recess activity that allows kids to go into the woods and use the forests' natural materials to build forts to play in. There is gentle supervision and only a few rules, most notably that you cannot exclude anybody from your fort. You are not likely to see any children testing the rules because they are too busy showing off their construction technologies to each other. Inside the school, an old mansion retrofitted for the needs of gifted and creative children, you will find intimate classrooms, a sunny ballroom, cool passageways and stairways, warm, friendly administrative offices, and an inviting library with resources ranging from wonderful old, leathery books to sparkling computer stations. Most striking is the constant conversation, laughter, and vocalized *Aha!* moments of teachers and students working in small groups. In each classroom, projects and interactive activities are underway—a science project where children are peering through a microscope at the structure of leaves they have gathered, a storytelling circle, or a kindergarten room with multiple play groups and teachers roaming, questioning, and encouraging their students. The students are lively and engaged, and teachers manage their classrooms deftly so that no child is left out and no child's enthusiasm is dampened. It is a utopia of learning and growth.

Most special schools for gifted children are private schools, university-based lab schools, or public magnet and charter schools. Private schools are very expensive but usually have generous scholarship programs; they tend to be located on prime real estate in affluent areas of cities or park-like suburbs. For parents of limited means, it is important to consider these schools despite the expense, because most of them are experienced and skilled in dealing with the needs of smart girls. One concern many parents will have is transportation; the school may be very far from home with public transportation unavailable. Again, don't despair before asking about transportation options. We were pleased to find that a group of parents had organized a taxi shuttle with the same, reliable driver for five kids that cost just a few dollars a day each.

University lab schools are usually outstanding as well and often reasonably priced or even free through an arrangement with the school district. They may, however, have entrance requirements and waiting lists to get in. Many university-based lab schools have long histories—such as the Hunter College School in New York City, which goes back a hundred years. These schools are often staffed by professors in gifted education, graduate students, and teachers in training, and are active in developing and evaluating curriculum for gifted students.

Charter schools are hit and miss; some are wonderful, some are not. Sadly, many states that allow charter schools have very little oversight, and too many have been organized by entrepreneurs more concerned with profit than with education. They may have alluring titles that include words like *academy*, *honors*, *leadership*, and *talent*, but the names don't necessarily mean that they serve bright students. Too many schools that show up on the lists of "Worst Schools in America" have these misleading titles. On the other hand, charter schools have been the only way that a school can be publicly funded, and in some states, gifted education teachers and parents of gifted students have come together to create a charter school with a vision of innovative education for bright students. We caution parents to investigate each school carefully. We know kids whose education and lives were saved by charter schools for bright kids.

Most schools for gifted students will require test scores, parent nominations, and teacher checklists for admittance. Intelligence test scores stabilize at around nine years old. This is because younger children are often more affected by the relationship with the individual administrator than older children, and because reading skills may not be fully developed enough for a fair assessment on group tests.[169] If the school has K-5 classes, usually additional indicators will be used. In a school devoted to the needs of gifted children, it is usually possible for smart girls to learn at their own rate in flexible arrangements for each subject area. In such a school, acceleration is not a dirty word, and grouping is often used for different levels of giftedness when needed, ranging from moderate to profoundly gifted. The faculty and administrators of these schools are usually active members of associations for gifted education and active users of relevant websites with constantly updated information. They enjoy new and effective strategies like problem-based learning; the use of technology is central, with online education used wherever children's special interests lead. Because parents are often the founders of the school, parental involvement is high and relationships between parents and faculty are usually very good. For smart girls who might go unnoticed and underserved in the regular public schools these schools are a place where they can thrive.

What about Homeschooling?

Forget everything you have heard about homeschooling—particularly the stereotype of the gun-toting, Bible-thumping, backwoods mom teaching her kids that dinosaurs and men existed together in the Garden of Eden. Gifted homeschooling parents could not be more different from the myths and stereotypes most people have of homeschoolers. They are not all mothers; they do not homeschool alone but usually have the support of a large gifted homeschooling community; and they often homeschool in addition to working in other occupations, often out of the home. Their gifted children interact with other gifted kids who share their interests and abilities, both in family get-togethers and online. They learn social skills while doing projects in the community, traveling with their parents, and interacting with children of many cultures as well as their parents' colleagues and friends. Most home-schooling parents made the decision to take over their children's education because the needs of their kids just could not be met in any kind of school in their locale. Profoundly gifted children who need radical acceleration, gifted children with uneven talents, and twice-exceptional children make up many of the students being schooled at home. For more information about twice-exceptional smart girls and their special needs, see Chapter 11.

For the smart mom with a gifted daughter, becoming a homeschooling mother presents a special dilemma. How does she encourage her daughter to have an unrelenting devotion to her intellectual goals if she, the mother, seems to have put her own goals on hold while educating her daughter? Many smart women have resolved that dilemma with grace and resourcefulness; they share the task of homeschooling with their spouse, thereby making it clear to their children that teaching is not just a woman's job. Many smart homeschooling mothers have integrated homeschooling into their vocational interests, by taking up free-lance writing, for example; others have found a new calling in homeschooling while some manage a blog, a business, or a career as well.

Rebecca McMillan may be one of the best-known homeschooling parents in gifted education. As the founder of *The Brain Café*, a Facebook venue, she shares resources about brain science, psychology, creativity, and education with 2,200 members, including researchers, psychologists, edu-cators, journalists, bloggers, parents, gifted advocates, passionate amateurs, and curious souls from around the globe. She also created and directs the online education unit for Gifted Homeschoolers Forum, a resource for homeschoolers all over the world.

She calls herself a "3rd generation feminist," who was self-supporting at age 17, put herself through college, and devoted herself to articulating the vision of social justice nonprofits. She and her husband have a marriage of true minds, supporting each other's vocations. After the birth of their first son, they knew within a year that he was highly gifted. Although she had intended to continue graduate school and work in nonprofits, "life had other plans" as Rebecca and her husband struggled not only to give birth to a second child but also to care for their aging, ill parents for more than a decade. The academic needs of their first son and the second, born equally gifted, clearly required that the family change course and find a way to provide for them at home. Here is what Rebecca says about why she chose homeschooling and how she manages it:

Homeschooling is consistent with our overarching commitment to honor and nurture the intellectual, psychological, and creative development and well-being of each member of the family in equal measure. Homeschooling is both a form of creative self-expression itself and is the educational context most compatible with a life built around creativity and self-expression.

With both boys, it was evident almost immediately that they were far from typical or average, though as first time parents, it took us longer to trust our conclusion regarding Will. At 18 months, he had a vocabulary of 300 words; by 20 months, he was speaking in full sentences; and just a few months later, was using such words as precarious, precipitation, cathedral, and more. We sent him to a progressive private school with multi-age classrooms that seemed to do a good job of nurturing creativity. While a very good fit on the social, emotional, and creative fronts, it was never enough for Will on the academic front. I began advocating for more challenging academics for him midway through his kindergarten year and never stopped. I also intensified my research on gifted issues. In 3rd grade, we finally had Will tested and observed by Linda Silverman, a psychologist specializing in profoundly gifted (PG). Through these first hand experiences and from abundant reading of the gifted literature and contact with other families attempting to educate their highly gifted (HG) or PG offspring, I came to realize that it was unlikely that we would be able to trust any school, public or private, to provide an education that would simultaneously meet Will's intellectual, social, emotional, and creative needs. During Will's last two years at Wildwood, I began pulling him out one afternoon a week to experiment with homeschooling and give him the time to pursue his musical interests.

Luke was born the summer before Will's fourth grade year. In no time, it was clear that Luke too was likely PG and would have unusual educational needs. As we confronted the likelihood of having two kids in private school, paying nearly $40K per year for an education that was nowhere near enough academically, we did some soul searching and came to the conclusion that it made more sense to homeschool, where our dollars would stretch further and we could make do on a single income. Scott accepted a position at a friend's production company in Dallas, and Will and I started full time homeschooling. At this point, Will was starting sixth grade *and Luke was two.*

Our approach was eclectic, to provide both of us with room to follow our creative muses. After just a year of lessons, Will was already serious about violin and had begun to compose after taking a music theory course through UCLA extension before we left L.A. He was also an avid reader and creative writer. He read Norse mythology and reenacted the Ragnarok on one of his computer gaming platforms. He was happy, engaged intellectually and creatively, and had plenty of time to explore his many interests. Fortunately, he was also responsible and self-directed as we had very few child-care options and Luke's antics kept me very, very busy! Though we both enjoyed homeschooling for those two years, Will was hungry for more social contact and he was even hungrier for more musical opportunities. When he found out that he could take two periods of orchestra daily at the local high school as well as continuing his violin lessons and youth symphony, he jumped at the chance. We accelerated him a year so he could start that fall. He started at the local high school as a 13-year-old freshman with additional subject accelerations. Homeschooling continued with Luke.

(Note: The family moved to North Carolina so that they could blend public school opportunities with homeschooling. Some schools allow homeschooled students to attend part time.)

We are now in our sixth year of homeschooling. Luke has read more Shakespeare than most educated adults. He's studied stream ecology; monitored local rivers; participated in archeological digs; collected data for UNC research projects; written hundreds of pages of stories; completed two years of high school-level English; studied French and Latin; participated in a gifted homeschooling co-op for five years; undertaken a two-year study of the history of science; completed an in depth study of Lord of the Rings; read hundreds of books; studied electronics, honors biology, civics, economics, current events, U.S. history, and world history; whizzed through elementary math; mastered algebra; dabbled in statistics; and immersed himself in The Hero's Journey.

Each of these projects provides abundant opportunities for me to learn and create on a daily basis while homeschooling and providing the support Luke needs to grow into a fully independent, engaged, and passionate student. Luke sees me apply myself with diligence and passion to my own projects, work, and learning. We read and study right alongside each other. We discuss the passages and ideas that intrigue and excite us. We strategize about how to solve problems in his work or mine. He watches as I throw myself into my research, get excited about new connections, follow my inner stream of consciousness toward new understandings, and struggle to shut out distractions as I write. I watch and encourage as he does the same. I post in The Brain Café as he practices or improvises on piano or guitar. We encourage, cheer each other on, analyze our failures, and celebrate our successes. We extend the same spirit of engagement and support to Scott who often works from home, writing, blogging, teaching, and doing phone consultations. Learning and work is integrated into the fabric of daily life for all three of us (four when Will was still living at home).

Feminist and creative values are embedded into the very way we have constructed our lives, pursue our interests, the work we choose, and the way we educate and raise our sons. No one's work is given priority over anyone else's. We respect each other's revolving and differing need for quiet, space, discussion, debate, engagement, and problem solving as legitimate parts of the learning process. Household chores are shared equitably. When one of us is busy, overwhelmed, or on a tight deadline, the other two pick up the slack. The entire dance is organic and born of mutual respect and commitment to equality. Each person's need for autonomy and creative expression is recognized, respected, and accommodated to the greatest extent possible. No one is asked or expected to engage in meaningless, soul-killing work. Throughout our marriage, Scott and I have allowed each other the freedom to pursue our creative interests and define our own path even if that meant we had to sacrifice financial security, take a financial hit, or move away from family and friends. There is little worse than watching someone you love, for whom creativity is as natural and important as breathing, deny themselves the time and freedom to create. No financial gain is worth that sacrifice. We have considered deeply, labored mightily, abandoned both conformity and normalcy, set aside careers, forged new paths, and invested heart and soul to provide Will and Luke with the time, space, and freedom they need to learn, discover their passions, and express themselves creatively.

Every step in the journey has been a marvelous adventure. As it turns out, homeschooling gave me the time and freedom I needed to discover and nurture my own passions as well. Funny that![170]

For families that want to homeschool, many new resources exist to assist them in the process. *Creative Homeschooling* by Lisa Rivero and *From School to Homeschool* by Suki Wessling provide a guide to parents who are considering homeschooling, as well as resources and suggestions for integrating homeschooling into family life.[171]

Home and Away—Busy as a Bee

The activity level of the gifted girl can come as a surprise to many parents.[172] Most gifted girls sleep less than other children, frustrating their parents by finding a hundred reasons to stay awake at night—a book they must finish, a game they must win, a dance routine that must be performed, a costume that must be found, and on and on. They want to wake up early, too, and bang around the kitchen or turn on the TV.

I remember my fascination with dawn. I wanted to be there to watch the stars fade, the sky grow grey, and the sun peek above the housetops. I was up, dressed, and out in the back yard while the dew was still on the grass. I brought bread and peanuts, threw them around me in a circle and then stood stock still, waiting for the sparrows, pigeons, and squirrels to approach me. I was Jungle Woman feeding the parrots and toucans. I was St. Francis, suffering the little animals to come unto me. I was a Lady of Green Mansions, communing with the spirits in the grass and trees. —Barbara

The right amount of sleep is indeed very important, because day-time learning is consolidated during slow-wave sleep. Children have much more slow-wave sleep than teens or adults, indicating that this is a critical part of their intense learning years.[173] Parents have a hard time negotiating bedtimes and waking times, and they usually find that the best solution is to figure out what is the least amount of sleep that makes it possible for her to get through school or weekend activities without fatigue and then make some safety rules around that length of time. Safety rules for girls under 10 might be: no going outside at night; no cooking on the stove at night; or no animals or friends in the house while the parents are still asleep. Making hard and fast rules, like "In your bed, lights out, eyes closed by 8:00 p.m.," is going to require more enforcement than most tired parents can muster up.

Girl Power and Its Products

Smart girls are naturally project-oriented, and every day a new plan emerges for a backyard laboratory or Shakespearean theater in the round. In competitive upper middle class households, parents often believe they have to provide many expensive and educational toys and games. Not only did the Baby Einstein videos start a trend for parents to start prepping their kids for college in infancy but now there are also products to support every aspect of Girl Power.

As women who have been involved in empowering girls for decades, we were delighted when societies around the world began to embrace images of girls that were strong, brave, and accomplished in children's media. From Japanese anime *Grrl Power* to *Dora the Explorer*, new girl icons emerged who could hold their own. Some of our enthusiasm soured, however, when marketers commercialized Girl Power products, and the girls depicted began to take on the usual stereotypes. Strong girls were too often portrayed as adorable, sexy, or just plain mean. Even science-oriented Girl Power products showed girls that they could learn science through perfume, makeup, or pink building blocks. In *Packaging Girlhood: Rescuing our Daughters from Marketers' Schemes*, Sharon Lamb and Lyn Mikel Brown show how the media played upon our fears about strong, self-directed girls by turning them into mean cheerleaders and bossy babysitters or renewed stereotypes of girls by making the feisty girl a secondary character in an otherwise boy-oriented story.[174] They also note that during the time a girl might be watching a program about a brave girl fighting her way to freedom or working for justice, she will be subjected to numerous commercials for feminine beauty products or pink, frilly toys.

The solution to all these mixed messages is to be very aware of what is being marketed to your daughter, to comment lightly, and to steer her toward the images of girls that are truly empowering. That means not setting up false divisions like good girl and bad girl but rather teaching girls not to be afraid of being judged. It means helping our daughters to see that they are so much more and can do so much more than they are being shown. Teaching smart girls to be critical viewers and consumers can start in childhood because bright girls often want somebody to articulate the discomfort they feel even when reading about or watching a show that is supposed to be for girls—but doesn't seem to be about them.

With regard to products for busy play, most smart girls are content with arts and crafts supplies, things to take apart, dress-up clothes from the thrift store, and dolls and animals that can be set up in a variety of scenarios.

A few coveted, heavily marketed products can help keep her from being totally uncool, the poor girl with the hippie mom who won't let her own plastic toys or watch DVDs, but you will see that your attitude of benign indifference is likely to be shared by her as she tires of simplistic, girlie toys. A cheap touch pad, smart phone, or laptop that she can use on her own may be a great investment, given the world of projects that it opens up—there are now easily a thousand apps for children. (Jungle Woman would have loved the Audubon bird song identification app and the Swahili language translation app.) Finally, keep in mind that your daughter is bombarded all the time with messages to buy stuff and become a consumer but that you are raising her to *produce* ideas, products, and services that will make a better world, rather than filling it with junk.

All of these self-directed activities are the good kind of busy. The bad busy is busyness of the over-scheduled or overworked child. In our earlier chapter on Millennials, we discussed the findings of several major studies about the over-scheduling of this generation. If you dig deeper into the studies of what children are doing today, you will see that much of the extra activity that is being observed is the increased activities of girls; we suggest that smart girls may be hit the hardest by expectations to be involved in every possible activity. Upper middle class bright girls may be expected not only to be achieving in school but also in myriad extracurricular activities. Middle class and poor smart girls must pick up all the domestic activities that their working parents or single moms cannot do. The stressed childhoods and busyness of smart girls can take many different forms.

School age smart girls in wealthy and upper middle class homes can expect to be involved in a wide variety of programs to increase their ability to enter the most prestigious colleges. As Chris Reardon, a scholar who studies inequality, points out in the *New York Times*:

> High-income families are increasingly focusing their resources—
> their money, time, and knowledge of what it takes to be successful in
> school—on their children's cognitive development and educational
> success. They are doing this because educational success is much
> more important than it used to be, even for the rich. With a college
> degree insufficient to ensure a high-income job or even a job as a
> barista, parents are now investing more time and money in their
> children's cognitive development from the earliest ages. It may
> seem self-evident that parents with more resources are able to
> invest more—more of both money and of what Mr. Putnam calls
> "Goodnight Moon time"—in their children's development. But even

though middle-class and poor families are also increasing the time and money they invest in their children, they are not doing so as quickly or as deeply as the rich.[175]

Parents, therefore, might be investing in test preparation skills for high-stakes exams; however, they also may be attempting to get all possible extracurricular activities in the schedule during the week to prove their daughters' well-roundedness.

It is our belief that test preparation classes are superfluous for smart girls and that attempts to make these girls well-rounded are wrong-headed. Rather than choosing all the activities that other parents are insisting are critical to well-roundedness, it is best to ask the bright girl, "What would you most like to learn to do that you aren't learning in school?" The answer may surprise you.

When I asked my nine-year-old daughter, Grace, what she would like to learn, she promptly answered, "Improv comedy." That was a challenge. There were no improvisational comedy troupes for children in Phoenix. Grace persisted, saying she would be happy to join an adult Improv group. So we searched for an adult troupe providing family-oriented comedy and sheepishly asked the director to allow her to audition. The audition theater was full of thirtyish, verbally gifted, extremely hyper males of every ethnicity imaginable. Grace's audition consisted of drawing an adjective and an occupation from a hat and meeting another actor on stage, who had also drawn two cards. She drew hypocritical and cowboy. We were taken aback. Did she even know what hypocritical meant? Her partner, a 30-year-old Hispanic man, had drawn obsequious and butler. She leapt on stage and yelled at the top of her lungs, "I ain't no phony cowboy! I'm a fur real cowgirl!" The butler entered and fawningly said, "May I bring you anything, Madame?" She screamed, "Get me ma guns!" He brought the invisible guns on an invisible silver platter. She yelled, "I'm the best gun in the West." She then pretended to shoot at the audience, stopped suddenly, spun around and fell to the floor, twitching in death throes from a supposed attack of shots from the audience. The audience roared. Audition over. Later, I apologized to the director for bringing a child to auditions when it was clear they didn't have kids. He said, "Oh, she's in all right. She has loads of talent. And no self-discipline whatsoever. Leave her to me." Thus began four years of comedy

training in which she thrived and learned better verbal sparring
skills than she ever could have in Girl Scouts and better teamwork
than she could have at soccer. —Barbara

Whether your daughter wants tuba lessons or electricity lessons, it pays to listen because she will be more committed to those activities that she chooses herself. If you insist on soccer and Suzuki violin because you believe that this will be best for her—and it is what the other girls are doing—she will prove you wrong.

One of the worst examples of a parent's misreading of a smart girl's needs is a single dad we knew who was infected with sports mania. In the working-class neighborhood where they lived, everybody was a little sports crazy already with a city team to cheer for in every sport, every season. Parents also rightly figured that a sports scholarship might be the only way to pay for college. This dad enrolled his daughter in every conceivable team sport—soccer, hockey, softball, and volleyball—and signed up to be assistant coach as often as possible. His reasoning was that if she tried out every sport, they would be able to figure out what she was best in and get her to higher-level teams. Every evening and weekend was taken up with practices and games. Dad was having a ball, but his daughter? Not so much. She said, "I know Daddy loves sports, and we do have a good time going to the games. But I don't like how the boys are so mean on the soccer team, and the girls on my softball team hate how I don't play as well as they do and make them lose games. I wish I didn't have to play so much, but I think Daddy would be upset if I didn't."

Sometimes smart girls themselves want to do everything and insist on being driven to each new activity. They might flit from one activity to another, never finishing a full year because they tire of it and want to go on to the next. When this is the case, some limitations are in order. Out-of-school activities are best limited to two, mutually-chosen, extracurricular activities. In addition, once an activity is started, it often requires a year or more to get up to enough proficiency to be enjoyable. While soccer might take a year, violin might take three or four years before the music sounds pleasant to the child's ear. It is important to take this into consideration and to talk with girls about the commitment that will be necessary. If a child wants to play a musical instrument, explain that you'll need at least a full semester commitment. There is probably more incentive to stick with it when a child joins orchestra or band because quitting would affect more than just her; all the instruments are needed to contribute to a larger group effort and performance.

Another kind of stressful over-scheduling stems from parents' over-worked lives. A majority of women in the U.S. will be single, working mothers at some point in their lives—this includes divorced and stay-at-home moms who suddenly have to find a way to make ends meet, as well as the impoverished urban mother who must work two part-time jobs and still doesn't have enough to get by without food assistance. In our earlier chapter on eminent women, we make it clear that most eminent women had early responsibilities in the family, and it is true that caring for siblings and sharing in the household chores is good experience for most smart girls. However, no girl should have to miss school to translate for her parents at the bank, or miss sleep to feed an infant, or help care for an aging grandparent round the clock; those girls who are forced into these inappropriate roles are likely to have debilitating stress symptoms. Parents who are overwhelmed need to seek the support of other adults, through extended family or a self-created extended family of friends. Rather than keeping the high-mortgage house in the suburbs, single moms might be better off moving near other single moms for mutual support and childrearing. Working parents who are struggling need to reduce their own stress in order to reduce their daughter's stress. Why is this such an important issue for smart girls? Unlike lots of kids, smart girls will usually try and succeed at being a parent, housekeeper, and nurse to the elderly—because they can. That tendency to adapt, to be resourceful, and to rise to any challenge may mean that the smart girl does not receive the parenting she herself needs; she misses having her own childhood and lives with loneliness, fear, and a feeling of being overwhelmed.

Alone Time

The importance of solitude comes up over and over in the stories of eminent women and the thoughtful women who pursue careers in arts, sciences, and humanities. Think of the endless hours Jane Goodall spent observing her beloved chimpanzees and the hours that J.K. Rowling spent dreaming and then writing about Harry Potter's world. None of this work would have been possible without a capacity for solitude. It is as children that girls need to learn the joys of being alone. In a society where girls are relentlessly encouraged to be likeable and popular, it is refreshing to the smart girl to have time out from all-consuming girls' groups. In their alone time, girls can dream, play out their own stories, and learn the first lesson of creativity—get away from the crowd.

Imaginative Play

From the earliest scholars of child development like Jean Piaget and Maria Montessori to today's psychologists who watch children at play, observers of kids have remarked that for children, play is serious.[176] Play is practice for work and adult roles. Play is for enacting and internalizing the values being taught at home, school, and the community. When girls are given too much guidance, too many directions for how to play, and too many rules for what to do when playing alone, they may never develop a sense of inner freedom and playfulness of spirit. Freedom to play also seems to improve school achievement.[177] Provide the bare minimum of objects and attire, model imaginative play, and then leave the room. The smart girl will think of something wonderful to do with them.

Nature

Not all schools can have Nueva School's wonderful forest, and not all neighborhoods have a natural park. Children need nature, and growing up without plants and animals creates a disconnect between humans and the Earth around them. Most women scientists began their careers as little girls who chased butterflies or gazed at the tiny world in a square foot of nature or sketched the natural environment. Georgia O'Keeffe remembers lying on a blanket and reveling in the colors of nature around her. Female leaders, whose future work was to be guiding other people, often first showed their capacity to nurture, teach, and lead by caring for animals. Find natural spots for smart girls to play, or bring nature inside by filling the home with plants and whatever pets are allowable. Go out and stare at the clouds and stars, count the birds in the neighborhood, and teach her the names of the living things around her and their relationships to one another. Even the youngest girls can experience the wonder of the vast web of being that is nature if they are just given the chance to participate in the natural world.

The Friendship of Books

Often the voice that eminent women remember best is the voice of their favorite childhood author. When people think that a smart girl's manners are remarkable, or her vocabulary advanced, or her opinions extraordinarily informed, it is often because of the books she has read. It is because that girl has counted among her friends some of the most brilliant, polished, and kindly people who ever lived—the authors of great books. She has worried, along with Anna Sewell (author of *Black Beauty*), that people are too often cruel and thoughtless in their treatment of animals, so she is unfailingly kind and attentive to her own and others' pets. She has followed the plight of Charles Dickens' impoverished heroes and now insists that her parents never pass a homeless person without a donation and a kind word. When girls are kept too busy out of school, they don't have time to meet these outstanding authors and to develop the lasting love of books that will help them to be independent learners.

The following shows just how powerful a relationship with an author can be for a smart little girl:

I was seven when I first picked out a book in our neighborhood library called The Silver Brumby, by Elyne Mitchell. How an Australian book about a wild horse got into a South St. Louis library, I will never know—but it changed my life.

Told from the horse's point of view, it was about a silver stallion named Thowra (an Aboriginal word for wind) whose lifelong goal was freedom from capture and the protection of his herd of mares. I read that book so many times that most of the stamps in it were mine, and I was furious when somebody else checked it out for an eternal two weeks. I lingered over every description of the Australian bush, every exciting scene of bravery and escape into freedom. Somehow, I not only internalized the love of this strange, exotic place but also the passion for freedom—the opportunity to run free, to seek new green pastures, and to help my herd to freedom. The day came when my Australian colleagues Glen Alsop and Leonie Kronborg would invite me to teach in Melbourne. Imagine my surprise when 40 years later I found that people in Australia adored Elyne Mitchell as much as I did! While signing books in a Melbourne bookstore, a man approached me and said, "Whatever brought you all the way to Australia?"

I replied, "Wild horses dragged me here! I love brumbies, and I want to see one someday!"

"Why, I know Mrs. Mitchell! I am a film director, and I worked with the company shooting The Man from Snowy River on her station in Corryong. Would you like to meet her?"

Soon it was all arranged. We spoke by phone, and the next year I was invited to spend a week with her at her lovely station (ranch) in the Snowy Mountains. That week was a dream come true. Mrs. Mitchell was now 86 years old and still writing her books about brumbies. Every day, we wandered over the hills and valleys in her Ranger; every night, we stayed up late sipping tea and talking. It was as if she were a long-lost aunt or a mother from another world; her voice was my voice, her ideals, my ideals. She had lived a remarkable, independent life as an author, rancher, and activist for Australia's wild horses. She had been happily married for several decades and had raised her children to be successful and fulfilled within a network of loving friends. In Mrs. Mitchell, I had not only a model but a dear friend. —Barbara

Supportive schooling with opportunities for acceleration, studies in a subject of interest, play and imagination, books, time in nature, a mentor—all of these are important for smart girls' development. No family or school can provide for all the needs of the smart girl, but the family who makes every effort to make time for reading and play, to create a special place to be alone, and to offer exposure to natural spaces will be rewarded with a livelier and happier smart girl. The school that provides individualized education that stresses challenge and provides for the deepening of the smart girls' special interests is likely to awaken the passion for learning that will follow her throughout her life.

CHAPTER 8

The Adolescent Smart Girl

The Change

What happened to the exuberant, confident little girl who used to stride as if on stage with every entrance into the room? Why did the little scientist abandon her laboratory and rock collection in the garage?

In the 1990s, public attention focused on the sudden shift that occurred in the self-expression of adolescent girls, and a number of the books written at this time had important implications for smart girls. Lyn Mikel Brown and Carol Gilligan showed how girls lost their authentic voices as they went through puberty. Adolescent girls, they said, stood at the crossroads; only a few continued with confidence in their opinions and values. The others seemed to lose faith in their own voices as they attempted to conform to an image of girls as shy, withholding, and modest.[178] In *Schoolgirls*, Peggy Orenstein described the extreme drop in self-esteem as occurring between 11 and 17.[179] In *Smart Girls, Gifted Women*, I concluded that the teen years were a danger zone when many smart girls left their career aspirations behind and plunged into the popularity game.[180]

Now, 20 years later, few studies of these issues can be found. Perhaps this is partly because adolescent girls have now caught up and surpassed boys in achievement in many academic domains. They constitute more than half of college students, and they are pouring into professional and graduate schools. A few studies show increasing aspirations and self-confidence. Everything has been fixed, right? Problem solved. Well, not really. Complexities and paradoxes abound in describing the development of gifted girls. David Yun Dai reviewed the literature on gifted girls' motivation for achievement and concluded that despite the advances in gifted girls' achievement, significant work needs to be done if we are to help them fulfill their potential.[181]

The American Psychological Association Task Force on Adolescent Girls (1999) sums it up by saying, "Declines in self-esteem during adolescence are not inevitable consequences of either pubertal or school changes. Both girls' and boys' self-esteem decreases during the high school years; but girls' self-esteem tends to drop more over time."[182] Adolescence is hard for everybody. Contrary to simplistic notions of the power of "raging hormones," it is not the changing hormones that are causing the emotional shifts, identity confusion, and difficult decision-making of adolescence. Although the pituitary hormones trigger the cascade of sexual hormones resulting in puberty, they are not directly causing behavioral changes. Instead, there are critical changes in neurotransmitters—particularly glutamates and dopamine. These neurotransmitters, produced in abundance during puberty, are linked to strong emotions and reactions to perceived rewards and stressors in the environment. This brings about a de-stabilization of mood so that experiences are felt much more intensely. Changes in the brain, particularly in the pre-frontal cortex, signal the growing capacity for self-regulation and impulse control; however, the growth in this area is nowhere near complete and won't be until about age 25. Even though gifted adolescents may be precocious in the development of their prefrontal cortex (which governs impulse and emotional regulation), there are still likely to be periods of asynchrony. This is why, as neurologist Judy Willis writes in *Inspiring Middle School Minds*, special attention must be paid to the levels of development in all areas—emotional, intellectual, and social.[183]

Attention, memory, organization, and information processing are all rapidly improving in the adolescent years, eventually resulting in metacognition, or the ability to think about one's own thoughts. What a paradox! Just as the abilities to regulate one's thoughts, emotions, and behaviors are growing, emotionality and the urge to take risks are also increasing.[184] The brain reaches the point of being able to solve problems using abstract thinking, but it also increasingly permits often painful self-consciousness.

Current research on self-esteem shows that all teens experience a drop in self-esteem, although girls experience a greater decline in body image and social self-esteem.[185] While adolescent girls' interests in achievement decline, that decline is less in girls than in boys. What does all this mean for gifted girls? Despite the horrors of popular media that depict teen girls as victims, most gifted girls will get through adolescence strong and self-confident. Intelligence is a protective factor that guards most gifted girls from many of the worst actions and allows them to avoid the riskiest situations.

I once had an uncomfortable experience at a conference for educators of gifted and talented students when I stayed to hear the speaker after my own presentation. I had spent the morning sharing all that positive psychology had to teach us about teaching and guiding gifted students. I spoke about resilience, creativity, hope, engagement in learning, the development of a sense of purpose in adolescents, and how we can enhance these positive forces in the lives of young gifted people. The speaker for the afternoon could not have painted a more different picture. For three hours, she talked about drugs—"They're everywhere! Gifted adolescents are smoking, drinking, doing marijuana and hard drugs in increasing numbers! Gifted girls are engaging in hookup sex, friendship with benefits, girl-on-girl sex for boys' pleasure, group sex, oral sex! They are getting pregnant and contracting STDs!" I don't know where the other speaker got her information because most of it was wrong. Despite the negative (and incorrect) message of the speaker, the audience was riveted, discouraged, and frightened—and my work of the morning was undone. —Barbara

The reality of the matter is that smoking is drastically declining, as is alcohol and drug use. Marijuana use in on the rise but still only at 11% by senior year for all adolescents. Some forms of STDs like HPV are rising, but most teens are using contraceptives. Even though about 20% of adolescents will have sex in early adolescence, the average age of first sexual experience for girls in the U.S. is 17. For most girls, intimacy takes place within a romantic relationship, and intimacy gradually increases with time and the development of the relationship.[186]

Why would professionals try to get teachers and parents worked up about sex and drugs and gifted girls? First, psychologists have long been guilty of focusing on pathology and deficiencies rather than strengths and protective factors, as positive psychologists continually point out. Out-of-control sex and drug use is simply more exciting for scholars than self-esteem and achievement issues. Second, one key aspect of sexism is portraying girls as victims rather than as agents who make choices—and sexism is alive and well in both popular and scholarly literature. Finally, persuading the parents and teachers of gifted girls that they are in trouble and need help makes jobs for psychologists and a wide variety of helpers.

You will see, however, that scholars who have actually studied large samples of gifted girls—from Lewis Terman to the *Study for Mathematically Precocious Youth*—discover that gifted girls are not only well-adjusted but also amazingly resistant to those scary aspects of adolescence such as substance abuse and risky sex. We have interviewed hundreds of gifted girls—including gifted girls who are considered at-risk. We found that although they had explored, experimented, and even run around with "sketchy" boyfriends for short periods of time, they never seemed to be at the party when the police arrived. One of the strengths of gifted girls seems to be the ability to have adventures while taking calculated risks. And usually their calculations turn out well.

Gifted girls' strengths are just as interesting as their problems—and helping a girl to discover her interests, develop her identity, and strengthen her resolve to attain her dreams is just as fascinating as helping girls with problem pregnancies and drug addictions.

Although gifted girls certainly encounter some difficulties—particularly in their schools—it is more appropriate to focus on their academic achievement, the development of their talents, their strivings for positive relationships, and their increasing sense of their purpose in the world.

Middle School Malaise

Whose idea was it to take every American child at 11 years old and throw him or her in with an enormous crowd of 11-15 year olds for several years of "social development?" In what other culture is it considered a good idea for early adolescents to be separated from responsibilities of younger children as well as the modeling of older adolescents? Where once gifted adolescent girls had clear reminders of their childhood around them and the presence of more mature teens to give them something to aspire to, now they are isolated into one mass of boys and girls going through puberty together.

The Middle School Movement took the nation by storm in the 1980s, and by 2000, middle schools made up of students age 11 to 14 were the major method of education delivery for pre-adolescents and young adolescents. From 1980 onward, U.S. schools moved children from a two-phase (K-8 and 9-12) to a variety of three phase models, such as K-5, 6-8, and 9-12. Now the system has spread to other countries. It is truly a movement, characterized by a strong ideology centered on the belief that early adolescence is a distinct developmental period, that middle school should primarily prepare young people for participation in a diverse, democratic society, and that collaboration, community, and teamwork should be emphasized over competitiveness.[187] All of these are fine ideals; unfortunately, the way they were put into practice turned most middle schools into intellectual wastelands and uncomfortable villages of puberty-induced drama for gifted girls.

Most parents whose gifted girls have had some degree of gifted programming in elementary school are stunned to discover that there will be no gifted education program services in middle school. In fact, if they are unfortunate enough to have administrators who are passionate supporters of the middle school movement, they will be told, "We don't believe in gifted education! We are educating the whole child, not just the brain! This is the time for your daughter to concentrate on exploring, growing up, and learning to collaborate with her peers." This is because most proponents of the middle school movement thought that the best way to achieve their ideals was with *heterogeneous groupings*; thus grouping by ability became anathema in middle school. Only in mathematics, where the differences in ability are so vast in a large middle school population that something must be done for very low performing students (under NCLB), will these schools offer some cluster grouping by ability. Of course, this is disheartening for the gifted girl who previously has been receiving opportunities to learn at her own pace. She now has to slow down. As far as the school is concerned, she is no longer gifted, and she may never hear the term again throughout her schooling.

Many gifted girls come home distressed when they learn that in nearly all of their classes, they will have *co-operative learning* or collaborative team projects. For the middle school proponents, this was perceived as the best way to allow active teens to get up and move around, along with learning teamwork skills. Cooperative and/or collaborative learning is based on heterogeneous grouping so that any group of four to six students will contain all ability levels. These are supposed to be democratic groups in which each child participates equally according to his or her interests and abilities. Even from the earliest years, parents of bright students complained that their gifted child somehow ended up doing all the work in these "team" projects. Educators concerned about gender bias noticed that girls seemed to get the dull, routine tasks, while boys got the exciting, exploratory, or leadership tasks.

One parent explaining a project on science careers described it this way: "So Max, the gifted boy, leads and gets the two other boys to go out and interview a couple of scientists. Two of the girls just sit and whisper together. Mari, our gifted daughter, tries to assign tasks equally but is ignored. The boys come back with scattered interview notes and refuse to do any of the required research, saying they have done their part. Mari is now worried about getting a failing grade if their presentation is so uncoordinated, so she does the research on biochemists, computer technicians, and sound engineers, cleans up the interviews, and develops a PowerPoint presentation with a part for each team member to read. She stayed up all night!" The risk, therefore, is that as a girl her voice will be overpowered by the boys, and as the gifted girl she will end up fretting about the product and doing much of the work.

Not all collaborative learning is awful, and many of the new Problem-Based Learning approaches, such as those developed by gifted educator Ginger Lewman, combine collaboration with rigorous learning of material needed to solve real problems.[188] However, it is important for parents to learn about these approaches and to explore when and whether they promote the learning needs of the gifted girl.

Another somewhat misguided notion is the idea that because early adolescence is a distinct developmental stage, these students should all be put together. It is indeed a distinct stage in which rapid transformations are taking place in the brain—from concrete to formal, abstract thinking—as well as within the body. Most cultures throughout history have considered the onset of puberty as a time for the entire community to come together to celebrate and support the gradual transformation of a child into an adult. It is the time to integrate the adolescent into the adult community, with new rights and responsibilities. More, rather than less, adult guidance is needed in these years, along with the clear communication of cultural values.

Perhaps this was what the middle school movement intended. But in practice, the fact that students now change classes means that they have at least five different teachers every day, too many to establish a close relationship with any one teacher. And teachers, who see at least 100 students per day pass through their classrooms, are too overwhelmed to invest additional time in individual students; they always have another class of 25 or more students coming in just 10 minutes. The result is that many adolescents are left to simply drift. In addition to all this, severe budget cuts in the last decade and the need to conform to Adequate Yearly Progress testing demands have arrested the development of the middle school movement ideals.

None of this is meant to be an attack on teachers, and parents should be aware that teachers no longer have the autonomy they once had to resist either government demands or policy makers' ideologies. In fact, it is the teachers who will —if they are supported—recognize high ability, provide rigorous and challenging courses, strictly enforce rules of full participation and credit for work done in collaborative problem-solving, and provide clear guidance toward achievement and mastery. These are the teachers who deserve our support because they do not simply throw up their hands in despair, saying, "These kids can't collaborate or do challenging work—their hormones are raging! Let's just let them be teenagers!"

The hope for every gifted girl lies in those individual teachers who make a difference. At the Intel International Science and Engineering Fair, I met teachers who had inspired middle school students to engage in science in the most profound ways—helping a girl to learn statistics so she could analyze her data, setting up mentorships at hospital and university laboratories, or officially chaperoning the school team. The examples are many. It is important to remember what psychologist James T. Webb often says in his talks about educating gifted students: "Just one good and caring teacher can inoculate a gifted child, making that child immune to the deficiencies and indignities of an entire system."

Talent Search to the Rescue

If one good teacher can make a difference, imagine what a program targeting the needs of gifted adolescents might do. Fortunately, a wide variety of options are available to bright girls after school and during the summer. It is in early adolescence that the Talent Search programs begin, and these have been a saving feature of the lives of thousands of gifted students. Talent Search programs are run by universities in several regions throughout the U.S. and internationally.[189] They provide high quality, accelerated, and enriched gifted programming during summers and online to middle school students who receive high scores on college entrance exams such as the ACT and the SAT while they are in seventh grade.

In the past, special programs were only available to students who scored at or above the mean for high school seniors; now, however, there are hundreds of programs offering challenging courses to students with a wide variety of criteria. Sadly, there are still schools that do not participate by encouraging gifted students to apply to these programs. In addition, the testing is expensive. Encouragement and support are vital; middle school gifted girls can feel intimidated about taking tests that are meant for high school juniors and seniors. Gifted girls are less likely to take advantage of these programs if they are not confident in their abilities and reluctant to take academic risks.

Teachers and parents need to make extra efforts to persuade girls to sign up for the ACT or SAT, to get online and apply to the Talent Search in their region, and to save up, along with their parents, the money for the application fees. Talent Search programs do transform lives. Gifted girls who participate are more likely to earn acceptance at selective colleges, to have high aspirations, and to go on to prestigious careers. Not the least of the Talent Search programs' effects are life-long friendships, maintained online, on the phone, and through visits.[190]

In addition to the Talent Searches, many other out-of-school and summer programs for gifted students are affiliated with colleges and universities, with school districts, and with state institutes and "Governor's Schools." An Internet search of "summer opportunities for gifted students" will yield long lists of camps and courses, and the one provided by Duke University's Talent Identification Program provides a searchable directory.[191]

Skipping High School

What about the girl who is so very intellectually different and so keen to forge ahead with her studies that she dreads high school? To the highly gifted girl who is ready for college study, high school might seem like a four-year prison sentence where she is captive in dull courses and surrounded by girls who are competing to be the prettiest and the most popular—a contest in which she has no interest. Even at 13, she may have already discovered the emptiness of consumer culture, celebrity worship, and the imperative that girls camouflage their brilliance. Such a 13-year-old, profoundly gifted girl may be idealistic, driven by a hunger to learn, and longing for a community of girls like herself.

Targeted at just such highly gifted young women are programs like the Mary Baldwin College Program for the Exceptionally Gifted (PEG). In *College at 13,* Razel Solow and Celeste Rhodes described the long-term impact of early college entrance and special guidance on the girls who attended the PEG program.[192] Naturally, many parents and even the girls themselves had trepidations about skipping high school and going straight to college. But this radical acceleration turned out to be exactly what these highly gifted young women needed for the development of their intellect and their feeling of a proper fit in the world; the specialized guidance and strong community supported the development of the young woman's sense of idealism, purpose, and aspirations.

If a highly gifted girl wants a coeducational accelerated environment, then programs like Bard College at Simon's Rock in Massachusetts, which is a combined high school and college institution, provides a chance for gifted students to forge ahead straight into college with a group of like-minded peers. A few universities also allow such radical acceleration, such as the Robinson Center for Young Scholars at the University of Washington, the Davidson Academy at the University of Nevada, and the Herberger Academy at Arizona State University. In fact, all universities these days are more open to the idea of gifted students needing to move ahead at a faster pace. Your own state university may accept younger students who have the ability to succeed.

Secondary School and Preparing for College

By secondary school, most smart girls are hitting their stride, gaining confidence, and becoming involved in a wide variety of activities outside of regular classrooms with less adult supervision. Extracurricular activities like sports, chess club, or yearbook give the smart girl an opportunity to explore and extend her talents that just aren't available in the No Child Left Behind curriculum in the U.S. Smart girls need both rigorous academics and a few, well-selected activities; at this point, only high schools in well-funded districts with substantial gifted education programming provide both. Currently, it is the specialized secondary schools, "exam schools," and residential high schools for gifted students that provide maximum opportunities for the development of talents. When opportunities are available, most academically talented gifted girls will maintain high academic achievement as well as hold leadership positions in school activities.[193]

Where once adolescent gifted girls fell behind gifted boys in their aspirations, now they continue to have high aspirations, planning for college and beyond while in high school. Given proper guidance, they know that they can strive for medical school, law school, and graduate school. They often have a career goal and at least a partial plan for getting there. Exploring their options for college is easier with the parental support and the financial means to visit various campuses, but it is important that girls begin thinking about it as early as their sophomore year.

In poor communities and underfunded schools, smart girls strive against the low expectations held for their peer group. Who survives these schools that provide so little? Our studies of talented at-risk girls, as well as studies of high-achieving minorities, showed that the adolescent gifted girls who had strong support of their families, who were provided with homes and safe out-of-school environments, and who were engaged in church and community activities were likely to survive and even thrive.[194] In African-American communities, the churches provided safe places to interact with both teens and adults and often offered musical and leadership activities that were missing at school. In many poor communities, strong athletic involvement provides not only a safe place but also a chance to stay healthy and strong. Athletic activities are a protective factor in reducing teen pregnancy, substance abuse, and exposure to violence.[195] For Hispanic girls, the extended family is a safety-net factor, and Hispanic teen girls who have the opportunity to participate in Quinceañera coming-of-age ceremonies gain a sense of belonging and an introduction to a dignified womanhood.[196] In Native American communities, tribal involvement, whether in talent pageants or traditional activities like ceremonial and intertribal Powwow dancing, provide a strong sense of identity and pride that protect gifted girls against threats to their self-esteem.   The American Psychological Association's Report, "Beyond Appearance: A New Look at Adolescent Girls," says:

> *Important sources of resistance to and liberation from negative cultural messages for adolescent girls include the following: a strong ethnic identity, close connections to family, learning positive messages about oneself, trusting oneself as a source of knowledge, speaking one's mind, participation in athletics, non-traditional sex typing, feminist ideas, and assertive female role models.[197]*

Nowhere is the role of the teacher as talent scout more important than the high school in a poor community; he or she must find the smart girls, challenge them to high aspirations, help them think about and prepare for college, and persistently advocate for them. A simple question like, "Have you ever thought about going to college and studying journalism or television broadcasting?" can be an important "seed" that helps them think about a possible future. Then these girls, too, have the opportunity to prepare for a time when they can realize their full potential.

Growing Identity and a Sense of Purpose

In adolescence, smart girls begin to discover their strengths and weaknesses, their unique pattern of talents, and the outlines of their future self. They continue their voracious reading, searching now not just for interesting characters and a good plot but also for signs of their possible future selves. Smart girls may even try on the roles they read in literature or see in the films and TV series they avidly follow. Being bright and creative allows them to vividly play these experimental roles, right down to the costumes and the colloquialisms of their character. It is a normal part of adolescence, but many parents may worry about sudden shifts in personality—because the shifts, so well-executed, can seem extreme.

As they try on these different roles and explore their identity, smart girls need accurate information about how their interests, needs, and values compare to those of other students and adults. Sometimes they may take a test to try to ascertain what their "true" interests are. Unfortunately, most vocational interest tests given in high school will not tell smart girls much they don't already know, because they are usually brief tests given mainly to determine whether a student is college-oriented or oriented toward a trade. Instead, smart girls will get much more relevant information from comprehensive tests like the *Strong Interest Inventory* or the *Career Circumplex* (available online at the Virtual Counseling Center http://vcc.asu.edu). These vocational interest tests will tell them how their personalities compare to those of people who are happy and successful in a wide variety of occupations, including the professional and high-level careers to which smart girls aspire. They need tests that are meant for college students, not only because they are more sophisticated instruments but also because they are normalized on thousands of bright students who are also college-oriented. In addition, gifted adolescent girls need the kind of complex and nuanced results they can get from personality tests based on the Big Five Personality Theory (described in Chapter 1) such as the NEO-PI-R and from value inventories such as the Values in Action survey, also available free online at www.viacharacter.org.[198]

Testing should be done at a university counseling center or by a masters-level counselor or doctoral-level psychologist with special training in the needs of gifted students. At both the University of Iowa and the University of Kansas, we have developed counseling laboratories specifically for the guidance of gifted adolescents; you can read about and seek assistance from the assessments and counseling strategies at www.belinblank.org and www. cleoslab.org.

Why so much emphasis on career guidance? Smart girls need to plan early for their future, and they need help defining their identity and purpose in life, as well as finding a career title that seems intriguing. For the last decade, we have worked to create career development strategies that help gifted and creative girls to identify those activities that lead to a state of flow consciousness where they feel at one with the work they are doing. Using flow consciousness as the touchstone, we integrate interests, personality, needs, and values into a profile that helps a girl to see precisely where her characteristics meet the needs of the world. An experience of intense vocational exploration like that at the Counseling Laboratory for the Exploration of Optimal States (CLEOS - www.cleoslab.org) is a way of discovering one's calling in life, rather than just looking for a career.

The Role of Advanced Placement, International Baccalaureate, and Honors Programs

Too often, the only gifted education programs available to bright students in high school are Advanced Placement (AP) and International

Baccalaureate (IB) courses and Honor Societies. As Holly Hertberg-Davis and Carolyn Callahan note, these programs amount to a "narrow escape" from boredom and social competition in high school culture.[199] Because these courses and honors usually come later in high school, freshman and sophomore gifted girls may continue to suffer the same neglect they experienced in middle school. On the positive side, AP courses do provide a valuable opportunity to move ahead through college level material, allowing the student with qualifying test scores to enter more advanced courses in college. The cost for the end-of-year tests are increasingly expensive and often out of reach for poor students in schools that do not subsidize the costs of the tests. Still, the cost to register for the test is less than the tuition cost of taking the course in college, so "testing out" through AP is still a worthwhile option. When they enroll in college, smart girls may or may not get a chance again to test out of freshman level classes.

Fewer girls than boys enroll in AP courses for Calculus, Physics, Computer Science, and other physical sciences that might be offered. Many theories have been proposed, and much research has been done, but it appears that by junior year, girls often feel like they don't have a place in those classes. They may dislike the masculine culture that is often characteristic of these fields, or they may feel there is not enough emphasis on the ways science can be a means of helping and caring for people. Worst of all, many gifted girls who have straight As mistakenly believe that taking an AP course will threaten their perfect transcript. Actually, most colleges would rather see a transcript with a somewhat lower GPA and a fair number of rigorous courses than a perfect 4.0 transcript with easy courses.

Because most secondary schools do not do enough to encourage gifted girls to sign up for AP courses outside of their comfort area, it falls to teachers, school counselors, and parents to make the effort to enroll smart girls and explain the benefits. In many ways, computer science and coding for software are the new "math filter" that filter young women out of opportunities for highly paid and highly desirable occupations. Four years of mathematics without computer science may not be enough to ensure admittance to technology-dependent college majors. Most smart girls are unaware that it is not just engineering that requires these technology skills. Increasingly, careers in journalism and communications require the capacity for website development that goes beyond just building from an existing template. Art, design, and architecture require the use of computer-assisted design that often involves developing one's own software. Even teachers of gifted often do not understand the importance of these "filtering courses" across a wider range of fields.

IB programs, available in many high schools and online, provide a comprehensive curriculum in *ways of knowing* and *theory of knowledge*. The curriculum is designed to be acceptable for admissions to colleges and universities throughout the world. The curriculum provides for fluency in a foreign language, four years of math and lab science, and a special project and essay that allow students to pursue their own interests as well.

Finally, honors programming can provide a chance for gifted girls to interact with bright peers and to be celebrated for their achievements. When combined with gifted education classes and special advisory times set aside for gifted students, they can keep gifted girls on track. Many secondary gifted education and honors programs also provide social and emotional guidance, helping bright adolescents to understand the implications of giftedness for their personal lives. The gifted education coordinator often becomes the go-to person for all manner of guidance, ranging from college planning help to personal guidance. When guidance counselors are overwhelmed with the needs of underperforming students, as is often the case, it can be a great support for smart girls to have a coordinator of gifted education to advocate for them. One school district we know calls this high school gifted coordinator a *Gifted Counselor/Advocate* with responsibility to do personal, academic, college, and career advising of gifted students, as well as organizing individual career shadowing and internship opportunities.

Dual Enrollment

Dual enrollment, where a student is enrolled in both high school and college classes, is allowed in many school districts, but parents are often unaware of this option. Usually, dual enrollment requires an agreement between the high school and a nearby higher education institution that stipulates how academic credit will be awarded. In some cases, the college course counts toward high school graduation; in others, the college course counts later toward college graduation. It is important for smart girls and their families to be aware of the policies in their district so that girls can take advantage of college courses that are either more advanced or deal with topics not covered in the high school curriculum.

Romance, Intimacy, and Sexuality

The current generation of smart girls has been bombarded with media images of precocious sexuality. Fortunately, most smart girls are savvy about media portrayals of women as sex objects and smart about how they negotiate romantic relationships. It is, nevertheless, distressing to any mother to see her daughter lying on the floor surrounded by fashion magazines, watching celebrities and "reality" shows on television showing women at their superficial worst, and playing video games where the females are impossibly busty, gorgeous warriors or princesses. In *The Lolita Effect*, M. Gigi Durham, a professor of media studies, describes how pop culture and advertising teaches young girls and boys many false illusions about sex and sexuality.[200] The effect of this media storm is the creation of several myths. Girls don't choose boys; boys choose girls, but only sexy girls. There's only one kind of sexy—slender, curvy, white beauty—and girls should work to be that type of sexy.

Most smart girls don't really believe these myths, but their behaviors can make it look as if they do. They can be at risk when they channel their considerable achievement drive into attempts to attain the kind of sexy beauty they see in the media. We agree with Durham that the best way of combating the media's portrayal of sexiness is for parents to talk with girls about the impact of these images. Parents can help girls understand the distorted reality of the media and support their daughters' development of their own healthy image. Websites such as Geena Davis Institute on Gender in Media (www.seejane.org) give accurate information about how women are portrayed in the media and make for good discussion.[201]

One of the best things about Durham's approach is that she doesn't paint girls as victims or as the passive recipients of boys' advances. Instead, girls should have a sense of agency and ownership of their own sexuality, and we believe this is what parents should strive to instill in smart girls. Prepare to be surprised how much smart girls already know, and prepare to discuss romance and sexuality as an equal, rather than as the authority on sexuality.

> *I had a recent comeuppance when I asked my young adult daughter about the impact of the Lolita effect in the media on her life. "Oh, I didn't pay much attention to the media. I learned about the Lolita effect by reading Lolita when I was 13. That gave me a sense that I could have agency over my sexuality just like she did." What?!*
> *—Barbara*

A sense of agency is a good thing—it means feeling in control of your own body and your own sexuality. On the other hand, smart girls as adolescents with yet immature judgment may dive headlong into relationships with "fixer-upper" boyfriends: the handsome, depressed outsider; the hoodlum with the golden heart; the weird, awkward guy who has trouble coming out of his shell—the kind of guys that make your eyes roll have a special attraction for brilliant girls who believe they can help these wounded birds to fly. Emotionally intelligent girls may be caught up in the thrill of the rescue; and creative girls need a project. Always remember during this time that she hasn't totally lost her wits. Talk with her about her motivations, be courteous and kind to the guy, and bring him into your household so you can keep the two of them close by! The parental impulse to throw him out the door seldom leads to anything but conflict and a deepening of their relationship, as centuries of romance literature have demonstrated.

We believe smart girls need access to positive portrayals of both romantic love and sexuality. Most gifted girls will eventually be in long-term relationships, and many will have dual-career marriages. Relationships in high school should prepare smart girls (and boys) for dual-career lives, egalitarian relationships, and shared domestic tasks. Neither old-fashioned dating, in which boys pay for everything and expect increasing intimacy, nor new models of "hooking up" without any expectations of commitment provide any helpful preparation for that future. We ask smart girls some of these questions concerning boyfriends: Does he go to your sporting events? Does he know what your career goals are? Is he happy when you have an achievement? Does he expect you to be strong and opinionated? Does he laugh at your jokes and listen to your stories? If so, he scores high on the Good Boyfriend-O-Meter.

For smart girls who have a lesbian orientation, the process of identity development is fraught with difficulty. Because many gifted girls are androgynous, that is, having as many traditional "masculine" behaviors as "feminine" behaviors, they may receive confusing cues from others or direct questions about whether they are heterosexual, bisexual, or lesbian. Lesbian gifted girls generally begin to wonder about their orientation around eighth grade, but according to a study by Jean Peterson, they are fairly sure of their orientation by 11th grade.[202] While in high school, many have passed through the stages of wondering, denial, or defensive masquerading to the eventual acceptance of their orientation. But the important people in their lives still may not have reached a stage of acceptance. Gifted lesbians must negotiate how, when, and even whether to come out to their parents and peers, which happens more often in high school than it used to. Despite their own self-awareness, it can still be a frightening and perilous process. Even in schools that have a culture promoting equality and tolerance, bullying and verbal cruelty are real dangers. Smart girls are more likely to have read about their sexual orientation and to have fewer misconceptions than the general public. They may have the knowledge they need but still feel lonely when there are few girls like them and when their school or home is opposed to equality for LGBT students. Participating in organizations that provide friendship and support to LGBT students can help smart girls with lesbian orientations to negotiate the difficulties of adolescence. More information on lesbian smart girls will be provided in Chapter 12.

Friendships can be just as difficult as romantic relationships for smart girls. They may have few friends who are as bright as they are or lack a peer group that is achievement oriented. The American Psychological Association Task Force of Adolescent Girls in 1999 said:

> *Early adolescence appears to be especially stressful on adolescent girls' friendships and peer relations, signified by a sharp increase in indirect relational aggression. More typical of girls and more distressful to girls than to boys, relational aggression, characterized by such behaviors as spreading rumors or threatening withdrawal of affiliation, appears to emerge as girls' attempt to negotiate current power relations and affirm or resist conventional constructions of femininity.*[203]

This point of view—that gifted girls are often engaged in a struggle with other girls about just what femininity is—can be very useful in discussing friendships with gifted girls. Too often when a bright girl's way of dressing, talking, or conducting a friendship deviates too much from what the most powerful girls have deemed the "proper" ways, the punishment is harsh indeed.[204] Smart girls shouldn't have to hide their giftedness from their girl-friends, yet the research on the social coping of gifted adolescents shows that gifted girls do sometimes feel compelled to hide their good grades or their intellectual interests.[205] This is where friendships with older, gifted girls or adult women can be very helpful; it is important to have an opportunity for bright adolescent girls to be with women who are confident in their abilities, proud of their accomplishments, and willing to talk about achievement with enthusiasm. Special summer programs for gifted girls can provide this but so can a mentoring relationship with a college woman through family or school networks.

Finally, there is the need of every smart adolescent girl for an "other mother"—a woman who shares her parents' values and dreams for her future but is often perceived as much cooler, smarter, and more sophisticated than her parents. Every culture has a role for a godmother because all societies recognize that often teens are willing to share confidences and hear the exact same advice given by the parents, as long as it is delivered by some other adult whom she thinks "gets it." Help your daughter to find her own godmother by setting up special events for her with your best women friends, her aunts, a neighbor, family friend, or special teachers or coaches in her life.

Avoiding Danger Zones

Although we've disparaged the alarmists who want us to believe that smart adolescents are in dire danger from drugs, sex, and extreme emotional sensitivities, it is important to point out some risks that are specific to gifted girls. These include too much openness to experience; perfectionistic anxiety; multipotentiality; rejection for being intellectually or creatively different; and losing boundaries because of high emotional intelligence.

The major personality trait of creative girls is openness to experience. This same trait that allows them to be open to novel ideas and to create original work also may predispose them to be *too* open to experience. These are the girls who are most likely to experiment with substances and sexual intimacy with unusual or deviant people; although they usually recover from thoughtless mistakes, they do need some careful, nonjudgmental advice about safety and psychological balance.

Multipotential gifted girls may try to be good at everything they do. Millennial adolescent girls suffer from greater stress and higher levels of anxiety than boys, and gifted adolescent girls are at risk of being over-whelmed.[206] Being multipotential—that is, having the capacity to excel in a wide variety of domains and activities—means being confronted with too many options. Smart girls in high school may find themselves not only striving to get As in every course but also to shine in cheerleading and sports competitions, to perform in all the school musicals and plays, and to lead in student government and activities. Their days are endless, beginning early with marching band, continuing through a full load of classes, going on to after school activities, and then home to homework; to this, girls from low Socioeconomic Status (SES) families add part-time jobs and family respon-sibilities. Exhaustion and stress-related illnesses are often the result. These girls—usually the academically talented Worker Bees—need help prioritizing their activities, letting some activities go, and most of all, learning to focus on those activities that fulfill their interests and deepest values. No amount of meditation and stress reduction exercises can help as much as opening up her daily schedule with times of rest and playfulness. We tell these girls, "Just because you're good at something doesn't mean you have to do it. Just because your friends are urging you to join doesn't mean you have to do it.

Even if your parents might be disappointed in your dropping cheerleading or choir—you need to make the case for your health and your well-being."

Smart girls who are trying to be everything to everybody are most at risk for absorbing societal and media demands that they be beautiful, thin, and popular. Eating disorders seem to affect gifted girls disproportionately, particularly those gifted girls in dance, performing arts, and individual athletic training. It may be, as we discuss elsewhere, that gifted girls are just better at the "rules" of an eating disorder—the minute calculations of calories consumed and expended, the iron will needed, and the constant self-monitoring. It may be that perfectionism, consciousness, and terrific fear of rejection all feed into the gifted girl's need for slenderness. It is important for smart girls, their parents, and their teachers to be vigilant for signs of the girl who won't eat or who disappears to the bathroom right after a meal. Eating disorders are serious and professional help is needed early in the process.

The nonconformity of profoundly gifted and creatively gifted girls often leads to rejection. Creative adolescent girls and highly gifted girls are also exceptions to the rule that most gifted girls are happy, well-adjusted, and popular. Both creatively gifted girls and highly gifted girls often cross the behavior boundaries that typically are aggressively enforced by their female peers. They can't help but talk about things that seem different, unusual, or just plain weird to other girls. When their interests include non-girlie topics such as science fiction, World of Warcraft, or graphic novels, other girls will often make fun of them. If girls choose to dress themselves in their own original creations, they have gone too far in the eyes of the girls in designer clothes. When highly gifted girls enroll in Math Olympiad or chess tournament, the popular girls just roll their eyes in disdain. Constant rejection is stressful even to the thickest-skinned nerd or outsider. Girls may need reminders that "The geeks shall inherit the earth" and that nerds in high school often go on to be high-status technology entrepreneurs in adult life, for example, Steve Wozniak, Bill Gates, Bill Clinton, Steven Spielberg, Natalie Portman, and Julia Roberts.

Highly gifted girls who also have Asperger's symptoms or a learning disability or any other kind of exceptionality may suffer particularly deeply in the social hothouse that is high school. Sometimes the behaviors from their suffering combined with their gifted behaviors may result in a diagnosis of an emotional disorder that is incorrect or only partially correct. Information on the needs of twice-exceptional students and the unique ways that giftedness combines with cognitive and emotional disorders can be found in the book *Misdiagnosis and Dual Diagnoses of Gifted Children and Adults: ADHD, Bipolar, OCD, Asperger's, Depression, and other Disorders.*[207] What these girls need most is a few friends who share their interests and with whom they can bond. There is safety in numbers, and creative girls and highly gifted girls with specialized interests can try to find each other online and across distances.

Girls who combine intellectual giftedness with high emotional intelligence may find themselves overcome with the needs of their many friends. The emotionally intelligent girl who has the healing characteristics of empathy and superb communication skills may find herself always called upon to help. Girlfriends text her all night long with their fears and anxieties, and boys lean on them for the kind of conversation they can't have with other guys. These girls may suffer from burnout of carrying their friends' problems. Adult helping professionals, like physicians and psychologists, need years of training to develop the objectivity and careful boundaries that prevent burnout. Adolescent girls may get caught up in helping others, but they don't have the maturity or training to deal with other kids' suicidal feelings, drunken disasters, and relationship collapses day in and day out. Parents need to watch for the signs of the overly empathic girl who is suffering from others' crises. Teachers and counselors can help by actually teaching some important peer mediation and peer counseling skills that include setting boundaries and knowing when to seek help from an adult.

When Smart Girls Fail

As much as we would like to predict smooth sailing and blue skies for gifted girls, there are times when the weather turns stormy. When a smart girl fails—whether she bombed a high-stakes exam or tanked on a weekly science quiz—the effects can be devastating. Almost immediately, she is likely to begin compromising her goals and downsizing her aspirations. Although many talented girls consider Bs and Cs the equivalent to failure, in this section we're talking about actual failure—as in getting an F.

Here is how a few smart girls describe their experience with failure:

Tara, age 14

> *"I'm scared of failing. After taking all of my science classes this year, I started thinking about nursing school instead of medical school. The first time I ever failed a test was on a biology test this year. At first I was disappointed, and then I tried to water it down for myself*

but it didn't work. I was like, I tried to not fail, but I still failed. I could have studied harder and longer, and I got an F anyway, and that's how life is.

"*Even last year during middle school, I was still thinking I would be a doctor. I didn't do badly in science last year, but it's not where I'm strongest this year. If I try to become a doctor, I might be more frustrated than anything. I want to get As in school. Getting a C is a passing grade. If I get a C, that's fine. But I don't want to go through school just passing. Last semester, I got a B in science and an A in math.*

"*I started ruling out medical school at the beginning of science class this year. I understand biology, but I don't understand chemistry and physics very well. I'm not strong in those areas, so I feel like I couldn't do those things in college. If I don't know the answer, but I know I can figure it out on my own, I don't say anything about it or ask the teacher. Or if everyone else understands something and I don't, I'm just like, yeah, I got it, too. And it only gets harder from here. I'm struggling a lot now, so I'll probably struggle a lot in the future. Now I'm thinking maybe I should drop science altogether. Science is just not where I'm at.*"

With Tara, we witness the effects that failure—or even the possibility of failure—has on a young woman's career aspirations, as well as the old problem of retaining girls in STEM fields. Her confidence in STEM, which was once robust during middle school, has diminished considerably now that she's in high school science classes. With the change, she has started downsizing her aspirations and compromising her goals for a career that seems easier, like nursing. Little does she know that 21st century nursing curricula and training are some of the most challenging. We are not suggesting that Tara should not pursue nursing *if that's really her first choice*, but we know she aspires to medical school. That's the problem. Tara, an excellent student and a top-performer in her class, has already begun to question her ability to be successful at college-level work in a scientific field—even though she earned a B in science and an A in math in the previous semester. It is quite possible that she may opt-out of STEM altogether and lose the perspective of herself as an innovative young woman who has the intellectual capacity to become a leader in a STEM career.

What do girls like Tara need? Tara needs to learn how to persist through the frustration that comes when she is learning concepts that do not come easily. She also needs to stop comparing herself to how she thinks other people are doing. Both are difficult tasks in highly competitive learning environments. She also needs to learn to ask for help privately when she doesn't understand key concepts—instead of faking her understanding, which is a common defense against appearing vulnerable or "dumb" to one's classmates.

Jenna, age 15

> *When I found out my test scores, I broke out in tears. I didn't know what failing meant for me and my future. I was just overwhelmed with emotions because I didn't know how to deal with it. I studied a lot but not enough. I thought I knew the information, but my mind went into a panic state. Even if you know the information, you can't remember because of the scary test. My brain started thinking, "Oh my gosh! I don't know this because of how the material is presented."*
>
> *Testing has never been easy for me. I didn't take what I could do seriously. I always thought that I'm bad at testing, so why should I try that hard? If I'm going to fail anyway, why try at all?*
>
> *I needed a wake-up call. I learned that you have to know the core and base of a subject so you can apply it in different ways. If you just learn how to see it in only one way, your brain spazzes out because it's like you've never seen it before. But when I use the base concepts, I can break down a problem and figure it out. After doing so badly on my exams, I've become a better student. I do all the homework on the day that I get it. I memorize for the sake of memorizing, and I'm learning that I have to take myself and my studies seriously.*

With Jenna, we meet a girl who didn't take her testing seriously. She says she studied; it seems she has the intellectual capacity to perform very well on the exams. But why didn't she? Usually when a smart girl doesn't take her studies seriously, it is a defense or coping strategy to protect against and to prepare for the very thing she fears: failure. Since testing has never been easy for Jenna, she's taught herself to prepare for failure. She is also dealing with test anxiety, which is common with smart girls. And she is spot-on when she says that her brain was "spazzing" out. During anxiety panic, the brain's executive functioning is reduced or even shut down, which makes activities that require logic and reasoning much more difficult.[208] To illustrate, imagine taking a test while wearing glasses that are a very wrong prescription, and you will understand a little what it is like to take a test with anxiety or panic.

What do girls like Jenna need? Jenna needs positive experiences with testing so that she can rebuild her battered self-confidence. To that end, she needs training on anxiety management and emotional self-regulation. If the anxiety persists, she might consider at some point talking with her physician about possible medications.

She also needs to understand that emotions can be contagious. In testing settings, emotionally intelligent people are able to sense other people's anxieties. Unfortunately, they often are not aware that it might be other people's anxiety that they are feeling and not their own (or a combination of both their own and others' anxieties). Learning how to block out or ignore other people during tests will be an important skill for Jenna to learn. If she also has a diagnosis such as anxiety or ADHD, her school's Disability Resource Center may be able to provide her with a private, distraction-free testing room.

Planning for College—Or Alternatives

At the latest, planning for college or alternatives should begin by 10th grade. The kinds of careers that smart girls aspire to require intense preparation, both in terms of academics and out-of-school experiences. Because there is no one-size-fits all plan for smart girls after high school, we want to return to the beehive analogy to give specific suggestions for the future of academically talented girls, creatively gifted girls, emotionally intelligent girls, and spiritually intelligent girls.

Academically Talented Girls

Academically talented girls, with their quick intelligence and great memory, traditionally excel in school, and like most gifted girls of high ability they are well-adjusted and have high aspirations. They have been leaders in many school activities—sometimes too many. By sophomore year, these smart girls need to begin to prioritize their activities into just a few that fit their strongest interests or that support their health and well-being. Most colleges don't care about three inches of fine print under the yearbook picture; they are looking for focus, for a student whose academic interests and out-of-school activities form a balanced, logical series of experiences that show development and expansion of academic talent over time. They are looking for rigor, for a girl who has challenged herself in nontraditional areas, who has taken risks, and who has demonstrated mastery of advanced concepts in each domain. Yes, of course, they are looking for high grade point averages, high college admissions scores, and great recommendations, but they also usually look for something unique or outstanding, such as a girl who has studied Mandarin since childhood, or devoted herself to a collection of photographic images of the Hollywood in the thirties, or won science or invention fair prizes.

One of the most distressing events for an academically talented girl is the day she receives her college entrance exam scores. Often, the scores do not seem to reflect her academic performance. While gifted girls receive the same or better grades in mathematics and science as boys in the classes in which they are enrolled, there is still a tendency for boys to outscore girls in math and science in standardized tests; often girls are shocked to find themselves in the 88th percentile when they fully expected 99th on ACT Math and Science or SAT Quantitative. This can lead to despair for the perfectionist or the girl whose identity depends on constantly being the best—unless she is prepared.

Since 1994, when David and Myra Sadker wrote the first edition of *Failing at Fairness,* educators have tried to understand whether gender bias, stereotype threat, or differences in boys' and girls' interests in math and science can explain the differences in these test scores.[209] It is certainly evident that most math and science examples are from the world of sports, machinery, or wagering in textbooks—things about which girls are generally less interested than boys. Studies of stereotype threat show that merely writing one's name and checking off *female* can lead to underperformance.[210] Something is going on, and it is not that "girls can't do math." Girls need to have information about possible bias in test items, stereotype threat, and how preferences shape performance.

> *I will never forget my daughter getting into the car after taking the college entrance exams. "How was it?" I asked. "Awful," she said. "There was an entire section where you had to read a story about a quarterback in a game and you had to answer math questions afterwards about the game. I don't even know what a quarterback is. It was stupid." —Barbara*

Help smart girls to avoid this by preparing them well, not just academically but also psychologically for these experiences. If possible, have her take the PSAT (necessary for National Merit Scholarships) and the PLAN to get practice. Test schedules are not always publicized at school, so bright girls and their parents need to check carefully on the websites of the PSAT and the PLAN to know when they will be administered. In addition, it is important to know which tests are required by the colleges to which she is applying.[211]

When it is time to apply for colleges, what colleges are best for academically talented girls? The choice comes down to practical issues such as size, distance, and financial aid as well as academic issues such as the quality of the professors and the availability of services and out-of-class activities. Because engagement with the college and faculty has been found to be the strongest predictor of persistence, gifted young women need colleges where they stand a chance of meeting and getting to know one or more professors, of being mentored, and of becoming involved in real research, service, or internship opportunities. That means that the Ivy League schools are not always the best choice, particularly the large ones with enormous graduate and professional programs where the graduate students often receive more attention than undergraduate students.[212] Liberal arts colleges with small or no graduate programs are likely to provide more individualized experiences and small classes with accomplished professors.

On the other hand, don't dismiss your state university system or that of other states. For young women with clearly defined interests, the chances of finding a mentor in her specific area of interest is higher with a larger faculty. In addition, many state universities rival the Ivy Leagues in specific areas of both humanities and sciences. Enrolling in an honors program at many state universities and taking nearly all of one's courses in honors can provide the equivalent of a much more costly small, private college education. For example, because the Honors College at the University of Missouri was founded by graduates of the University of Chicago, the well-known Humanities Sequence of four semesters gives students the opportunity to have a University of Chicago education in philosophy, literature, arts, music, and history integrated into one set of courses. Cohort programs, special residence hall floors related to student interests, and scholarship halls all provide a chance for gifted girls to work with intellectual peers in a living-learning community.

It is unfortunate that high school college guidance counselors are so overwhelmed with responsibilities that their college guidance often consists of merely informing students about deadline dates and getting them registered for the college preparatory courses. Parents with the financial means often consult Independent Educational Consultants Association (ICEA) (www.iecaonline.com).[213] Research by the IECA has shown that the investment in an educational consultant pays off; the right information can help prevent expensive investments in college from going wrong when the institution's glossy brochures don't match up with the reality of life on campus. These consultants are required to visit 50-100 college campuses and have an extraordinary fund of knowledge. Some even specialize, for example, in the arts, music, or leadership. In addition, choosing the right rankings and college guides is an art. *U.S. News and World Report* rankings, although useful in early stages of exploration, often miss some great colleges that don't do the kind of self-promotion and numbers games that are required for high rankings. Peterson's guides are helpful but shouldn't be taken as gospel. Information gained first-hand from visits is important, but every parent must be aware that an indifferent orientation guide or an overbearing admissions official can sway their adolescent daughter's opinion toward the negative even when the college is actually a good match. The first impression should not be the only variable taken into account. Use guidance counselors, gifted education teachers, and consultants; read specialized books about college majors; and seek out information from parents of other gifted students and from students themselves. There are a few books on college planning for gifted students, including Sandra Berger's *College Planning for Gifted Students: Choosing and Getting into the Right College*. Elizabeth Loveland's *Creative Colleges* provides details about colleges that specialize in the fine arts, music, and performing arts.[214]

What about Women's Colleges?

Only about 2% of women in higher education attend women's colleges, but according to all the research, this is unfortunate for gifted young women. Since their founding, women's colleges have produced more scholars and leaders than co-ed colleges. Single-sex education was a controversial topic during the 1990s, with even the American Association for University Women saying that its positive impact was mainly the result of the high SES of students and the small classes. You will still hear those findings used against women's colleges. More recent, large-scale, very well-designed studies, however, have confirmed that there is something quite special and very positive about women's colleges. For gifted women—particularly highly gifted women—this may be the best option for a challenging and fulfilling college education. Jill Kinzie and her colleagues summarized studies of women's colleges like this:

> *Women attending women's colleges are 1.5 times more likely to earn baccalaureate degrees in the life and physical sciences or math than women at coeducational institutions. Compared with their counterparts at coeducational colleges and universities, women attending women's colleges exhibit greater gains in such cognitive areas as academic and intellectual development, intellectual self-confidence, and self-perceived academic ability.*[215]

Kinzie's study showed that women's colleges were superior to coeducational colleges for women on almost every measure of student engagement, including academic challenge, critical thinking, meaningful experiences, interaction with faculty, and satisfaction with the college experience.

Creatively Gifted Girls

Girls who are creatively gifted may need a different path for college planning. Creatively gifted girls often prefer careers in art, design, music, writing, and scientific and technological invention. Many are interested in unique careers that combine the arts with sciences and technologies, sometimes called STEAM (Science, Technology, Engineering, Arts, and Mathematics).

No traditional college education is going to fully meet the needs of highly creative students. Many creative students languish in general education courses because of their tendency to achieve only in courses that interest them, their nonconformity to gender norms, and their drive for exploration, problem-solving, and hands-on experience. They are bored with the conventional college culture. Creatively gifted girls need to be encouraged to get into higher education environments where their creativity will be nourished rather than squandered. For girls interested in arts and design, this means specialized colleges for the arts. Many parents will balk at this idea, saying, "First get your general education at the state university where you can get in." Wrong! The highly-focused, creatively-gifted student, particularly with moderate grades and scores, who is forced to endure an ordinary college is more likely to drop out than the one who goes straight into the arts, music, or invention. Parents also worry that the investment will not pay off, thinking that arts education is a luxury. It is not a luxury, and arts and entertainment are huge industries where students who attend specialized schools are much more likely to gain employment.

Art and Design Colleges

Don't be fooled by for-profit "art institutes" because they are usually geared toward low-performing students willing to take out huge loans to learn from underpaid instructors that advertise how they will help students develop their portfolios. Creatively gifted girls need to start building their portfolios in high school. Many of the best secondary schools for the arts provide the best preparation for art institutes and colleges, teaching students knowledge and skills in the arts as well as the capacity for enduring critiques and building a unique portfolio. Knowing that most creative students have uneven achievement scores, the best art schools such as the Rhode Island School of Design, the School of the Art Institute of Chicago, and Cranbrook

Academy of Art de-emphasize both grades and achievement test scores in favor of the quality of the art and presentation given to admissions officers on National Portfolio Day. The website at www.portfolioday.net describes that event and provides a list of most art colleges and art departments at universities. Are these elite colleges affordable? Some of the most prestigious schools have the largest merit-based scholarships, so it is important to apply regardless of one's financial situation; in addition, many colleges have work study, cooperative study, and paid internships that help students get through. Wook Choi's book, *Art College Admissions,* is a helpful planner for portfolios and applications.[216]

Musical Conservatories

Juilliard, Eastman School of Music, and Berklee College of Music are legendary for producing some of the world's greatest musicians in classical, jazz, and contemporary music; in addition to these are a wide variety of specialized music schools throughout the world, some of which are outstanding for particular instruments, vocal music, genres, or master teachers. Like art colleges, these institutions want students with demonstrated potential in music and are less interested in college grades. A music or performing arts high school is often the best way to prepare for higher education in music; otherwise, intense involvement in music at school, in the community, and with a music teacher is critical. It is important for the smart girl to play and perform well, but she must also learn auditioning skills, including overcoming performance anxiety, and practice skills that make long (2-4 hours a day) practice sessions productive. Most conservatories offer financial aid with the most prestigious offering substantial scholarships. At Yale's School of Music, all students are provided with scholarships.

Technology

For the creative girl who wants to be an inventor, opportunities abound. Female inventors are very rare. Women make up less than a fifth of the graduates of engineering, industrial technology, computer science, and physics programs; those who go on to postdoctoral work, to product development teams, and to patenting are true survivors of a male-dominated world. Because of this, engineering colleges and institutes are eager for young women; scholarships are plentiful and recruitment is intense. Although young women must be above average in verbal ability, it is the Quantitative scores on the SATs, the Math and Science scores on the ACT, and AP courses in Calculus, Advanced Calculus, Physics, and Computer Science that are of interest to the top programs. The great science and engineering colleges offer undergraduates early opportunities to get into the laboratory; these include Massachusetts Institute of Technology, California Institute of Technology, Stanford, and University of California, Berkeley.

Writing Programs

Creative writing programs are usually located at colleges and universities with great graduate programs and well-known literary magazines, where guest and resident writers are experienced and already known for their poetry, short stories, novels, and plays. The admissions requirements for those outstanding programs located at large universities like University of Iowa and University of Arizona are the same as those for all undergraduates; smaller schools with famed programs such as Hamilton and Alfred will be interested in verbal scores and portfolios of good writing. Smart girls who are interested in writing should attend summer institutes for creative writing such as the Sarah Lawrence summer workshop; they should build a diverse portfolio of writing in a variety of genres and work closely with English teachers and professional writers while in high school to hone their writing ability. Fields such as science writing, technical writing, graphic novels, and cartooning require combinations of skills and often are featured as stand-alone programs or specialties at a small number of colleges and institutes. When a girl's interests are extremely focused, she should find the training opportunities that precisely match her genres and her interests.

Emotionally Intelligent Girls: Healers and Leaders

Many emotionally intelligent girls, whether caring and empathic or influential and extraverted, do not want to wait all the way through college to get an opportunity to try their hand at healing and leading. They need a higher education institution that will allow them service-learning and leadership opportunities. For girls who want to be health professionals, first-rate pre-med programs will offer them early opportunities to work in medical and hospital settings. Pre-vet and animal science programs that get young women involved immediately in working with animals and the people who love them will let them experience both the caring side of veterinary medicine and the very real and often difficult side that is animal abuse and euthanasia.

Most great pre-med and pre-vet programs are associated with teaching hospitals for people or animals. One of the best options for gifted girls with very strong achievement scores and science preparation are the BS/MD programs that offer accelerated and combined bachelors and medical degrees. Boston University, Northwestern, and Kent State are all examples of schools that have these combined programs and that provide many early opportunities for practice. Finally, smart girls who want to be psychologists, counselors, or social workers need to seek out those schools with the strongest service-learning programs, as well as the undergraduate institutions with the strongest academic departments. Helping professions are dominated by women, so there will be many role models and mentors on the faculties for gifted young women. Berea College and the College of the Ozarks emphasize direct service to others, the University of Maryland, College Park stresses social leadership, and universities such as Brown and Oberlin focus on social justice issues.

For emotionally intelligent girls who were born to lead, early opportunities to influence, direct, and manage others are important. Participation in debate clubs prepares smart girls for the argumentation that is critical in law and politics, and often the colleges with strong debate programs also have leading academic departments in political science and government. Gifted girls who want to be accepted to the top political science and pre-law programs need to go where the laws are being debated and made: the state capitals and Washington, D.C. Georgetown also notably prepares a disproportionate number of politicians and diplomats. Girls who want to work in nonprofits and nongovernmental organizations abroad need to seek out specialized undergraduate programs in nonprofit management and international relations.

The business world remains the one where the glass ceiling is still holding firm; if a gifted girl aspires to be a top CEO, she will need to attend one of the top ranked business schools and become involved in entrepreneurship and management at the earliest opportunities. Notre Dame, University of Virginia, and Washington University usually take top honors in these areas in the U.S. News and World Report listings. Finally, it bears repeating that girls who want leadership opportunities are going to thrive in women's colleges and universities; freed from the competition with male voices, women can seize the chance to lead in all college activities.

DIY Education, Gap Year, and World Wide Education

The Millennial gifted generation is the first in history to walk away, in increasing numbers, from traditional college education. In *DIY U: Edupunks, Edupreneurs, & the Coming Transformation of Higher Education*, Anya Kamenetz describes the explosion of alternatives to college.[217] The new Massive Open Online Courses (MOOCs) offer the chance for gifted girls to take free college courses online from professors at leading universities.

The courses range in quality from extraordinary to awful; most people need to sample many courses for a few sessions to determine which ones they want to complete. There are both for-profit companies, like Coursera and Udacity, and nonprofits like Edx that provide certificates of completion and, increasingly, college credit. Because so many gifted adolescents already have experience with online learning, using MOOCs for a large part of their post-high school experience is quite doable and comfortable. For many smart girls, the expansion of online courses is like a world-wide party of intellectual fellowship and nourishment. It is now possible for a young woman to get credit from an accredited university and even complete her entire education online. Although older people worry about the source of the credit and the accreditation, you will find that many employers don't care about the source of the degree, as long as the skills are there—particularly in any technology or business-related field. In addition, many gifted students don't care about getting a diploma because the kind of work they want to do is building their own business, whether alone or with friends. We encourage smart girls—especially the creative, entrepreneurial, self-starting types—to at least explore some of these alternatives.

The Gap Year

Perhaps the idea of an idyllic, ivy-covered campus with small classes, engaged students, and enthusiastic professors is still part of the smart girl's dream of the future. If she can get accepted to this kind of college, the only downside is that while she is spending four years in cloistered circumstances, other young women her age are traipsing all over the world, farming on an Israeli kibbutz, fighting violence against women in Kenya, and teaching English in China. The Gap Year is an alternative for the student who has a definite plan to complete college but also has the urge to see the world. Many students do their Gap Year between high school and college as a way of discovering more about the career direction they want; some just want to learn more about the world's cultures and amazing places. The Gap Year can just as easily come during college if the institution will allow time off— which most do. Many colleges have the option of a semester or a year abroad, particularly in foreign language programs, and those are an alternative to a do-it-yourself Gap Year.

In any case, the Gap Year—if fully integrated into an educational plan—can be a valuable complement to traditional education. Many organizations offer Gap Year programs, as well as guidance in choosing the right program. Gap Year fairs are scheduled internationally so that heads of Gap

Year programs can meet and talk with students about the possibility. Learn more about the Gap Year here: www.usagapyearfairs.org. We encourage parents to be open to the Gap Year approach as well as other nontraditional travel and experiential combinations.

Finally, there is the option of just walking away from college altogether and starting a business, becoming a farmer, or creating art and music. Women earn less than men, and high school graduates earn much less than college graduates. For increasing numbers of smart girls, going to college—at least immediately—makes no sense to them. For the smart girl who is independent, nonconforming, mature, and purpose-driven, creating a life that is not based on what employers want may be the right alternative.

I am a farmer as well as a professor, and I have hosted young people from the World Wide Opportunities in Organic Farming (www. wwoofinternational.org). The young women who come are sturdy, committed idealists, often from big cities around the world, who want to learn to sow, cultivate, and harvest crops in a sustainable way. They live on farms in houses, tents, and dorms, providing help in return for room and board. Programs like these allow young women to see the world in a safe way and to meet other enterprising agriculturalists. I also helped to found a Makerspace, (makerspace. com/makerspace-directory) where young artists and technology enthusiasts come together to learn from each other in informal classes in 3-D printing, stoneworking, silkscreening, robotics, and all kinds of visual technologies. —Barbara

The goal of many of these innovators is to create prototypes of products and services to show to investors or to enter onto crowdfunding sites like Kickstarter and Indiegogo.[218]

Many teachers and parents will find it difficult to be supportive of a young woman who wants to take a chance on alternatives to traditional college. According to J. Brooks-Gunn, parents tend to become more vigilant about potential social and behavior problems and less concerned about achievement during adolescence.[219] Parents of girls are generally more protective of them than they are of boys; they are concerned about safety, financial loss, and loss of direction. In addition, most parents and teachers had traditional educations themselves, so they can't imagine what an educational and training plan that involves a wide menu of experiences might look like—or what it will be worth. No matter how risky a gifted young woman's dreams of a do-it-yourself education may seem, it is important to listen to her and question her supportively. We believe that if a gifted young woman can produce a plan—with a rationale, budget, timeline, and proposed outcomes—then she is ready for the challenge of a do-it-yourself education.

Smart Girl Profile | Jasmine, age 15

Jasmine is a 15-year-old European-American girl who attends Arizona State University's Herberger Young Scholars Academy. She has served in leadership positions at the Academy, including student government and the yearbook committee, and she often organizes activities that the entire school community participates in. She has a deep interest in global women's issues, sociology, and anthropology. She is, however, confused about her career plans, and she also thinks that she is a poor leader. Since she is a natural counselor, her classmates come to her for advice and her honest opinion, which she doles out in a reasonably sensitive manner (unless she's overwhelmed, and then, like other verbally gifted girls, she blurts out whatever she thinks without the benefit of her filters). She has a high energy level and a vivid imagination. Her career assessment highlights social and enterprising interests, which suggests that she has the potential to pursue entrepreneurship or leadership in areas of teaching, psychology, social activism, or global studies.

In one interview, Jasmine said that when she was a little girl, her 5th grade teacher called her *mouse*, owing to her small voice and quiet demeanor. That is quite different, however, from how others see her today. These days, she's an extravert—talkative, gregarious, and full of positive emotions. She can be really fun to be around with such an effusive personality. Yet there are times when she is a bundle of nervous energy and struggles with dark, existential issues of meaning and purpose in life. She tends to be self-conscious and as a result can be sensitive to even mild correction; criticism tends to generate feelings of embarrassment. There are times when she is confident and sure of herself but just as many times when she contends with a wobbly self-esteem. Jasmine's greatest challenge is to take herself and her gifts seriously. She also needs to expand her understanding of leadership to include examples of socially-intelligent leaders. Once she does this, she will likely come into her own as a leader.

In Her Own Words by Jasmine, age 15

What are your greatest strengths? *Since I've felt the harshness of people not wanting to include me, I try to include everyone. Empathy is one of my strengths—if someone is having a hard time, I try to relate to whatever the problem is. Family, friends, and even boys count on me to give advice. I give outside opinions, and I tell them exactly what I think. I also have a lot of positive emotions that help in stressful situations, especially in school. Having someone who's positive helps bring up other people's moods. If I have positive energy, people will absorb it and help them feel better.*

What qualities would you like to cultivate? *When I get stressed or when I don't feel good about myself, it's hard to get out of it on my own. I need someone who can set me on the right track again. It's like trying to get through a maze when you've got so many different places you can go. A helping hand can mean the world of getting out of a bad situation.*

On dealing with anxiety and existential issues: *I get physically sick when I'm anxious. I don't feel depressed, but I notice that no matter how many friends I have around me, sometimes I still feel lonely. I have an empty feeling, kind of like when you realize that your life amounts to dying. Because in the end, everyone dies. I sometimes wonder: Why am I going to school? I'm going to die anyway. Yet, whenever it hap-pens, it always catches me off guard.* (Note: In our experience, such existential anxiety is not uncommon among gifted girls, neither is the striking candor with which they describe their inner worlds.)

On Leadership: *Leadership is a chance to prove yourself, but if the people you're leading don't respect you, it reflects badly on you. Leaders are confident in themselves, they know what they're doing, and they could lead an army into war. They have a kind of "I know I'm good" and I-know-I-can-do-it attitude.*

I don't feel that I'm good at leading people. I don't feel respected by the other students. But I'm willing to try new things. Being extraverted helps me communicate with people, even though my communication skills fail me sometimes. There are times when I want to separate my work from my friends, but at school I can't do that. I think my class-mates see me as a peer rather than a leader. It sucks because being in leadership roles takes a toll on friendships and it impacts my vision of the world; it seems like a duller place. It feels like I'm never doing a good job. Subconsciously, I think I don't want leadership roles, but I feel guilty about saying anything to the teachers.

What's your advice for other Smart Girls? *Learn from your mistakes, but also learn from your successes. Which means that once you know that it works for you, use that strategy again. When you fail, it might be hard at the time, but with confidence and help from others, a failure is an opportunity to learn and to improve. If you're not confident in yourself, you can't do the best work that you're capable of. Just because you don't see the whole plan for yourself right now, you still have to believe that you are going to do great. You have to believe that the struggles and successes are going to build you up to be the amazing person you want to be. You can make the world what you want it to look like.*

What's your heart's desire right now? *In the long term, I want to help people. Maybe through making a contribution in medical research or by working with kids with ADHD and helping them to be the best they can be. I want to help other people fulfill their purpose.*

Conclusion

The period of a smart girl's life that begins with the great change of puberty and ends with the completion of high school is a tumultuous time. The decisions she makes now will affect her throughout her life. Some smart girls may begin to plan for college while still in middle school if they want to go to elite colleges and go on to professional and graduate education. The relationships that she explores with friends and romantic partners will be the outline that she may follow as an adult; even some of these friendships will last a lifetime. The values and interests she acquires during these years will be instrumental in developing her identity—which she will carry for years. If she identifies as a scholar, an athlete, a leader, an artist, a musician, or a techie, that identity will prepare her to seek the mentors and training she needs. If she identifies as a fashionista, a romantic, a rescuer, or a socialite, she will lose the opportunity to walk away from the crowd and become her own unique self. Most important of all, she may lose the opportunity to fall in love with an idea and devote herself to the realization of her talents through her deepest values. Guiding a smart girl through adolescence means holding her responsible to her dreams and making a solemn pact to support her as she finds her vision of the path to her future.

CHAPTER 9

Smart Women in College: Danger Zones and Paths for Success

Here is an interesting experiment: Go to Google Scholar and type in *College Women*. Google Scholar will give you the articles that scholars are reading in this subject area. If you are a parent or teacher who has invested a lifetime into supporting the goals of your smart girls, you are likely to be horrified. You will see five articles on sexual victimization (one on its relationship to alcoholism), two on eating disorders, two on problems with self-efficacy, and one on women being the majority in college enrollments—and that is just on the first page! Keep scrolling and you will simply see more of the above, on and on, with sexually transmitted diseases as a topic by the third page of citations.

What is going on here? The good news is that women now far outnumber men on college campuses.[220] Why is the bad news—sexual victimization, eating disorders, alcoholism, and low self-efficacy—the apparent major topic to scholars who study college women?

An article in the *Atlantic Monthly* by Kate Bolick claims that these problems are indeed rampant and that they are interconnected.[221] Because women outnumber men on college campuses, these issues arise because men define the terms of relationships, an occurrence she says arises in any society with a sex ratio tilted toward women. Put another way, the presence of so many women, most of them delaying marriage but eager for relationships, means that men have much more power to have relationships on their terms—which, in most American colleges, means multiple sexual relationships with attractive women in the context of partying, alcohol, and sexual victimization. For females, it means more time spent in pursuit of romantic goals, usually including dieting, exercise, makeup, clothes, and endless conversations about romantic strategies that often ensue. Did we invest all this time, energy, and emotion in our daughters' education and guidance just to have them go to college to lose their minds—and often their emotional balance—in some kind of romance meat-market?

Okay, it is more complex than that. First of all, we have to realize that scholars who study women have always been engaged in "deficit" thinking—that is, the idea that women are lacking in something, have problems, and are deficient in key abilities and resources compared to men. Even in scientific publications, good news does not excite the readers the way bad news does, so there is a bias in what people study. Second, even though there are indeed some awful things happening to women in college, there are many, many women who are avoiding the hazards and danger zones. Third, the story of smart women's experiences in college is simply much more nuanced than that.

What are the milestones and danger zones for smart women in college? How can this generation of women keep their dreams intact while enjoying all that coming of age in the new millennium has to offer? First, we must understand the characteristics of bright young women as they enter college, the barriers they encounter, and the pathways toward adulthood they can choose.

A Paradoxical Combination of Characteristics

Smart young women enter college with a puzzling and contradictory set of characteristics. They have higher grades than men throughout school. They enter with higher achievement test scores in verbal reasoning, English, language AP tests, social studies tests, and they are just about even in mathematical reasoning except at the very highest end of the distribution of scores where males still outnumber them.[222] For many gifted women, however, there is a disconnect between their actual ability and their confidence in their ability to achieve their goals. Although college women are changing in the direction of higher self-efficacy and increased confidence in their abilities to succeed in college courses, many gifted college women have lower self-efficacy than their male peers of the same ability level. Longitudinal studies comparing gifted women and gifted men in high school and young adulthood found more females than males decreased their perception of their giftedness.[223] Second, college women's aspirations are higher than they have ever been, with more women intending to enter graduate school, medical school, and law school than men. Nevertheless, in studies where college women compare the time they spend on their academic goals versus their romantic goals, it is clear that, unlike college men, women are spending more time and energy on their romantic goals. One study found that the very mention of romantic goals had a negative impact on college women's motivation to enter STEM fields immediately following.[224] Finally, smart college women are seizing leadership positions in college, becoming active in everything from sports to debate clubs and more engaged in extracurricular activities than at any time in history.

They are, nevertheless, still highly involved in supporting the activities of men in their lives. Many studies, including those with ethnic minority women, have continued to show the strong impact of gender relations on career aspirations; for example, many Hispanic college women spend inordinate amounts of time helping their boyfriends with housework and homework. In one nationwide study of college women, Linda Saxe and her colleagues found that college women took responsibility for housekeeping and family-related tasks that were virtually absent from the lives of college men.[225]

In the study with Karen Multon, Sharon Robinson-Kurpius, and Marie Hammond, we found that women in STEM majors were aware that many women dropped out of science because of relationship, marriage, and family issues, but they believed that this would not happen to them.[226] On the other hand, many also believed that not engaging in any relationships was necessary to succeed in STEM careers. College women do not seem to connect their present assumption of inequitable roles in their relationships with future compromises of their career goals. Demonstrating the often sad reality of that connection is important if we want to help them to avoid its effect and persevere.

The conflicts about women's roles that are so prevalent in society today are apparent in the lives of college women: high abilities vs. low confidence; high aspirations vs. romantic distractions; and strong leadership in college activities vs. a passive role in a relationship.

Several pathways are available to gifted college women; how they negotiate—or fail to negotiate—these pathways will determine the careers, economic status, and independence for much of their adult lives.

The Party Pathway

For those women who never aspired to popularity, perfect attire, and perpetual fun, the party pathway looks nightmarish. For smart women who successfully danced down this pathway, it is remembered fondly as the best years of their lives when they were sought out by desirable, high-status men, when they had close friendships with sorority sisters or hall mates, when they did the minimum amount of schoolwork, and life seemed utterly carefree. The party pathway is organized and promoted by fraternities, sororities, student organizations, and friend groups. It involves a plethora of social activities that usually feature alcohol, socializing, sexual hookups, romance, and sometimes drugs; these are central to college life for people on the party pathway, and academics are peripheral. As Elizabeth Armstrong and Laura Hamilton found in their study of a "party floor" in a women's dorm, the party pathway definitely has its winners and its losers.[227] Those women who are bright and wealthy are likely to come through the experience of the party pathway unscathed. This is for a number of reasons. First, they have networks of family and friends who are all familiar with college life and who can tell them the easiest courses and majors. Many well-off gifted women will be told to major in business, communications, or education so that they can keep up a high grade point average while still having fun. They can be more adept at walking the tightrope between sexual freedom and "sluttiness," and they are more likely to understand the subtle nuances of the culture. They have access to the required name-brand clothing and cosmetics and are able to use the party pathway to attain the "polished femininity" that will make them desirable as romantic partners and successful in careers that require fashionable, good-looking, extraverted women. If this woman graduates with little preparation for a job, she can return home, or she can be supported by her parents while she does internships in big cities.

For middle class and lower middle class girls, no matter how gifted, the party pathway can be a disaster. These young women are usually working and paying tuition with student loans, so failure in a course means substantial financial loss. The pressure of trying to have the right clothes and accessories can lead to overspending and running up credit card debt. Lacking networks of college women in their family and among friends, they don't know the subtle rules of the hookup culture; as a result, they run the risk of sexual assault and alcoholism, as well as being labeled as a slut. When their partying gets out of hand and they fail their courses, there is no one to advise them or help them get back on their feet academically, emotionally, and socially. Armstrong and Hamilton, in *Paying for the Party*, describe how these women are sometimes forced to leave school, return home, and go to community college and work. Many of the women who lost their way on the party pathway end up with diminished social mobility rather than the enhanced opportunities that college is supposed to give.

The message of *Paying for the Party*—as well as many other studies of college culture—is clear for gifted women. It is a very risky path, particularly for those who do not bring financial resources to college. It is also risky for smart girls who actually came to college intending to follow a career dream and improve their chances in life but were pressured by peers into choosing a major they cared little about. Even for the winners—the bright, wealthy girls who keep respectable grade point averages—danger may lie ahead. In her *Atlantic Monthly* article "All the Single Ladies," Kate Bolick shows how the tendency of women to put off marriage and engage in casual romance throughout their 20s—thus extending their college behaviors of networking, socializing, and moderate engagement in careers—has left many bright women with little power to choose the kind of relationship or career they want. Those who have found a satisfying career, a happy, sustainable relationship, and a supportive circle of friends are the lucky ones.

As psychologists at college counseling centers, we have worked with many bright and talented young women who suffered unintended consequences of the party pathway. They wore the right clothes, went to the right parties, belonged to the right sororities, and dated the right boys. But they came to counseling because their grades—and their self-esteem—were suffering. The young women typically came in with symptoms of anxiety or depression. They struggled with eating disorders, relationship drama, and alcohol abuse. Some were trying to recover from a DUI or sexual assault.

With the proper psychological support, as well as a change in their primary environments, talented girls on the party pathway can recover and redirect their energies toward a meaningful and healthy college experience. How? By helping them refocus on the reason that they entered college in the first place; by providing them with new skills that help to manage and regulate their emotions; and undoubtedly, by cultivating a positive relationship with a counselor who can not only relate to their experiences but also show them another way of living their college lives.

Smart Girl Profile | Nika, age 21

Nika, a senior in a demanding journalism school, was a smart writer with the pragmatic sensibilities of an editor-in-chief in the making. On the party pathway, she was a pretty girl on campus, a member of a popular sorority, and dating a fraternity guy. By all outside appearances, it looked as though she had her life together, but she came to counseling with symptoms of depression, coupled with constant fighting with her boyfriend. On top of that, her college roommate was in the chaotic throes of an eating disorder. Nika's writing was suffering. She got a C in a journalism class, which in J-School is akin to failing. Her self-confidence was shattered.

Early in counseling, she did not improve. She revealed that when she was a child, her father had committed suicide. When she herself began experiencing persistent suicidal thoughts, she decided to hospitalize herself. After a few days, she stabilized and began to recover with the combination of psychotherapy and psychiatric medications. In counseling, she began to reprocess her past trauma. Over the course of six months, she regained her sense of purpose and her joy for writing. As she reclaimed her self-confidence, she began to talk about the future. She broke up with her boyfriend and prepared for graduation. She stated, "One day I realized that there was more to life than college parties. That's when I started taking my work seriously." Just before graduation, she came to her final counseling session with great news. She had landed an amazing internship at her favorite magazine. She was headed to the East Coast right after graduation. Her symptoms of depression were gone, she'd learned new skills to help her cope with life's stressors, and she'd developed a sense of self-confidence that would support her in the next part of her journey.

The Striver Pathway

The "Striver" role, named this by sociologists who studied campus cultures, dates all the way back to the time when the new land-grant universities first began admitting students—students whose families had never been to college.[228] Even today, these first-generation college students come from middle class or poor families and are usually members of an "outsider" group—most often rural, racial, or religious minorities. They come to college to get a degree that will allow them to better themselves, their family, and their community. Often, strivers believe that they must choose a major that is practical or professional and that will afford them a high salary when they graduate. Strivers have no interest or time for partying because they are serious and driven. They usually have to work, so they also have little involvement in extracurricular clubs.

Many gifted young women attending college are strivers, and often strivers are in the top ranks of their high school classes. Programs like the McNair scholars and the Gates Scholarships have targeted first-generation college students, making it possible for high-ability, high-achieving students with little financial means to go to college. For smart young women, the striver pathway means majoring in practical majors like education, social work, or nursing. The many new STEM scholarship programs also appeal to strivers because STEM majors are likely to lead to high-paying jobs right after graduation.

The striver role has fewer perils for smart young women because the seriousness and industriousness of this pathway actually protect them from the sexual victimization and drunkenness that can take place at parties. These young women usually either delay serious relationships or seek committed relationships with supportive partners, and they are more likely to seek help when they are struggling with writing or math. Most campuses offer tutoring services to help students succeed. Professors appreciate the conscientiousness of strivers and reward their hard work with opportunities for mentoring.

There are, however, some risks. Sadly, many of these overburdened young women cannot take advantage of opportunities like internships and undergraduate assistantships. This is where the perils lie in the striver's pathway; these strivers may miss out on many experiences that round out a college education. They may not have time for the art, music, and theater events that are so enriching for first-time college students. They may avoid rigorous or skills-oriented courses that may endanger their grade point average—and therefore their scholarships—but many of these courses are valuable for learning how to live more balanced lives.

Another peril comes from the perfectionism, anxiety, and stress that accompany many strivers' drive to succeed. When you know that your failures not only affect you but your family and community as well, it can be a heavy burden indeed.

Smart Girl Profile | Carlie, age 18

From a well-being perspective, strivers are some of the most challenging young women to support in counseling. Carlie—smart, high energy, and actively involved on campus—worked diligently in her classes and maintained a 3.8 GPA. As a senior, she still lived at home. Although she would have liked to move out, she felt pressure from her older sister and her father to live at home to avoid saddening her mom.

Carlie had been dating a guy whom she called supportive, but when she talked about him, her voice wobbled and she became defensive, saying, "He's a really nice guy!" Carlie is highly agreeable, which means that she said *yes* to everything that her professors and advisors asked of her. Her cheerful smile and enthusiasm masked the mounting stress from juggling too many projects. During her last semester, she dropped the ball on a few big projects. Her classmates were frustrated and, rather than addressing her mistake, Carlie began avoiding the people who wanted to support her—including her counselor.

When her counselor finally (gently) corralled her to find out what was going on, she described how she had multiple competing priorities, including the most important: her senior thesis. The counseling work with Carlie focused on the advantages and disadvantages of saying *yes* to everyone. She said, "If I say yes, then they won't be disappointed," but when she neglected projects she had committed to, she said, "Then I feel really guilty that I forgot and people get mad at me. Plus, I'm worried about making sure my mom and my boyfriend are happy."

Counseling strategies to address the problem of over-commitment focused on practicing two important phrases that every striver needs to use regularly: 1) "I'm sorry to disappoint you, but I can't commit to another project right now;" and 2) "No." Additionally she needed to recognize that, for her, guilt was an emotion that signaled she had overcommitted and that she needed to prioritize her activities and decide which ones to drop so that she could focus on her thesis.

Subsequently, she communicated with several people to whom she had made commitments, and within a few weeks, she had completed her thesis, graduated, and headed off to her Master's program. Will over-commitment still be a problem for Carlie? Probably. Like other strivers, she will need to continue to practice saying *no* in order to prioritize her activities based on her values and goals. She will need to be continually mindful of her tendency to want to please others before taking care of herself.

The Engaged Pathway

There is another pathway that strivers can aim for that is just as focused, but much richer in experience. This pathway provides a meaningful alternative to the party pathway for all smart women, even the most privileged. Studies have shown that the students who are most likely to complete their college degree are those who are persistently engaged in the pursuit of intellectual growth and the discovery of a purpose in life.[229] These students are also conscientious and industrious, but rather than settling for what they perceive to be a practical major, they throw themselves fully into a major that answers their deepest questions. That does not mean they avoid areas sometimes thought of as less challenging, such as education, nursing, or social work. It means that they choose these majors out of the love of children or the desire to heal or support social justice, rather than expedience. They can be found throughout the university, in all majors—wherever they have found ideas that are meaningful and appealing and professors they admire.

Even for first-generation or poor students, it is possible to pursue the engaged pathway by working in work-study jobs or community jobs that directly relate to their major. Often, engaged students are sought out by professors as assistants, and most of these professors can help them find the financial aid they need. Engaged students like these take the advice of their mentors and choose a few "risky" courses that promise deep learning and key experiences. Most important of all, these students join student groups that are not only related to their interests but also provide a sense of community and a source of support through tough times. For example, minority students can live on a residence hall floor that is diverse and focused on the needs of these students; architecture students can join a student-led design studio; language students can join a language circle or housing group to practice their new language. Some of the most engaged students are those who work side by side with faculty on social causes, such as the science students who work together in an environmental advocacy group.

Engaged students are likely to avoid the pitfalls that some smart women encounter in romantic relationships because they are in love with their ideas and not likely to turn their back on their intellectual development. The allure of falling in love is tempered by the search for a partner who shares their values and dreams. As a result, engaged students are more likely to be in relationships that are equitable and mutually respectful.

There are few perils on this pathway, other than the very valuable struggles that occur to the sensitive, smart student when confronted with the true complexities of art, humanities, science, and service to others. Engaged students are indeed likely to have crises of meaning as they grope for that one direction that will provide meaning in a complicated world. With other engaged students and trusted faculty members for support, college is a place to be absorbed in this struggle.

Smart Girl Profile | Katie, age 23

At 18, Katie started college with the goal of opening a small tech business in her home town. Little did she know how her goals would grow. During her sophomore year, she addressed 10,000 new students during the university's Welcome Week. In her junior year, she was elected president of the WiSE Leadership Program, a vibrant student organization for women in STEM. Subsequently, she was voted Homecoming Queen, which meant that she demonstrated exceptional leadership potential and offered outstanding service to the university community. Now in her senior year as a Graphic Information Technology major with a minor in Technical Entrepreneurship, her career opportunities have expanded exponentially. Yet even Katie, who has been focused on her career development from the beginning, has doubts.

In Her Own Words by Katie

When you think about your future after graduation, what's your greatest fear? *Not being able to start my career—and make the changes I want to see happen—immediately. Not being able to do what I set as my goal immediately, not being able to find the success I'm looking for. I'm also afraid of having to sit in a 9-5 job in a box (a cubicle), not being able to interact with people and clients. What's scarier to me than being unemployed is having a job doing pointless work in a pointless place.*

What barrier do you think could stop you from achieving your goals? *Employers who won't give me the chance or take the risk on me because I don't have the experience of other, more experienced workers. Another barrier is not getting the opportunity to shine.*

What's your greatest hope? *That I'll have the opportunities to do what I want and my path will be clear and easy to follow. I want something that is so breathtaking that it feels like I've gone the right way.*

What keeps you up at night? *The future. I think about everything. I imagine all possibilities. My mind wanders in both directions. It's exciting and overwhelming.*

What's something bad that could happen? *That I can't get a job I enjoy or that I move somewhere and hate my job, but I would have* *to stay until I find something else. I worry about being stuck and not being able to grow in a position.*

Where do these worries come from? *My worries come more from seeing other people struggle, more so than from my own personal history. I hear stories about college students who don't get jobs or who wind up working for lousy companies—media influences mostly. It's what everyone says to you. The job outlook is so bleak and I can't help but listen to what everyone is saying. But I've never had any of those experiences personally.*

How do you protect yourself against negative influences from the media and your peers? *By maintaining a positive outlook and knowing that I'm still moving forward in the direction of my goals. I have to remember that a pause isn't a full stop and that there are going to be lulls and peaks in my career. You keep going up, but you might hit a little plateau. And I have to remember that there's never been a point in my life where I didn't have options.*

The Creative Pathway

Finally, there is the creative pathway. For young women who are creatively gifted, the engagement pathway is a rewarding one. But what if her particular college or university does not provide the mentors or opportunities for the engagement she needs? If coursework is unchallenging and no student organizations exist that speak to her interests, the creative student may take the pathway so many inventors, artists, writers, and musicians have taken in the past—the one she creates for herself.

Keira, a young art student, began an art major because her life as a troubled teenager had been changed by an organization devoted to teaching arts to at-risk youth. In college, she found to her despair that her art professors had little interest in community arts, so she began her own organization of art students who wanted community involvement. She invented her own curriculum by taking online courses and independent study in public art. She joined Films for Action, an organization made up of filmmakers devoted to social justice issues. She remains deeply engaged in her art.

Josefina, from a small women's Catholic school in Brazil, wanted to be involved in environmental activism, but her limited curriculum and small faculty could not help her. She created a website (first teaching herself web development skills) that would match Brazilian students with environmental organizations in their area, and within a few months, she had 6,000 readers of her blog and many active participants. She succeeded in creating a forum for others who shared her passion.

Creative young women often need to invent their own college majors; to change the institutions; to combine travel and community experiences with coursework; or to use online learning to fill in the gaps they perceive in their education. Many creative young women drop out of college to begin their own business or take the scenic route by going to school part-time and engaging in their innovative work the rest of the time.

Women on the creative pathway often find that their peers view them as outsiders or slackers. Parents of smart women on the creative pathway are often doubtful and worried. Will she ever complete a degree? Will she be able to get a job with a degree in avant-garde Asian literature? Even professors may be annoyed by the creatively gifted woman's seemingly narrow focus or lack of interest in the professor's work.

The skepticism with which others view the creative pathway is one of the perils of this course; parental and academic support may fade as her pathway becomes less comprehensible to others. In addition, a major difficulty for creative women is the lack of knowledge or relevant information when they want to manage their own education and training entirely themselves. Mentors are essential to women on this pathway, particularly mentors who understand the structure of knowledge in her disciplines of interest, the hoops to jump through, or the politics of the domain. Because many creative young women have been disappointed by teachers and professors, they may try to go it alone—but a supporter, mentor, or sponsor can prevent her from going off course. On the other hand, the creative pathway is now more attainable than ever with Mass Open Online Courses (MOOCs) and liberal arts colleges that encourage self-developed majors. The creative pathway, managed well, can put the smart young woman on the fast-track toward fulfilling her passion, beginning her business, or entering a precise occupational niche for which she has trained herself.

Hope for the Future: A New Generation of Smart Young Women in STEM

Even though women are now the majority of college students, they are still the minority in most science and engineering majors, and as they continue their college career, women are much more likely than men to drop out of these majors. Some scholars have suggested it is just a matter of preference; gifted women prefer people-oriented careers and gifted men prefer thing-oriented careers. Somehow, professors of STEM fields have not gotten across the message that science helps people. Other scholars, for decades, have explored the areas of women's potential "deficits"—low math or spatial ability, lack of confidence, or lack of self-efficacy. All of these variables are hard to change, whereas environmental variables, such as access to mentoring and science experiences, are not.

In 2006, along with my colleagues Karen Multon, Sharon Robinson-Kurpius, and Marie Hammond, I began an ambitious project to discover how scientifically talented women's relationships, achievements, and distance from privilege affected their intention to persist in college, their confidence in their major, their self-efficacy, and their hope for the future. That's a lot of variables! We believed they were all important, but we also suspected that the large body of research on women's persistence in STEM placed too much importance on women's internal barriers. In fact, most of the literature implied that the problem with women's persistence lay in their low self-efficacy—that is, in their lack of confidence in their abilities in math and science. We believed that this kind of research, which focuses only on women's deficiencies, was outdated. We had seen how powerfully external variables, like women's status in society (distance from privilege) and their ideas about relationships affected their desires to continue their studies in these challenging fields.[230]

We wanted to know if the gender relations that were so problematic in the 90s and "Culture of Romance" described by Holland and Eisenhart were the same for gifted women in STEM fields of this generation.[231] We brought in hundreds of young women to take a questionnaire measuring our chosen variables. Our college women were wonderfully diverse, pulled from a historically Black college, a university with a large Hispanic population, and a university serving many rural as well as suburban women.

What we found was hopeful indeed. First, we found that the *distance from privilege* concept was an important one; and second, that upper class and very poor women were less likely than lower middle class and middle class women to want to persist to graduation in science, technology, math, and engineering. There was an interesting twist, however: lower middle class women who had somehow received *social capital* were most hopeful and confident about their STEM careers.

What is social capital? It is the networks and experiences that make you feel like you belong and give support in your endeavors. Many of our persisting female students had come from working, blue-collar families that had managed to provide them with rich experiences in science—car trips to interesting natural places and science museums, summer and after-school activities that encouraged them in STEM fields, and a home life where books and access to online learning experiences were plentiful. The results regarding the upper class women as less persistent were somewhat puzzling. Perhaps because their need for income was not as pronounced, those in their adolescent environment did not provide reinforcing support in the same way or the same quantity as the middle class.

Gender relations, which encompass all of women's attitudes and experiences with romantic partners, also proved to be a fertile ground in our investigation. There was a substantial group of gifted young women who believed their career goals and romantic goals were equally important. Nearly all of these confident, persistent women planned to delay marriage until after their education and early career. Most of them also believed that their current partners were supportive of their career goals. Knowing how often women in STEM get sidetracked later by marriage decisions and childbirth, we understood that there was a certain amount of idealism and even naiveté in our participants. In our interviews, we often heard statements like, "Oh, I know how women get derailed by relationships, but it won't happen to me. My boyfriend supports my career goals."

Finally, we discovered that self-efficacy was only a weak predictor of women's persistence, confidence, and hope for the future. This generation of gifted college women does not seem to suffer the same level of worry and fear about their competence that previous generations did. On the other hand, maybe researchers have just placed too much emphasis on what is wrong with women, rather than what is wrong with college environments. For college women to fulfill their passion for science, they clearly need to enter college with many positive experiences of science in the family and in school already under their belt, with equal or greater ambition for career goals than relationship goals, and the focus to find the college environment that will support their dreams.

What Is Being Done to Attract and Retain Women in STEM?

Young female inventors and engineers often struggle with how to be taken seriously in their work. If they're too chipper, too accommodating, or too feminine, they run the risk of being overlooked for promotions and key responsibilities. For instance, one young woman confessed that she had dyed her naturally blonde hair to a darker shade of brown so that the men in her department wouldn't see her as a dumb blonde. Another attractive woman wears glasses rather than contact lenses when she's presenting her ideas, for the same reason.

Other young women make no apologies for the Hello Kitty notebooks and pink pencil bags that they bring to their Differential Equations class. They say that the boys in their classes initially are shocked. But when the girls measure up—scoring the highest in the class on quizzes and exams—the boys take notice. The women engineers we work with tell us that they're used to being questioned and doubted. But over time, as they prove themselves, their self-confidence improves—as does their ability to make innovative contributions.

How can we ensure that young women in STEM know that they belong in engineering and science programs? That their perspectives are essential to advance the areas of engineering, technology, and design? One solution would be programs like the WiSE Leadership program at Arizona State University.

WiSE Leadership for Women

The mission of WiSE—Women in Science and Engineering—is to gather, guide, and advance young women who are pursuing careers in science, technology, engineering, and mathematics. Rather than focusing solely on a young woman's career development, WiSE provides a holistic approach to female leadership development in STEM using concepts from positive psychology and optimal development to address the social, emotional, and career development of talented college women.

There are three types of activities in the WiSE curriculum:

1. WiSE Career Stories: Interviews with professional women & community leaders to build a network of support and connections.

2. WiSE Social, Emotional, & Career Development Workshops: Focus on positive psychology concepts such as mindfulness practices for stress management, emotional self-regulation, career decision-making, identifying strengths, goal-setting, and creating mission, vision, and purpose.

3. WiSE Career Choices & Leadership Summit: An annual gathering of women in STEM for hands-on experiences with science and technology and sessions on career decision-making and social/emotional well-being.

Several key concepts called WiSE Career Choices are built into the WiSE Leadership curriculum. These WiSE Career Choices are:

1. Say *yes* to new experiences, even if you can't see how an opportunity logically relates to your career; your intuition will become more accurate as you gain knowledge and experience.

2. Find a mentor, but know that you cannot force a mentoring relationship. Most successful mentor-protégé relationships begin spontaneously over a shared interest or passion. You can help yourself by putting yourself into new experiences where you have an opportunity to connect with potential mentors.

3. Study abroad and learn a second language. Spending time in another country expands your understanding of the world—and there is even evidence that you become more spontaneous and intuitive in your decision-making.

4. Never let money be the reason you say *no*. There is power in decision. Once you decide that you want to have an experience, you can seek economic support from family, friends, and scholarships. There is always a way to finance your dreams, even if it is not immediately obvious to you.

5. Raise your hand in class, rather than whispering the answer to your friends. Smart women often disappear in the classroom, choosing not to compete or participate. Every time you whisper the correct answer behind your hand rather than saying it aloud, you rob yourself, your classmates, and your professor of your intelligence and wisdom. When you speak, speak with conviction, not qualifying your statements with "Maybe," or "I could be wrong, but…" Don't make statements that sound like questions, with a higher doubtful tone at the end.

6. Take yourself and your goals seriously. If you don't, no one else will either. Tell everybody what your major and your career goal is without apology or excuse for your choice.

7. Have conversations with people who are different from you. Don't limit yourself to a small group of friends; instead expand your circle to include interesting and creative people who add something unique to the conversation.

8. Take classes in world religions, philosophy, and women's studies so that you can develop a broader perspective on how other people think. Do this even if you're majoring in a STEM field.

9. Pay attention to how you feel and learn how to manage your emotions. Stress, anxiety, and depression each have a way of thwarting well-being and success. Your emotions will tell you if you're on the right track or not. When you're feeling happy, enthusiastic, and focused, you're exactly where you need to be. But if you're feeling anxious, depressed, or lonely, then you need to do something to change it.

10. Stay connected. When you're under stress or overwhelmed, you might withdraw from social circles. Instead, reach out to your mentors and professors. Let them know you need extra support. You don't have to do it all alone. First of all, it's no fun. And second, you deprive the people who care about you the opportunity to support you.

11. Be on the lookout for serendipity. Putting yourself into environments and activities in which you are more likely to make connections that positively grow your career can lead to unforeseen opportunities. There's a phrase for this phenomenon. It is called planned happenstance, and it is at the heart of a career that is informed by engagement and intuition.

12. Know your creative flow and focus on your strengths. When you feel flow, go with it, even if it means staying up late. Find that sweet spot where your strengths are just equal to the challenge of your work.

13. Understand your personality, including what sets you apart from other people and what might trip you up as you begin your career path.

14. Envision your future. Imagine yourself 10 years in the future, using your strengths, being in the flow, and contributing to the world as a positive force.

15. If these rules seem hard or intimidating, seek out a counselor or psychologist for coaching and support. She can help you learn to manage fear or anxiety that appears when you're stretching yourself. You'll need to learn this important skill so that you can take advantage of opportunities that will help advance your career.

Smart Girl Profile | Anna, age 20

Anna, a 20-year-old European American, was a sophomore on the party pathway, though she was majoring in mechanical engineering and loved math and design. She became a founding member of the WiSE leadership program. At the first meeting, the conversation focused on big questions—those pressing issues that the girls had about their futures as women in STEM fields. Anna's question went straight to the heart of the matter. She said, "I want to know who I am and what I'm here for...I want to know why girls in my engineering classes play dumb so that guys don't feel intimidated by us."

Smart college-age women have a deep need to know and understand themselves. One of the first WiSE workshops focused on *how to get engaged*—a play on words, to be sure, to describe the research on the culture of romance and the ways that young women downsize their career aspirations and fall in love with young men rather than with ideas. When Anna mentioned that she might get a master's degree after college graduation and someone asked, "Why not a Ph.D.?" Anna shrugged in response.

When Anna stopped attending WiSE meetings, her friends became concerned. It emerged that Anna had a new boyfriend, also an engineering student. Though ASU is an enormous institution of 60,000 students, the polytechnic ranch campus was much smaller; students and faculty smiled and said hello to one another, whether known or not. It is very hard to hide at Poly. As a student worker, Anna spent her free periods in the career center, helping students with their resumes and interviewing skills. After giving her some time, the head of the WiSE program tracked her down to ask why she had stopped attending WiSE meetings.

It came to light that her boyfriend did not want her to attend the WiSE meetings; he thought she should stay at home with him instead. She said, "When I mentioned that I was thinking about getting my Master's degree in Engineering, he told me that he wasn't going to get his Master's degree and that a girl shouldn't have higher degrees than her boyfriend." That's when she stopped attending meetings and began slipping into a traditional role. They had talked about getting engaged and were moving in together. They'd bought a dog.

The head of the program decided not to bring up the statistics or to admonish her not to succumb to the culture of romance. Instead, she opted for acceptance and love for this young woman who really just wanted to know who she was and why girls had to play dumb so boys won't be intimidated.

Several weeks later, she called, sobbing. She had broken up with her boyfriend and moved out. After leaving her boyfriend, she reconnected with her WiSE team and refocused on her academic goals with great enthusiasm. She took the Graduate Record Examination (GRE) that spring and met a new member of the engineering faculty who created a position for her on her research team. Soon thereafter, Anna was accepted into doctoral programs at two top universities. One, located on the east coast, flew her out and hosted her interviews. She also revealed that an elite engineering program in the Midwest had re-opened its admissions process so that she could apply. They had just called to tell her that she'd been accepted into the Ph.D. program in Engineering Education on a full assistantship. She would be paid to get her Ph.D.!

WiSE helped save this young woman's dreams. Without a community of high-achieving, bright and supportive young women, without a leadership curriculum that helped her to stand up for herself and her dreams, and without her willingness to reach for the opportunities in front of her, she would have probably been okay, but not great. Quite possibly, she would have been trapped in the beige life of mediocrity—the most discouraging place of all for talented young women to exist. She is now in the fourth year of her Ph.D. program.

Smart Girl Profile | Sonia, age 21

Sonia, a 21-year-old Latina, is a senior in Mechanical Engineering in the College of Technology & Innovation. She is vice president of the WiSE Leadership Program and a key member of the university's student government. In her studies, she consistently scores at the top of her class, and she loves math, physics, and engineering. In the summer following her junior year, she participated in a summer internship at Honeywell.

As a little girl at age six, she won awards for her interpretation of van Gogh's *Starry Night*, which still hangs in her parent's home in

Texas. As a young adolescent, she moved with her family to France, where they lived for five years. She is fluent in English, French, and Spanish. A socially-intelligent leader, she is positive, gregarious, and assertive. Her engaging leadership style makes it easy for others to follow. Sonia's need for achievement sets her apart from the majority of her peers; she has high aspirations and works hard to achieve her goals. In her work, she is diligent, purposeful, and has a strong sense of direction in her life.

In addition to being a talented engineer, Sonia is also spontaneous, highly intuitive, and possesses a vivid imagination and a willingness to challenge the status quo. For Sonia, it is not enough for her products to be functional, they must also be beautiful. For example, she reacted to the appearance of the energy-efficient stoves that her male classmates designed and sent to a community in Africa: "They're ugly! Even if you're poor and you live in a remote village in Africa, the women still will want to prepare food on stoves that are beautiful! Everyone deserves to be surrounded by beautiful design, regardless of their station in life."

What will Sonia do after she graduates? Right now, she is passionate about the design and function of airplanes, and she would like to focus on aerospace engineering. Sonia is an example of a woman well on her way to becoming an innovator.

CHAPTER 10

Lean In or Opt Out? The Evolution of Adult Smart Women

The 20s: Full Steam Ahead

After college graduation, most smart young women go on to graduate school, professional school, an internship, or work in their field. Bright young women today are pouring into postgraduate education, making up more than half of law and medical school classes and three-quarters of social science and humanities graduate classes. Studies of recent high school valedictorians, however, show that today's gifted women tend to attend less selective colleges than gifted men just as they did 10, 20, and 40 years ago. This tendency to choose less selective colleges for undergraduate study also then influences the selectivity of the postgraduate institutions to which they can aspire. It is a case of the so-called *Matthew Effect*, the phenomenon of accumulated advantage, named for the declaration in the biblical book of Matthew that the rich get richer.[232] For example, young people who choose selective colleges accumulate the advantage of the Ivy League name on their resumes, which then makes them more impressive to selective graduate and professional schools and future employers.

So why do academically talented women, even valedictorians, go to lower status colleges? We don't know. We can only speculate that the same desire to avoid competition and risk of failure that prevents some girls from taking advantage of special summer programs for the gifted is also at work here in their choice of college. In addition, the biases of guidance counselors may cause them to advise girls against choosing the colleges to which many gifted boys aspire, such as MIT and Stanford. Making a college choice is one of the most important decisions a young, gifted woman will make, but the decision must be made when she is still a teenager. If she is unsure of her direction, uninformed about the vast market in higher education, and unassisted by counselors, educational consultants, or savvy family members, she may make a poor decision and aspire to a lesser education than she deserves.

Though they enroll in lower status graduate and professional schools, gifted young women are in full-steam ahead, usually progressing rapidly and achieving excellent grades. They seldom marry while in graduate school, and the rigors of advanced training often mean fewer social events and smaller social networks. Loneliness and stress are a fact of life for many female graduate students, med students, and law students. Their study groups or intern cohorts become their dating pool, their friendship base, and their only source of support. For highly curious intellectually gifted young women, this can feel like a sudden narrowing of their world of ideas and experiences.

After advanced training, smart women often delay marriage with the intention of establishing themselves in a career first. The United States recently reached the lowest marriage rate among its young people in history.[233] This doesn't mean, however, that gifted women are not in long-term romantic relationships; about 80% of gifted women *are* in romantic relationships after college, and bright young women still take their boyfriends or partners' plans into account when planning where to go to graduate school or deciding where to accept a job or internship.[234] What *has* changed is that young professional women are willing to have commuter relationships and long-distance relationships while completing graduate or professional study.

And then, Marriage

For smart young women in their late 20s and early 30s, the pressure to both marry *and* have a successful career is immense. Most talented young women expect that they will be able to have children, a career, and partners who will share equally in the household responsibilities. At our career workshops for smart and creative students, the overwhelming majority of our young women wrote in the *Perfect Future Day* section about their visions of forthcoming dual-career bliss. Yet, we were taken aback by how many young men—about a third—envisioned a stay-at-home wife. It is hard to imagine that so many bright men will find stay-at-home wives. More than ever before, both men and women work outside the home, though women continue to take on more than 50% of the childcare and homemaking tasks.[235] Although dual-career couples do have higher satisfaction, the path to dual-career bliss involves a great deal of negotiation.[236]

When smart young women marry, too often they get caught up in the bridal industrial complex. It is the little girl princess craze all over again but with a much higher cost to everybody involved.[237] From the poorest women to the wealthiest, all are led to believe—by the happy ending of every chick flick and armies of wedding planners—that a wedding is the most important day of her life. So the rituals begin—the expensive engagement ring, the engagement party, the bridal shower with gifts from the registry, the dress, the bridesmaids and their dresses, the dress rehearsal dinner, the expensive hall, the band, the ceremony, someone to perform the ceremony, the reception, etc. For some smart women, the competitive urge and the need to achieve will be channeled into making that day a triumph—but a triumph of what? Some couples will rebel and elope on their own and others will plan a casual, fun wedding with their friends in mind. For most smart women, however, the dual awareness of the consumerist avalanche of wedding demands and the desire to please everyone in the family will cause her to be engulfed in an exhausting race to the day of the marriage. The entire performance seems intended to rob her not only of the intimacy of the moment but also of her identity as an independent, strong woman with goals and dreams for herself.

Then there is the issue of the name change. Sociologists have studied the impact of name changing with interesting results. From the late 70s until the 90s, there was a steady upward trend toward women keeping their maiden names, especially among women in professional, academic, and creative fields. Then in the 90s, as bridal mania reached a peak, the trend leveled off. Even though almost half of women in Ivy League schools, a majority of academic women with publications, and most performers keep their maiden names, the trend has reversed among other groups of women.

Name changing does have consequences, according to the researchers. Claire Etaugh and her colleagues studied how people perceived women who kept their own name versus those who took their husband's names. They found that people assumed a woman who kept her own name was more agentic—that is, more active in the world and more in charge of her own goals—than women who took their husband's names, who were viewed as being more communal, valuing relationships and harmony.[238] The choice of a name is a powerful signal; choosing to keep one's name, or at least hyphenate it, tells people immediately that this is a woman who is creating and keeping her own identity. It is important that young gifted women are not pressured to change their name as a sign of commitment to the marriage because that is not what it conveys to those who are evaluating her self-confidence and goal-orientation.

Finally, finances and money management are important issues to negotiate. The new bride is often encouraged to combine bank accounts and credit cards; but in dual-career couples, with dual incomes entangled, every purchase becomes a negotiation. Probably the most important foundation of a smart woman's autonomy, after the right to decide upon her own timing of pregnancy, is the right to earn and manage her own money. Linda Hirshman offers three rules for women: first, prepare yourself to qualify for good work; second, treat work seriously; and third, do not put yourself in a position of unequal resources when you marry.[239] She explains:

> *The first rule is to use your college education with an eye to career goals. The best way to treat work seriously is to find the money. Money is the marker of success in a market economy; it usually accompanies power, and it enables the bearer to wield power, including within the family. ...If you are good at work, you are in a position to address the third undertaking: the reproductive household. The rule here is to avoid taking on more than a fair share of the second shift.[240]*

Although these words may seem quite mercenary or selfish, there will come a time in the life of the smart woman when she needs to make decisions that require financial resources, decisions that involve no one but herself—an investment in her own business, travel she may need to promote her work, or even a retreat that she desperately needs and wants. When she has money of her own, she can make these decisions quickly and smoothly. By the time a smart woman is in her 20s, she should have established her own banking accounts (in addition to any joint household account) and should involve herself in household financial decisions, including tax planning and preparation and retirement saving.

Smart women need to be able to manage the practical aspects of their finances, such as earning, investing, saving, spending, and paying off debt. However, there is an often-overlooked psychological aspect of money that influences how well a woman actually manages her finances. Money evokes the same emotional reactions—anxiety, worry, helplessness, fear—from adult women that math does for many smart girls. Put another way, the smart girl with math anxiety is likely to become a smart woman who hates dealing with money. Rather than learning how to manage their emotions around the subject of money, some gifted women relinquish control of their finances or ignore their money situation altogether. Either choice is disempowering and dangerous to their futures.

What is a solution? When a gifted woman has access to money, she has more choices and more freedom. Although money isn't everything, money does affect almost every aspect of life. Money is currency, a means of exchange, and a marker of success. We recommend that smart women develop a friendly, empowered relationship with money. Learn how you are best suited to make money; find out how to negotiate your salary and ask for raises or promotions; and finally, discover how to overcome the challenges that you have when it comes to spending, saving, or earning money.

Smart Women in Their 30s: Exhaustion and Extreme Jobs

Leaving Science

For decades, millions of dollars and thousands of hours of scholars' time have been spent trying to increase the number of women in STEM. Since the publication of the first *Smart Girls*, enormous progress has been made in keeping middle school girls interested in STEM careers, in encouraging girls to take advanced courses in high school in these fields, and in increasing the numbers of girls majoring in STEM. However, leaks in the pipeline remain; they have just moved further down the line. Now the leaks happen in college. Women drop out of STEM majors (except biology) in greater numbers than men; in graduate school, women stop with the Master's degree; and most unfortunately, at the post-Ph.D. and M.D. phase, women still often achieve less than men. In fact, the "leakiest" part of the pipeline is at the post-doctoral level.

In summarizing the results of an extensive study of women in academe, the 2004 NSF report, *Gender Differences in the Careers of Academic Scientists and Engineers,* said:

> *We find evidence that female scientists and engineers are less successful than their male counterparts in traveling along the academic career path. Some of this disparity appears to be related to differences between the sexes in the influence of family characteristics. Typically, married women and women with children are less successful than men who are married and have children.*[241]

What this means is that the major barrier encountered by women scientists is not their lack of ability or accomplishments; it is the fact that they find that the years in which they are supposed to be racing toward promotion and tenure are precisely their prime years for marriage and childbearing.

Despite these clear findings, scholars continue to try to find the reasons for women's exodus from the highest levels of STEM achievement in their inner lives, rather than in the context of their work. The reasons given for the exodus range from ridiculous to amazingly complex. Let's start with the ridiculous.

Innate Differences? Ridiculous!

Former Harvard president Larry Summers once asserted that "innate differences" are responsible for the shortage of women at the highest levels of academia. His provocative comments, published in every medium, sparked a heated discussion on why women are not in top math and science positions. It was then necessary, once again, for women scholars to rush in to repair the damage his remarks made to a generation of smart girls. Elizabeth Spelke and Janet Hyde provided research insights into the question of whether or not inherent sex differences were in fact responsible for women's absence in top positions.[242] Even though they analyzed hundreds of studies of sex differences and published their findings in leading scholarly journals, the popular press was not interested.

Are biological differences the cause of fewer eminent women scientists? The short answer is *no*. Hyde's research supported the *gender similarities hypothesis*, which established that men and women are similar on most, but not all, psychological features.[243] The hypothesis, in brief, is that there are likely to be more psychological and intellectual differences within a group of women than there are between a group of men and women. What psychological differences that do exist seem to pertain to physical strengths, such as throwing distance, and physical violence, both of which become markedly different at puberty. So much for pop psychology's sweeping generalization that "Men are from Mars, Women are from Venus."

In addition, scholars know that anything they write about sex differences—no matter how trivial those differences are—will almost certainly be published. So when the mathematics achievement gap closed, psychologists busily pursued other possible differences that might account for women not staying in science, like "spatial-rotation skills," the ability to visualize an object from different perspectives.

That is not to say that there are no stable differences between men and women, but they do not seem to be so much biological as cultural. For example, in Western cultures, males place more value on high salaries, taking risks, and the prestige of their organization, whereas females place more value on satisfaction at work, respecting colleagues, and comfortable conditions in the workplace. In non-Western countries, the prejudice against women as leaders makes the cultural barriers toward success particularly difficult to navigate.

Then there is the *self-efficacy hypothesis*, which states that women don't feel confident enough in their science and math abilities to persist in those fields; given all the hype about sex differences, that might seem like a good hypothesis. A new book by Katty Kay and Claire Shipman explores the studies that show that women, no matter how competent they are, tend to underestimate their abilities while men overestimate their abilities. As a result, women negotiate their salaries less often and ask for less. They aspire to jobs only when they have 100% of the qualifications, whereas men will apply for jobs for which they only have some of the qualifications. Finally, although women leaders are highly rated, they are punished socially for overconfidence. All of these are important findings that explain why women ask for so much less than they deserve.

The problem is, if you look only at individual factors like confidence or self-efficacy, they are sufficient to describe some of the "leakage" from careers, but not much. When you add in environmental variables, like mentoring, social networks, supportive universities and workplaces to the equation, *the individual variables simply wash out*. In fact, women in STEM academic careers often lack support for combining family and career, and part of the support they seem to need is more knowledge about ways that successful women academic scientists do manage family and career, skills to negotiate for balance in the workplace, and equitable roles in the family.

Just Choices and Preferences? Hardly

Stephen Ceci and his colleagues believe that the problems concerning discrimination and sexism in STEM workplaces have mostly been resolved and that women are just making the choice not to go forward with their careers.[244] In an exhaustive study of hiring practices and editorial practices, they found no evidence of women being passed up or of discrimination in scholarly journals. They said:

> *This situation is caused mainly by women's choices, both freely made and constrained by biology and society, such as choices to defer careers to raise children, follow spouses' career moves, care for elderly parents, limit job searches geographically, and enhance work-home balance. Some of these choices are freely made; others are constrained and could be changed.*

> *That women tend to occupy positions offering fewer resources is not due to women being bypassed in interviewing and hiring or being denied grants and journal publications because of their sex. It is due primarily to factors surrounding family formation and childrearing, gendered expectations, lifestyle choices, and career preferences—and secondarily to sex differences at the extreme right tail of mathematics performance on tests used as gateways to graduate school admission.[245]*

Parenthood affects work preferences, especially for females. Women, before they became mothers, placed the same amount of importance on short hours and flexible schedules as everyone else; now 10 years later after becoming mothers, they rate these things as much more important. Taking a leave of absence is especially difficult in STEM fields because of the shorter durability of knowledge—that is, STEM research advances more rapidly, and ideas are modified, expanded, or upended frequently. Indeed, with respect to high-level STEM positions. Ceci says:

> *Returning to work is not the issue, rather it is returning to work at the same level that is the focal issue. Furthermore, when these shifts in values occur among partners who earn high incomes, acting on these changes in priorities becomes more feasible. For example, there is evidence that assortative mating among highly intelligent people has the consequence that women who would otherwise be eligible for careers in the highest echelons pull out of labor force participation at rates higher than comparable men do because their husbands' incomes are sufficient.[246]*

We are concerned, therefore, that Ceci and his colleagues are making the same mistake that so many have made who only study women in the early stage of their careers—a time when women are still being accommodating, thus telling everybody they are making a free choice. Too often, women perceive themselves to be making a choice when they are actually making the best of a difficult situation, and using their congeniality, good adjustment, and resourcefulness to adapt to their husband's career goals.

Follow-up studies of the mathematically precocious young women have also suggested that those women who did not follow the high-powered STEM-oriented paths of their male counterparts were merely expressing their preferences and choices for particular domains or lifestyles.[247] It may be that even though these young women had extraordinary abilities in math, they just weren't passionate about STEM fields and were drawn to more people-oriented careers. On the other hand, it is always important to consider the possibility that even the most brilliant women believe they are making a choice to follow a less challenging path, when they are actually responding to the many pressures and barriers that women experience in STEM fields.

The Home Front and the Support Needed

Steven Rhoades and Christopher Rhoades managed to get behind the scenes in their surveys of the households of academic faculty. They found that the partners of male professors worked fewer hours than the partners of female professors. For male professors, 36.3% had non-working spouses compared to 2.8% of female professors. Only 12% of male professors took paid parental leave as opposed to 69% of female professors. Of the 12% of male professors who did take paid parental leave, almost all did less than half of the childcare. In contrast, all of the female professors taking paid leave reported doing the majority of the childcare.[248] As we shall see, there is more than meets the eye to women's choices and preferences.

Women who want careers in STEM need support at each transition. In choosing a career, which is the first milestone, self-efficacy may be important. At the second milestone, persisting to graduation with a STEM major, environmental supports such as mentoring and provision of information may be more important. At the third milestone, the final year of graduate or medical school, decisions must be made about postdoc education; and at the fourth milestone, the transition from postdoc to principal investigator, issues of family/career combinations and the promotion and tenure path become most important.[249] The women who succeed are those who have support on the home front. As Linda Hirshman, author of *Get to Work* says, "Only when women make it necessary for men to take on a fair share of the family labor will they do so."[250]

So far, we have focused on STEM careers. Recently, however, the discussion has expanded into just about every other arena where smart women might work.

Growing Thorns in the Arts

Such a huge amount of attention is given to women in the STEM fields that one might think that women in all other fields were doing just fine, that equality of opportunity reigned, and that extraordinary creativity in art, music, creative writing, and performance is being rewarded. Nothing could be further from the truth. In fact, gifted women are further behind gifted men in creative fields than in almost any other domain of work.

Until auditions for positions in major orchestras were blind—that is, when the player was hidden—judges notoriously chose male performers over female performers, and only a tiny fraction of composers and orchestra conductors are women.[251] Even more egregious is the fact that musical institutions are free to discriminate against women if they can come up with other reasons to do so—such as harmonious relations among the members or aesthetic appearance of the orchestra. The Vienna Philharmonic, for example, does not hire women players because they believe it interferes with the "aesthetic" created by their all-white, all-male orchestra. In the ballet world, women seldom rise to the post of choreographers. Female ballet dancers are taught from their first troupe that they are replaceable, while males are encouraged to develop their individual styles. Only about 8% of the artists featured in exhibits at the Museum of Modern Art are women.[252] I remember storming down to the reception desk of MOMA and saying, much to my kids' embarrassment, "So is the Museum of *Women's* Modern Art down the street? Where are they?" Any list of great novels or short stories will include very few women authors—even very recently. Here are the figures: only eight of Modern Library's 100 greatest novels, 14 of Time Magazine's 100 good reads, and eight of the New York Time's 100 greatest novels are by women.

Women artists, musicians, dancers, and writers struggle to be taken seriously; their lower salaries and sales mean that they must work harder to survive financially in occupations that are already risky and difficult. Neither the public nor critics seem ready to acknowledge women's work in the arts as equal to that of men's. In addition, there are few protections for creative women in organizations and institutions in the arts; many of the academic and corporate policies that have existed for decades to prevent discrimination and sexual harassment are alien to arts establishments.

Women who decide they will have careers in the arts need "thorns" a lot more than women in other fields. Is it any wonder that on personality tests they score as disagreeable? Young women not only need to try for the best degrees possible at arts institutions but must also somehow find a way to get faculty to take them seriously, to mentor them, and to promote their work. As independent artists, writers, and performers, they need strong entrepreneurial skills and thick skins.

Marylou Streznewski, in her book about gifted adults, divided adults into strivers (high-testing, teacher pleasers), superstars (people who are taller, healthier, handsomer, wealthier, happier, and nicer than most people, as well as more accomplished), and independents (creative intellectuals who follow the beat of their own drums, regardless of the consequences).[253] Her book suggests two other characteristics needed by women in creative fields: first, they must cultivate their independence; and second, they must give up on praise or external reward as a measure of their quality. Only by being fiercely autonomous, aggressive, and enterprising can women persist in their creative work.

Business, Politics, and Professions

More than a few efforts have attempted to discover not only the factors that keep women out of top positions but also the variables that cause them to leave their careers in the first place. The conversation started in 2003, when journalist Lisa Belkin wrote *The Opt-Out Revolution*, which explored the reasons that high-achieving women were choosing motherhood over work.[254] Four years later, Pamela Stone wrote *Opting Out? Why Women Really Quit Careers and Head Home*.[255] Her in-depth interviews with bankers, scientists, physicians, and attorneys revealed that professional women were being *pushed out*—rather than opting out—of their work places.

Around the same time, retired attorney and professor Linda Hirshman argued that when educated, elite women make the decision to leave the workforce, they not only create their own glass ceilings, but they also harm society by withholding their talents. She offered a strategic plan, which included this advice: "Use your education to prepare for a lifetime of work; take work seriously; stop electing governments that punish women's work," and "Never know when you're out of milk." The last suggestion means this: Don't put yourself in charge of keeping the inventory of food, the schedule of social events, or the list of chores that need to be done. Even if a partner is helping out with 50% of the actual tasks, being the only person who must be the task-master and keeper of domestic information is stressful. It puts the woman in the position of being the "default mode" for domestic tasks; if she knows what needs to be done and when it needs to be done, it is too often just easier to do it herself. For example, a woman who knows the baby's schedule may wait for the baby's nap time to take a shower, asking her husband, "Can I take a shower? Just listen to the baby monitor," while her husband, blissfully unaware, just steps into the shower when he feels like it.

Sheryl Sandberg joined the conversation in 2010 when she delivered a popular TED-Women talk and introduced her own ideas about why there are so few women leaders. In her 2011 commencement address at Barnard College, Sandberg said, "We will never close the achievement gap until we close the ambition gap." The way to close the ambition gap, she advised, is for women to *lean in* to their careers. When Sandberg's book, *Lean In: Women, Work, and the Will to Lead,* was published in 2013, she wove together research, personal stories, and professional advice about the problem of why there are so few women leaders and what can be done about it.[256] She encouraged women to pursue their goals and to ultimately close the ambition gap that continues to exist at the highest levels of leadership.

Sandberg also addressed work-life balance or the myth of *having it all,* which she says is dangerous to women. In an interview with Oprah Winfrey, Sandberg notes, "Having it all is the worst. No matter how much we all have and how grateful we are for what we have, no one has it all, because we all make tradeoffs every single day, every single minute."[257] Basically, because of the tremendous pressure on women to do it all, most wind up comparing themselves to others and fall short of their own expectations to be a good mom, a good worker, and a good partner.

Soon after *Lean In* was published, the media was abuzz with an apparent controversy that positioned Sheryl Sandberg against Anne-Marie Slaughter, the former Director of Policy Planning for the U.S. State Department. Headlines juxtaposed Slaughter's perspective with Sandberg's. Why? Because Slaughter wrote an op-ed piece called *Why Women Still Can't Have it All* after spending two years in Washington before she returned to her faculty position at Princeton.[258] In the article, Slaughter writes, "I'd been the one telling young women at my lectures that you *can* have it all and do it all, regardless of what field you are in. Which means I'd been part, albeit unwittingly, of making millions of women feel that *they* are to blame if they cannot manage to rise up the ladder as fast as men and also have a family and an active home life (and be thin and beautiful to boot)." Like other well-established organizations, the U.S. government continues to function in a traditional way: long hours, little paid leave, and little tolerance for flexibility. Unlike the conversations (and actions) toward an increasingly humane work environment that are taking place in the business and technology sectors, Slaughter is one of the first women to comment on the government's unresponsiveness to the changing demographics of public servants.

As it turns out, Slaughter and Sandberg are in the same camp regarding the myth of having it all. Whereas Slaughter focused on the institutional barriers in extreme jobs (the long hours, little paid leave, and low tolerance for flexibility), Sandberg's focus is on internal barriers—the things that women do to stop themselves reaching for top leadership positions.

In summary, it seems that *having it all* is to adult smart women what being *well-rounded* is to smart young girls. By trying hard to be everything, they risk missing the mark regarding optimal development and eminence. Rather than focusing on having it all, we encourage talented adult women to focus on their unique strengths and to seek support with the other aspects of life—i.e., child care and household chores—that require their time and attention.

Opting Out

According to Pamela Stone, who wrote *Opting Out*, women often decide to quit the workplace because of inflexible working conditions rather than the attraction of staying home. Behind the scenes at work, too, a complex picture emerges.

Women are more affected than men by the extreme jobs that involve long workweeks, travel, unpredictability, tight deadlines, wide-ranging responsibilities, and 24/7 client demands. Sylvia Hewlett in her book, *Extreme Jobs*, wrote:

> *Dual-career couples in extreme jobs have a two-body problem. When spouses have similar credentials, they can both end up competing for seniority at work (more pay, a better title) or seniority at home (more support, fewer chores). Either way, male needs are often prioritized. Something has to give, and it is often the women's career dreams. Surprisingly, though, most gifted women say farewell to their ambitions with grace, finding ways to achieve their calling and fulfill their values in other ways. They adjust—because gifted women, besides being intelligent, tend to be very well adjusted. In her heart, however, she may feel something that is neither resentment nor bitterness.*[259]

What she feels, we suggest, is quiet resignation and sadness.

Shame and Disillusionment vs. Opting In—With Support

In a recent conversation with Felice Kaufmann, who has chronicled the lives of the Presidential Scholars whom she has followed since 1968, she said:

> *Nobody prepares these kids for life's storms...Gifted women often feel like they have been put up on a pedestal, idealized, and set up as models for others. Nobody talks about the shame amongst gifted women who just couldn't deal with the insane demands of their work. There is shame in having your wings melt because you got so much closer to the sun.*[260]

At one 20-year high school class reunion, a woman—who had graduated fourth in her class and was a talented vocalist and actress—chatted with her friends. When asked about her latest projects, she said, "Whenever I felt that urge to create or to do something new, I got pregnant. Now I have five children." When asked about her music, she said that she had always wanted to create an album of original songs. Interestingly, at the 25th high school class reunion, she reported that she had just finished producing her first original album. Only when she realized that by having children she was not fulfilling her motivation to achieve did she begin to take her career as a musician seriously.

On the other hand, another woman we spoke to married her husband during her third year of medical school. They waited to have kids until after both had finished their residency programs, passed their boards, and established themselves in their health care organization. Raising two little girls and working in a growing practice left her exhausted. She told her husband that she wanted to quit her job and be a stay-at-home mom. Rather than passively agreeing, her husband said, "I know you don't really want to quit your job. You're just tired, and you don't make great decisions when you're tired. If you quit your job, not only will you regret it, but you'll also be bored." She decided that she would not quit her job. After getting through the rough patch of raising her children, she received a second Master's degree from Northwestern University. Just a few years later, she's now a leader in healthcare technology and the medical advisor for a national political leader.

We share this story, not only to highlight the accomplishments and persistence but also to note and acknowledge her husband's support of her career. He could have easily told her that it was her choice and she could quit if she wanted to (his salary was enough to sustain the family lifestyle), but because he believed in her work and knew her well enough to know that it wasn't what she really wanted, he chose to honor her hard work toward establishing herself as a leader in her discipline. These two have established a way of doing things that enables both of them to reach their individual goals, while at the same time honoring their shared vision for their family. This is an example of what Sheryl Sandberg means when she says that the most important choice a smart woman will make is who she marries.

The Mommy Wars

What happens to smart women in their 30s? Some run into a wall of extreme jobs and marriages in which well-intentioned partners don't quite hold up their part. They move to part-time positions or less challenging jobs, and some who are married to well-paid partners step out entirely to raise their kids. No matter what choice they make, they are now in the front lines of the Mommy Wars. Supermoms and psychologists who believe in *attachment parenting*—the notion that if a mother doesn't snuggle her baby constantly from birth and nurse the baby for four years that the poor child will develop an *attachment disorder*—accuse the working mom of harming her child in some way. Of course they are ignoring thousands of years of human evolution during which fit young mothers have always worked while siblings and grandparents and others cared for the infants. Then there are the working moms who are not only often burdened with double shifts of working and homemaking but are also laden with guilt.

On the other hand, the mothers who choose to stay at home are told to get to work, to buck up, and just cope—without any help from her community, her government, or her family. They feel guilt as well, not only because they are not achieving in the workplace but also because of the awareness that they are leading privileged lives.

For smart women, whether staying home or working part-time or full-time, there is tremendous joy in having children. Despite the fact that parenting and raising children makes impossible the more linear path to eminence taken for granted by gifted men, most gifted women name their children as their life's greatest joy. In fact, researcher Kristin Perrone tells us that parenting tends to increase life satisfaction and leads to meaningful relationships.

What about the less privileged gifted women? Sarah Kendzior, writing about the current economic situation for women in the U.S. says there are no Mommy Wars, only money wars. Most women, she has found, are neither opting out nor opting in; they have no options other than to struggle to survive economically. She says:

> But for nearly all women, from upper middle-class to poor, the 'choice' of whether to work is not a choice, but an economic bargain struck out of fear and necessity. Since 2008, the costs of childbirth, childcare, health care, and education have soared, while wages have stagnated and full-time jobs have been supplanted by part-time, benefit-free contingency labour.[261]

Smart women who are from poor backgrounds and minority women are often disgusted by what one of my African-American doctoral students called "white women problems." Laughing about the Mommy Wars, she said:

Well, black women have always worked. My mother took care of white women's children for 10 hours a day while trying to raise three of us on her own as a single mom. Believe me, she never complained, because her mother had done the same. She went to the suburbs on a bus to work all day, and we were expected to help each other out, before and after school. When she got home, no matter how tired she was, she checked our homework and she tucked us in and told us stories or sang to us. She helped us to stay focused on our ambitions. Now I'm a psychologist and my sister is a successful head of a nonprofit. My brother is a nurse in Ghana working for the same nonprofit. So don't even talk to me about the problems of guilt of smart women who stay home![262]

Most smart women don't talk about guilt and shame in their 30s, and they can even be extremely defensive about their choices to opt out or slow down. They believe that despite all the extreme job structures at work and domestic pressures at home they made the choice freely to reduce their ambitions and trim their dreams. This was certainly the case with the gifted women in the original *Smart Girls*, who not only insisted that they had quit work because they simply wanted to but also decided that they weren't really that gifted anyhow. They thought it was a choice. Here is where gifted women so often differ from average women. They are so intelligent and resourceful that they find a way to make the best of their diminished dreams and persuade themselves and everybody else that all is well, that they love the choice they have made, and that they have never been happier.

The Lucky Ones

Then there are the lucky ones—the ones who made continual progress in careers that allowed maximum flexibility and autonomy; who married partners who truly did half of the domestic work and believed in the smart women's calling in life; and who found a network of support for childrearing in family, friends, and excellent preschool and schooling. These are the women who did not have a job subject to financial collapse and somehow never had to deal with neurotic or bullying supervisors. They made it through their 30s with their dreams intact.

There are also increasing numbers of smart women who are not married and choose to stay single throughout their 30s. Most of them are women who have fallen in love with an idea, and that idea drives their daily lives. They do their part, they prosper in business and professions, and they work for and receive tenure in academe. Because they have never opted out or slowed down, they begin to reap the rewards of their contin-uous progress—financial stability, satisfaction in their achievements, and an established community of colleagues and friends. These are the smart women who benefit from the Matthew Effect; the more they achieve, the more opportunities they receive for continued achievement, and they sail into their 40s, feeling like the ground is firm beneath their feet.

Kristin Perrone represents a new generation of faithful chroniclers of the decisions made by gifted adults. Her findings about the life choices of gifted women are remarkably similar to those of past scholars, including Carol Holahan who found that academic and career success was associated with joy in living, life and work satisfaction, competence, and self-esteem.[263] Similarly, Perrone discovered that gifted women who made early decisions about college had fulfilling career goals, significant relationships, as well as greater life satisfaction; they also reported being happy, proud, and satisfied with their relationships as well as with their financial success.[264] Perrone's findings regarding the link between romantic relationships and life satis-faction were consistent with studies of gifted adults during the 1970s and 1980s. Basically, the decision to commit to a romantic relationship was not just a major life decision for many gifted adults; it also led to greater life satisfaction and successful long-term marriages and relationships.[265] What stands out is the importance of deliberateness in choosing both career *and* relationship.[266] Those smart women who treat both of these aspects of life as equally important and equally worthy of deep reflection, planning, and careful decision-making seem to have the most satisfying lives.

40s: The Midlife Crisis and the Journey into the Self

> *"It is never too late to be what you might have been."*
> —*Mary Ann Evans, known by her pen name George Eliot.*

Midlife Crisis

There comes a point in a smart woman's life when she wonders, "Is this all there is?" As she reviews her life, she recalls moments or even entire years in high school and college when she was fulfilling her potential, times when she was self-possessed in the best of ways. She was responsible to herself and making the most of her gifts. Back then, she performed in school plays or spent hours in the dark room developing her black and white photographs. As she practiced her piano pieces, she dreamed of the day when she could have her own apartment in the city, with an elegant blue duvet cover on her bed and a cat. Or perhaps her daydreams included medical school or writing a book or international travel for business. Perhaps she imagined herself the leader of a global organization—something grand and influential—a position that would make a difference in the world.

But then, for many smart women, life happens. And instead of finding the cat and shopping for the apartment and the duvet cover, instead of searching for international positions or writing best-selling books, she slowly begins to settle. First she meets a boy—her college sweetheart. They fall in love and get married. She promises herself that she can still fulfill all of her dreams now that she's married. But then the student loans are due, or her husband gets a big promotion, and she picks up the burden of responsibility, practicality, and reality. Instead of writing, she reads novels and nonfiction; she posts reviews on Good Reads and interacts with other used-to-be writers. Her dreams of international business travel become travel images pinned to her Pinterest boards. Her love of photography morphs into myriad scrapbooks that she creates for the children she doesn't even have yet.

In her quiet moments, if she's honest with herself, she feels deeply disappointed—not just with herself, but with life. After all, how could life play such a cruel trick by showing her what's possible in her imagination but then relegating her to an ordinary reality?

Let's take a stay-at-home mother with teenage children, for example. It seems strange to her that she has teenagers because she can still remember herself at 16—vibrant, hopeful, and focused on her own future. As her daughter starts high school, she wonders where the time has gone—and what she has to show for it. She tries to make life about her kids. They are good kids and she is proud of her efforts to help them develop into successful people. She knows that being a stay-at-home mom is considered high status, particularly for European-American women; it is an acknowledgment that she *has* a choice and she's chosen her family. But the trouble with being a stay-at-home mom is that your children take you for granted. They show little appreciation for you—and suddenly your choice begins to feel like a sacrifice. Like many stay-at-home moms, she's been relegated to chauffeur, referee, and laundry maid—roles tantamount to those of a slave girl rather than a queen. It is not that she doesn't love her kids; it is the fact that she knows in her heart that there's more to life than picking up another person's dirty underwear. She begins to feel resentment and frustration with increasing frequency. It is not long before a plan begins to form. In her private moments, she wishes that she had followed her heart and studied abroad when she was in college. But a shortage of money and her parents' practical nature outlasted her dreams. She longs for a life where she doesn't worry about what other people think. She wishes that she had the courage to reclaim the dreams that she had as a teenager. She is tired of living through her children. She wants something for herself that is exclusively hers—work that challenges her mind, feeds her soul, and helps the world. She is tired of compromising her desires for the sake of her family. It is not that she doesn't love them, but a little voice in the back of her mind keeps asking: *But what about me? Is this all there is?*

Smart women who don't fulfill their missions tend to suffer from depression and anxiety. They question their purpose in life and find the typical reasons unsatisfying. Many come into a place of understanding that they can no longer be satisfied with an ordinary existence and feel pressed to contribute to their communities through leadership and service. When a gifted woman comes alive to her purpose, there is often a sense of urgency that surpasses what is ordinarily called internal motivation or obligation. Instead, she experiences an internal knowing that she has no other choice except to fulfill her destiny. Psychologists often encourage women to remember that they do have choices, but in the case of a smart woman on a mission, there seems to be an existential element that drives them forward, despite great pain and the possibility of failure. It is as though the price of choosing *not* to follow one's mission is too great to bear. Kate Noble, in a beautiful book on gifted women's development called *The Sound of the Silver Horn*, names it "The Call to Awaken."[267]

At first, a smart woman may attempt to compromise with herself. She will tell herself that life is not so bad, that the people around her love and support her. She will make an extra effort to maintain the status quo and dive fully into her current life with great gusto. Her efforts to ward off the quiet, yet persistent, call to awaken will be successful for a little while. She will be able to ignore what is in her heart—her desire to leave her job, to divorce her emotionally-distant spouse, to change her life. Many days she may get depressed, but it seems like a small price to pay. She is willing to compromise her own happiness for the sake of what she has helped to create so far. What she misunderstands is that her spirit will have its way, with or without her permission. Instead, she refers back to the rules of her childhood, rules that were designed to keep her safe, but actually just kept other people happy. In her mind, she hears old voices telling her, "Don't be selfish," "Don't get too big for your britches," or "Don't shirk your responsibilities." If she reflects, she will see clearly that there were no rules in place—not really, anyway—that would allow her to become more and more herself.

Then one day, she makes a decision.

Dissatisfaction, Restlessness, and Spiritual Awakening

At 40 years old I discovered that the strongest feelings I could experience were those of annoyance and fatigue. This came as a surprise because I thought I had been destined for more dramatic emotions. Having lived life in a headlong rush toward my goals, I suppose I was expecting to feel some kind of wild satisfaction in having achieved them. Instead, I felt like a ball, pitched through the air in a gorgeous, speedy arc, only to fall to the ground, roll a few times, and stop. —Barbara, Letters to the Medicine Man[268]

The symptoms of a woman's spiritual awakening resemble the feeling of being surrounded by beige walls in a suburban house that has become too small: It is bearable, yet subtly and undeniably oppressive. Exhaustion, irritability, discouragement, and depression are common experiences of gifted women, just before the inevitable shift. It is as though she can suppress the call of her soul, but only for so long. Though it sounds dramatic, sooner or later, there comes a time when she must listen, or perish. Rather, bringing one's self to the brink of change again and again without choosing to honor the transformation takes a toll on one's spirit.

Smart women seem to need continuous growth, and often that growth comes as a spiritual or philosophical transformation in midlife. There are instances when external circumstances—religious upbringing, stress, and friends' and colleagues' attitudes contain and suppress growth. Other times, a smart woman's own investment in the status quo—the way things have always been—will impede her evolution. As one wise therapist said, "At times, the painful familiar is more comfortable than the unknown." Edging one's way toward self-actualization is a tedious and sometimes scary undertaking, yet a necessary one for spiritual awakening. Some might call it courageous, but courage is what other people label the force behind having no real choice but to grow.

At my 20-year class reunion, I was surprised to find that the same women who had been so cheerful and insistent about their happiness as homemakers had changed; some had experienced bitter divorces, some had suddenly been forced to support down-sized husbands, and some had been struck by illness or disability. Most striking was the sense of awakening and their bold determination to move forward, no matter what might happen. At that time, it had seemed that only women who had been unable to achieve their dreams and

goals experienced a midlife crisis. That was incorrect. By the time we
were all 49 years old—the lone achievers, the dual-career strivers,
the super professionals, the stay-at-home moms—had almost all
experienced a midlife crisis. For me, it was a doozy. —Barbara

Yes, all the follow-up studies agree—for Terman's gifted women, valedictorians, Presidential Scholars, and former gifted education students—most gifted women in their early 40s who had opted out or reduced their aspirations are less financially stable, less satisfied with their lives, and less ready for the changes that comes when children leave home. We would expect those gifted women to be in crisis; after all, they did everything their society told them to do and were punished for it in public opinion and in their bank accounts.

But what about all those incredibly successful women who *had it all* in their 30s? Perhaps the biggest surprise in the stories and the research on smart women is that even the women who *leaned in* experienced a midlife crisis. If you return to the stories of eminent women, it is clear. Jane Goodall's story perhaps tells it best because even after she followed her passion, married an equal, and had a remarkable child, witnessing her beloved chimps engaging in the first warfare seen by a human sent her into a spiritual crisis that she documents in *Reason for Hope*. Similarly, high achievers like Sheryl Sandberg stepped back and said, "What am I doing?" and began to write the book about her struggles with *having it all* that would speak to a generation of women entering their 40s. Grethe Cammermeyer discovered in her 40s that, in spite of her success in the military and her model military marriage, she could no longer deny her deepest self as a lesbian. She fell in love with a woman and became an advocate for LGBT rights in the military.

So for most smart women, the midlife crisis is inevitable. How strange that we often have to turn to popular literature to understand what is going on, rather than scholarly literature. When the Baby Boomer generation of talented women reached midlife, the shelves of bookstores sagged with New Age books about spiritual journeys, but most of the psychological literature was silent. What is it that is so scary to scholars about the spiritual journey?

I will never forget the audience at the American Psychological
Association as I gave my Fellow Address. I am sure they were
expecting the usual review of all the impressive research leading
up to some rather narrow conclusion about some aspect of career
development, feminist theory, or talent development. Instead, I
launched into the story of my experiences learning Native American
spirituality: my transformative experiences in a sweat lodge

ceremony, my apprenticeship in shamanic healing, my descent into depression as I struggled to somehow integrate my spiritual life into my work and family life, and the inevitable transformation that occurred. My conclusion for my colleagues is that we could no longer afford to ignore spiritual intelligence as a concept that needed articulation and exploration. Most of the audience members sat there agape, as if they had just witnessed my falling off the dais and my brains spilling out on the floor. Equally strange, and quite meaningful to me, was the fact that so many female colleagues contacted me privately later to tell me about their own spiritual experiences and their fear of disclosing them. We were all afraid to lose credibility with our colleagues by entering this messy domain of unquantifiable experiences. Although I was indeed shunned by many of the hard-core scholars who thought I had gone batty, I will be forever grateful to my current colleagues—and collaborators like Kate Noble and Robyn McKay—for recognizing that one can have a spiritual transformation without losing one's commitment to science, or for that matter, one's commitment to sanity. —Barbara

Kathleen Noble documented the stages of the journey in her books *The Sound of the Silver Horn* and *Riding the Windhorse,* and countless women have written memoirs that recount the path.[269] The crisis—and the call to awaken—might begin with an unexpected loss or an insurmountable barrier of the kind we have described in extreme jobs. For the high-achieving smart woman, it is terrible to encounter a problem that cannot be solved with intelligence and creativity. The further you have progressed in life without any significant failures, the more difficult it is to admit defeat.

For some smart women, however, the sudden dissatisfaction seems to come out of nowhere. In that state of dissatisfaction, they are vulnerable—in a good way—to surprises. A bioscientist will discover yoga, something she never would have tried in her rush to the top. A businesswoman will read an article that touches her soul about women in Kenya who are trying to start their own businesses, and suddenly she finds herself flying to Africa to help. A woman who has spent her life as a medievalist, surrounded by scholars, will fall in love with a cowboy.

This is how the transformation happens, and life has to change radically for the woman on a new journey. Suddenly, the need to achieve simply for the sake of more money or higher status disappears. The need to take care of everybody else's needs at the expense of her own growth fades. Remarkably, most gifted women have the ability to go through this transformation while still being attentive to the needs of their family and continuing to work. Only a few have cataclysmic changes that end in a change of work, a change of partner, and a move to another place. Many smart women change their lives in place. While J.K. Rowling was transforming into the most successful writer in the world, she was caring for her daughter and her dying mother. While Hillary Clinton was transforming from First Lady to a Presidential candidate, she held her family together and carefully nurtured her daughter's passage into womanhood. What seems to hold smart women together throughout their crisis is their devotion to their purpose in life, as expanded and refined by their time in the fire.

Smart Women in their 50s and 60s—Giftedness Will Have its Way

In their 50s, many smart women seem to be just getting started. That was certainly my experience at my 30-year reunion gathering. I will never forget the surprise of seeing some of the women in my gifted class who had been struggling at 40 with difficult marriages, childrearing, and job dissatisfaction (the group I called *overwhelmed* in their 40s) who had become nothing short of dazzling. In *Smart Boys*, I contrasted the women at the reunion with the men—most of the women were lively, attractive, and engaging while most of the men seemed tentative, less physically fit, and aging. What on earth had happened in 10 years? Among the women who had been overwhelmed or just getting along at 40, one had gone from homemaker and part-time worker to vice president of a Fortune 500 company. One had gone from an ugly divorce and poverty to a Master's degree in Social Work and a thriving practice. Another had become a dramatic, passionate teacher of gifted students. Giftedness will have its way, I said to myself.

Despite all manner of setbacks and struggles, these women had used their adaptability to transform their lives and create a new narrative. For bright women, meaning-making in this decade later in life is a powerful motive.[270]

Entrepreneurship—Leaving the Organization

For many smart women in their 50s, entrepreneurship became the way to fulfill their passion when the corporations, practices, or universities they worked for seemed to be impediments to both the achievement of their dreams and to personal growth. For women who had been stranded by divorce or an empty nest, entrepreneurship was a way of making a new life. Not only did these new, woman-led enterprises lead to innovation and productivity, they also provided smart women with the opportunities to use all of their talents and skills.

Smart Girl Profile | Sara, age 60

Sara has a Ph.D. in Mechanical Engineering—she is an expert in her field. Several years ago, she sold her multi-million dollar technology company and began casting about for her next project. Sara studied engineering in the early 1980s, a time when women who took advanced math classes were flatly told, "You don't belong here." Yet, she persisted. She is extraordinarily brilliant, but her intellect alone is not where her success arose. She is also profoundly intuitive, serious about her work, and good-humored besides. She plays Rachmaninoff like a concert pianist; she's well-traveled, stylish, and optimistic about the future. Her abundance of positive emotions, good humor, and polite demeanor seem to mask her powerful need to create, explore, and discover. Sara has been financially successful, and she is happy to talk about her successes. In addition to her doctorate, she continues to pursue knowledge. She has an MBA from the University of Chicago and more recently has been learning 3D printing and graphic design at a state university.

After she sold her business, she struggled for a time to find her place in the world of work. Her friends, many of whom were employed as engineers, seemed confused by her early retirement. They seemed not to understand that her financial circumstances enabled her to take time off to strategize her next move as an entrepreneur. As a young inventor, Sara discovered that complete concepts would come to her in a fully-formed "download." She quickly learned that if she could "see" the final product in her mind's eye, it would quickly take on physical form. Now that she is in her 60s, her approach to innovation has evolved. She is still driven, but now she seems more intentional in her creative pursuits. She seems to enjoy designing for its own sake, rather than being driven to create out of hunger for achievement. She is a woman who is satiated by her past accomplishments, yet still intent on bringing her next vision into reality.

Smart Girl Profile | Tessa, age 51

Tessa made choices throughout her adult life that advanced her career. She went to Harvard as an undergraduate, and after working for a few years returned for her MBA. As a little girl, she imagined herself as a queen and is actually a distant relative to ancient Chinese royalty. She has all the right qualities for leadership in international business; she is open to new experiences and thrives on travel. She delights in teaching complex topics in economics and leadership to large audiences. Far from being intimidated, she takes disagreeable leaders on as a challenge and loves to win them over. She is humble, yet proud of her accomplishments. She was the Chief Financial Officer of a global organization when she walked into her boss's office early one morning and handed in her letter of resignation. She left at a time when her industry was under fire for its ethical practices. It wasn't that she did not like the work. She just wanted to do something different. Maybe she would write a book or host her own talk show or become a consultant for organizations similar to the one she was leaving. After taking a six-month hiatus, she trained as an executive coach. She is finding life outside of the corporate machine to be both exhilarating and frightening. The structure, annual bonuses, and other perks of leadership at its highest levels make returning to work appealing. Yet, she remains focused on blazing her own trail.

How does a smart woman in her 50s leverage the power of social media, online marketing, and entrepreneurship? How does she adapt to life challenges?

Adapting, Creating New Narratives, Finding Meaning

By age 62, the women in Terman's study had separated into clear groupings—lifelong homemakers, career women, and those who had done a combination of both.[271] The most surprising finding of the study was that the single, older, childless gifted women were the happiest; the next happiest were those who had combined career and family. The homemakers who had never had income-producing work were the least happy. It would have been very hard to anticipate this result when the women were in their 30s, happily letting go of their goals. Those women who had held onto their goals—which several studies of aging bright women label as *purposiveness*—were satisfied with their lives, happy, and positive about aging.

Felice Kaufmann's follow-ups of the Presidential Scholars of 1968 provided rich texture to the outlines provided by the Terman studies. She and Dona Matthews, in their article about the follow-up, called the period of life in gifted women's late 60s "Coming into Their Own."[272] These women never tied financial success to their definition of achievement. Kaufmann once said, "Some barreled right through, and some had a direct shot to emeritae in academics or went on achieving in law and medicine. The salary differences are significant; throughout their lives, these women made much less money than the men, yet they were still better off than the rest of population." What is surprising is how smart women held onto their dreams throughout the storms of life and came to value their work very differently. It seems that achievement alone lost meaning for them. Only those actions that were connected with deeply held values—no matter what the outcome happened to be—gave a sense of satisfaction. Older smart women came to the realization that they might never receive public recognition for their accomplishments, that less talented people might have gone further in salary and status, and that paradoxically, many of the barriers to public achievement had led them into more satisfying directions in life. They were rueful and funny about some of the complications in their lives; they had adapted with humor and new narratives. Here are some of their comments:

- ❖ I was supposed to set the world on fire. I am thankful that I have not set my hair on fire. Well, there was that one time with the hot-water heater pilot light…

- ❖ I married the wrong man, and it lasted 20 years.

- ❖ The great tragedy of my life was not that it failed, but that it succeeded so well.

- ❖ I expected children and a synergistic relationship; that didn't happen.

- ❖ My divorce is one of my greatest accomplishments, but they don't give awards for that.

- ❖ I expected more glamour, but such glamour as I have now seems too much effort.

- ❖ I expected to be prominent in some field, but I gave that up when I left education.

- ❖ I am just a wage slave, but there have been times when I have said, 'I can't believe they pay me to do this work!'

- ❖ I have learned that there is no limit to what you can accomplish if you don't care who gets the credit. I also still don't like the limelight very much. So while I love accomplishing goals, I prefer to deflect credit to others. I have collected my share of awards over the years, and I am grateful for each one. But I no longer aspire to be the head of anything or the best of anything. I like being able to make a difference—in an organization, in someone's life—but I do it now purely for the joy of it.

❖ My attitudes have, not surprisingly, become more nuanced over the years. I realize that academic and professional recognition are not the same as achievement, that professional achievement and making a contribution are not the same, and that at the end of the day, making a contribution is more important than acknowledged accomplishment or achievement. I can make small and large contributions to those around me by treating people kindly and with respect, by helping students to grow and to recognize their accomplishments and their potential, by helping groups to function well together, and by creating personal/social activities with good food and wine in which people enjoy their time together. I realize that professional contributions can be small and unacknowledged and still be valuable.

For those women who had married and had families, most regarded their children as their major achievement—their "crowning glory" as Kaufmann put it. Putting together both the Terman study and the Presidential Scholar study, it is clear that single women without children are extremely happy, but those smart women who do have children usually regard their children as their major source of happiness.

Elderly Smart Women

What youthful mother, a shape upon her lap...
Would think her Son, did she but see that shape
With sixty or more winters on its head,
A compensation for the pang of his birth,
Or the uncertainty of his setting forth? —William Butler Yeats

Yeats in his poem "Among School Children" confronts his own aging and gives us a striking image of a mother imagining her baby as an old person. Parents and teachers of gifted girls seldom imagine their daughters beyond college years or young adulthood. Mothers wish for a good education, success at work, and the pleasures of family life for their daughters, but do we ever consider what kind of old woman we would like her to be? Do we ever consider how our teaching and parenting might be shaping not only her youth—but to some extent—her aging?

Intelligence is indeed linked to good health and life satisfaction in old age, but what else does the distant future hold for smart girls? At the end of their lives, the Terman women were still happy and satisfied compared to the general population, but ill health did take its toll on happiness by the time the women were in their 80s. In fact, attention to physical health and adaptation to diminished abilities was significantly associated with happiness and satisfaction. Positive attitudes toward aging had long-term consequences; those women who showed positive attitudes towards aging while in their 60s were better off physically and psychologically in their 80s.

Adaptation to new circumstances and regulation of emotions were the major strategies used by elderly gifted women, according to Carole Holahan, who continued the study of Terman's students into their old age.[273] In other words, those smart women who had attained equanimity and serenity were those who had learned to manage negative emotions and nourish positive emotions. Reading about how these bright, elderly women coped psychologically brings us back to the importance of mindfulness—the acknowledgment and acceptance of emotions and a focus on the present moment. Felice Kaufmann talks about how the female Presidential Scholars prepared themselves for aging in surprising ways.[274] After years of intense productivity, many of these women had what she called *dramatic retirements*—some quit high-powered jobs to do art and play their musical instruments, and some quit just to walk the beach. The more creative the choice of retirement activity, the happier the women seemed to be.

Reading about the elderly lives of gifted women and feminist pioneers, one cannot escape the observation that the reward of a lifetime spent overcoming barriers while following one's passion—that is, falling in love and staying in love with an idea—was an ending of wisdom and peacefulness. Annemarie Roeper—founder of one of the first schools for gifted children and of the *Roeper Review*, one of the most important journals in the field of gifted education—is one of the few people to have written about "growing old gifted." She pointed out that in modern times the elder years have been extended longer and longer, but no roadmap, no model exists for what to do with those extra years. The problem, she believed, is even more acute for the "old, old" gifted—those in their 80s and 90s. She said:

> *Even into our 70s, there is little time to ponder life, death, and eternity—mankind's eternal concerns. We postpone these thoughts until later. But upon arrival in one's early 80s, the road that we have been traveling—once well lit, well-described, and well-worn— begins to peter out, until we are left standing in a field, no longer sure of the way. Older old age has not been well described well except as a lack of young age. Now that I am 87, I feel that I am*

on virgin ground, and there is not much, as far as I know, that can
help me and others cope with our experiences.[275]

After examining the losses that are inevitable—of health, freedom, status—she goes on to say that there is indeed one very important task for the elderly gifted, and that is to accept the unanswered questions and mysteries of life.

> *So my conclusion is that when you reach the age beyond old, your*
> *only reality is the unknown. This has actually always been true,*
> *but many have been able to avoid it up until this point. We don't*
> *even really know the past or the present, let alone whether what one*
> *feels as a living Self will remain as such or transform into further*
> *unknowns. Integrating these understandings as a reality may be*
> *the definition of "beyond old age."*
>
> *Gifted elders have to keep their minds trained carefully and*
> *keep on using them. In fact, I think that preservation of the mind*
> *has an additional task: It serves to maintain the Self and its inde-*
> *pendence. Keeping a sharp mind becomes a way of preserving one's*
> *freedom and control. Just as I consciously watch every step I take*
> *so that I won't fall, I watch every thought I think so that I can keep*
> *control. But the need for control is also a form of mistrust. There*
> *is a point at which we must give up that control, and the only*
> *people to whom we can trustingly give it up are those who love us*
> *unconditionally.*[276]

Finding that balance, then, between preserving freedom and trusting others when one can no longer be independent is important to gifted women aging well. Smart elderly women are sources of wisdom even as they seek the final wisdom of acceptance of the mystery of the universe. Smart girls and women can learn much from elderly smart women if they embrace not only their stories of the past but also their struggle to understand the nature of mortality and immortality.

Conclusion

As we complete this long journey through the adulthood of the smart woman, from the full-steam-ahead 20s to the wise and balanced end of life, there are several important lessons to be learned. First, no matter how talented and well-prepared a young woman might be in her field, she can still be derailed by her tendency to adapt to society's expectations about relationships and marriage. She can still, in this time of changing roles for women, find that she does not have enough financial, family, and workplace support for her dreams. The only pathway that leads to the fulfillment of her talent is that of refusal to adjust to conflicting societal expectations for her gender role, and the courage to demand from her family, workplace, and society true equity and support for her goals. She has to use her brilliance and wisdom to set her own goals and create her own journey. What gives smart women the strength they need to persevere is their love of an idea. A true vocation is not a job or a career but rather a calling—this powerful idea helps women to avoid the trap of worrying about whether the measure of her success is salary, status, or the opinion of others. The choice is not whether to lean in or opt out. It is to actualize one's deepest values through one's calling, or to suffer the sadness of not having fulfilled that calling. A job, a credential, relationships, and a marriage can all be taken away; a vocation, a commitment to an idea, can never be taken away. The message is clear for adult smart women: Self-actualization is not optional.

CHAPTER 11

Twice-Exceptional Girls

Twice-exceptional girls are those who have a disability but are also gifted. This could be a very bright girl who is blind or deaf or has cerebral palsy. More often these days, though, twice exceptional refers to people whose giftedness is combined with at least one *cognitive* disability; this include disabilities such as ADHD, Autism Spectrum Disorder, and other specific learning disabilities or psychiatric disabilities, such as Bipolar Spectrum Disorder, Oppositional Defiance Disorder, depression, or anxiety. Smart girls who are twice exceptional are particularly likely to have their intellectual abilities and talents overlooked; most often educators, parents, and even the girls themselves focus on what they cannot do—their disability—and fail to recognize and develop what they can do.

Diagnosis of twice exceptionality is often quite difficult; it is not a job for a family physician or a psychologist or psychiatrist who does not have training in both giftedness and mental disability. What makes diagnosis so very difficult is the probability of misdiagnosis based on insufficient information and observation, and as a result, sometimes the giftedness is overlooked, sometimes the disability is unnoticed, and sometimes both are passed over. The disability can mask the giftedness and the giftedness can mask the disability. Here are some of the problems that arise in diagnosing twice exceptionality:

Overlapping Profiles of Behaviors

It may be surprising to some, but many of the behaviors of giftedness actually resemble or overlap behaviors that are common with disabilities. Examples abound. The intense activity of a bored smart girl trying to stimulate herself by stirring up other kids in class with an off-task game or project may look like ADD with hyperactivity. The dreamy, spaced-out behavior of a smart girl fantasizing about her favorite book in order to tune out the drone of a lesson learned long ago looks like simple ADD without the hyperactivity. The loud, enthusiastic lecturing of a smart girl who has found a topic that fascinates her can appear to be the same as the obsessive lecturing and inattentiveness to others' cues of a child with Autism Spectrum Disorder. The long hours spent awake working on coding a new app and the frenzied attempt to meet a self-imposed deadline may look like mania. And a smart girl's strong preference for reading alone rather than physical and social activities may seem like depression. The list could go on and on.[277]

Too many smart girls whose behaviors simply deviate from other girls because of their intellectual interests, creativity, and independence are labeled with a disability. Context is critical. We have seen many girls who were considered difficult, noncompliant, and obnoxious in the regular classroom suddenly become enthusiastic, gregarious, and engaged in summer classes and camps for gifted kids.

The lesson is clear for parents and teachers who don't want a misdiagnosis based on overlapping behaviors: Always diagnose and treat the giftedness first. Challenge the smart girl intellectually with a group of gifted peers for an extended period. If the disturbing behaviors disappear or diminish greatly, then it is quite possible that a label of a disability is a misdiagnosis. Sadly, a misdiagnosis can follow a girl throughout her schooling, causing detrimental self-fulfilling prophesies; if teachers expect to see ADHD or depression, they are likely to focus on those behaviors that confirm that expectation.

Giftedness Masking Disability

On the other hand, sometimes a disability is really there, but it can be overlooked because a girl is bright enough to manage at least average schoolwork, even though her disability prevents her from showing the extent of her talents and perhaps even hides the presence of her disability. The struggle of a smart girl to mask her learning differences is exhausting—and she may not even know that she is struggling. When a girl has the ability to learn and reason rapidly, as well as the creativity to think up new ways of solving problems, she will often live with a learning disability for a long time before it is discovered. A smart girl with a specific learning disability such as dyslexia may use intense listening, memorization, and guesswork so well that teachers and parents cannot tell that she can't make out the words on the page properly. A smart girl with ADD, inattentive type, will be constantly late, careless, and absent-minded, but she will always have a last minute rush that produces something brilliant by the deadline or an imaginative, humorous excuse for her dereliction. Possibly more dangerous in the long run is the smart girl who has learned to mask her depression and anxiety with a vivacious, high-performing exterior self that prevents others from seeing the misery she is enduring.

Why do smart girls so often mask their disabilities? Because they can—and because girls have been socialized not to inconvenience others or make a fuss. Often, they are simply unaware of their differences, and they accept the constant struggle as a normal condition.

Different Behaviors in Different Contexts

Many twice-exceptional girls are perfectly happy, well-behaved, and busy at home with few issues or problems. In a safe and loving home, her parents intuitively meet her special needs despite not having named them. The smart girl with Asperger's symptoms may enjoy her hours alone or on the computer, and her parents support her solitary ways by giving her lots of space. When she turns to them with her current obsession—perhaps mapping Monarch butterflies on their migration—they are happy to obsess along with her, getting involved and excited about the project. They may even have a touch of Asperger's themselves and simply view themselves as a "geeky family." The difficulties come when teachers begin to report to parents that the student has a variety of disturbing tics at school, such as arm flapping and loud gulping; that other kids avoid her because she lectures them and says odd and sometimes cruel things to them; and that she ignores tasks in order to do her own thing. The parents may have a hard time believing she is the same girl that they know at home and suspect the teacher of exaggeration or deceit. At home, without the expectations of teachers and the distractions of peers, she may show little evidence of her disability.

However, when under pressure and hyper stimulation of noisy classmates and many changing tasks, she may become terrifically anxious—and the odd tics and blurting out strange sounds emerge. Without a knowledgeable teacher and school psychologist, things can go from bad to worse quickly—for the girl, her parents, and her teacher. This is the story for so many twice-exceptional girls: the accommodating home life in the early years, then the shock of the school environment that brings out the worst behaviors, then the conflicts between teacher and parents, and eventually the intervention of administrators.

Learning about Twice-Exceptional Girls

A solid foundation of knowledge is vital for both parents and teachers of twice-exceptional girls. Parents can find support and information in

SENG (Supporting Emotional Needs of the Gifted) parent support groups; teachers can find classes and professional development at many state and national gifted education conferences. The 2e Newsletter (www.2enewsletter.com) is an excellent primary resource with its website, newsletter, and book series. Bridges Academy (www.bridges.edu) in California is a prominent 2e school and its 2e Center for Research and Professional Development is well regarded. *Misdiagnosis and Dual Diagnoses of Gifted Children and Adults: ADHD, Bipolar, OCD, Asperger's, Depression, and Other Disorders,* by James T. Webb and his colleagues in neuroscience and cognitive psychology, is a good place to start learning about the complexities of this population of gifted children.[278] As Webb and other authors note, much less is known about twice-exceptional gifted girls than boys with the same issues. Many disorders such as ADHD, Autism Spectrum Disorder, and Oppositional-Defiant Disorder are much more prevalent—or at least more often diagnosed—in boys than in girls in general. So it is very important for parents and teachers to go the extra step of learning how these disorders show themselves in gifted girls from the few scholarly articles that are available to them.

Caution in Using Gifted-Specific Theories of Development

Although the literature on overexcitabilities is very popular in gifted education, particularly as a way of understanding misdiagnosed and twice-exceptional gifted people, the idea that gifted children and adults have different development, neurological structures, and reactions is still theoretical. As explained in Chapter 1, *overexcitabilities* are considered to be psychobiological tendencies of gifted people to be highly responsive to stimuli in a number of different areas—psychomotor, sensual, emotional, imaginational, and intellectual.[279] Most of these overexcitabilities seem to overlap with Big Five personality characteristics: aspects of imaginational and intellectual overlap with openness to experience; psychomotor reflects impulsive aspects of non-conscientiousness; and sensual reflects the overly sensitive aspects of neuroticism. Unlike the Big Five Personality Theory that has been extensively researched, O-E theory is based on small samples and case studies and does not have decades of research with tens of thousands of subjects; nor does it have supporting evidence of cross-cultural, genetic, and neurological validity.

The concept of overexcitabilities, based on the Dabrowski theory of developmental potential, provides a way of thinking about gifted individuals that makes them seem like they have a special path, a potential for a higher realm of human experience, than persons of average ability. We agree that high intelligence does indeed open up doors to extraordinary human occurrences of peak experiences, transcendental states, and engagement. It is the curiosity to seek access to all the greatest sources of wisdom that makes this possible, we believe, rather than any special cognitive or neurological differences.

Too often labeling a gifted child with particular overexcitabilities clouds diagnosis of twice exceptionalities and implies that serious symptoms of cognitive disability, anxiety, or mood disorders are somehow normal or even signs of giftedness. This can result in another kind of misdiagnosis because it is a *missed diagnosis* where an actual disorder is overlooked. On the other hand, there are some ways in which high intelligence can indeed both trigger and amplify disorders such as depression. Existential depression will be described later as a special case of depression in gifted people that requires more than the commonplace therapy.

A Different Face of ADHD

The greatest problem for smart girls with ADHD is discovering it. Most ADHD research has been done with boys, and it is well documented that it is under-diagnosed in girls.[280] The diagnosis of ADHD means a child experiences inattention, or hyperactivity and impulsiveness, or a combination of the two according to the *Diagnostic and Statistical Manual of Mental Disorders* (DSM-5). There are three subtypes of the disorder: where it is predominantly inattentive (ADHD-PI or ADHD-I); where it is predominantly hyperactive-impulsive (ADHD-HI or ADHD-H); or where the two are combined (ADHD-C). Felice Kaufmann, Layne Kalbfleish, and Xavier Castellanos have described how ADHD affects gifted children and how it can be treated, and Megan Foley Nicpon and her colleagues review some of the most helpful studies that describe identification and treatment for ADHD gifted students.[281]

Girls most often show their disorder as attention deficit *without* hyperactivity.[282] Smart girls who have ADD without hyperactivity are disorganized, absent-minded, messy, late, and scattered. They hop from one activity to another and are easily distracted from a task. Finishing any project is nearly impossible once they become bored with it.

Most teachers and parents know the male stereotype of the hyperactive child very well, but they have little awareness or knowledge of female types of ADD and ADHD.[283] If a girl does not act out, behave boisterously, disrupt the classroom, and defy the teacher, she is not likely to be diagnosed. Research shows, however, that the impact of ADD on preadolescent girls may be more severe than for boys.[284] If the girl lives in a stimulating home where her constantly shifting interests, messiness, and wackiness are not only tolerated but considered part of her creativity, then her parents may not know of her ADD until a troublesome event of poor judgment, such as forgetting to go to the tryouts for a play she desperately wanted to be in or failing to turn in an important project.

Smart girls with good social skills and high creativity also can use their charm and quick problem-solving to get out of one jam after another. They can whip together a project at the last minute, persuade a teacher to give them extra time, or wheedle parents into pleading for extra credit when their points don't add up because of absences or tardiness. Bright girls learn many ways of coping with and camouflaging their ADD, often telling themselves that someday in the future they will get organized, but still using shortcuts at the present. As Ed Hallowell, author of *Driven to Distraction*, said, "For the ADD person, there is just *now* and eternity, and nothing in between."[285]

Girls with ADD are at risk for a wide variety of other difficulties and disorders.[286] Smart ADD girls, whether with and without hyperactivity, are often rejected by other girls who don't like to play or socialize with them because of their unpredictability. Feminine gender roles require girls to be neat, punctual, and compliant with authority, and smart girls with ADD are usually none of these. Often, male teachers will like them more than will female teachers, especially female teachers who prefer traditional gender role behavior.

Most children with ADD or ADHD seem to have an inflated idea of their abilities, particularly in their weakest area. They have learned to cover up their problems with bravado. Smart girls with ADD will often insist on very challenging projects because they are intuitively aware that they have the intellectual skills, but they are perpetually unaware of how their disorganization will sabotage their best efforts. The end result is low self-esteem and despair, usually masked with gaiety and seeming unconcern. By adolescence, girls with undiagnosed ADD have often dug some serious holes for themselves with uneven grades, risky behaviors, and a marginalized peer group.

Fortunately, with early diagnosis, family support, professional counseling, and perhaps carefully adjusted medication, most smart ADD girls can succeed. The creative fields of art, music, and dramatic arts are particularly good ones for women with ADD, and even academic areas where they can find flow experiences will be welcoming. Smart girls with ADD and ADHD, even with good life-skills training and medication, will likely always need caring support for their underlying feelings of shame and sadness. More important though, they will need environments where their liveliness, fearlessness, and creativity can thrive. For ADD smart girls, fine arts and performing arts camps are a joyous experience, and special schools for the arts bring them in contact with lots of kids like themselves. Even peers and teachers who don't suffer from ADHD are likely to be more tolerant and more willing to see the strengths of these girls.

Creative women with ADHD will often describe the "gift" of ADHD. One woman colleague said, "It made me different. It made me unafraid. Because I was rejected by other girls, I had to live in my own world, and I ended up creating my own art therapy business in the same way—by choosing to be different and helping others like me to have courage to create."

Mood Disorders

Mood disorders are severe or prolonged mood states that disrupt daily functioning. The DSM-5 divides mood disorders into two categories: Depressive Disorder and Bipolar Disorder. Major depression is a single severe period of depression, marked by negative or hopeless thoughts and physical symptoms. Depression is not sadness or a negative reaction to a bad experience. It is a serious condition that involves changes in sleep patterns; feelings of sadness, grief, worthlessness, hopelessness, shame, and guilt; fatigue and physical symptoms; difficulty with concentration and decision making; and disturbed or irrational thinking.

Bipolar disorders are conditions in which people experience two extremes in mood. They alternate between depression and mania or hypomania, which is an extremely high-energy, optimistic state without delusions. Mania is a clearly abnormal elevation in mood that is excessively cheerful with wild, grandiose ideas, extreme energy, and sleeplessness. The person is enthusiastic and talkative to the point of wearing everybody out. Occasionally, the high energy is channeled into irritability and anger. In a severe manic state, young women are likely to have terrifically poor judgment, go on spending sprees, abuse drugs and alcohol, and engage in inappropriate sexual relationships.

Hypomania is not as severe as mania and does not cause the level of impairment in work and social activities that mania can. In fact, hypomania is a very common characteristic of creative people; entrepreneurs, innovators, artists, and writers benefit from the feeling of being wide awake, energetic, courageous, and exuberant in their ideas. Hypomania for smart girls is only dangerous when it leads to exhaustion and fatigue-related illnesses (like mononucleosis and walking pneumonia) or when it turns into full-blown mania. Sometimes a person's hypomania can be triggered into full-blown mania by a stressful event or by two or three sleepless nights (like during finals week).

Finally, persistent depressive disorder is a frequently occurring negative mood that does not seem related to particular events, but brings a loss of energy, interest, and engagement over a long period of time. Some people seem to have a temperament that predisposes them to this mild sort of depression. In smart girls, such dysthymia is often accompanied by dysfunctional perfectionism, eating disorders, and social isolation.

Are smart girls more likely to have mood disorders than other girls? The answer is complex. Most studies of gifted children who are in gifted education classes, summer camps, and programs for gifted children are found to be better adjusted than average students. In addition, from Terman's studies of high-intelligence children to today's studies, it has usually been found that high intelligence is associated with good social adjustment, low incidence of mental disorders, better health, and higher well being. On the other hand, from Leta Hollingworth's studies until today's studies that examine different levels of giftedness, the findings are consistent that as intelligence increases past the 99th percentile of intellectual ability, people are so different from their peers that they experience a wide variety of emotional reactions ranging from mild chronic depression to occasional major depressive disorder.

In addition, studies of creative individuals often showed a high incidence of Bipolar Spectrum Disorders, once called Manic-Depressive Disorder, among creative writers, artists, and musicians.[287] Unfortunately, most of those studies were done with small, select groups of creative individuals, often those who actually sought help.[288] As a result, the relationship between creativity and mood is still unclear; broader, well-designed studies are needed to resolve the centuries-long controversies about the relationship of creative genius to mood problems.

It is safe to say, however, that *something* is going on with highly gifted and highly creative people that prompts them to suffer from gloomy depressions or disruptive mood swings. Whether the links are genetic and neurobiological, stress-related, or some combination doesn't really matter to the person experiencing these awful moods; what matters is that mood disorders can diminish the realization of potential and ruin academic achievement, careers, and relationships. Gifted young women with mood disorders are more likely to experiment with substances in order to self-medicate, but they are likely to deteriorate rapidly while maintaining the appearance of normalcy and to experience eating disorders or other physical symptoms in addition to sadness and morbid thoughts. Criticality of others and self-criticism are often the first signs of a descent into a depressive disorder, with the depressed mood following on the heels of a long bout of criticism of self and others.

James T. Webb has suggested that bright people, particularly the more idealistic ones, are predisposed to special forms of mood disorders such as existential depression.[289] In *Searching for Meaning: Idealism, Bright Minds, Disillusionment, and Hope*, he describes the overwhelming sadness that occurs when a strong intellectual awareness of the problems of the human condition—disease, poverty, environmental destruction, violence and war, aging, and the inevitability of death—is coupled with a sense of individual helplessness to do anything about it.

Gifted girls from a very young age have the ability, though perhaps not the equanimity required, to read the news reports of the day, to watch disturbing videos, and to pore over the sad history of "man's inhumanity to man." A 10-year-old girl might be able to read the accounts of Nazi concentration camps by survivors, watch the horrors on film, and even read historian's analyses, but at age 10, not only does she feel she can't do anything to prevent these things, but she may also lack the emotional and cognitive maturity to process and integrate this disturbing information.

Gifted girls are profoundly upset by hypocrisy, and the news is often full of people pretending to care about justice or equality but working for the opposite. When the subject of the news is the role of women, gifted girls listen and watch attentively. What is it like to be 11 and read about rape, kidnapping, forced marriage, female genital mutilation, and bride burning in the international news? What does it mean to a 7-year-old girl encouraged by her teachers and parents to be curious and achieving, but the other girls depicted in the media are merely cute and nice? Smart girls realize that they are handicapped in their desire to take action against inhumanity, hypocrisy, and injustice, not only by their age but also their role as second-class citizens in much of the world. To transcend the anger and despair of existential depression, gifted girls need help searching for meaning and hope.

In the chapter on eminent women, we showed how gifted and creative women fell in love with an idea—and suddenly had the strength to go on. Sometimes that idea is indeed, as it was for Sonia Sotomayor, the idea of justice. Sometimes the idea is not related to overcoming the evils of the world but to creating more beauty, order, or knowledge instead. Noticing and describing some aspect of the universe becomes a way of making sense of some small corner of the vastness. Just experiencing the flow of consciousness that comes with creating a new essay or painting is often enough to give a smart girl hope. The original existentialist, Jean-Paul Sartre, said, "Be engaged." And that is good advice for smart girls.

Strong emotions, including mood swings, can benefit girls and help them be engaged. At the CLEOS counseling project for creative people, we have found that a mild form of bipolar disorder—where mood swings between hypomania and mild depression—are actually an advantage for creative work when deliberately managed by the person. Hypomania aids the writer, artist, or musician in the early stage of creativity, when ideas flow freely and unusual connections are made. In the hypomanic state, the artist has energy for long days and nights at work and the motivation to complete the project. When the project is complete, the artist falls into exhausted sleep, only to awake in a dysthymic, low mood—which happens to be great for editing, evaluation, and revision. The earlier carefree, fearless mood is replaced by criticality, concern for detail, and the need to repair gaps or flaws in the project. Is it any wonder that moderately bipolar people are drawn to creative work—or that creative work is best accomplished by moderately bipolar creative people? That is why we work with creative people to *manage* their moods, rather than to simply strive for a constant even state. Ups and downs are fine, if they are somewhat predictable, planned for, and effectively used for the right kind of work. When they break through into serious depression or mania, then medication and psychotherapy may be needed.

Anxiety Disorders

Anxiety is a normal reaction to stress and, when mild and short-lived, can enhance performance. Athletes, performers, and people who are effective test-takers know that an optimal amount of tension is necessary to get charged up for a challenge and they learn to enjoy the increasing arousal and anticipation of competition.

For some people, however, anxiety can become prolonged and intense—and it loses its functionality. Extreme anxiety is difficult to control because most of the person's attention is simply on immediate survival, rather than on clear thinking and problem solving. For smart girls, anxiety is often related to overly high expectations of oneself or attempts to fulfill the impossible expectations of others. Anxiety often is experienced along with depression. The types of anxiety currently recognized by the DSM-5 and which may be experienced by smart girls are: Anxiety Disorders, Obsessive-Compulsive Disorder, and Trauma and Stressor-Related Disorders. Generalized Anxiety Disorder (GAD) is one of the most common anxieties experienced by smart girls; it is a pervasive state of worrying and tension about everyday matters, along with a belief that it is uncontrollable. GAD is only diagnosed when it has lasted longer than six months. People with anxiety disorders sweat, fidget, tense their muscles, and experience nausea, headaches, or other physical symptoms. Panic disorder, which often goes along with other anxiety disorders, is characterized by sudden bursts of fear, the desire to flee, heart palpitations, and rapid breathing that may be unrelated to any identifiable trigger. A large proportion of young people who go to emergency rooms with panic disorder had been taking prescribed or un-prescribed anti-anxiety medication and then suddenly stopped, setting off an awful rebound. Social anxiety is an increasing fear and nervousness that arises from being around other people, especially when having to ask for help, make a phone call to a stranger, or enter a roomful of people. Smart girls and young women may associate this anxiety with going to school, taking physical education classes, or participating in disliked after school activities, particularly when they have been rejected by other girls.

Given that girls and young women have all of the above anxiety disorders at twice the rate of boys and men, parents and teachers should be alert for the signs of anxiety in gifted girls.[290] Smart girls have legitimate issues to be anxious about, particularly when they are required to spend all day in regular classes. Just being bored can lead to such a high level of anxiety that the girl may feel like a caged animal; she cannot find anything in the lesson to interest her and is not allowed to pursue her own interests. Being different from other girls—by virtue of being highly gifted and unable to hide it or highly creative and not wanting to hide it—can put smart girls in danger of bullying and cyberbullying. Knowing their vulnerability, bright girls might come to dread school and avoid being in any situation that can give other girls an opportunity to bully them. In this way, legitimate sources of stress that are not addressed can lead to overreaction and generalization—and a state of anxiety that is unbearable. With counseling and practice, however, smart girls can learn to manage their thinking in ways that reduce their anxiety to manageable levels.[291]

Obsessive-Compulsive Disorder (OCD) ranges from looping, repetitive thoughts or behaviors that are barely noticeable to others to obsessions and compulsions that are crippling to the person. Some of the more common ones include hand-washing compulsions, physical or psychological rituals such as counting tiles in the ceiling or chairs in a room, or repetitive tics such as arm flapping and grunting. OCD tends to occur later in females than in males and symptoms are less severe in that the behaviors are usually less aggressive and less intense.[292]

Two important aspects of OCD are first, that the sufferers know that the obsessions or behaviors are irrational, and second, they believe they must engage in them. In fact, for many people with OCD, the ritualistic behaviors are a way of coping with the obsessive thoughts. There is a normal period of childhood between four and seven when most children have obsessions or compulsions, and children with active imaginations can come up with some unusual rituals to calm their anxious, repetitive thoughts.[293] Some childhood cases, however, seem to be related to strep infections and the OCD can come on very suddenly and feature severe tics and obvious repetitive movements; these are called PANDAS (Pediatric Autoimmune Neuropsychiatric Disorders Associated with Streptococcal infections).[294] Although still in early stages of research, parents and professionals should be alert to this possibility.

For parents of smart girls, it is important to remember that simple perfectionism, cleanliness, and tidiness are not the same as OCD. In fact, there is such a thing as healthy perfectionism, a positive attitude about doing one's best that is common in bright students.[295] Only when obsessions or compulsions become dysfunctional—such as taking up at least an hour of her time and interfering with other activities—do they represent OCD; unfortunately, a smart girl can come up with many rationalizations and arguments for maintaining her compulsions. OCD usually responds well to counseling, though progress can be slow.

Trauma-related disorders occur when a girl has been exposed to an overwhelming experience that is just too much for her coping skills. This can include loss of a significant person, exposure to violence, sexual, or other abuse, presence at a disaster, or any number of frightening situations. Although most bright girls have good coping skills, even the most resilient smart girl can become painfully anxious when too many stressful events occur one after another. The stories of eminent women often include times in their lives when they had traumas and trauma-related anxieties. What remains a mystery is how so many smart women not only eventually coped with anxiety but transcended it to become "better than well." This is the hope we must hold out to gifted girls who suffer from anxieties of all kinds—that bright women like themselves have found themselves not only healing but also finding meaning and purpose as they transformed their suffering into action and creation.

Autism Spectrum Disorders

Autism spectrum disorders involve delayed or abnormal functioning before the age of three in one or more of the following: social interaction; communication; and restricted, repetitive, and stereotyped patterns of behavior and interests. Until recently, symptoms of social awkwardness and restricted interests without intellectual delays were called Asperger's Syndrome, but in the new DSM-5, all of these disorders will now be called Autism Spectrum Disorder (ASD). Sadly, many gifted young people who are merely uninterested in social relationships and have a grand passion for a particular topic—like engines, dinosaurs, horses, or science fiction—will be labeled as autistic or as suffering Social (Pragmatic) Communication Disorder, a disorder that is newly listed in DSM-5.[296]

True ASD usually includes symptoms such as repetitive routines or rituals, peculiarities in speech and language, inappropriate emotions or social behavior, and problems reading nonverbal cues such as facial expressions, intonation, or postural behaviors of others. Young people with ASD also often have clumsy or uncoordinated motor skills.

Another diagnosis that might mislabel gifted kids is *subthreshold autism* or *atypical autism*, because of its milder symptoms or symptoms in only one domain, such as social difficulties. However, a great many smart girls have perfectly good social knowledge and skills—but they deliberately choose not to use them in order to be left alone to read or think. In adolescence, with their increasing interest in peers and romantic relationships, smart girls can seem to suddenly blossom into normal, socially active teens. Even if your daughter has been diagnosed accurately since she was very young as having classic autistic behaviors, remember that she can have a happy and fulfilled life if she is allowed to pursue her special interests, develop her expertise, and escape society's demands that everybody be sociable. See Temple Grandin's many books and articles to understand the true potential of gifted autistic girls.[297]

Getting Help for Twice-Exceptional Girls

Focus on the Giftedness or Talent

In many developed countries, mental health systems for children are well established and often free or low cost. In the U.S., however, mental health care is difficult to find, expensive, and often inexpert. In addition, finding appropriate treatment for smart girls with any of the disorders we have discussed means first finding a psychologist with expertise in giftedness, or at least one that is willing to learn about giftedness. The Hoagies website

keeps a current list of psychologists at www.hoagiesgifted.org/psychologists.
htm. There are, in addition, many psychologists with expertise in gifted
education at universities and in communities not on this list. Consult with
the coordinator of gifted education at your school or a faculty member in
the gifted education training program at a local university. Be aware that
most school counselors spend their time with low-performing students, and
most school psychologists spend their time in testing students with learning
disabilities, so your best bet in your school is the gifted educator.

Why should you start with a psychologist with expertise in gifted
rather than with your family physician? First of all, your family doctor
probably has had only a short period of training in psychological diagnosis
and treatment—perhaps one rotation of a few months—whereas clinical
psychologists have four or more years of training in these areas. Second,
very few family doctors have any expertise in identifying how giftedness
interacts with the wide variety of disorders, how it may mask disorders,
or how it may be mistaken for disorders. In fairness, we must say that
this lack of training and expertise goes for most psychiatrists, psychologists, counselors, licensed psychiatric nurses, and social workers as well,
and parents may have to help educate these otherwise quite competent
professionals. Psychologists, too, are less likely to suggest medications
too quickly. Psychologists in most states do not prescribe medication,
but if your daughter needs psychiatric medication, a psychologist with
expertise in gifted usually can make a referral to a physician with similar
understanding. If your insurance requires a visit to your primary care
physician for a referral, simply tell them that you would like a referral to
one of the psychologists recommended by gifted educators, and then go
forward from there.

Read and Become Educated

Parents and educators will need to gather a lot of information about
giftedness and related areas. Remember that there is a lot of pop psychology
and misinformation on the Internet. Be cautious! Information about mental
health issues is best gleaned from the National Institute of Mental Health
website (www.nimh.nih.gov/health/publications/index.shtml) or from
National Association for Mental Illness, an advocacy group (www.nami.
org). The Supporting Emotional Needs of Gifted (SENG) website (www.
sengifted.org) provides many free, downloadable articles, as well as a list of
recommended organizations and helpful books. The National Association
for Gifted Children (http://www.nagc.org/resources-publications/resources)

and the American Psychological Association (www.apa.org/education/k12/ gifted.aspx) also have resources for social and emotional needs of gifted. Megan Foley Nicpon at the Belin-Blank Center for Gifted Education has summarized much of what is known about twice-exceptional gifted students in her articles.[298] Susan Baum has described a variety of giftedness/ disability combinations and suggested ways of helping these students to achieve their potential.[299] Parents who persist will be able to find the information they need.

Slow Down and Breathe

When symptoms or unusual behaviors emerge in your daughter or when a friend or teacher gives you an unsolicited diagnosis for your daughter, the first thing to do is just slow down and breathe. All children have emotional outbursts, behave disruptively, and challenge authority occasionally, and gifted girls tend to be quite strong-willed. Your smart daughter, with her advanced vocabulary and wide knowledge, may seem like a small adult—until she blows up over nothing, makes unreasonable demands, or insists on dressing and acting very strangely just for fun. Take time to listen to her. Is she depressed or enjoying alone time? Does she have ADHD or is she just bored? Is she reciting mathematical facts because she has ASD or is she just in love with numbers? Share your concerns, share information with her, and go slowly. If you are concerned that she is twice exceptional and are not sure what to do, we suggest you consult with a pediatric neuropsychologist, an expert in twice-exceptional gifted, and other parents of twice-exceptional kids. Find out everything you can and then, with the help of caring experts, design an academic and treatment program that will build on your smart girl's strengths.

CHAPTER 12

Privilege, Power, and Talent: Minority Smart Girls

When most people think of the word *gifted*, the ideas of *elitism* and *privilege* come to mind. Although educators of gifted children react with dismay when they meet this criticism from their friends and colleagues, there is a kernel of truth to the association of giftedness and privilege. That is because, as anybody can observe, most children who are labeled *gifted* and placed in gifted programs in schools are indeed white, upper middle-class students. Students who are from cultural and ethnic minorities are distinctly underrepresented, and we are losing many gifted girls from those groups because of this.

In a country like the U.S. where people are increasingly sensitized to the extreme gap between the rich and the rest of us, the idea that children of the wealthy are most likely to receive special opportunities for gifted rankles. As Joy Davis points out in *Bright, Talented, and Black*, even in the poorest African-American communities, bright, creative children exist and often emerge and shine within their communities, but they may never be identified and labeled in our underfunded schools.[300]

Sharon Kurpius and I learned, in our 10-year long gender equity studies with talented at-risk girls (TARGETS), that there is no shortage of Hispanic, Navajo, Apache, Pima, and Hopi girls who are rapid learners and quick problem-solvers—but often the ways they manifest their abilities were not those on which they were being tested. To be bilingual at four years old or to memorize hours of Native American chants and ceremonies at age 12 were not recognized talents—despite the extraordinary value of those skills to their communities. It is so frustrating to have to continually remind

241

people that intelligence and creativity are everywhere throughout
the human community. —Barbara

The extreme lack of privilege has clear and strong implications for impeding a child's potential. It is obvious even in infancy that hunger, fear, restricted environments, and unstable home settings can begin to dismantle the potential for achievement and creativity for desperately poor children. No amount of fiddling with standardized tests to make them less biased will stop the dance of genes and environment that begins even before birth. In fact, nonverbal tests based on Raven's Progressive Matrices and other attempts to create less biased tests for minority students have been disappointing.[301] Privilege enhances the bias. Children who have good nutrition, loving parenting, and enriched, safe communities will be able to capitalize on their opportunities. Their intelligence will literally be nourished through good diet and expanded through exposure to varied and plentiful information. Their creativity will be encouraged and nurtured through music lessons, arts exposure, and access to technology. Like the previous examples of the Matthew Effect, as the years go by, the gap in achievement grows larger as the enriched grow richer.

Privilege is a word that privileged people don't like because it implies that they did not work hard for what they have. Certainly, it is true that many eminent and prosperous people have worked hard, but few succeeded without having the head start that privilege can provide. Many privileged people simply assume that other people could have what they have if they just worked hard enough, but even if it were true (and it's not), children should not be held responsible for their parents' failings. People who have benefited from being white, or male, or wealthy, or living with their nation's citizenship and major language are often blind to what it is like not to have the extra advantages that come along with being the dominant people in a society—the ones with power.

My colleagues, Karen Multon, Sharon Kurpius, Marie Hammond, and I set out to understand the interplay of talent and privilege when we developed our Distance from Privilege scale for our NSF project "Milestones and Danger Zones for Talented Young Women," and we discovered that we had an immense task ahead of us. We learned, first of all, that objective privilege is not as important as perceived privilege—that is, the distance people believed themselves to be from the dominant groups in society affected their behavior more than the observable differences. So we had to develop a measure that asked young women how they felt they rated in the eyes of their society—how acceptable they believed their particular identity was.

Second, we learned that a great many factors came into play in people's minds when judging how far they were from privilege. For African-American girls, it was race that seemed to separate them most from privilege; for Muslim girls, it was religion; for Hispanic girls, it was citizenship or language differences; and for white girls, it was gender and attractiveness. For rural girls, it was their geographic location. For lesbians, it was sexual orientation. From our early findings, we constructed a scale that asked girls about their gender, race, socioeconomic status, language, sexual orientation, citizenship, religion, age, attractiveness, geographic location, disability status, and intelligence, and then we considered how those factors influence gifted girls.[302] *—Barbara*

The Special Case of Race

It is no secret that minority girls, with the exception of Asian-Americans, are underrepresented in U.S. gifted programs.[303] Smart girls who are members of minority groups, both in the U.S. and internationally, are less likely to be identified as gifted or provided special programming to encourage their talents. Gifted education programs may not have curricula that are culturally sensitive, so that minority smart girls don't have models in the literature they read and the images they see of success and accomplishment. In the U.S., each recognized minority group has its own challenges in navigating education for bright students. The fact that "race" is even considered a biological reality rather than a social construction makes a society less likely to recognize the brilliance in people who are considered "other" by virtue of the color of their skin.

African-American Smart Girls

In the U.S., race is usually considered to be the most powerful, visible predictor of acceptance and approval, no matter what your talents or personality characteristics might be. That is what Martin Luther King meant when he said, "I have a dream that my four little children will one day live in a nation where they will not be judged by the color of their skin but by the content of their character." Many African-American girls grow up believing that their skin color is too dark and their hair isn't very acceptable, and even if their own families celebrate blackness, the media will make it difficult not to see that the majority of women depicted in media have white skin and light-colored hair. They see that others expect them to be "Jezebels" who are sexy and seductive, to live in homes headed by single mothers, to be poor, and to accept that they are not expected to achieve.

African-American girls know all the stereotypes from an early age. When Kiri Davis was in high school, she began interviewing other African-American teens about their experience of being black girls.[304] In college, she repeated the famous "Doll Experiment" first performed five decades earlier by psychologist Kenneth Clark. In the doll experiment, four-year-old black children are shown a white doll and a black doll and asked, "Which is the good one? Which is the bad one? Why?" The majority of black children, even five decades after desegregation, still chose the white doll as the "good" doll and the black doll as the "bad" one—stunning evidence of the powerful effect that is called *internalized racism*.

Kiri Davis's film *A Girl Like Me* is one of the best ways of understanding what it is to be a black girl in America.[305] In this film, one can see a strong illustration of how internalized racism leads to problems with identity. How does an African-American girl achieve in school if she believes that to achieve is to "act white" and that to comply with teachers is to betray her own friends? How is she to approach achievement tests when she believes she is just being set up, once again, to show how black people don't achieve?

Frank Worrell, a researcher on the issues of African-American gifted students, advocates for focusing on the strengths of these students, as well as their resources for resilience. In his studies, he found that those African-American students who have dual identities—both as an African-American and as an American—seem to have the most success. Worrell has made it clear that the gap in achievement test scores between African-American and white students is not the result of bias in the tests; instead, he says, it reflects the long-standing gap in actual achievement related to the differences in sociocultural and individual issues of these students.[306] Although bias in tests is not a cause of the differences, buying into negative stereotypes and racial identity can contribute importantly. That is why his work supports the idea that African-American students need help countering their internalized negative stereotypes by claiming dual identities as well as understanding and acting on their strengths.

In a study that my colleagues and I conducted of very bright minority students who had scored in the 95th percentile on the ACT, we found that many African-American gifted students claimed that their greatest accomplishment during high school was "just surviving." They had survived and thrived, according to them, because of their family support, their heavy participation in their churches, their teachers' confidence in them, and because important adults kept them safe from the violence, drugs, alcohol, and the despair of the surrounding community. Our follow-up of these high achievers in college showed that the most successful ones had resolved their identity issues by proudly claiming their racial identity, joining with African-American students and faculty in social change organizations, and challenging stereotypes with their achievement. "I had something to prove became the theme of the research."[307] —Barbara

Paradoxically, there is some evidence from an early AAUW study in 1991 that African-American girls were less likely than white girls to lose self-esteem during their teen years; the authors of that study believed that African-American mothers effectively taught their daughters that their true worth might not be judged fairly and thus helped them to be more sophisticated than white girls in understanding racism and sexism.[308] It is interesting, too, that many more African-American women than men attend and graduate from college, and that they are incarcerated much less often than African-American men (1 out of 6 African American men are in correctional institutions).[309] They are more likely than white girls to learn independence because they learn to expect that they will have to work all their lives. Joy Davis and Donna Ford, who have written extensively about the strengths of African-American girls and women, conclude that these young women have potential far beyond what has been expected, measured, or identified.[310]

To be black, gifted, and female is to deal daily with the paradox of outer powerlessness and inner strength; although teachers and parents can never resolve the paradox for these girls, they can emphasize their strengths and show them ways to overcome their lesser power through education, enrichment, and passion for an idea.

It should be noted for our international readers that the barriers encountered by African-American girls with American racism will have parallels for girls descended from slaves in countries such as Brazil and Haiti. Wherever people have been brought unwillingly in servitude to another country, their descendants suffer the lingering scars of racism for generations afterwards.

Native American Smart Girls

I have had such profound experiences with the Native American girls with whom I worked that I was propelled into an entire new area of study of Native American languages, culture, and religion. Only when I had learned enough Navajo, Apache, and Lakota language, as well as how to honor the spiritual traditions of my Native American friends did I fully recognize both the immense barriers and amazing strengths of Native American gifted girls.
—Barbara

It is a sad commentary about schools that most Native American gifted students are taught by white teachers and selected for gifted education by white specialists. Many of the teachers on reservations only speak a few words and phrases of the languages of their students, despite a decades-long push for the reclaiming of Native American languages. A wonderful exception to this was the leadership of school principal, neuroscientist, and Navajo holy singer, Harold Begay in Tuba City. Harold Begay and C. June Maker, in *When Geniuses Fail: Na Dene' (Navajo) Conception of Giftedness in the Eyes of the Holy Deities*, showed how Native American views of giftedness and education can differ profoundly from European American conceptions.[311] Among the Navajo, giftedness is perceived as a special maturity, or *hoya*, that is a gift from the sacred deities. The gifts are described as follows:

Ayoo Ba'iiliil—Extraordinary transcendent power to cause effect.

Ayoo Ba'iideelni—Skill to cause a consequence in concrete and immediate matters.

Ayoo t'aa doole'i nizhonigoiil'I—Exceptional ability to always do things or make things in the right way, exemplifying highly desired character values.

A girl considered gifted by the Navajo may have a special capacity for healing, a role as caretaker of Earth and its beings, or a gift for being a family provider. She may have proficiency with the symbols and ways of communication with the deities and the ceremonies that bring health; a skill for peacemaking through empathy; a skill for leadership through consensus and self-discipline; or skills in traditional arts, cuisine, handling of livestock, making the home structure, storytelling, and teaching. Within a family or community, a child's gifts are noticed and observed carefully by elders who gradually introduce the child to adult knowledge and skills appropriate to the child's gifts. Begay describes the complexity and care that is taken, for example, in the teaching of dry painting, with symbols represented by as many as 10,000 words.

Smart Native American girls on reservations are hindered by the devastation of their communities through poverty, poor nutrition, alcohol, drugs, gangs, and gambling addictions. The girls with whom I worked usually had several alcoholics in their immediate families, had witnessed domestic violence, and had been solicited by gangs and drug dealers. Despite these impediments, the smart Native American girls in our study had achieved *A*s in their math and science classes and had won talent contests and beauty pageants (a very different kind of pageant focusing on traditional skills and beautiful demeanor). They had also worked part-time, acted as the major caretakers for siblings for long periods of time, participated in important roles in traditional ceremonies and Powwows, and had aspirations to become leaders of their community.

With 561 federally recognized tribes, nations, and communities of Native Americans, we have an extreme diversity of native languages, history, traditions, and worldviews. Native American gifted children may speak only English; they may have learned their tribal language as their first language, often from grandparents, and speak English as a second language; or they may speak English but learn their tribal language in school. Many of these students are multilingual; for example, many Navajo students understand other Athabaskan languages such as Apache and use some of the Hopi language and the Spanish of their neighbors.

Each tribe has a history that may cover thousands of years of residence in the same place, or a removal from their homeland, or having both land and customs devastated and families dispersed. For many Native American children, the grief resulting from the loss of culture is unresolved through generations. The high rates of poverty, substance abuse, domestic abuse, and unemployment seem to be strongly related to the loss of cultural traditions. The majority of scholars agree that the key to well-being for Native American youth is not assimilation into the dominant culture but rather an education that embraces the tribal culture as well as providing skills that allow young people to succeed in the dominant culture.

Hispanic-American Smart Girls

Like all demographic designations, Hispanic-American is socially, not biologically, based; it is neither a race nor a distinct ethnicity. This group of smart girls includes Mexican-American girls, the largest group, as well as girls whose families originate in any Spanish-speaking country: Puerto Rico, Cuba, Guatemala, Nicaragua, Dominican Republic, or even Pacific Island Spanish speakers. Many generalizations have been made about Hispanic Americans, but in the rapidly changing urban areas where many have migrated, generalizations start to weaken as acculturation (the process of learning about and participating in the new culture) increases and traditions are lost or changed. Some of the generalizations applied to Hispanic gifted girls assert that they are more family-oriented than other groups, that they are less achievement-oriented, and that their culture is much more religious, patriarchal, and sexist. New research on Hispanic families shows that while there is some truth to these generalizations, usually formulated for first-generation immigrants, there is much more complexity than others originally assumed. Maureen Neihart, who studied poor, Hispanic adolescent gifted, said:

> *Gifted students from lower-socioeconomic backgrounds may be encouraged to work hard in school but discouraged from pursuing a college education or from taking accelerated classes. Parents may tolerate the pursuit of high achievement only as long as it doesn't interfere with earning a paycheck or with responsibilities at home. In low-income families, there may be a greater expectation to marry young and secure a job rather than go to college. Some low-income families may not view college as worth the financial sacrifice. In families where no one has college experience, adults are not aware of financial aid resources that would make college possible, nor are they aware of ways to prepare for college admission.*[312]

In our own study of Mexican-American and Central American gifted girls, we found it to be true that many families did not have much knowledge of the educational and occupational structure of the U.S.—but were proud of their daughters' achievements. The strong influence of the father is considered to be the mark of patriarchal Hispanic families; however, most of the girls in our study were not discouraged by their fathers from achievement. A more in-depth look at Hispanic families shows that girls and boys are indeed treated differently, particularly in first-generation families. The differences are mainly in the number of privileges, chores, and money given; girls have fewer privileges, more chores, and less money. They are, nevertheless, encouraged to do well in school. We found that Hispanic girls were particularly close to their mothers, especially when they were single mothers; these girls wanted their moms to be proud, and they also wanted to do everything they could to help and support them.

In the last decade, the English-Only Movement was seen by Hispanics as a direct threat to their culture and community. Most research has shown that education that allows a child to transition from native language to the new language with respect for the first language and culture is the most effective form of education.[313] Both bilingual education and a structured English immersion are effective if the school provides continued, dedicated support for emergent language learners.[314] One form of prejudice against Hispanics that has emerged is the attempt by legislators in several states to shut down any form of bilingual education programs, to force all children into English-only classrooms and schools and even to forbid the teaching of multicultural courses that include information about Mexican culture.[315] Advocates for English-only claimed that bilingualism demotivated students from learning English. Nowhere is that claim more untrue than in the case of gifted Hispanic girls, most of whom learn English at an astonishing rate. Although the primary issue facing recently-migrated, Hispanic gifted girls is that of performing in a new language, the greater verbal ability of girls and the rapidity with which smart girls learn means that English is usually quickly acquired. This is why so many little Hispanic girls become the translators for entire families. The prejudice that non-English speaking Hispanics encounter is strong, and most Hispanic children are eager to learn to avoid the humiliation they encounter in many communities.

Citizenship privilege is intertwined with language and cultural privilege for Hispanic-Americans. In cities like Phoenix, Arizona, Spanish-speaking (and even Hispanic-looking) people were targeted by the county sheriff for interrogation and arrest; people who even looked like Mexicans had to be careful to carry proper identification.[316] If their parents are undocumented, children often feel a crippling fear that they may be discovered; many Hispanic, undocumented children dread going to school or even being seen too often outside of their house. Bright girls living in the shadows seldom have the opportunity to show their talents.

Another issue for gifted Hispanic girls is mobility. Hispanic families move much more often than other families in the U.S.; sometimes it is for greater opportunities and other times it is to avoid risky neighborhoods and bad schools. Every time a girl changes schools, the transition is difficult. It is important to remember that when children perceive the move to be for greater opportunities and better schooling, then the transition is much less difficult than if they feel forced to move.

Stereotypes of Hispanic women, or Latinas, break down at the college level. Once they have made it to college, Latina smart women are likely to be high achievers, strivers who are focused and engaged. They often are more individualistic and independent than was expected by their professors, and their ambitions are frequently at odds with the low expectations that others may have of them.

Gifted Hispanic girls need support for their strengths. For example, a girl who can learn English in one year can probably learn other languages easily as well. It is remarkable how often extraordinary linguistic ability is taken for granted in these girls. Families may not know how to support the strengths of their daughters, and given the differences in treatment of boys and girls, it may be important to encourage mothers and fathers to give their daughters more independence and privileges—particularly when that means attending special programs for gifted students and college preparation programs.

One of the most successful programs in which we participated was the Hispanic Mother-Daughter program, where mother and adolescent daughter pairs attended banquets at Arizona State University and learned together what is needed to prepare for college. Not only did the program increase the number of Latinas going to college, but also a number of mothers then went to school with their daughters.

Traditions that provide support are important. For example, an over-whelmingly Catholic population has indeed sometimes encouraged *marianismo*, the belief that females should be pure as the Virgin Mary, nurturing, loving, forgiving of errant males, and tolerant of suffering. In our observations, many Hispanic girls find the church is a place of learning and support for a more active perspective.[317] In the veneration of Our Lady of Guadalupe, many gifted Latina Catholic girls see a role model, not of passivity, but of power, serenity, and strength. The tradition of the Quinceañera—the celebration of the girl's 15th birthday—is a strong tradition in many Hispanic families. Although it can be just a big, happy birthday party, it can also be a time to celebrate the achievements of a young woman's life and the anticipations of more to come. Parents of Hispanic smart girls can use this important rite of passage to strengthen their daughter's identity as a leader.

Asian-American Smart Girls

Asian-American girls often carry the heavy burden of the Model Minority stereotype, a commonly held myth in the United States that all Asian-American students are super high achievers who do little except study and who are utterly obedient to authority.[318] The stereotype of the Model Minority can raise the anxiety levels of Asian-American girls; this has been added to by the uproar surrounding the publication of the *Battle Hymn of the Tiger Mother* by Amy Chua.[319] Amy Chua claims that the strict, authoritarian, hard-driving parenting of Asian families is what leads to the success of Asian children. The Model Minority stereotype is related to a few facts and a lot of misconceptions—as is the Tiger Mother stereotype.

One fundamental fact is that Asian-Americans, particularly those from China, Taiwan, Korea, and Japan, tend to be overrepresented rather than underrepresented in gifted education; they are often in the top percentiles of achievement tests, in grade point averages, and in mathematics and science competitions. Scholars offer many suggestions for why this is so, but what has been well established is that Asian-Americans, unlike African-Americans, are in the U.S. by choice, rather than their ancestors coming as slaves. If you think about what kinds of people voluntarily immigrate to another country, it is clear that they are likely idealists who value achievement and can envision a different way of life—all of which suggest that they are likely to be brighter than average and to have family traditions of achievement. In addition, it is clear that, on average, Asian-American families place much more emphasis on education as a pathway to success and on academic achievement as a sign of family honor. Asian-American smart girls, therefore, are expected to be high achieving, good at math and science, and hard working in order to avoid shaming their parents.

However, like so many generalizations, the stereotype is not entirely accurate. Not all Asians immigrated just because they wanted to. Those Asian-Americans whose families came here as refugees—some of them from mountain clans of Cambodia like the Hmong or very poor villages in Viet Nam—are less likely to be high achieving.

Another fact that challenges the stereotype is that Asian-American daughters of second and third generations immigrant parents are less likely than those of the first generation to have internalized traditional Asian values of conscientiousness, hard work, modesty, and the subjugation of individual desires to the needs of the family. Many Asian-American smart girls today are so far removed from the culture of their origin that they don't speak the language of their family's culture; they know little of the traditions; and they have internalized the values of American mainstream culture. In addition, many Asian-American smart girls do not fit the stereotype of being math and science nerds; in our minority gifted study, for example, a higher number of the girls were interested in fine arts and design than in math and science. In fact, many Asian-American girls defy the stereotypes by becoming artists, actors, and writers who express themselves powerfully and even outrageously. Think of Yoko Ono, artist and widow of John Lennon, who at 80 years old continues to produce edgy, *avant-garde* performance art.

Another stereotype is that all Asian-American gifted students go to Ivy League colleges. Although they generally are high achievers, Asian students now attend a wide variety of colleges and universities. In fact, Asian-American students are so extraordinary in their academic achievement that many colleges have tried to limit their numbers—an attempt at balance that may be a new form of discrimination. In a study of academically talented, we were surprised to see that proportionally fewer Asian-Americans were offered scholarships to prestigious universities; because of the lack of college financial support, many Asian-American, straight-A, high-scoring gifted girls must now apply to lower-level institutions.[320]

The stereotype of the driving, harsh, punitive Asian-American parent presented in the Tiger Mother book is an exaggeration, even according to author Amy Chua and her daughters. Asian-American parents do, in general, however, have high expectations for their children and a low opinion of many aspects of American culture. In one study, according to Chua, Chinese immigrant mothers said that they believe their children can be the best students since "academic achievement reflects successful parenting," and that if children did not excel at school, then there is a problem and parents are not doing their job. Asian-American smart girls probably do attend fewer social events and study more than other girls, but it is unlikely that they are forbidden entirely from parties, sleepovers, and dating.

Earlier in this book, we have shown that girls' cultures are not often conducive to achievement and that other girls can be bullying and cruel to smart girls. The restraint and negative view held by Asian-American families toward the American media and pop culture actually may be a good thing for smart girls—especially when it protects them from images of girls as silly, vain, and obsessed with romance. In addition, when moderate forms of Asian parenting styles are used—such as insisting that children keep trying for mastery—then the result is often more confidence and desire to achieve. For example, many bright girls don't like the practice that is needed to gain expertise with a musical instrument. Once they have achieved basic mastery, however, they begin to find great joy in their music and are glad they had to practice so many hours. Many worry that this kind of parenting is bad for self-esteem; however, Chua and many others note that America's obsession with self-esteem may not have allowed children the solid self-confidence that comes with mastery and expertise.

On the other hand, the problems that Asian-American smart girls face in trying to live up to the Model Minority stereotype include anxiety, perfectionism, and fear of failure, according to Margie Kitano.[321] Psychologists, who once lumped all forms of perfectionism together, have begun to see that there are both negative and positive aspects of perfectionism. When achievement becomes so critical to one's identity that anything less than 100% is a failure, all sorts of negative psychological issues crop up, especially crippling anxiety for Asian-American smart girls. On the other hand, some forms of perfectionism, like defensive pessimism, may work for these students. *Defensive pessimism* is an attitude in which the girl thinks, "I won't do well on this test unless I study really hard." For many girls, this is actually a useful stance; it may lead to some overzealous studying but results in high achievement. Interestingly, the anxious wish to be high achieving does not necessarily carry over into other areas of life, so that many smart girls are able to study hard and perform at high levels while also being relaxed and easygoing in social and recreational pursuits.

Socioeconomic Status (SES)

SES is shorthand for social class—a combination of education, income, and occupation. SES is related to things that will make a person's life good or tolerable on the one hand, or full of struggle on the other. Low SES children have less enriched environments, are read to less often, and enter kindergarten already behind high SES children in school skills. In addition, low SES children often have poor nutrition; more exposure to toxins, such as lead in paint; more illnesses, obesity, and behavioral problems; are subject to more abuse and neglect; and are punished and bullied more often than high SES children.[322]

Not surprisingly, the achievement gap between white, black, and Hispanic students is overlapped by the gap in SES. Low SES students often attend substandard schools in dangerous neighborhoods. Although experienced teachers can help raise achievement of low SES children, school experiences of students in low SES schools are much less beneficial than those of students in high SES schools. Low SES adolescents go to college in lower numbers and go to less prestigious colleges than high SES students.[323]

For most readers, none of these facts are surprising, but a real surprise, according to Sean Reardon, is that in the last 30 years in the U.S. and most of the world, the gap in achievement between rich and poor has widened enormously—not just because of the conditions under which the poor live, but because the wealthy are investing much more in their children's preschool education, support services for schooling, and college educations.[324]

All of this means that a smart girl from a low SES family has a long and often difficult way to travel to reach the center of privilege and power. Against the powerful forces of SES, she has one advantage—her intelligence. That advantage will either grow as a result of loving and safe families, enriched preschool education, challenge in excellent schools, good choices of extra-curricular activities, and college preparation—or it will diminish. The stories of many eminent low-SES women are largely stories of good fortune—a parent or relative who invested in early education; a source of stimulation, particularly found in books; a special teacher or mentor; a chance to succeed in school; and an opportunity that opened the gateway to college and beyond.

In addition to these special gifts in their environments, eminent minority women also had resilience, an ability to bounce back from stress, conflict, and loss. Most important, they had the power that comes from an inner passion; falling in love with an idea at an early age seems to provide the strength and resilience needed. We suggest that falling in love with an idea and discovering a purpose in life might work in combination with other special advantages to help a smart girl overcome the ravages of poverty.

Sexual Orientation

Although facts and figures about lesbian youth are often lost among LGBT statistics, girls who identify as lesbians are at higher risk for a wide variety of difficulties compared to both heterosexual girls and gay boys. In a nationwide, representative sample of adolescents in high school, girls who were attracted to girls or who identified themselves as lesbians were both more likely to engage in risky behaviors such as running away, drinking, and truancy, and more likely to be punished for it than other girls who did the same things.[325] About 17% of girls felt same-sex attraction and about 14% identified as lesbian/bisexual. These girls experienced family conflict and violence more often than heterosexual girls, and they experienced rejection and conflict as a result of coming out. Girls who do not come out, who try to change their orientation, or who hide it from most people are at risk for depression and anxiety. For smart girls, being lesbian in orientation means being doubly different; during adolescence, this double difference can be particularly hard.

Lesbian adolescents are more likely than heterosexual females to have been bullied, expelled from school, stopped by police, and even arrested. Other pediatric studies have shown they are more likely to have health problems, eating disorders, and obesity. Given the history that many lesbian adolescents have had with sanctions and punishments, as well as the fact of poorer health, it is not surprising that they would feel distant from privilege and power.

When smart lesbians belong to religions or ethnicities that are negative or punishing toward LGBT orientations, they are particularly at risk. A smart adolescent girl, with her capacity for deep reflection, questioning, and sensitivity, may find herself in an internal struggle for identity as well as an external struggle with the teachings of her religion and her community. In a community where homophobia runs deep, the smart girl may grow defensive and deeply isolated.

On the other hand, according to histories of lesbians in the last century, these girls and women usually had higher aspirations and intentions for careers than heterosexual girls. Unfortunately, lesbian adolescents who have attended schools where there was harassment with few protections were less likely to plan to go to college. Schools with supportive educators provided a greater sense of school community overall, and those lesbians who attended supportive schools had higher average GPAs and fewer missed school days than other LGBT students.[326] Lesbian young women who find supportive communities in college often discover a culture of their own where they feel safe and free to develop their talents. Athletic participation, involvement in LGBT rights activism, and engaging in reflective writing about their lives all can help smart girls to cope with the denial of privilege that results from their orientation.

Attractiveness

For smart girls, physical attractiveness is one of the most powerful determinants of a sense of well-being. Girls' subjective sense of how distant they are from the ideal facial features and body weight may create not only psychological distress but can also lead to extremely self-destructive behaviors, such as cycles of extreme dieting, anorexia and bulimia, and complete social withdrawal. In *The Body Project*, Joan Jacobs Brumberg describes American adolescent girls' obsession with facial beauty and perfecting the body, but in the era of globalization, these obsessions also have been exported around the world.[327]

Cross-cultural studies show that similar faces are seen as beautiful around the world. Skin condition, regular features, and symmetry seem to be associated over generations with health, and therefore it makes sense that certain faces would seem to signal health. Both males and females respond more positively to beautiful faces. People who are generally physically attractive are not only judged as more competent than other people from the time they are small children, but they also develop more positive traits over time.

In a major study that examined previous research on attractiveness, Judith Langlois and her colleagues found that:

> *(a) Raters agree about who is and is not attractive, both within and across cultures; (b) attractive children and adults are judged more positively than unattractive children and adults, even by those who know them; (c) attractive children and adults are treated more positively than unattractive children and adults, even by those who know them; and (d) attractive children and adults exhibit more positive behaviors and traits than unattractive children and adults.*[328]

Their findings were some of the first to undo the maxims that are often told to girls such as, "Beauty is in the eye of the beholder," and "Beauty is only skin-deep." The truth is, beauty has an extraordinary impact on one's life and does indeed create an unfair advantage—or disadvantage.

When it comes to obesity, the stigma is overwhelming; it is almost the last socially acceptable form of prejudice in developed nations, and fat girls and women—as well as those who merely think they are fat—suffer greatly. This is in contrast to past generations and underdeveloped countries where extra weight was valued as a sign of health. Large studies, based on the representative sample of U.S. adolescents, found that overweight girls are at risk for a wide variety of problems, from bullying to depression, low self-esteem, and suicidal thoughts. Although fat boys and girls experience negative perceptions and judgments, girls are hit much harder and take it more to heart; there is simply much more pressure on girls and women to be thin. In fact, the fear and sadness surrounding feeling overweight is so great that young women who spend most of their day around attractive women have a greater tendency toward depression than those who spend time around more normal-sized women.[329]

There is a modest correlation between estimated intelligence and attractiveness; a beautiful face can provide a "halo effect" that makes the attractive woman seem smarter than others.[330] For smart girls, however, this small association between intelligence and attractiveness is a double-edged sword. On the one hand, many smart girls are likely to be healthier, stronger, and more attractive than other girls—so that they have an additional boost in judgments from others. On the other hand, smart girls who are not also attractive may be overlooked or presumed to be less intelligent than their better-looking peers.

What if the smart girl is *not* pretty and thin? What if she is pimply and overweight? In that case, her intelligence on the one hand may help her achieve scholastically, but it may also work against her by giving her the skills she needs to torment herself more effectively with elaborate diet plans, punishing exercise, skin-treatment regimens, and constant self-monitoring of her looks. Smart girls may carefully study nutrition information in order to find the number of calories in any food in order to avoid consuming them; they can estimate the value of every exercise. When we add the strong achievement motivation of many smart girls to these abilities, we have a recipe for a severe eating disorder. It is no accident that so many of the dying anorexics on the hospital wards are high I.Q. girls.

To be unattractive and overweight as a girl or woman is to find oneself a long way from privilege. The advice given to girls, as always, has been to lose weight; however, the evidence is so overwhelming that diets do not work that most pediatricians, nutritionists, and advocates for overweight people have changed their approach. In a recent and striking paradigm shift, health experts (but not the media) have called for new strategies called HAES— Healthy At Every Size. Linda Bacon, in her book about HAES says that this new way of being healthy means changing mindsets about body image to acceptance rather than self-hatred, to the use of intuitive or mindful eating that has long-term well-being as its goal rather than weight loss, and to the use of pleasant exercise and creative activity to maintain both physical and mental health.[331] After decades of an upward trend both in obesity and body shame in women, perhaps there is hope for decreasing the distance from power that comes from the burden of unattractiveness. Smart girls and women need to challenge society's images of beauty, just as Linda Bacon is doing, by exposing the prejudices toward women who are considered unattractive. Smart girls and women have the power of their wit, verbal skills, and empathy to confront the stereotypes of body size and facial beauty. The Geena Davis Institute on Gender in Media website and Amy Poehler's Smart Girls website provide many ideas about how gifted girls and young women can get involved in changing how the media portrays women.[332]

The Power of Religion

Most of the world's religions have sects that assumed the inferiority of women as a fundamental part of their traditions; yet, gifted women have emerged into eminence within all religions, even as mystics and prophets.

Although feminists like Simone de Beauvoir saw religion as antagonistic to women's urge to self-actualization, other feminists have worked within religious traditions to promote equality for women. We believe that it is not religion per se that prevents smart girls from attaining their highest potential but rather those elements within a religion that require the obedience of women to men and the subjugation of women's goals to men's.

Smart girls and women have demonstrated remarkable coping strategies for pursuing their educational and vocational goals even within the most traditional religions. Margie Kitano, in her studies of gifted international women, found that women from traditional backgrounds either found ways to rebel (refusing to marry an old man she was given to and running away from home), to enlist the help of family (a brother agreeing to work so that the sister could go to school), or to cope by going as far as possible academically while strictly observing the appropriate behaviors for women.[333] In the U.S., religions vary greatly in the degree to which they proscribe intellectual advancement and vocational aspirations for women, and families within a religion vary greatly with regard to how much they adhere to the religion's traditional roles for women.

To determine how distant from privilege a girl might feel as a result of her religion, one has to consider the following questions:

❖ Is the religious group more interested in nurturing women's spirits or does it emphasize controlling their behavior?

❖ Does the religious group welcome or at least tolerate expanding roles for women in the workplace or does it insist on a few, narrowly defined traditional roles?

❖ Does the religious group allow sexual agency with women in charge of their own bodies or does it require the repression of women's sexuality?

❖ Does the religious group believe in education as a path to fulfillment for women or is it suspicious of women's education?

In addition, girls can feel distant from privilege when their religion is stereotyped by others, when they are a distinct, visible minority, or when their religious practices are seen as strange or unacceptable. Of course, all of these factors can come into play; for example, a Somalian immigrant girl in the U.S. whose family still secretly practices genital mutilation might feel disempowered both by her religion that requires her to suffer and by the surrounding general culture that views her religion as barbaric.

The Geography of Opportunity: Urban, Rural, and Suburban Lives

In his book, *The Rise of the Creative Class*, Richard Florida first uncovered the facts that many creative people understand intuitively: Smart, creative people cluster together in particular cities and regions.[334] Living in a particular area will determine the quality of your school, your access to cultural opportunities, your chances of meeting potential mentors, your opportunities to join groups of like-minded people, and finally, your academic and career opportunities.[335]

Jane Piirto, who writes about the development of creative people, says the single most important thing a writer can do is move to New York City.[336] In addition, scientists and technology experts gather in clusters like in Silicon Valley and the North Carolina Research Triangle; the chances of a young woman meeting a scientist or inventor are much higher if she lives in those regions. Similarly, more musicians (not just country musicians) live in Nashville and more actors in Los Angeles than anywhere else in the U.S. because of the many recording studios and venues. Artists and comedians gravitate to Chicago and New York City; business entrepreneurs congregate in the Southwest.

Smart girls who grow up in rural areas find multiple barriers to the development of their talent, not least of which is the stereotype of the redneck girl. Television portrays rural people as ignorant, bigoted, and rowdy; people mock country accents and ways of speaking. Bright girls with strong, Southern accents are often dismissed as dumb. Even the prizes won by smart girls in rural areas for their raising and showing hogs, cows, and sheep in 4-H clubs are ridiculed by urbanites. Despite the fact that these girls will have more difficulty having their talents taken seriously by urbanites, most smart girls from rural areas are inevitably encouraged to move as far away as possible from family and home and to never return. Craig Howley is an outspoken critic of the discrimination faced by rural gifted and by the relentless encouragement to abandon the rural area. Gifted students, he says, who love the rural life and want to be stewards of their farms should be encouraged to return to their roots and to realize their potential outside of the urban vocational world.[337]

Because many gifted girls live in areas with very low college attendance rates and women tend to marry at a young age, they may see few alternatives. Often, they have not been exposed to a variety of career options except those they see in town and on television. If they do go to college, they may feel like outsiders, particularly if the party pathway is a strong force.

Finally, many more principals and teachers from rural areas themselves may not be familiar with gifted education strategies; sadly, one study found that many teachers and principals in rural schools were opposed to gifted education.[338] As a result, rural smart girls will need special social and cultural capital to overcome their distance from privilege. This could include online learning opportunities, travel, college visits, and a chance to meet other gifted students at summer camps and seminars.

The Importance of Social and Cultural Capital

Of all the ways in which smart girls can be distant from—or close to—privilege, we have only reviewed those most common in American and Western societies. For each girl and each culture, a different combination of factors will determine whether she will be nurtured or ignored by powerful people. Only by asking smart girls about all of these characteristics and how they perceive them as affecting their chances of gaining privilege and power can we learn the subtleties of perceived status in society.[339]

The key to overcoming perceived lack of privilege is not to try to persuade young women that they are wrong. To pretend that sexism, racism, SES gaps, heterosexism, and "looksism" don't exist will only cause girls to look inward for the sources of their failures and to subsequently blame themselves. When girls internalize society's disdain for their sex, race, class, sexual orientation, or looks, they come to see themselves as bad, unworthy of love, and unable to succeed. When we confront these things straight on, we help smart girls to see that many of the bad things that have happened to them are not their fault. When we show smart girls the ways in which they are different, we can also help them to name and understand those differences.

Bright girls from an early age understand the complexities of human behavior better than other children, if they are carefully explained. When we help them understand the fact that being put down, bullied, or treated unfairly is often because of social differences, then girls are empowered to take control of the conditions of their lives.

What we have found most useful in solving the problem of distance from privilege is helping smart girls gain *social capital* and *cultural capital*. Social capital encompasses all the family support, friendships, alliances, networks, and groups that help you feel like you belong and allow you to play a more powerful role in society and in achieving your goals. These networks also include parents' friends, religious communities, and social organizations. Cultural capital is the knowledge and skills that come from exposure to fine points of the dominant society that one needs to get along with others in relevant groups—and that includes such things as learning the manners, language, attire, preferences in products and services, and aesthetic tastes of different subgroups (called *code-switching* by many minority scholars) and by participating in opportunities experienced by privileged people like museum visits, travel, and campus life. In fact, probably the most important finding of our NSF Study, *Milestones and Danger Zones*, was that social and cultural capital, particularly for lower middle class girls, was associated with self-efficacy, hope, confidence in a chosen major, and intention to persist.[340]

In addition to gaining capital, smart girls need straight talk about the role of money and finance in their lives, because that is the foundation they will need to realize their potential. Money can buy social and cultural capital by allowing access to experiences and places where privileged people live, work, and lead—and eventually, cultural and social capital can lead to financial security. From the lives of eminent women, it is apparent that these women often possessed not only intelligence and creativity but also sufficient social and cultural capital to raise their confidence and propel them forward. Providing smart girls with social and cultural capital can overcome many of the problems posed by their sex and gender role.

CHAPTER 13

Passion: What Lights
the Smart Girl's Fire?

Working with accomplished children, adolescents, and adults for our careers, we have seen the role that engagement plays in the productivity of these people. In fact, the sheer level of energy, fervor, and intensity that science fair winners, young artists, budding writers, and eminent people of all types put into their chosen domain of work is a bit fatiguing even just to witness.

Scott Barry Kaufman's book, *Ungifted, Intelligence Redefined*, is an amazing march through extensive writings about intelligence, creativity, motivation, and just about every cognitive behavior known to humans. He deftly presents research and shows how often *gifted* does not translate into achievement and how often supposedly "ungifted" people—people who do not score well on conventional intelligence tests—actually do achieve eminence in their fields. The strongest take-away message of the book was this: "Intelligence is the dynamic interplay of engagement and abilities in pursuit of personal goals."[341] Here is someone who really understands that abilities without engagement do not produce much beyond lackluster, mediocre achievement.

Other scholars have observed this intensity and tried to understand it, and we will review some of the theories and research of people who have tried to understand the passion that underlies the work of eminent people. We examine the concepts and mechanisms that are often used to describe the motivation of highly accomplished people. Many will be familiar to educators and others familiar to psychologists. We have tried to pull together the various explanations of passion all in one place, with our reflections on how they apply—or don't apply—to smart girls and women.

Is Passion Just Task Commitment?

Joseph Renzulli's Three-Ring model of giftedness held that gifted people are those who combine above-average intelligence, creativity, and task commitment.[342] It is easy to see that most eminent women combine these three characteristics. Task commitment, says Renzulli, is motivation turned into action—perseverance, endurance, hard work, as well as self-confidence and a fascination with a special subject. These are all "non-intellective" factors in success, according to Renzulli.

That comes close to explaining passion. Unfortunately, the vast majority of educators over the years who learned about the Three-Ring model took task commitment to be simple conscientiousness or motivation applied to *all* tasks. This meant that those children who turned in messy papers and late assignments, who never seemed to be on time, or who simply underachieved in the tasks required by the teacher would never be considered gifted in this interpretation of the model. The teacher might never find out that in the area of the student's passion, the student is the very model of conscientiousness.

In various interviews of eminent women, immediately striking is that their own work—whether writing, research, or leading an organization—was characterized by extreme attention to detail and persistence. Did this apply to everything they did? Their housework? Not so much. Their attention to their clothing and appearance? Not really. Their attendance to any tasks not related to their passion was, in fact, pretty slapdash.

In smart girls, we have seen the same *selective conscientiousness*. If a bright girl obsessed with anime, or equine dressage, or robotics never gets a chance to share her work in this area with teachers, then her ability to focus on a task, attend to details, and get things done may never be noticed or recognized. In addition, girls are more likely to express ADD as carelessness, lateness, and sloppiness—so if nobody sees her at work on her drawings, or her riding, or her robots, she will probably be labeled as an ADD child, rather than a determined, creative person. When teachers observe only classroom behavior and try to evaluate a gifted girls' conscientiousness and task commitment, they may be missing out entirely on the selective conscientiousness that will come in handy when she is a woman putting her passion first.

Is Passion Explained by Overexcitabilities Theory?

Many writers in gifted education have seized upon the overexcitabilities theory to describe and explain the intensity they saw in gifted children.[343] Most of the research has sought a link between high intelligence and high scores on a measure of overexcitabilities, but this methodology, according to a review by Sal Mendaglio, may lead to confusion about the identification and development of talent in smart girls.[344] The researchers saw that gifted children could be intensely engaged in several domains and, based upon *Dabrowski's Theory of Positive Disintegration*, theorized that these domains corresponded to neurological propensities called overexcitabilities. The domains—psychomotor, sensual, imaginational, intellectual, and emotional—correspond loosely to definitions of kinesthetic intelligence, creativity, academic ability, and emotional intelligence. As noted earlier, each one overlaps to some degree with personality traits such as impulsivity, sentience, openness, achievement, and instability of emotions. The problem with the use of this theory is that its components conflate those characteristics that are usually called abilities, personality traits, and arousal levels in most psychological science. Perhaps it is not so much Dabrowski's original theory or the scholarly research of giftedness that are at fault but the intense popularization of the concepts of "sensitivities" and "intensities" that can easily be misinterpreted.

We worry that describing smart girls as sensitive and intense implies a kind of fragility and need for nurturing that has been the stereotypical female upbringing. Overexcitabilities theory, taken to the extreme, would seem to make smart girls into hothouse flowers whose delicacy must be protected. We are concerned that parents and teachers who believe the overexcitabilities theory will overprotect and over-help smart girls when they often need the opposite kind of guidance. Sal Mendaglio and James Webb, who have both written about parenting highly sensitive children, both warn against overprotection as a response to the gifted child who is highly sensitive and responds intensely to frustration.[345] In fact, according to Mendaglio, Dabrowski viewed anxieties and depression as opportunities for growth and saw "advanced development" as an achievement of people who had worked through conflicts between their sensitivities and the demands and pressures of society.[346]

As we have shown in our portraits of smart girls and eminent women, most bright women have indeed worked through these conflicts. They manage and direct their energy and motivation very well. The majority of creative people are stable and self-controlled. Creative adults may be accomplished in spite of their sensitivities and emotional intensity, not because of them. Describing gifted children as being overly active, sensitive to sights and sounds, obsessed with ideas, and unable to control intense emotions seems to make a virtue of distressing conditions; this also creates the possibility of misdiagnosing autism or neuroticism as signs of giftedness. Wanting to see autistic behaviors as perfectly normal aspects of giftedness makes them no less distressing to the child. If emotionality (such as frequent tantrums and crying episodes) is seen simply as a sign of giftedness, underlying depression and anxiety could go untreated.

Smart girls and young women need assistance with learning self-regulation, management of moods, and methods of reducing unwanted behaviors—so that they can be empowered to fulfill their goals. The use of this theory, therefore, to explain passion and intensity could lead to over-protection, over-helping, and the failure to recognize or seek remediation for symptoms of depression, anxiety, autism, and ADHD.

It is unlikely that overexcitabilities—or sensitivities and intensities—drive the actions of smart women. Instead, their motivation seems to come not from neurological propensities to respond more intensely but rather from a deliberate choice to regulate their emotions in the service of their chosen work.

Is It Mindset?

Carol Dweck, in three decades of research on motivation, turned her interest toward what happens when children are constantly told that they are gifted.[347] The results of her experiments show that kids who believe they are gifted usually also believe that any task is a test of their giftedness; therefore, they are eager to engage in tasks that show their brilliance and unwilling to engage in tasks that might expose their flaws or inabilities. She calls this the *fixed mindset*—the belief that giftedness is fixed, that intelligence can neither grow nor be diminished.

On the other hand, she says, children who have a *growth mindset*, one that leads them to believe that intelligence is not fixed but can be expanded through effort, will develop an ability to pursue goals in which they cannot be assured of success. They will try to improve by sustained practice, exploration, honing their skills, and seeking information and help.

As we and others like Scott Barry Kaufman have shown, intelligence is indeed *not fixed*. From prenatal environment until senescence, intelligence is either being nourished or starved. Giftedness grows through both external opportunities to learn as well as the person's own efforts to expand knowledge and perfect skills. We agree with Dweck's statement that intelligence is not fixed and that giftedness as a label can do harm if a child becomes devoted to simply maintaining the label. In maintaining and focusing on the giftedness label, gifted children may not have the opportunity to learn frustration tolerance, persistence, and resilience.

Where we differ is on the impact of the mindset theory on girls. It may be that gifted girls *do* need reassurance that they are, in fact, gifted. In the case of women and other groups who are less privileged, it is probably not a fixed mindset that causes them to lose faith in their abilities. Many of those gifted girls never do believe they are gifted in the first place, despite the evidence of their label and their outstanding performance. Because girls are socialized to camouflage their intellect and our society persists in seeing intellectual achievement as masculine, they can have a very fragile intellectual self-concept. Additionally, as can be seen from the valedictorian studies and from the first *Smart Girls* follow-up, too many young women unfortunately lose confidence in their intelligence and giftedness as they enter college and adulthood.

Tracy Cross and his colleagues documented various ways that gifted children cope with other kids' attitudes and behaviors toward giftedness.[348] Many females, they find, tell others that their good grades are just luck or they downplay their giftedness as a factor in their success. As they get older, they may begin to feel like impostors, as Pauline Clance and Suzanne Imes described in their book *The Imposter Phenomenon*; women's identity as caring, sociable, compliant people just does not fit with an identity as achieving, aggressive, and nonconforming individuals.[349] Carol Dweck's own work in the 1980s showed that young women tend to attribute their good grades to external causes (e.g. luck) and their bad grades to internal causes (being dumb), while young men tend to attribute their good grades to internal causes (high ability) and their bad grades to external causes (a bad teacher or a boring class).[350] The result is that men keep persisting, even when getting Cs, and women give up. Dweck's current conclusion, however—that we should never tell children that they are gifted—is not appropriate for girls and young women.

In a study of thousands of gifted boys' and girls' attributions of success and failure, Susan Assouline, Nicholas Colangelo, and their colleagues emphasized the implications of their repeated findings that gifted girls, unlike gifted boys, doubt that their success is the result of giftedness:

> *The girls had to meet the same standards as boys for entry into all the programs and thus there is no reason to assume differentiation in the sample by ability. A higher percentage of girls chose "I work hard" (long-term effort) over "I am smart" (ability) for success. Is this a "humbleness factor" and, perhaps more so, a hesitancy to*

assess oneself accurately? We see potential negatives for girls who do not accurately recognize their academic abilities. They may be more tentative about undertaking challenges or putting themselves in competitive situations. We encourage research on gifted girls to assess how they approach highly challenging tasks and competitive situations compared to boys.[351]

Girls certainly need to be told that they have high abilities but not simply as a label that anoints them as "gifted." Informing girls about their abilities should include the following components:

1. The information should be precise. E.g., "Your verbal abilities, according to this test, seem to be around the 95th percentile. Your math abilities seem to be in the 99th percentile. The test is saying that if you are in a room with 100 other kids your age, that you will probably be better at reading, writing, and thinking with words than 95 of the other kids. You will be better at doing the math assignments in your grade better than 99 of the other kids."

2. The information should be time-limited. E.g., "Right now, this is a snapshot of your abilities compared to other kids your age. If you keep on learning and working the way you have, you will probably continue to be in the gifted group."

3. The information should take into account gender, social, and cultural variables that can account for differences in achievement. E.g., "Lots of people believe that girls can't do as well in math as boys—but that is totally untrue! African-Americans like us are often told we aren't high achievers, but look at Mom and Dad and you! We had lots of advantages that other families don't have, so we do just as well or better than white people on tests."

4. The information should include your family's definition of gifted-ness. E.g., "The school says you are gifted, but different schools and programs all have their own way of deciding who they are going to call gifted. We believe you have unusually high abilities because even when you were a little girl, you learned really quickly and you were so curious about the world! In our family, being gifted means being good at learning and really trying to take in as much about the world as possible."

5. The information should clearly show how giftedness relates to responsibilities and social relationships. E.g., "Just because school work is easy for you doesn't mean other kids aren't working hard enough. They are probably working just as hard as they can. You got a special head start in life because of your abilities and all that we and your teachers have done for you—so you need to use your abilities to help make the world a better place."

When girls are told precisely how they are gifted—that they can choose to increase their abilities; that the label of giftedness given by the school depends on lots of social and cultural factors; and that in the family, there are clear definitions and responsibilities for gifted people—they are more likely to have a solid sense of their intelligence. So it is not an either/or thing where girls either believe that intelligence is fixed or that it can grow. Instead, girls need to have faith in their intelligence as a *foundation* for further learning, as well as the desire to persist in challenging the boundaries of their abilities.

Is It Grit?

Angela Duckworth and her colleagues wanted to ascertain the differences between high achievers and moderate achievers, and they discovered that hard work, persistence, and task commitment were just as important (or more so, in their samples) as ability.[352] Even with high natural ability, effort is needed. Once smart young women reach a point in their musical, intellectual, or artistic training, their natural abilities to learn need to be supplemented with lots of hard work, and they need to transition to a different style of study and practice. Most smart young women make that transition gladly, learning the strategies for learning just as quickly as they learn everything else.

If bright women enter college and cannot find an idea that they love or a purpose in doing well, however, then they are at risk for bypassing the transition to the hard work needed for excellence. If they have only ever achieved for the sake of achievement, not in the service of a passion, then they will likely just drop out of a tough course. They are unlikely to try new learning strategies, like getting a tutor or memorizing key equations. Their failure is not a failure of mindset or grit but a failure in the search for meaning.

To us, grit is just a new name for the same old idea that it is perspiration, not inspiration, that produces accomplishment, that effort is more important than ability, that hard work will win out, and that people who achieve are those who have grit. The trouble is, many gifted kids believe that it is not true. In their lives, they have succeeded many times without hard work or much effort at all. Del Siegle and Betsy McCoach suggest that we teach our gifted children to underachieve by failing to challenge their abilities.[353] By the time smart girls go to college, their academic progress has been so effortless that they are often starving for an opportunity to be challenged, to stretch their wings. Not only are most smart girls not resting on their laurels, they are dying to make an effort.

Of course, people of average ability need to work hard to achieve at the levels that gifted women can achieve pretty easily, and nobody with an average intelligence score is trapped by that score forever if she is willing to engage in sustained effort, practice, memory training, and myriad other learning strategies. There is plenty of room in every profession and discipline for people who have worked really hard to increase their talents and skills—but there is also room for those people for whom academic work comes naturally, and the opportunity to challenge themselves at last is exciting.

Is It Flow?

Mihaly Csikszentmihalyi did much to change the way we think about the lives of creatively eminent people by introducing the world to the concept of *flow*.[354] Flow is a state of consciousness, just as dreaming, rational thinking, and meditation are states of consciousness. Unlike these other states, however, flow shares both aspects of the rational state of mind and an almost trance-like state. Almost everybody who has gotten to the point of expertise in any field, whether cooking or calculus, knows what it is like to feel as though every action comes intuitively and naturally. In this state of mind, there is a surge of energy and suddenly you feel at one with the work you are doing. You lose track of time. For example, you begin writing late at night about a topic you know extensively and feel passionately about—and suddenly, you look out the window and it's morning. You forget about your physical needs, whether it is hunger, thirst, fatigue, or needing to stretch. You forget about your anxieties. The present moment, you, and your work are all that is.

How do people enter into a flow state? Csikszentmihalyi learned that this consciousness state happens when people are functioning at the limits of their abilities—when their skills are just equal to the challenge facing them. That is why flow occurs most often in creative fields when people have reached a point of expertise. It is hard to go into flow as a musician when you are just beginning to learn chords on a guitar or as a beginning artist when you are just figuring out the way that pigments blend together.

With less complex skills like driving a car, we all go into a flow-like state as long-practiced movements and thorough knowledge make us drive in a semi-conscious state (How did I get all the way home? I wasn't even thinking!). For eminent people, years of gathering knowledge and practice come together as they engage in the work that challenges them. They get excited about a new idea, start working at it, and then they are in flow.

An amazing aspect of flow is that it feels good. Neuroscientists have tried to pinpoint everything from the gamma bursts in the brain of the *aha!* moment to the cascades of dopamine (the motivation chemical) that come pouring into the brain when experts are in a state of flow. Nobody really knows why we evolved to have this marvelous consciousness state, but it seems to be the power behind the grand innovations and accomplishments of humankind. Creatively eminent people seem to have lots of experiences of flow; it is so satisfying that they keep seeking greater and greater challenges in order to have that next flow state.

Does flow explain the passion of the eminent woman? It comes very, very close because it captures the importance of curiosity and constant search for more knowledge and skills, the willingness to surmount environmental and personal barriers, the desire to engage for long periods of time in the activity, and the lifelong pursuit of challenge. We believe that flow is a great explanation of the motivation to follow and attain one's goals and dreams.

There is more, however, to what smart women feel when they find the idea that drives them to seek and find greater knowledge and skills, when they feel a passion that makes them impervious to society's negative judgments, and when they commit their lives to a calling or life's vocation. We believe that the best way of describing catching fire, driving forward, and creating meaning is the falling—and staying—in love with an idea.

In Love with an Idea

It seems clear that the passion of eminent women for their chosen work is more than simply task commitment, overexcitabilities, flow, mindset, or grit. Overexcitabilities alone do not explain the capacity of eminent women to regulate their emotions in the service of their work. Task commitment, mindset, and grit have too much overlap with the plain old personality trait of conscientiousness.

Conscientiousness is very much associated with general academic achievement and doing well in all subjects, but conscientiousness is famously inversely correlated with creativity. We propose that this is precisely because eminent people—those who are not only expert but also skilled with the eminent kind of creativity—are selectively conscientious. They apply themselves 100% to their passion, using planning, strategic use of their resources, hard work, and attention to detail. With regard to tasks that are not related to their passion, they are less conscientious. Domestic tasks, personal grooming, and attendance at meetings that do not concern their goals are likely to take a back seat to tasks related to their passion. Perfectionism, for them, has one place and one place only—in the service of their passion.

That is why we prefer to fall back upon E. Paul Torrance's lovely expression—falling and being in love with an idea—to describe the energy that propels smart women toward eminence.[355] Smart women's passion looks a lot more like being in love than a dreary obsession with doing all things perfectly. Torrance knew that the secret to discovering and nurturing a passion was not being well-rounded but being devoted to one's mission in life. When women are in love with their idea, it is very similar to falling in love with a person. First comes *curiosity*—"What is this about? What is going on here?" Then, *engagement*—"I'm going to take a leap of faith here and jump in, learning everything I can and putting lots of effort toward making this work." The woman begins to have flow experiences when her expertise has reached the point at which she can achieve that state of consciousness where her work has a feeling of blissful, unbounded, challenge. And finally, *passionate commitment*—"I want to take on this mission in life, forsaking all others."

One amazing thing about falling in love with an idea is the way it energizes one's work—suddenly staying up late to work is fun, finishing references or framing a painting perfectly is a satisfying kind of perfection, and working while others are playing seems like a higher form of play. Just as when one is in love with a person, no little task or flourish seems too much. The follow-through required for eminent productivity is similar to the thousand daily courtesies that form the substance of a successful marriage—and is no less enjoyable.

There is one very important way in which falling in love with an idea differs from falling in love with a person. An idea will never abandon you. You can lose a marriage, a job, or even your children as they move on with their adult lives—but your idea is there for you. It is no wonder that so many single, gifted women in their 80s who had lifelong careers they loved felt so little need for marriage or children. They had discovered the secret of joy that is always there waiting for the gifted woman—that falling in love with an idea can provide a lifetime of emotional sustenance and constancy.

Does falling in love with an idea preclude the possibility of intimacy, family, and community? Only when a partner sees the woman's passion as competition for his or her time and energy, when a family sees a mother's goals as less important than everybody else's, or when a community cannot accept the driven, focused smart woman. On the other hand, many, if not most, of the eminent women we have met have found partners who not only support their work but also adore their loved one's passion for their work. Most eminent women have found creative ways to have children and build a family; their children grow up, seeing Mom not just as the person who sacrifices herself for their goals but as another person whose goals are also worthy. Falling in love with an idea is not without conflict and loss, but in the end, those women who hold fast to their passion tend to be satisfied with their lives and proud of their achievements, their marriages and families, and the community that has supported them.

Self-Actualization and Optimal Development

It seems to us that falling in love and staying in love with an idea is the surest path to self-actualization. What is self-actualization? Abraham Maslow, one of the first great humanistic psychologists and motivational theorists, saw self-actualization as sitting at the top of his pyramid of human needs.[356] Most of us were introduced to Maslow's hierarchy of needs in introductory psychology classes. In his formulation, people have basic needs that, when met, allow them to seek satisfaction of the next layer of needs that, when met in turn, cause the next level of needs to emerge, and so on.

In the first, basic set of needs, Maslow puts basic physiological needs like air, water, and food that humans must have to stay alive. The next set of needs are safety and security, when most humans seek a secure place, safe from environmental and human threats. In the next layer of needs is belongingness; he believed that when humans have basic and safety needs met, they seek the company and intimacy of other humans. Then humans could seek self-esteem through achievement. And finally, after a person has consolidated achievements to the point of satisfaction, that person would feel the emergent need for self-actualization.

Since that time five decades ago when Maslow proposed his hierarchy of needs, motivational researchers have explored almost every aspect of the hierarchy except self-actualization. Although many would argue with the placement of the needs in the hierarchy, most psychologists agree that they are all important to motivation and full development of human potential. But self-actualization—perhaps because it seems so difficult to articulate and describe—usually doesn't get much attention. Edward Deci and Richard Ryan's Self-Determination Theory never mentions self-actualization, although there are bits of Maslow's idea in their notions of autonomy.[357] Their theory, which could be considered the current major theory of human motivation, proposes that all humans universally seek the following:

- ❖ Competence—the need to control the outcome of one's actions and experience mastery.

- ❖ Relatedness—the need to interact, be connected to, and experience caring for others.

- ❖ Autonomy—the need to be a causal agent of one's own life and to act in harmony with one's integrated self.

We do not believe that the needs in Maslow's hierarchy or Deci and Ryan's self-determination model are enough to guide the smart girl toward self-actualization. Certainly, as we have pointed out in the chapter on privilege, meeting basic needs is important to the flourishing of intelligence into achievement. It appears, however, that eminent women often set aside or deliberately ignore their needs in order to plunge ahead into their work. If Malala had been concerned about safety, would she have chosen to continue promoting girls' education after being shot by the Taliban? If J. K. Rowling had been fixated at the level of meeting needs for belongingness, why would she have written the Harry Potter novels? (Although perhaps she met her needs for belongingness by inventing her own world of wizards.) Most eminent women went long periods of their life without some of their basic needs being met. Marie Curie admitted that she nearly starved to death in her quest to understand the nature of radioactivity. It also seems like most eminent women are driven by something more than merely acting in harmony with their "integrated self." The passion that drives eminent women directs them not only to empower themselves but also to empower others through their work with such things as knowledge, beauty, political or economic power, or freedom. Their passion transcends safety, comfort, and the recognition or disapproval of others. What, then, is self-actualization as we conceive of it? It is development toward the following goals:

1. The realization of talent. The gifted girl needs to explore her talents and, as an adolescent, decide upon one or perhaps two talents she is going to develop and integrate. She needs help prioritizing her talents on the basis of her strongest interests. Which talent domain piques her curiosity and makes her want to learn more every day?

She needs to seek mastery of the knowledge and skills in her chosen domain. She needs to choose the most rigorous courses and focus her extracurricular and summer activities on further development of her talent. If she has decided to integrate two talent domains, she will need mastery in both of them. As a young woman, she needs to seek higher education and advanced training wherever the best experts and mentors are available and challenge herself to persist in even the most difficult courses. She needs to pursue the graduate or professional education that will hone her skills and provide access to the most prominent networks and clusters of talent in the field. As a young woman, she needs to continually seek the new knowledge that will inform her quest and choose jobs with a long perspective. What jobs will allow her to fulfill her talents the most? What jobs allow the most advancement, as well as the most autonomy to create the life she wants?

2. Building on strengths and regulating weaknesses. The gifted girl needs to strengthen the personality traits that serve the pursuit of her goals, and then she must recognize and regulate her weaknesses. Those traits that de-stabilize her mood and misdirect or split her in different directions impede the development of the habits she needs for her calling. If she is conscientious, she needs to strengthen that trait and seek careers that allow her attention to detail, industriousness, and seriousness to be used to the fullest. If she is open to experience, she needs to find places where she can be creative. If she is extraverted, she needs to perform and express herself to others; if introverted, she needs to seek a vocation that allows for some quiet and contemplation. If she is anxious, she must learn ways of soothing herself; if she is too dependent on others, she needs to gradually wean herself away from the crowd. If she is distractible and unable to meet a deadline, she must learn to focus her attention and manage her time. As gifted women develop their identity to the fullest, they begin to see how they can transform their weaknesses into strengths. The anxious young woman learns to re-frame her anxiety as anticipation and excitement. Eleanor Roosevelt, a shy, anxious introvert, transformed her negative feelings about herself into a new, vivid understanding of what it is to be a marginalized person—and devoted herself to human rights.

3. A daily focus on deeply held values. The gifted woman must nurture a constant intention to fulfill her deepest values, not only in her work but also in her daily life. If her deepest value is beauty, then she must not only create art in her spare time but also find opportunities every day to create more beauty in the world. If her deepest value is wisdom, then she must read and learn every day and share information with others. If her deepest value is prosperity, then she must not only attend to her finances every day but also find ways of creating financial value through her enterprises in the world. Those values that rank low in her priorities are those underlying the activities or requirements she chooses to resist or ignore. For each woman, the activities she chooses to engage in to fulfill a particular value may be entirely different from another's path. One young woman fulfills her values in nurturing children by becoming an educator and another might become an engineer who designs safer car seats for infants. The important thing is that she asks herself every day: How will my actions today fulfill my deepest values?

4. The pursuit of transcendence. The gifted woman can use flow and mindfulness to discover what is her personal ultimate meaning of life. The search for one's life's meaning is assisted by the fulfillment of values while trying to answer the question: What am I here on Earth to do? Falling in love with an idea is just the beginning of that quest; how one chooses to integrate the love of that idea into a healthy, happy, and satisfying life is the work of a lifetime. Flow experiences point the way. By tuning into flow experiences, a young woman can discover what activities feel right and the path on which she feels she was meant to be. Mindfulness, the practice of getting into the present moment and focusing awareness on one's inner experiences, allows a woman to notice the signs of anti-flow—the feeling of a pinch, like when your shoes are too tight. When she is engaged in an activity that makes her feel "not right" or just plain awful, she needs to focus on the feeling and find out exactly what is leading her away from her flow. Mindfulness doesn't just provide warning signs that one is on the wrong path, it also allows one to fully enjoy the moment when on the right path. By stepping back and fully experiencing the moment, one can acknowledge the richness of the present and open oneself up to awe. The teacher who is in the flow of teaching, when she and

her students are engaged in a beautiful dance of learning so intense that nobody wants to leave class, can take a moment afterward to savor the experience. The writer who finishes a perfect chapter can stop, breathe, and feel awe at the way the words seemed to channel through her. Increasing flow experiences and using mindfulness pave the way for those times of transcendence that Maslow called *peak experiences*. Peak experiences are those wondrous moments of joyous, awe-filled awareness when one suddenly feels a sense of harmony and interconnectedness with all being. People often describe transcendent moments as reconciliation of polarities— being certain about one's place in the universe while maintaining a deep awareness of an underlying mystery; feeling like one knows everything and nothing at the same time; feeling unspeakable ecstasy tinged with the sadness that it must end; being fully alive while being aware of one's mortality. We don't think that self-actualization should be just the realization of intellectual potential or the fulfillment of strengths and values—it should also involve the opportunity to have these feelings of connectedness and mystery that make suffering along the way worthwhile.

That is why our model of women's talent development reaches beyond the attainment of expertise, leadership, or eminence in order to become a model of the varied paths toward optimal development and self-actualization. Bright women deserve the chance not only to achieve what men have been able to achieve throughout time but also the chance to search for meaning and ultimate truths—the chance to be fully human.

CHAPTER 14

A New Model of Talent Development for Smart Girls and Women

It is clear that giftedness alone does not guarantee achievement, life satisfaction, or self-actualization. Giftedness is expanded or limited by a girl's given demographics and how she perceives them, especially in regards to distance from privilege. Giftedness is focused through specific abilities, which are then tempered by personality, interests, and values, and energized by passion and engagement. Giftedness develops through these filters into the spheres in which women can develop toward self-actualization: personal and public.

Two decades ago, Kathleen Noble, Rena Subotnik, and Karen Arnold created a model of female talent development that was to provide a new understanding of giftedness and girls.[358] For the first time, they brought together the existing research on how females might fulfill their potential, and used the ideas of foundations, filters, and spheres. Foundations were the "givens" in a girl's life, such as her giftedness and her personality traits. Filters were the ways in which those givens were shaped by talent domains and opportunities. Spheres, or contexts, were the places where the work took place—public or private.

During the last 20 years since this model, we have been working to further define its terms, refine its concepts, and add new discoveries. We have tried to take the best from other models of talent development, such as the domain-specific talent development ideas of Dona Mathews and the recent Subotnik, Olszewski-Kubilius, Worrell model.[359] We examined Sally Reis's model of gifted women's talent development, which includes both internal and external barriers.[360] Our model of smart girls' and women's talent development integrates old and new scholarship in ways that point directly to guidelines for smart girls and women who are on their way toward optimal development.

Figure 14.1. A Model of Talent Development for Smart Girls and Women*

Foundations	Demographics	Individual Characteristics
	Distance from Privilege	Abilities
		Personality
		Values
		Love of an Idea
Filters	Opportunities	Talent Domain
	Legal Rights	Arts
	Gender Relations	Humanities
	Social and Cultural Capital	STEM
	Education	Teaching/Caring
	Career	Business/Law
		Spiritual/Religious

Spheres	Personal	Public
	Personal Growth	Professional achievement
	Family	Entrepreneurship
		Scholarship
		Leadership

*An expansion of Noble, Subotnik, and Arnold's Model of Female Talent Development

Foundations

Demographics and Distance from Privilege

How a young woman perceives herself to be positioned with regard to privilege and power is fundamental; it is the basis upon which she will build. Noble, Subotnik, and Arnold, in their 1999 model, added a completely new idea that none of us had seen before: the distance a female must travel to get close to the center of privilege and power in her domain. In their formulation, for example, a poor Navajo girl who graduates as one of only 15% who finish high school on a reservation where healthcare and education are difficult to obtain may be as gifted as a wealthy, white, suburban girl who receives a master's degree. In other words, the difficult circumstances girls have to overcome to fulfill their potential are as much a measure of their giftedness as intelligence and achievement scores.

> *Karen Multon, Sharon Kurpius, Marie Hammond, and I were so intrigued by this idea that we began to research each component of privilege. In developing our instrument to assess people's perceptions of their privilege, we learned which aspects of privilege seemed important to each of the groups we studied. Based on previous multicultural research and the findings from our first groups, we determined that gender, race, socioeconomic status, language, religion, attractiveness, citizenship, age, sexual orientation, disability status, and geographic location encompassed most of the ways that people can perceive themselves as valued, or not valued, by society. How far they perceived themselves from the societal ideal was a good measure of how many and how high the barriers they saw hindering their success. We studied the relationship of distance from privilege to achievement, self-efficacy, hope, and persistence, and we found distance from privilege to be a powerful variable. —Barbara*

Abilities + Personality + Values

In our Beehive model, presented earlier in this book, we showed how general intelligence overlaps and combines with specific abilities and the personality traits that underlie emotional intelligence, creativity, and spiritual intelligence. We based our Beehive model on the assessments and interviews of 500 gifted students, all nominated for their creativity in five domains.[361] Using statistical methods of factor analysis and cluster analysis, we discovered groups of students who shared common personalities and interests. We found that values—our sense of what is right, true, and important in life—added a little more information that was helpful in figuring out career paths. For adolescents, it is often values that point the way to falling in love with an idea. Although values overlap personality, they are not as heritable as intelligence and personality traits. Values are, after all, not directly inherited biologically; values are what every family consciously or unconsciously begins to communicate and inculcate from the time a child is born. Each combination of intelligence, personal traits, and values, if recognized and nurtured, can lead to the wonderful variety of experts, social leaders, innovators, and spiritual leaders that make up the beehive of society.

When gifted students had a combination of high academic ability, conscientiousness, and a strong value for achievement, we found that they were most interested in careers as experts—physicians, accountants, lawyers, and professors. Their career path was clear; they would require strong high school preparation in both verbal and mathematical skills, excellent colleges, and a degree from a prestigious graduate or professional school. Many of them also had practical skills and interests and loved engineering and computer technology. These students were more introverted than the others in the study and seemed perfectly happy tinkering around making computers do their bidding. These students fell into the category of Worker Bees and Forager Bees.

A second cluster usually had divergent thinking abilities in addition to spatial, verbal, and mathematical abilities. The personality trait of openness to experience added to their intelligence, and they had strong values for knowledge, wisdom, and beauty. These students were the Procreator Bees, those who were most interested in creative careers and needed guidance concerning the invisible career ladders in creative fields. They needed help figuring out how to get into art institutes, musical conservatories, and specialized programs. They also needed help learning to manage their considerable impulsivity, moodiness, and nonconformity so they could survive the intense training ahead.

Still another group of students combined high academic ability with agreeability, extraversion, and strong values for altruism and nurturing; these students were most interested in humanitarian service and teaching professions—the Honey Bees. Often, these gifted students were a little embarrassed to be aiming for teaching and counseling because so many people had told them they were too smart to go into teaching. (Naturally, that is upsetting to those of us who teach and counsel.) We affirmed their career goals, however, and showed them how to keep their aspirations high and seek the most challenging, progressive teachers' colleges, social work schools, and psychology majors.

A fourth group of students, who combined high ability with extraversion and values for action and accomplishment, were natural speakers and persuaders who loved being in the spotlight. There were many debaters and political volunteers in this group, as well as students who had already started their own businesses. They were interested in leadership and entrepreneurship. They had the social skills of Honey Bees and the achievement orientation of the Worker Bees. We helped them understand where the best schools of business, pre-law, and international relations were located and affirmed their participation in the clubs that they loved. It was interesting that many of the most accomplished high school athletes fell into this group as well. Although few planned careers in athletics, they saw athletics as a key to scholarships, and many girls told us how their involvement in athletics had led them to be interested in teamwork, leadership, and coaching of athletes. For these women, we often suggested business and management careers in the sport they loved.

Another tiny group of students—10 in all—had an unusual combination of very high scores in openness to experience, introversion, agreeability, and the highest scores of all on our test of *absorption* (easily entering consciousness states like meditation, flow, and ecstasy). In one of our experiments using biofeedback machines, these students were exceptionally competent in closing their eyes and moving their minds back and forth from alpha state (relaxed) to beta (busy mind) to flow (a combination of alpha and beta states). These students' career goals were: a priest, a missionary, several alternative healers, rabbi, Sufi master, and leader of Transcendental Meditation. What else but spiritual intelligence could they be expressing? These students embodied the elements of the Queen Bees, and together with them, we explored the pathways to the careers that they wanted—divinity school, advanced spiritual training, and naturopathic and alternative therapy institutes.

The combination of abilities and personality has been found to be quite predictive of the careers that bright women select.[362] Even 50 years after bright women at Mills College were first tested, their personalities were still clearly linked to the directions their vocational lives had taken.

Even if a young woman has the ability, personality strengths, and values needed for a certain career, these do not ensure that those positive characteristics will develop fully. For that, engagement is necessary. Scott Barry Kaufman says: "Engagement and ability are inseparable throughout human development, dynamically feeding off each other as we engage in the world."[363]

Love of An Idea: Curiosity, Engagement, Passion, Vocation

As we highlighted in the last chapter, motivation is the energy that drives one's abilities toward talent development and actualization. In the beginning, that motivation in the smart little girl will look like curiosity that gradually becomes directed toward a particular set of interests. As the gifted woman discovers the idea with which she is falling in love, she becomes engaged in her education and career. As she experiences flow more and more often and has mindful experiences of the exhilaration of her work, her motivation becomes passion. By the time she is an adult, her motivation is the energy that drives her sense of vocation or calling. Her love of an idea is both her touchstone that reminds her of who she is and her source of strength and resilience.

Filters

Beyond a girl's demographics and level of privilege, there are barriers as well as opportunities set up by her government, her family, her community, her school, her higher education, and her job that will filter the development of her talent.

Legal Rights

In the original model, developed in a time and place where legal rights for women were increasing, the rights given to women by the government were not considered. As political and economic upheavals increase in the U.S. and throughout the world, the status of women in a particular country becomes vital to understanding how women's talents will be developed or discouraged. These rights—to learn to read and go to school; to travel independently without a male escort or even to drive a car; to live, work, and play in the same space as a male; to have sexual desires and choose a partner to marry; to choose when and if they want to have children; to divorce; to practice a religion; to work in a chosen job; to live alone or own property and to stay or leave at will; to have one's own bank account and credit; and to be protected from violence, abuse, or rape—all vary from country to country and government to government. In these cases involving basic rights, women are the primary victims of laws that discourage, disrupt, and deny girls the chance to grow into independent, achieving, and accomplished women. For gifted girls and women in democratic or progressive countries, it is possible to engage in activism for legal rights such as those that protect them from sexual harassment and pay discrimination. For women in patriarchal, authoritarian cultures, being an activist like Malala can be life-threatening. Until gender equality is reached throughout the world, legal barriers will continue to filter out women's talents.

Gender Role and Gender Relations

In developing our model, we needed to consider the powerful impact of the Princess Industrial Complex, the Culture of Romance, and the Wedding

Industrial Complex, all of which influence attitudes and behaviors relating to women's intimate partners. Whether female talent will be actually nurtured depends on many factors, and gender role is one of the most influential.

Female gender roles are the expectations that a culture has for how girls and women are supposed to look and behave; gender relations are how a girl or woman enacts those roles in relationships. Although cultural expectations do not have the force of law, they are still powerful and pervasive. From media, family, and peer groups, girls learn early how girls are supposed to look and behave. Whenever and wherever girls are expected to be less curious, less engaged, less achieving, less active, and less free in constructing their own destiny, then gender roles will bend the arc of girls' lives away from the realization of their potential.

The ways in which girls and women are socialized (by their families, friends, and culture) to behave with intimate partners has an extraordinary effect on their future career and life choices. If they are socialized by tradition to put the needs and goals of the men in their lives before their own, they will often make choices against their own interests. A high school girl may decide against a scholarship to an Ivy League college in order to attend the same college her boyfriend is attending. Many college women surrender to the party pathway and reduce their aspirations. A young woman who marries in graduate school is more likely to choose part-time work for an extended period to support her husband's career. Then there are women who are so exhausted by her high-demand, non-family-friendly career that they drop out to raise the children while the husband pursues his goals. All of these women are being influenced by family, society, and traditional values regarding gender relations. Those young women who challenge traditional gender roles, who expect equity in their relationships, and who expect support for domestic tasks and family life from their partner are more likely to fulfill their career and achievement goals.

Social and Cultural Capital

Social and cultural capital can make up for many privations of youth. Even if a girl is born far from privilege and perceives herself to be distant from power, family and social network support and knowledge of the culture can make up for the difference between herself and more privileged girls. When smart girls from rural or poor urban neighborhoods are brought to college campuses or workplaces, helped to feel a sense of belonging there, and shown all the ways that they, too, can aspire to better occupations, then they are gaining cultural capital. When smart girls from less privileged homes are introduced to teachers, youth workers, and professional people who can serve as mentors, they are acquiring the social capital they need to feel confident around powerful people.

Educational and Career Opportunities

Educational opportunities for schooling, training in specific skills, higher education, and graduate and professional education are the opportunities that need to be acted upon. If a girl is offered a place in a Talent Search summer program but doesn't perceive it as important to go, or if a young woman gets admitted to an elite women's college but doesn't bother to consider a single-sex school, these opportunities are wasted and she pays a high opportunity cost. Offers of admission and financial aid—even special recognition of talent—all play an important role in filtering young women's talents. Mentors, role models, hands-on career education experiences, and career counseling all are needed for the optimal education.

Lots of scholars have debated how much education and experience are needed for expertise in a domain, with ideas like *10,000 hours* and the *10-year rule* being thrown out there.[364] It is unlikely that every talent develops at the same rate in every domain. Scott Barry Kaufman says, "There are no '10-year rules' or 'creativity thresholds' in which a person must attain a certain amount of knowledge or score above an arbitrary level on a standardized test to attain their goals."[365] Education and training that allows rapid progress at the woman's own pace is the best pathway for the development of her talent. Telling a smart girl that it will take 10,000 hours to mastery may take the wind out of her sails just as she embarks on her adventure; in addition, for many bright girls, the time may be much shorter.

Career opportunities include not only the actual jobs that a smart young woman gets but also the career education, internships, and volunteer experiences that might lead her to a career. Once employed, these filters become a chance to advance through merit and productivity, to gain a career mentor or supportive supervisor, and to exercise autonomy, decision-making, and leadership. If self-employed, women need incubator or entrepreneurial assistance, financial resources and investors, and a market for her products or services. When all of these are in place, a career can move a woman toward her goals; if too much is lacking, she may become stagnant or stuck. Educational and career opportunities, however, are not a matter of relentless hunting for chances to move ahead, nor are they simply the result of random chance. Career theorist John Krumboltz uses the term "planned happenstance" to describe the importance of being in the right place and being around the right people for "chance" opportunities to emerge.[366] Smart women need to learn how to plan for fortunate happenstance, so that they will be there when the opportunities emerge.

Talent Domain

Every domain has its own pathways and gatekeepers, whether it is visual arts, performing arts, humanities, STEM fields, business and law, teaching and counseling, athletics, or spiritual occupations. Fine arts have portfolios; performing arts have auditions; humanities and STEM have differing curriculum vitae; business and law have resumes; and teaching, counseling, and ministry require evidence of practice skills. Rena Subotnik provides a model based on studies of experts that showed the clear distinctions in the kind of training experiences required by each domain.[367] Each talent domain filters talents by determining how a person's talents will be challenged, promoted, and judged as expert or eminent. Finally, talent domains will determine lifestyle and life course—where and how one will work and live.

Sphere

Personal

Most career development theories do not even consider the sphere in which talents will be expressed; it has always been assumed that men will express their talents in the public domain, producing ideas, goods, and services to society. Those of us who try to understand women's career development must always wrestle with the personal vs. public spheres of influence and production because until this last century, women were not expected to manifest their talents in the public sphere. Recall that half of Terman's gifted women were homemakers because they had been socialized to apply their schooling, college education, and personal strengths to creating homes and raising families. Today, people like to talk about the choice to stay home to raise children, but as we have seen, many women don't have a choice except to work, and the crazy requirements of extreme jobs persuade many women to "choose" to stay home when they are worn down to the point where they must escape. Many women who work in minimum wage jobs realize that, with daycare costs, they are only making a few dollars a week. They might as well stay home and do their best to pursue their calling from their home office until their children go to school. Many gifted women are homeschooling their gifted children by themselves because it is impossible to get the schooling their children need and the father's work is less flexible. Only in Scandinavian and European countries where childcare is subsidized by the government for all families and parental leave is paid can women truly and freely choose to work or stay home.

Whatever the conditions, we have always urged women to move forward with their vocation, whether paid or unpaid, at home or in the public sphere. No matter how difficult the job market or working conditions, a true calling is not dependent on having a job or having equitable domestic arrangements. Even if a woman cannot find work as an anthropologist, she can continue to read the scientific literature and perhaps participate in scientific conferences. If a woman cannot find a way to survive in the business workplace with its rigid structures, she can become an entrepreneur from home. If in the course of homeschooling, she discovers a way to increase her own knowledge or develop technology skills in ways that will support her calling, then she is still living her mission.

The key, we believe, is either to *lean in* to one's work or *move forward* with one's vocation by any means necessary. Acknowledging that the childrearing years are exhausting and difficult, women can insist on equitable sharing of home chores and childcare and push their organizations for greater flexibility while still leaning into their careers. When that can't work because of the lack of a partner or institutional support, then the woman has to move forward with her career by continuing her education, her professional involvement, and some form of productivity in her chosen field at home. She will still need the support of family members, friends, or a cooperative childcare to have the alone time that she needs for the development of her art, business, or scholarly life.

The home and family sphere is likely to be a temporary one—so any woman stepping out must keep up with changes in her domain so that she can be ready to re-enter with intensity and confidence.

There is another temporary sphere that we debated a long time—the sphere of personal growth. Can a woman realize her talent, fulfill her values, and self-actualize entirely by herself? We thought of contemplative nuns and women seeking psychological or spiritual growth. We considered Emily Dickinson, laboring alone on her poetry that she believed might never be read, and we agreed that it is possible. For many women, however, personal growth is a phase of life—particularly in midlife—when she withdraws from the public sphere and concentrates on healing psychological distress, seeking a new narrative for her life, or finding connectedness through nature or spiritual practice. It was hard for us to think of any woman staying forever in the realm of personal growth—because it seems inevitable that the result of healing or discovery of connectedness is a re-birth of one's calling in life.

Our suggestion is: Don't stop there too long. Get back on your feet, recognize your relatedness to the universe, and get on with your work in the world.

Public

Subotnik, Olszewski-Kubilius, and Worrell say that eminence should be the goal of education for gifted children, and we agree that a rigorous, challenging education leading toward mastery of a domain will provide smart girls with the most options in life.[368] We don't agree that eminence should be the goal of one's life or one's career development. Eminence will always be in the eye of the beholder—that is, in the eyes of the gatekeepers of a talent domain. As long as women are closed out of those domains by foundations and filters that prevent them from the full expression of their talents and strengths, then eminence is not a goal that will bring life satisfaction. Besides, eminence is an extrinsic goal, one that lots of people other than the individual can influence or control; a calling is an intrinsic goal, and the individual remains the final judge of its attainment. The gender role socialization of men often leads them to seek extrinsic goals like prizes, tenure, and eminence—and they often bitterly regret the pursuit of that goal when the cheering stops.[369] Nobody whose life goal is attainment of fame, riches, or recognition is likely to ever attain that goal of self-actualization because they have had to twist their own personalities, compromise their values, and forget their personal dreams to meet the approval of others.

When the goal is instead optimal development and self-actualization, it is amazing how much women can accomplish for the public good. The smart girl or bright woman who pursues her interests, develops her talents, and falls in love with an idea nearly always ends up in the public sphere— sometimes to their own surprise, like J. K. Rowling. Even the mystic and the private poet must eventually put words to the page, and if her talents are great and her passion strong, the probability is that those words will eventually come to light for someone else to read.

We have added several other spheres because in the beehive of life there is room for many roles. One can find optimal development as an *expert professional*, using one's talents to the fullest by sharing one's expertise with students, patients, and clients. Some experts will find within themselves the desire to lead other professionals or advocate for their profession to the public; if they have emotional intelligence, they will probably succeed. Even the most creative inventor or artist might not be interested in eminence but will choose to be an *individual entrepreneur* in order to be in control of their own career development. Thus, entrepreneurship should also be a domain of expression of talent.

Finally, some women just cannot escape becoming eminent, even if they never dreamed of reaching the apex of their domain. They have it thrust upon them, by virtue of their genius and their passionate involvement with the idea with which they have fallen in love. They have had the solid foundations, they have found their way through the filters, and they have been fortunate enough to realize their full potential in a domain that not only let them in but also recognized their worth. Eminence is power, and one's love of an idea can inform the use of that power. Self-actualizing women do not stop with the attainment of eminence in their field. In the words of Felice Kaufmann, "They just barrel on through." They use their eminence to empower others.

CHAPTER 15

Suggestions to Guide
Smart Girls and Women toward
Optimal Development

Research, theorizing, and model building are important but so are practical suggestions for guiding smart girls, for smart women who want to reach for optimal development, and for the professionals who help them. These recommendations will help parents and teachers build on the foundations of optimal development.

For Parents | The Preschool Years

1. Give your little girl a head start in health. Encourage lots of active play outdoors and sunshine; provide many healthy, delicious food choices; and promote as much sleep as she needs to be in a happy mood most of the time.

2. Dress your daughter for active play. Resist the Princess Industrial Complex gently with awareness, patience, and provision of alternatives. Teach her that, for most of us, being a princess is not a viable career option.

3. Read to her every night and share not just the mechanics of reading but also your love of learning.

4. Allow her to play with a touchpad and show her how to find pictures, puzzles, and games that she likes.

5. Allow her to play with lots of materials and tools for making things—not just crayons and paper but clay, metals, fabrics, liquids,

and of course, dirt! Think 3-D, not just 2-D play. Make some toys together. Make a sailboat, a doll, a musical instrument. Toys like *Goldie Blox*, Lego-like toys that encourage girls in the area of design and engineering, are perfect for this age.

6. When you use numbers, speak them aloud, whether counting, measuring, or finding a TV station.

7. If you speak two languages, be flexible and use both languages in the home.

8. When she shows signs of interest in reading, celebrate her interest and find her the books and media that she likes to read.

9. Teach her how to say what she is feeling and to ask for what she needs. These are two of the most important emotional skills you can give your smart girl. When she is having a meltdown, stay calm and simply ask: What are you feeling right now? If she does not know, give her a couple of options. Say: "Some people might be feeling mad or sad or frustrated." When she tells you what she is feeling, then ask, "What do you need right now?" At first she probably won't be able to tell you, so give her options again. Say: "Some people might need to take a time out, or to take a breath, or to go run up and down the stairs to get rid of their energy. Which one do you need?" When she tells you what she needs, give her the time and space to receive it.

10. Choose daycare or preschool carefully—the most expensive option is not always the best. The best for your little girl is one that is open to different learning rates, that has a diverse group of teachers and students, that provides active, outdoor play, and that doesn't enforce nap time, just quiet time. Avoid preschools that segregate girls' and boys' play.

11. Surround her with an extended family—even if you have to create it yourself from best friends and neighbors. Let her have the experience of growing up in a mutually supportive community with lots of people who care for her.

12. Outdoor play is not just about getting exercise. It is her first introduction to the physical world around her. Show her the plants and animals of your backyard and neighborhood. Name them and introduce her to their needs and habits.

Kindergarten through Fifth Grade

1. Make sure she goes to kindergarten when her mind is ready, rather than just the age that most children go; when she is reading, drawing, counting, categorizing, let her go. If the school has rigid guidelines that refuse her at an early age, then challenge those rules or invest in private kindergarten until she can be accepted at the appropriate grade level.

2. Take her for testing if there are early gifted programs, but remember: These tests are not stable or particularly accurate until about nine years of age. If your family belongs to a less privileged group, it is likely that her scores will be an underestimate of her abilities. You are the best judge of her abilities because you have observed her development.

3. Provide her lots of alone time and the independence and resources she needs to choose her own activities.

4. Avoid informal all-girl playgroups, sleepovers, and other extended, unsupervised time in same-age girl groups where popular girls' culture is enforced. Find informal groups of intellectual and emotional peers where she can find her "sure shelter."

5. On the other hand, a formal, well-organized girl group with a strong mission to support girls' dreams, like Brownies, 4-H, or YWCA, is a good idea *if* she enjoys the group. Help her learn the friendship skills of listening, kindness, and sharing.

6. Model egalitarian relationships in your family.

7. Provide lots of opportunities to meet adults and children of different races, cultures, languages, orientations, and social classes. Bring the world to your home so that she will be comfortable in the world.

8. Start a second language while she is still very young through formal instruction, immersion in another culture, or informal instruction at home.

9. Start a musical instrument while she is very young, allowing her some choice of instrument after a period of exploration. This too can be done formally or informally through a neighbor or friend.

10. Teach her to be proud of her body and the things she is physically capable of learning and doing. Emphasize the skills she wants to learn and only engage in early team sports if she chooses them and enjoys them.

11. Seek opportunities for accelerated learning, and ask that your daughter be able to learn at her own pace at school, through differentiation, clustering, or self-contained classrooms. However, do not expect that your school can provide everything she needs.

12. Do not over-help, overprotect, or oversee all of her activities. Let her take risks, and let yourself be uncomfortable sometimes.

13. Help her to keep her connection to nature. It is a chance for you to teach her about her relationship to the Earth and the universe around her. Show her the rivers, lakes, and underground caves where water comes from. Show her the plants and animals that feed us or have become our companions, and help her see the connections and communities of living things. Show her the stars at night, and teach her about the millions of other suns that light other worlds.

Middle School

1. Try to find a middle school that has a program for gifted education or at least one that acknowledges differences in learning abilities and allows for differentiation.

2. Prepare your daughter for puberty not only by teaching her about the physical changes but also in terms of how it might change how people respond to her. Teach her to love and respect her growing and changing body, despite your or her embarrassment during these discussions.

3. Resist the cultural sexualization of middle school girls by discussing advertising and media portrayals. Help her choose clothing that is fashionable without objectifying her. No sexy selfies.

4. If she must be on Facebook, Tumblr, Pinterest, Instagram, or other social media sites, set limits about privacy settings, content, and the types of people she is allowed to interact with. For example, only she and her friends should be able to interact. No interaction with strangers without parental supervision—another good rule. Give examples of the kind of content that you like and approve.

5. Help her find an older girl or young woman who is achieving and confident to be her friend and mentor.

6. Sign her up for the testing for the Talent Search program, and encourage her to go to the summer programs for which she qualifies.

7. Take her on trips to museums, science centers, theater, dance performances, and natural areas such as state and national parks.

8. Engage in family volunteer work for religious organizations, charities, and nonprofits.

9. Invite adult friends who are intellectuals, well-traveled people, artists, and leaders to your home for social events that include her.

10. Take her along to conferences and conventions related to her interests, and introduce her to professional people.

11. Help her choose just a few out-of-school activities that will increase her talents and leisure skills.

12. If her musical, artistic, performance, or athletic skills have reached a point where her teacher recommends a new level of instruction, find a master teacher and help her understand how this more challenging and rigorous instruction will help her in the long run.

13. As her gender identity and sexual orientation emerge, support her with information, emotional connection, and understanding.

14. Be clear about what you expect in a romantic partner for her, and stick to boundaries you have set; for example, you must meet and spend time with any serious love interest. Rather than forbidding particular relationships, reinforce positive, equitable relationships with attention, invitations, and praise for your daughter's good choices.

15. Expect some bad judgment, emotional flare-ups, sadness about romance and friendships, and challenges to family rules. Maintain a friendly, reasonable, no-drama stance toward these. Steer clear of labeling behavior too quickly as mental illness, and avoid medication unless recommended by a qualified psychologist or physician who works with bright children.

16. Girls' peer groups at this age are fraught with drama; girls who were pleasant friends as children might become bullies or negative opinion leaders. Encourage your daughter to choose achievement-oriented, confident girlfriends from among her intellectual peers whose parents share your values.

17. Don't expect your daughter to be the main babysitter, meal-maker, and housekeeper when you must be away after school; some responsibility when parents must work is good, but not all of the responsibility of parenting roles.

18. If you lack financial resources, recognize that almost all programs for gifted young people have a source of scholarship money. Use your networks to discover company scholarships, assistance from youth or religious groups, and independent crowdfunding sites like Kickstarter.

19. If she is a member of a race, class, religion, disability group, language group, or size group, it is time to talk about how these social labels interact with both her sex and her giftedness. Introduce her to the ideas of privilege and power, and help her understand how discrimination and prejudice can become internalized. Teach her about stereotype threat and self-efficacy, and assure her that she does not have to yield to stereotypes and societal expectations.

20. Teach her about the meaning of flow, and as she gains expertise in school subjects or outside activities, help her identify that feeling.

Older Adolescence

1. Begin serious planning for college or post-secondary experiences by sophomore year. She should take the preparatory exams for SAT and ACT; she should sign up for AP courses and exams at school or online.

2. She needs career counseling from a counselor or vocational psychologist who understands the needs of gifted girls. Find lists of resources at the NAGC website, nagc.org/get-involved/nagc-networks-and-special-interest-groups/networks-counseling-guidance, and Hoagie's website, www.hoagiesgifted.org/counseling.htm, and use them. Check www.cleoslab.org and www.smartcreativehappy.com for information on counseling for creatively gifted girls.

3. These years are the ones in which she is most at-risk for eating disorders, stress disorders, and risky behaviors. Distinguish between experimentation and habit, and between situational stress and chronic conditions like depression or anxiety. Discuss how being smart can make these problems worse. Take her to a psychologist for gifted girls if her problems are interfering with her schoolwork and her enjoyment of life and school.

4. On the other hand, these are the years when she may fall in love with an idea. Watch for it! As she gains mastery over knowledge and skills in a field, as she delves deeper into ideas that intrigue her, support her 100%. Rather than spreading out your resources trying to support four different expensive out-of-school activities, focus your resources on the area in which she is growing her passion. Talk about flow and values and how they help her to identify an idea worth loving.

5. Help her find mentors at colleges, universities, or institutes with interests that are similar to hers. By 16 years old, she can volunteer or take part-time work assisting professors or professionals, if you help her to design a proposal. There is no reason for her to be working in fast food or retail jobs when she could be earning the same money working for a professional who might never have considered a teen assistant until asked.

6. Make a plan with her for college or institute visits, and make financial support part of that plan. Be clear about what the family has to spend, and help her prepare a federal aid (FAFSA) form so that she understands the investment you are both making. Get help from college counselors finding private scholarships as well. She should go to the institution with the best professors who are engaged in her interest area, not the best colleges from some list.

7. It is likely that she will prefer older friends and college students rather than age peers. Of course, this is problematic if she has romantic relationships with partners older than 18, which puts both her and the partner at legal risk. Help her understand the risks while recognizing and trusting that most gifted girls make good decisions about relationships with older friends.

8. Let her go to college early if she is prepared and wants to go. For many highly gifted and creative girls, high school culture holds little to interest them once they have completed their requirements.

9. Consider college courses while she is still in high school or even dual enrollment in high school and college. Massive online courses allow exposure to excellent professors and a chance to try out different subject areas.

10. If she wants to try a Gap Year or a DIY college approach, make sure that she outlines a plan with timelines and expected outcomes so that she doesn't end up drifting or losing confidence in her goals.

11. Now that she is ready for adult literature, share your favorite authors as well as the classics she didn't read in high school. Show her classic films and discuss current popular culture. Introduce her to the websites that feature women artists, writers, scientists, and leaders and read the overlooked work of women together. Become intellectual companions, which is one of the best ways of transitioning from parent-child to parent-young adult relationships.

College Years

1. She will need a safe haven for a while. Don't move, change her room at home, or completely re-model until she has had a chance to get her footing out in the world.

2. Be there for her emotionally, recognizing the intensity of the transition.

3. Let her handle meetings with advisors, financial aid counselors, and other college personnel by herself.

4. Allow her to choose her own living arrangements; if she refuses residence halls or sororities, it is probably for a good reason: She doesn't want to be a part of college social culture. On the other hand, she may have found exactly the right residence hall or sorority that supports her goals and welcomes smart women; be open to that possibility as well.

5. Make your home a place she is happy to bring new friends.

6. Her college experience is not your college experience; many of the things you treasured she will ignore or resist, so let her have her own way of finding her intellectual and emotional home now that she is away.

7. Remember her entire generation is likely to marry late if they marry at all, so refrain from asking about it. Support her in her choice of lifestyle and community, no matter how different it might be from your own.

Advice for Smart Girls in Elementary and Middle School

1. It is okay to be different from other girls. It's not just okay, it's great.

2. Do you like to read and think a lot about what you read? Ask all the grownups you like about what they liked to read when they were your age.

3. What kind of adventures do you like—outdoors, at the library, at the playground? Plan a little adventure every day. Let your parents go along or help you plan.

4. Ask your parents for one place in your home where you can go to be alone, even if it is just a place you make yourself. Practice spending time on your own, reading, thinking, collecting things, experimenting, and writing down your thoughts.

5. Think and write about the girls you like in books, on TV, and online. Which ones don't you like? Which boys do you like? Dislike? You don't have to like the boys or be like the girls you don't like, even if everybody else thinks they are great.

6. If other girls talk about how they look all the time, forget about it—you're young. Just run around, get lots of exercise, eat less junk food than you want, and get outside every day.

7. What would you like to be when you grow up? Nowadays girls can be anything they want to be—it didn't used to be that way. So think up the most exciting, interesting things you could do and learn all about the people who are doing those things.

8. Think about when you grow up. How will you do things differently from what grownups are doing right now in the world? Write about the world you want to grow up in.

9. Do you want to change something about the world right now? Start a club and make your voice heard.

10. Find other kids who like the same things you do—even if they are younger, older, boy, or girl—and ask your parents to help find kids like you to hang out with.

11. What kinds of things have you tried that are hard for you? Think of one thing you are really bad at doing, try it out, and work at it. Even if you never get to be the best at it, you can have fun doing it and laugh at yourself when you goof up.

Advice for Smart Teens

1. Never go on a date where you try to look as beautiful as possible for a guy and he pays for everything. It can create expectations or a feeling of obligation. It is okay to go out with someone and just hang out together, or talk on the phone or online about everything in the world, or go see things together that are cool and interesting. Just don't get into a thing where he always pays for you. Why should he? Besides, you're equals. Don't let yourself be treated otherwise.

2. Never go on an extreme diet. Dieting keeps girls from being powerful, active, and engaged in the world because they are busy starving themselves to death. Most diets will starve your spirit as much as your body. Eat delicious, beautiful food, most of it plants. Do some crazy, wonderful exercise that you love every day, preferably outdoors—not a work out.

3. Learn how to name and manage your emotions. When your hormones flare up and your body seems out of control, there will be times when you will feel like laughing, crying, screaming, and curling up in a fetal position all in the same moment. Emotions are normal. However, when your emotions run wild too often, it is a sign that you might need to talk with a professional counselor or psychologist who specializes in gifted girls about how to regulate your emotions. The good news is that regular exercise, mindfulness practices, yoga, and deep breathing all help with emotional self-regulation. Also, just being able to say what you are feeling and ask for what you need is very empowering. Try it and find out for yourself.

4. Hang out with smart, funny people who make you feel happy to be alive. Hint: If they never care to talk about your ideas and interests, they probably don't care about you, right? And they might not be the best people to have as friends.

5. Is somebody insulting you or talking trash about you to your friends all the time? Welcome to the world of human beings. Think about how the most clever, strong, heroic, selfless character in fiction would deal with that person. Forget about drama or online public exchanges—just get above that stuff.

6. If your school is like some post-apocalyptic wasteland of non-learning, start researching online for how you can get the education you need, and begin lobbying hard for a place where you can learn, in the real world or online. Really talk with your parents about this, and listen to their concerns as well as making your case.

7. Read the classics in science, history, and literature, and find everything that is new and edgy in popular culture. In films, books, and videos, use the Bechdel Rules: first, at least two characters are women; second, they talk to each other; and third, they talk about something other than men.[370]

8. Start planning your future now. Think of all the things that are worth living or even dying for. These are your values. Do you value nature, beauty, service, peace, equality, spirituality, wisdom, creativity, and freedom? Now think of some careers where you can make those values come alive. Find out what it takes to get to those careers.

9. When you fall in love with an idea, follow it anywhere; if you haven't found an idea to fall in love with yet, start looking. Find ways to travel, to meet people from many different cultures, to meet people whom you admire, and to volunteer for causes you believe in.

10. Do your parents treat you like a princess or a resident genius? Don't let them. Start thinking of them as human beings and figure out how you can help them out because life is difficult for most parents. Do your part around the house. If, on the other hand, you seem to be doing too much—like staying home from school to take care of a little brother or sister or helping in the family business so much you don't have time for homework—that is not okay; let them know about it.

11. Choose just a few out-of-school activities that relate to your strongest interests and that challenge you—really challenge you. Don't try to do everything or be everything to everybody. And don't buy

into the idea that you have to be well-rounded. Get into summer programs that extend your knowledge in ways you can't get at school—a foreign language, a technology course, an art, music, or writing camp, or a leadership camp. Consider some all-girls activities that will connect you with strong female leaders.

12. If you are thinking that you have to choose a college or a career based on what you are the best at—whether it is math, athletics, writing, music, art, or whatever—stop thinking that way. You are probably talented enough at all kinds of things to get to the top of the field with enough effort, so choose your pathway based on what activity gives you a sense of flow, not just what you are good at.

13. Find out about money and how you can have your own bank account. Forget about fast food and big box store jobs. What are you going to learn there? Who is going to mentor you? Find a professional person, a leader, or an adult doing something you admire and ask that person to pay you minimum wage to assist him or her in some task. Organize their library, make calls for them, run errands, or do chores for old people who have retired from jobs you admire.

14. If you think you might be bisexual, transgender, or lesbian, now is the time to talk about it with your parents or a teacher you trust, preferably who is a member of an LGBT alliance so you can avoid discrimination.

15. If you are heterosexual, follow the unofficial McKay Law of Boyfriend Evaluation when choosing a relationship:

    • Does he go to your games, performances, or competitions?

    • Does he know your career goals?

    • Is he as smart as or smarter than you so that you don't have to spend a lot of time in your head correcting his facts or grammar?

16. Do not date for a boy's potential. A romantic relationship is not supposed to be a boyfriend improvement project. If your boyfriend smokes pot, drinks too much, plays video games until the early morning hours, skips school or slacks in his classes, or if, when you tell people about him, you finish by saying something like "…but he's got a lot of potential" or "…but he's a really good guy,"

then it is time to break up with him. Remember this: People show you who they are. It is not your job to change them. It is your job to believe them. And walk away from the ones who don't enable you to fulfill your own potential.

17. Do not get pregnant. That is the single most important thing you can do for your future education and career opportunities. Do not even get into a position of being scared that you might be pregnant—that just robs you of energy and happiness and creates anxiety so that you can't concentrate. Do not even think about having sex without contraception. Not even once.

Advice for College and Graduate School Women

1. When choosing a college, use your intuition, but let your intuition be informed by a lot of information. Most important: Is there somebody at that college who teaches or does research in exactly the area that you love? If you are into exotic animal veterinary medicine, you need to go to an undergrad pre-vet or animal science program where there is a faculty member doing regular work in the field with exotic animals. If you love the German language, make sure that more than two courses are offered in German. Consider a women's college if you want more leadership opportunities.

2. Know your values. Your values are the ideals and guiding principles that you hold precious and dear. Use them to inform your intuition and guide your decisions. And remember, values are not the same as morals.

3. Know your creative flow. What intellectual or creative activities cause you to lose track of time and become so completely absorbed that you forget everything else? What activities challenge your mind and spark your imagination? These are the activities that should be at the center of your career. Passively looking at other people's photos, comments, and images on Facebook, Pinterest, and Instagram are usually ways of zoning out, not creative flow.

4. Begin identifying your mission. Know that your mission will evolve over the course of your lifetime. You should start to understand what you are uniquely suited for and how you can contribute to the world in a meaningful and creative way.

5. Manage your stress. If you notice that you're anxious, down, worried, or can't sleep, take yourself to the campus counseling center and work with a counselor on stress management skills. Also talk about the things that are bothering you.

6. Get to know your campus career center staff. In fact, find ways to hang out at the career center so the staff can get to know you. They are there to help you prepare your resume and find internships and study abroad experiences. And they are usually really nice people, too.

7. As you take your general courses, do not be surprised if you suddenly fall in love with a different domain. It happens all the time—and gifted students tend to change majors early and often. If you find yourself going into a state of flow while working on a lab experiment, writing a midterm paper, or completing an art project, that is a good signal that this is something you should be doing.

8. Find a mentor. It is nice if a mentor is in the exact field that you are interested in, but what really matters is that there is a faculty member who takes a personal interest in you and wants to help you achieve your goals.

9. Raise your hand and mean it. In college classes, it is easy to hide in the back of the class and whisper the correct answers to your best friend. It is far more scary to say the answer out loud in front of the class because you might be wrong, but it is an important action. Raise your hand with enthusiasm in order to get your professor's attention. Let him or her know that you are interested in exploring the topic by participating in class discussions. Don't hedge and qualify all your comments and act as if you were asking a question rather than making a statement.

10. If you get a C in a class—or even if you fail a class—it is not a sign that you're not as smart as you thought you were. More likely, it is a sign that something else is going on in your life that needs attention. Maybe your parents just split up. Or perhaps something bad just happened to you or you fell in with a party crowd. Talk with a counselor, mentor, or your parents about what is happening in your life. Most important: Do not disengage from the world. Get the support you need so that you can bounce back quickly.

11. Join student groups in areas related to your interests. Don't just join social groups. Have fun, but don't get caught up in the party pathway. Not going to college? If you are doing a Gap Year, a DIY education, or a mixture, have a clear plan, a mentor, objectives, and portfolio showing the accomplishment of your objectives.

12. Avoid the culture of romance. Hang out with women who can talk to each other about ideas, accomplishments, and dreams—not just about relationships with men and beauty tips. When your friends define themselves by their relationships with men, call them out on it.

13. Become involved in a cause and work for social change; you will never be as free again to express your values through social and political action.

14. Get as many scholarships and grants as possible so that you do not have to rely upon student loans for most of your education; consult a professional educational consultant who specializes in scholarship searches, or make a friend in the financial aid department. If you work, keep your hours under 20 every week, and try to keep the work in your area of interest.

15. Try for the most prestigious internship at an organization that will not use you as slave labor. Carefully investigate, and talk to people who have done these internships. Create a portfolio. Save the results of every paper and project that you do in an online portfolio of experiences.

16. Plan your future relationships as carefully as you plan your career. Explore relationships with friendly, smart partners. Learn the difference between sex and love. Look for clues that this partner has a history of equitable relationships, supports your career goals, and admires your passion. Are your goals as important to him as his goals are? The best friends and intimate partners for a smart young woman are those with whom she has the best, longest lasting, and most exciting conversations. If you are bored, worried, or annoyed too often, get out of there.

17. Fall in love with an idea. Identify something that pisses you off, that compels you to stay up late into the night researching and reading, or that makes you so mad you could scream. Find the

idea that seems to you the answer to all the questions you have had. A topic that evokes your passion is worthy of your love. Then set about to solve a problem related to that idea. Find new ways to bring beauty and function into the world. Start a movement. Create an app. Make art and music that expresses your love of your idea.

18. Get engaged to your career. Work actively toward the fulfillment of your values. Make a promise to yourself to commit to your work and your way of life.

Adult Smart Women

1. If you haven't found the idea with which to fall in love, it is not too late. You will need to go back to the last time you felt a sense of flow—the last time you felt fully at one with the work that you were doing. Start there and re-acquaint yourself. Then plunge into a new field of endeavor with all your heart.

2. Accept and relish change. If it has been a long time since you reveled in scientific discovery, writing, art, music, leadership, teaching, or service, then you will need to recognize both how you have changed and how that profession has changed. Are you still in love with the idea? How has your love for it transformed?

3. Take stock. If you have been going full steam ahead in your career and find yourself overwhelmed, stop and ask yourself:

   • How am I contributing to my mission and purpose in life?

   • How does this contribute to the loving support I have built around me?

   • How does this contribute to the things I need to do to support my mission?

   If what you are doing does not contribute to any of these, say *no.* Stop doing it.

4. Set limits. If you have a partner, your relationship won't need constant negotiation if you establish some non-negotiables. What must you absolutely have in your life, not just to survive, but to thrive? What does your partner need? What does an equitable relationship mean to you? What does it mean to your partner?

5. Go to workshops, but use caution. Do not get over-involved. Smart women can be precocious in their personal development, speeding through workshops and retreats, gathering new information with the enthusiasm of a scholar, and processing their experiences aloud as they go. There is always a danger in getting caught up in a perpetual self-help cycle where a woman explores and examines her life in such depth that she becomes lost.

6. Support other smart women. Find them, build a community, and take the time to keep up with each other.

7. Mentor girls and young women. Pay a smart girl to assist you in some task. She can organize your library, make calls for you, run errands, manage your website, or run your social media campaigns.

8. Plan your family. If you have children, do it in your time in your way. You choose the method of childbirth, the method of feeding, and the schedule. It is your body and your life. Be as creative as you need to be in order to work and nurture your children. Be as demanding as you need to be to get your colleagues, administrators, and organization behind you.

9. Keep up with your field. Avoid stopping or dropping out for more than a year unless you have both a clear plan for how you will stay involved in your profession or discipline during this time and a clear plan for re-entry.

10. Plan your finances for both short- and long-term goals. Do not stop or drop out without your own bank account and enough savings to purchase what you need for your continued professional engagement. Did you save for professional travel and expenses during your time off?

11. Strive for a healthy lifestyle that involves good nutrition, healthy exercise, solitude, spirituality, social support, and romance—all of these can provide a foundation for your vocation.

12. Know your legal rights and demand them. Work for equality and justice for yourself and for the women who are coming up behind you.

13. Plan for your own mental health. Find a psychologist, counselor, or leadership coach who understands smart women.

14. Try not to be too "well-adjusted"—that is, too agreeable, compromising, and resourceful in meeting others' needs. Having a few "thorns" may defend you against those who would ask you to compromise your goals and values.

15. Practice selective conscientiousness. Give yourself 100% to your chosen mission; be perfectionistic, precise, and persistent. Learn to do activities that are not related to your mission half-way or just well enough. Surround yourself with people who love you and support your mission.

16. Remember your connections to the universe. When you are alone, sad, or afraid, go into nature and look for the inspiration and awe that will help bring perspective back into your life. There are few hurts so deep that the love of animal friends and the beauty of growing things cannot heal.

Recommendations for Professionals who Work with Smart Women

To assist smart women in the stage of career development where they are ready to fall in love with an idea and get engaged, we recommend that professionals focus on the following topics. Here are some issues and strategies to work on together:

1. Create a timeline of the past that details and processes social, emotional, and career milestones, including career goals, marriages, divorces, children, promotions, depression, anxiety, and anything that may have impacted how she views herself and her future.

2. Assess strengths, values, and personality, but emphasize areas of creative flow.

3. Examine the psychology of financial success consciousness, as well as the kind of relationship with her finances that will support her mission and purpose.

4. Practice some behavioral strategies, such as mindfulness, to manage symptoms of guilt, depression, and anxiety.

5. Identify key archetypes in the Female Hero's Journey as Kathleen Noble describes in her book, *The Sound of the Silver Horn*, in order to have a heroic figure to aspire to.[371]

6. Use movie-therapy and bibliotherapy through films and books with strong feminine leads.

7. Suggest retreats that promote optimal states of being, such as equine-assisted coaching, mindfulness or yoga retreats, spiritual retreats, adventure experiences including trapeze, horseback riding, skydiving, and travel abroad.

8. Explore ways of increasing creative expertise and mastery, whether in dance, music, art, coding, consciousness, language lessons, or other tools of the many domains of talent.

9. Use personal well-being activities such as massage, exercise, and yoga in support of their goal of being strong and fit.

10. Develop a personal mission statement so that she can state her mission in life in 25 words or less. Then integrate all of the above activities into a map of the future that shows what she must do this week, this month, and this year to attain her vision.

CHAPTER 16
Conclusion

How a nation treats its smart girls is a measure of that nation's future prosperity. How a nation nurtures the talents of smart women is a measure of its commitment to freedom, equality, and the well-being of all of its citizens. Across the world, we stand at the threshold of a new era for humankind. For the first time since we became *Homo sapiens*—the wise ones—women have the ability to determine when and if they will have children in countries that support birth control and reproductive freedom. For the first time in recorded history, women in most developed countries have the right to earn money and own property. Just a century ago, women had little control over if, when, and how they gave birth. According to historical studies in medicine, the typical woman in the U.S. in the late 19th century had six pregnancies that resulted in a live birth, one or two miscarriages, and one or two children who died in childhood.[372] If you were unlucky enough to use Victorian maternity hospitals where doctors did not wash their hands when delivering, you had a one in eight chance of dying in childbirth.[373]

Now consider all the theories about why more women didn't achieve eminence—ranging from sex differences in intelligence to women's supposedly natural inclination toward nurturing—and most of these theories seem rather obtuse from the perspective of human history. Until recently, few smart girls had a chance to develop into eminent women—their lives were one long cycle of pregnancy, childbirth, nursing, and tending to sick children or other family members. Those few gifted women who attained eminence were single, childless, or privileged women with maids and nannies.

Now, however, smart girls have the opportunity to fulfill their potential in most developed countries. In sharp contrast, in countries like Afghanistan, bright girls must fight for the right to read; in India, teen girls must fear for their lives if they marry without a large enough dowry; in central Africa, women and infant mortality is similar to that of a century ago. It is truly the smart girls who live in places that allow them control of their bodies and their incomes who will lead the way to the new global society where all talents are recognized.

What do we need to do as a global society to develop the talents of our smart girls?

First, We Have to Find Them

As educators, advocates, and policy-makers, we need to cast a wide net to find smart girls from every nationality, race, ethnicity, orientation, and religion. To cast a wide net, we have to consider any girl who learns rapidly and solves problems in any domain as a smart girl. Parents and teachers need to have the courage to advocate for the smart girl's right to be identified for special programming that will meet her needs and propel her forward. We need to target even the eccentric, disagreeable ones with all the wild ideas—because those girls are likely the creative ones. Creativity knows no boundaries of race, class, gender, disability, or any other imagined category devised to divide us. Somehow, even in our most impoverished communities, there are still children who are curious, who are engaged in their own learning adventures, and who are in love with creating. It might be that little overweight girl who goes off by herself at recess to read, ignoring all the other kids. It might be that tall, scornful, girl with pink hair who doodles all through class. It might be the girl in the wheelchair who knows everything there is to know about videogames but doesn't do her homework. She is an intellectual survivor who has found that writing or making things or coding or drawing cartoons is making life livable. On the other hand, it might be the nice girl who smiles and raises her hand when nobody else does because, well, she feels sorry for the teacher when the class sits in sullen silence and she is the kind, nurturing girl to whom all the kids turn for help. This one is the emotionally intelligent smart girl whose tendency to be easygoing leads others to underestimate her. Do not let people misjudge the value of her extraordinary interpersonal skills. Once or twice in a lifetime, you will meet that smart little girl who seems wise beyond her years, who ponders the great philosophical questions, and who seeks knowledge not only in books but through her dreams and visions. She is the spiritually intelligent smart girl, who may transform our society with her transcendent vision. Find all those girls and then nurture them.

We Need to Challenge Them

Ask, "What are you drawing? That looks amazing!" "Tell me about that book you're hiding in your lap. What's it about? What do you like about it?" "How did you figure out how to make that facial recognition app—it works great!" Find out what she wants to know about that topic and give the gift of knowledge. Slip her a book to read. Tell her where she can find an animation software program. Show her an article on Japanese cultural influences on early Nintendo games. And keep the conversation of challenge going, every day. Remember that it is important to give her precise, clear feedback about how her abilities compare to those of other children at this point in time, and help her find the kinds of challenge she needs to keep her abilities growing strong.

Advocate for early admission to kindergarten, acceleration, grouping, clustering and differentiation, honors programs, AP classes and IB programs, dual enrollment—in short, every possible means by which she can be academically challenged. Challenge doesn't just come in academics; smart girls need to be challenged creatively and spiritually. They need to be challenged to be strong and fit and to regulate their difficult emotions.

We Need to Guide Them

Share your enthusiasm for her passions with everyone in the family and with friends and colleagues. Find a friend who knows something about her interest and introduce them—that is social capital. Look for afterschool programs or a summer camp that fits; find a local library, museum, or college where she has never been and take her there—that is cultural capital. Raise scholarship money online, from your friends, and from the community for those programs—that is yet another kind of capital. Talk about careers and help her find the invisible pathways. Follow up! Say, "What are you doing now? What's your latest project? I'd love to see it!"

It is not enough to create accelerated programs that speed up girls' education; we have to guide the missile. Smart girls need specialized career and personal guidance that takes into account their unique needs. They cannot make their life decisions solely based on what they are good at or what they are interested in because they might be good at everything and interested in everything. They need to be encouraged to make their life decisions based on their most deeply held values, and they need to choose majors and careers that will allow them to have the most experiences of flow consciousness. Finally, smart girls do not make their career decisions in isolation from relationship decisions. Young women need help understanding gender relations—that is, how their relationships with significant others will impact their life choices and their eventual life-satisfaction. Help smart young women to envision and plan for a future with egalitarian partners or a future of fulfillment in single life, rather than promising a romantic fairy tale that just happens by falling in love one day.

We Need to Love Them

We need to love smart girls when they refuse to fulfill our dreams for them—whether we dream of normalcy or eminence for them. She is not on this Earth to live up to her teachers' or parents' goals but to fulfill her deepest values through the realization of her unique potential. Loving smart girls means focusing on their strengths rather than harping on their weaknesses. Is she willfully underachieving? Can her refusal to achieve be a sign of her courage in a society that expects all girls to do as they are told? Can that courage be channeled into achievement in the service of an idea? Is she sharp-tongued and biting in her humor? Could this be a sign that she knows how to defend herself from being swept up in mediocrity or mass opinion—and can that capacity be channeled into defense of a just cause? It is easy to love the perfect little princess who fulfills all of our societal expectations for a girl—but it is just as important to love the wise-cracking, smart girl in the dirty jeans or the provocative neo-punk girl in black mesh stockings. Given what we have learned about eminent women, the ugly duckling does grow up to be a swan—on her own terms.

We Need to Let Them Alone

Can we please just stop making smart girls go to play dates, sleepovers, birthday parties, soccer games, dance academy, cheerleading tryouts, and sororities *if they don't want to go?* Can we allow them to play by themselves, to live in a world of fantasy, and to be best friends with books without worrying that they won't learn social skills? Is there any evidence that a smart girl will learn social skills by being forced to play with girls who hate her because she is different? Can we stop buying them stuff and expecting them to become happy consumers of clothes and makeup? Can we talk with smart young women about the intellectual project that consumes her morning and night rather than wheedling information out of her about potential romantic partners? Isn't it time to recognize that, given women's longer lifespan, most smart women will spend at least a part of their lives alone—and that this can be a time of transformation? We need to help smart girls realize that many gifted women lead satisfying, happy, love-filled lives as single women. Let women connect in their own ways to the people they have chosen to love. Let them, if they choose, connect to the voices of the past—in history, philosophy, science, and literature.

Let them, if they choose, connect to a greater voice, the voice of the mysterious universe all around them.

References

Alvarez, J. (2007). *Once upon a Quinceañera: Coming of age in the USA*. New York: Penguin.

American Association of University Women. (1994). *Shortchanging girls, shortchanging America*. Washington, DC: AAUW.

American Association of University Women. (2000). *Tech-savvy: Educating girls in the new computer age*. Washington, DC: AAUW.

American Psychological Association. (2010). Education and socioeconomic status. Retrieved from http://www.apa.org/pi/ses/resources/publications/factsheet-education.aspx

Armstrong, E.A., & Hamilton, L. T. (2013). *Paying for the party: How college maintains inequality*. Cambridge, MA: Harvard University Press.

Arnold, K. D. (1995). *Lives of promise: What becomes of high school valedictorians: A fourteen-year study of achievement and life choices*. San Francisco: Jossey-Bass.

Arnsten, A., Mazure, C. M., & Sinha, R. (2012). Everyday stress can shut down the brain's chief command center. *Scientific American*. Retrieved from http://www.mc3cb.com/pdf_articles_interest_physiology/2012_4_10_Stress_Shut_%20Down_Brain.pdf

Aronson, J., Quinn, D. M., & Spencer, S. J. (1998). Stereotype threat and the academic underperformance of minorities and women. J. K. Swim, & C. Stangor, (Eds.), *Prejudice: The target's perspective* (pp.83-103). San Diego, CA: Academic Press.

Assouline, S. G., Colangelo, N., Ihrig, D., & Forstadt, L. (2006). Attributional choices for academic success and failure by intellectually gifted students. *Gifted Child Quarterly, 50(4)*, 283-294.

Bacon, L. (2013). *Health at every size: The surprising truth about your weight*. Dallas, TX: BenBella Books.

Bailey, S. D., & Ricciardelli, L. A. (2010). Social comparisons, appearance related comments, contingent self-esteem and their relationships with body dissatisfaction and eating disturbance among women. *Eating behaviors, 11(2)*, 107-112.

Barnett, C. (2013). Top 10 crowdfunding sites for fundraising. *Forbes.* Retrieved from www.forbes.com/sites/chancebarnett/2013/05/08/top-10-crowdfunding-sites-for-fundraising/

Baron, I. S., & Leonberger, K. A. (2012). Assessment of intelligence in the preschool period. *Neuropsychology Review, 22(4),* 334-344.

Bates, T. C., & Rock, A. (2004). Personality and information processing speed: Independent influences on intelligent performance. *Intelligence, 32(1),* 33-46.

Baum, S. M., & Reis, S. M. (Eds.). (2004). *Twice-exceptional and special populations of gifted students (Vol. 7).* Newbury Park, CA: Corwin Press.

Begay, H., & Maker, C. J. (2007). When geniuses fail: Na-Dene'(Navajo) conception of giftedness in the eyes of the holy deities. In S. N. Phillipson, & M. McCann (Eds.), *Conceptions of giftedness: Sociocultural perspectives,* (pp. 127-168). Mahwah, NJ: Lawrence Erlbaum.

Belkin, L. (2003). The opt-out revolution. *New York Times Magazine, 26,* 42-47.

Berger, S. L. (2006). *College planning for gifted students: Choosing and getting into the right college.* Waco, TX: Prufrock Press.

Bergin, D. (2002). The role of pretend play in children's cognitive development. *Early Childhood Research and Practice, 4(1).* Retrieved from http://ecrp.uiuc.edu/v4nl/bergen.html

Bes, F., Schulz, H., Navelet, Y., & Salzarulo, P. (1991). The distribution of slow-wave sleep across the night: A comparison for infants, children, and adults. *Sleep, 14*(1), 5-12.

Bekker, M. H., & van Mens-Verhulst, J. (2007). Anxiety disorders: Sex differences in prevalence, degree, and background, but gender-neutral treatment. *Gender Medicine, 4,* S178-S193.

Blehar, M. C., & Keita, G. P. (2003). Women and depression: a millennial perspective. *Journal of Affective Disorders, 74*(1), 1-4.

Bloom, B. S., & Sosniak, L. A. (1985). *Developing talent in young people.* New York: Ballantine Books.

Bolick, K. (2011). All the single ladies. *Atlantic Monthly, 308(4),* 116-136.

Boon, J. (2012, October 9). Pakistani girl shot over activism in Swat valley, claims Taliban. *The Guardian.* Retrieved from http://www.guardian.co.uk/world/2012/oct/09/pakistan-girl-shot-activism-swat-taliban

Borland, J. H. (2012). Problematizing gifted education. *Fundamentals of Gifted Education: Considering Multiple Perspectives,* 69.

Brenner, M. (2013). The target. *Vanity Fair.* Retrieved from http://www.vanityfair.com/politics/2013/04/malala-yousafzai-pakistan-profile

Brody, L. E., & Mills, C. J. (2005). Talent search research: What have we learned? *High Ability Studies, 16(1)*, 97-111.

Brooks-Gunn, J., & Zahaykevich, M. (2013). Parent-daughter relationships in early adolescence: A developmental perspective. In K. Kreppner, & R. M. Lerner (Eds.), *Family Systems and Life-span Development*, (p. 223). New York: Psychology Press.

Brown, L. M., & Gilligan, C. (1993). Meeting at the crossroads: Women's psychology and girls' development. *Feminism & Psychology, 3(1)*, 11-35.

Brumberg, J. J. (2010). *The body project: An intimate history of American girls*. New York: Random House.

Burks, B. S., Jensen, D. W., & Terman, L. M. (1930). *The promise of youth; Follow-up studies of a thousand gifted children (Genetic studies of genius volume III)*. Paolo Alto, CA: Stanford University Press.

Butler, C. H., & Schwartz, A. (Eds.). (2010). *Modern women: Women artists at the Museum of Modern Art*. New York: The Museum of Modern Art.

Calderón, M., Slavin, R., & Sánchez, M. (2011). Effective instruction for English learners. *TheFuture of Children, 21*(1), 103-127.

Cammermeyer, M. (2010). *Serving in silence*. Bloomington, IN: Author House.

Ceci, S. J. (2009). *On intelligence…more or less: A biological treatise on intellectual development*. Cambridge, MA: Harvard University Press.

Ceci, S. J., & Williams, W. M. (2011). Understanding current causes of women's underrepresentation in science. *Proceedings of the National Academy of Sciences, 108(8)*, 3157-3162.

Chamorro-Premuzic, T., & Furnham, A. (2008). Personality, intelligence and approaches to learning as predictors of academic performance. *Personality and Individual Differences, 44 (7)*, 1596–1603.

Choi, W., & Rhee, J. (2012). Art college admissions: An insider's guide to art portfolio preparation, selecting the right college, and gaining admission with scholarships. New York: W&J.

Chua, A. (2011). *Battle hymn of the tiger mother*. New York: Penguin.

Clance, P. R., & Imes, S. (1978, Fall). The imposter phenomenon in high achieving women: Dynamics and therapeutic intervention. *Psychotherapy Theory, Research and Practice. 15(3)*. Retrieved from http://www.paulineroseclance. com/pdf/ip_high_achieving_women.pdf

Colangelo, N., Assouline, S. G., & Gross, M. U. (2004). *A nation deceived: How schools hold back America's brightest students* (Vol. 1). Iowa City, Iowa: University of Iowa. Retrieved from www.accelerationinstitute.org/nation_deceived/

Colangelo, N., Assouline, S. G., Kerr, B. A., Huesman, R., & Johnson, D. (1993). Mechanical inventiveness: A three-phase study. *Talent development: Proceedings of the Wallace Symposium*. Scottsdale, AZ: Great Potential Press.

Costa, P. T., & MacCrae, R. R. (1992). *Revised NEO Personality Inventory (NEO PI-R) and NEO Five-Factor Inventory (NEO FFI): Professional Manual*. Lutz, FL: Psychological Assessment Resources.

Crosnoe, R. (2011). *Fitting in, standing out: Navigating the social challenges of high school to get an education*. New York: Cambridge University Press.

Cross, T. L. (2005). *The social and emotional lives of gifted kids: Understanding and guiding their development*. Waco, TX: Prufrock Press.

Cross, T. L., Coleman, L. J., & Stewart, R. A. (1993). The social cognition of gifted adolescents: An exploration of the stigma of giftedness paradigm. *Roeper Review, 16(1)*, 37-40.

Csikszentmihalyi, M. (2009). *Creativity: Flow and the psychology of discovery and invention*. New York: HarperCollins.

Csikszentmihalyi, M. (1980). Some paradoxes in the definition of play. In A. T. Cheska (Ed.), *Play as context* (pp. 14–26). Champaign, IL: Human Kinetics.

Dai, D. Y. (2002). Are gifted girls motivationally disadvantaged? Review, reflection, and redirection. *Journal for the Education of the Gifted, 25(4)*, 315-358.

Daniels, S., & Piechowski, M. M. (2010). When intensity goes to school: Overexcitabilities, creativity, and the gifted child. In R. A. Beghetto, & J. C. Kaufman (Eds.), *Nurturing creativity in the classroom*, (pp. 313-328). New York: Cambridge University Press.

Davidson, J. W., & Edgar, R. (2003). Gender and race bias in the judgement of Western art music performance. *Music Education Research, 5(2)*, 169-181.

Davis, J. L. (2010). *Bright, talented, and black: A guide for families of African American gifted learners*. Scottsdale, AZ: Great Potential Press.

Davis, K. (2007). *A girl like me* (film). Brooklyn, NY: Reelworks Productions. Retrieved from Media Matters http://www.youtube.com/watch?v=YWyI77Yh1Gg

Deci, E. L., & Ryan, R. M. (2004). *Handbook of self-determination research*. Rochester, NY: University of Rochester Press.

Digital History. (2014). *Childbirth in Early America*. Retrieved from http://www.digitalhistory.uh.edu/topic_display.cfm?tcid=70

Dijkstra, P., Barelds, D. P., Groothof, H. A., Ronner, S., & Nauta, A. P. (2012). Partner preferences of the intellectually gifted. *Marriage & Family Review, 48(1)*, 96-108.

Duan, L., Chou, C., Andreeva, V., & Pentz, M. (2009). Trajectories of peer social influences as long-term predictors of drug use from early through late adolescence. *Journal of Youth & Adolescence, 38(3)*, 454–465.

Duckworth, A. L., & Quinn, P. D. (2009). Development and validation of the short grit scale (GRIT–S). *Journal of Personality Assessment, 91(2)*, 166-174.

Duncan, N., & Owens, L. (2011). Bullying, social power, and heteronormativity: Girls' constructions of popularity. *Children & Society, 25(4)*, 306-316.

Durham, M. G. (2009). *The Lolita effect: The media sexualization of young girls and what we can do about it.* New York: Penguin.

Drife, J. (2002). History of medicine: The start of life, a history of obstetrics. *Journal of Postgraduate Medicine, 78*, 311-315.

Dweck, C. S. (2006). *Mindset: The new psychology of success.* New York: Random House.

Dweck, C. S. (1986). Motivational processes affecting learning. *American Psychologist, 41(10)*, 1040-1048.

Elkins, I. J., Malone, S., Keyes, M., Iacono, W. G., & McGue, M. (2011). The impact of attention-deficit/hyperactivity disorder on preadolescent adjustment may be greater for girls than for boys. *Journal of Clinical Child & Adolescent Psychology, 40(4)*, 532-545.

Ellick, A. (2012, October 9). My 'small video star' fights for her life. *New York Times.* Retrieved from http://thelede.blogs.nytimes.com/2012/10/09/my-small-video-star-fights-for-her-life/?_r=0

Emmons, R. A. (2000). Is spirituality an intelligence? Motivation, cognition, and the psychology of ultimate concern. *International Journal for the Psychology of Religion, 10*, 3-26.

Ericsson, K. A. & Charness, N. (1994). Expert performance: Its structure and acquisition. *American Psychologist, 49(8)*, 725-747.

Erwin, J. O., & Worrell, F. C. (2012). Assessment practices and the underrepresentation of minority students in gifted and talented education. *Journal of Psychoeducational Assessment, 30(1)*, 74-87.

Etaugh, C. E., Bridges, J. S., Cummings-Hill, M., & Cohen, J. (1999). Names can never hurt me?. *Psychology of Women Quarterly, 23(4)*, 819-823.

Faigenbaum, A. D., & Myer, G. D. (2012). Exercise deficit disorder in youth: Play now or pay later. *Current Sports Medicine Reports, 11(4).* 196-200.

Feist, G. J. (1998). A meta-analysis of personality in scientific and artistic creativity. *Personality and Social Psychology Review, 2(4)*, 290-309.

Ferriman, K., Lubinski, D., & Benbow, C. P. (2009). Work preferences, life values, and personal views of top math/science graduate students and the profoundly gifted: Developmental changes and gender differences during emerging adulthood and parenthood. *Journal of Personality and Social Psychology, 97(3)*, 517-532.

Fey, T. (2011). *Bossypants*. New York: Hachette.

Filippeli, L. A., & Walberg, H. J. (1997). Childhood traits and conditions of eminent women scientists. *Gifted Child Quarterly, 41(3)*, 95-103.

Finn, C. E. (2012). Young, gifted, and neglected. *Education Next*. Retrieved April 15, 2013 from http://educationnext.org/young-gifted-and-neglected/

Flanagan, D. P., & Alfonso, V. C. (1995). A critical review of the technical characteristics of new and recently revised intelligence tests for preschool children. *Journal of Psychoeducational Assessment, 13(1)*, 66-90.

Florida, R. L. (2012). *The rise of the creative class: Revisited*. New York: Basic Books.

Ford, D. Y. (1995). Underachievement among gifted and non-gifted black females: A study of perceptions. *Journal of Secondary Gifted Education, 6(2)*, 165-175.

Freeman, K. A., & Walberg, H. J. (1999). Childhood traits and conditions of eminent African American women. *Journal for the Education of the Gifted, 22(4)*, 402-19.

Friedan, B. (2010). *The feminine mystique*. New York: W.W. Norton & Company.

Friedman, T. L. (2008). *Hot, flat, and crowded: Why we need a green revolution—And how it can renew America*. New York: Macmillan.

Gagné, F. Y., & Gagnier, N. (2004). The socio-affective and academic impact of early entrance to school. *Roeper Review, 26*, 128-138.

Gallagher, J. J. (2004). No child left behind and gifted education. *Roeper Review, 26(3)*, 121-123.

Gallagher, J. J., & Reis, S. M. (Eds.). (2004). *Public policy in gifted education* (Vol. 12). Thousand Oaks, CA: Corwin Press and National Association for Gifted Children.

Gardner, H. (1983). *Frames of mind: The theory of multiple intelligences*. New York: Basic Books.

Ge, X., Natsuaki, M. N., Neiderhiser, J. M., & Reiss, D. (2007). Genetic and environmental influences on pubertal timing: Results from two national sibling studies. *Journal of Research on Adolescence 17*, 767.

George, L. G., Helson, R., & John, O. P. (2011). The "CEO" of women's work lives: How Big Five Conscientiousness, Extraversion, and Openness predict 50 years of work experiences in a changing sociocultural context. *Journal of Personality and Social Psychology, 101(4)*, 812.

Gilligan, C. (1982). *In a different voice: Psychological theory and women's development* (Vol. 326). Cambridge, MA: Harvard University Press.

Gilmore, B. (2008). *Academic advocacy for gifted children: A parent's complete guide*. Scottsdale, AZ: Great Potential Press.

Gnalauti, E. (2013). *Back to normal: Why ordinary childhood behavior is mistaken for ADHD, bipolar disorder, and autism spectrum disorder.* Boston: Beacon Press.

Goertzel, V., Goertzel, M. G., Goertzel, T. G., & Hansen, A. M. W. (2004). *Cradles of eminence: The childhoods of more than 700 famous men and women.* Scottsdale, AZ: Great Potential Press.

Goleman, D. (2012). *Emotional intelligence: Why it can matter more than IQ.* New York: Random House.

Goodall, J. (1996). *My life with the chimpanzees.* New York: Simon and Schuster.

Goodall, J., & Berman, P. (1999). *Reason for hope: A spiritual journey.* New York: Hachette.

Grandin, T. (1990). Needs of high functioning teenagers and adults with Autism (Tips from a recovered autistic). *Focus on Autism and Other Developmental Disabilities, 5(1),* 1-16.

Gross, M. U. (2002). "Play partner" or "sure shelter": What gifted children look for in friendship. *SENG Newsletter, 2(2),* 1-3.

Habib, N. (2011, November 4). 14-year-old girl wins Pakistan's first peace prize. *CNN.* Retrieved from http://www.cnn.com/2011/11/24/world/asia/pakistan-peace-prize

Hallowell, E. M., & Ratey, J. J. (2011). *Driven to distraction: Recognizing and coping with attention deficit disorder from childhood through adulthood.* New York: Anchor.

Halpern, D. F. (2011). *Sex differences in cognitive abilities.* New York: Psychology Press.

Halpern, D. F., & Cheung, F. M. (2011). *Women at the top: Powerful leaders tell us how to combine work and family.* West Sussex, United Kingdom: John Wiley & Sons.

Halsted, J. W. (2009). *Some of my best friends are books: Guiding gifted readers from preschool to high school.* Scottsdale, AZ: Great Potential Press.

Haroutounian, J. (2002). *Kindling the spark: Recognizing and developing musical potential.* New York: Oxford.

Hertberg-Davis, H., & Callahan, C. M. (2008). A narrow escape: Gifted students' perceptions of Advanced Placement and International Baccalaureate Programs. *Gifted Child Quarterly, 52(3),* 199-216.

Hewlett, S. A., & Luce, C. B. (2006). Extreme jobs: The dangerous allure of the 70-hour workweek. *Harvard Business Review, 84(12),* 49-59.

Himmelstein, K. E., & Brückner, H. (2011). Criminal-justice and school sanctions against nonheterosexual youth: A national longitudinal study. *Pediatrics, 127(1),* 49-57.

Hinshaw, S. P., Owens, E. B., Zalecki, C., Huggins, S. P., Montenegro-Nevado, A. J., Schrodek, E., & Swanson, E. N. (2012). Prospective follow-up of girls with attention-deficit/hyperactivity disorder into early adulthood: Continuing impairment includes elevated risk for suicide attempts and self-injury. *Journal of Consulting and Clinical Psychology, 80(6),* 1041-1051.

Hirshman, L. R. (2007). Get to work: And get a life, before it's too late. *ADVANCE Library Collection,* 133.

Hoagies gifted education. (2013). Retrieved from http://www.hoagiesgifted.org/tests.htm

Hoagies mathematically gifted. (2013). Retrieved from http://www.hoagiesgifted.org/math_gifted.htm

Holahan, C. K., & Velasquez, K. S. (2011). Perceived strategies and activities for successful later aging. *The International Journal of Aging and Human Development, 72(4),* 343-359.

Holland, D. C., & M. A. Eisenhart. (1990). *Educated in romance: Women, achievement, and college culture.* Chicago: University of Chicago Press.

Hollingworth, L. S. (1942). Children above 180 IQ. *The Teachers College Record, 44(1),* 56-56.

Hollingworth, L. S. (1926). *Gifted children: Their nature and nurture.* New York: Macmillan.

Hong, E., Greene, M., & Hartzell, S. (2011). Cognitive and motivational characteristics of elementary teachers in general education classrooms and in gifted programs. *Gifted Child Quarterly, 55(4),* 250-264.

Horowitz, H. L. (1987). *Campus life: Undergraduate cultures from the end of the eighteenth century to the present.* New York: Knopf.

Howley, C. B. (2009). The meaning of rural difference for bright Rednecks. *Journal for the Education of the Gifted, 32(4),* 537-564.

Hrdy, S. B. (1999). Mother nature: A history of mothers, infants, and natural selection. *New York Times.* Retrieved from https://www.nytimes.com/books/first/h/hrdy-mother.html

Hudson, J. (2012). *I got this: How I changed my ways and lost what weighed me down.* New York: Penguin.

Hughes, J. (1985). *The breakfast club.* [Film].

Hyde, J. S. (2005). The gender similarities hypothesis. *American psychologist, 60(6),* 581-592.

Hyde, J. S., & Linn, M. C. (1988). Gender differences in verbal ability: A meta-analysis. *Psychological Bulletin, 104(1),* 53.

Hyde, J. S., & Mertz, J. E. (2009). Gender, culture, and mathematics performance. *Proceedings of the National Academy of Sciences, 106(22)*, 8801-8807.

Iddings, A. C. D., Combs, M. C., & Moll, L. (2012). In the arid zone drying out educational resources for English language learners through policy and practice. *Urban Education, 47(2)*, 495-514.

Jamison, K. R. (1996). *Touched with fire*. New York: Simon and Schuster.

Jarvin, L. & Subotnik, R. F. (2006). Understanding elite talent in academic domains: A developmental trajectory from basic abilities to scholarly productivity/artistry. In F. A. Dixon & S. M. Moon (Eds.), *The handbook of secondary gifted education*, (pp. 203-220). Waco, TX: Prufrock Press.

Jaschik, S. (2005, February 18). What Larry Summers said. *Inside Higher Education*. Retrieved from http://www.insidehighered.com/news/2005/02/18/summers2_18#ixzz24frZmNQl

Johnson, N. G., Roberts, M. C., & Worrell, J. E. (1999). *Beyond appearance: A new look at adolescent girls*. Washington, DC: American Psychological Association. Synopsis retrieved September 1, 2013, from http://www.apa.org/pi/families/resources/adolescent-girls.aspx

Kamenetz, A. (2010). *DIY U: Edupunks, edupreneurs, and the coming transformation of higher education*. White River Junction, VT: Chelsea Green Publishing.

Kaufmann, F. A., Kalbfleisch, M. L., & Castellanos, F. X. (2000). *Attention Deficit Disorders and gifted students: What do we really know?* Storrs, CT: National Research Center on the Gifted and Talented, University of Connecticut.

Kaufmann, F. A., & Matthews, D. J. (2012). On becoming themselves: The 1964–1968 Presidential Scholars 40 years later. *Roeper Review, 34(2)*, 83-93.

Kaufman, S. B. (2013). *Ungifted: Intelligence redefined*. New York: Basic Books.

Kelly, K., & Grant, L. (2012). Penalties and premiums: The impact of gender, marriage, and parenthood on faculty salaries in SEM and non-SEM fields. *Social Studies of Science, 42(6)*, 869-896.

Kendzior, S. (2014). Mothers are not 'opting out'—They are out of options. Editorial opinion in Online *Al Jazeera*, retrieved 4/1/2014 from http://www.aljazeera.com/indepth/opinion/2013/08/201381615448464851.html

Kerr, B. A. (1985). *Smart girls, gifted women*. Dayton, OH: Great Potential Press.

Kerr, B. A. (1997). *Smart girls: A new psychology of girls, women, and giftedness*. Scottsdale, AZ: Great Potential Press.

Kerr, B. A., & Cohn, S. J. (2001). *Smart boys: Talent, manhood, and the search for meaning*. Scottsdale, AZ: Great Potential Press.

Kerr, B. A., & Colangelo, N. (2001). Something to prove: Academically talented minority students. In N. Colangelo, & S.G. Assouline (Eds.), *Talent Development IV*. Scottsdale, AZ: Great Potential Press.

Kerr, B. A. & Colangelo, N. (1988). The college plans of academically talented students. *Journal of Counseling & Development, 67*(1), 42-48.

Kerr, B. A., Colangelo, N., Maxey, J., & Christensen, P. (1992). Characteristics of academically talented minority students. *Journal of Counseling & Development, 70(5)*, 606-609.

Kerr, B. A., Kurpius, S. E., & Harkins, A. (2005). *Handbook for counseling girls and women: 10 years of gender equity research at Arizona State University*. Mesa, AZ: Nueva Science Press.

Kerr, B. A., & Larson, A. (2007). How gifted girls become eminent women. In S. Lopez (Ed.), *Positive Psychology Perspectives*. New York: Praeger.

Kerr, B. A., & McAlister, J. (2001). *Letters to the Medicine Man: An apprenticeship in spiritual intelligence*. New York: Hampton Press.

Kerr, B., & McKay, R. (2013). Searching for tomorrow's innovators: Profiling creative adolescents. *Creativity Research Journal, 25(1)*, 21-32.

Kerr, B. A., & Multon, K. D. (2014, December). Gender identity, gender role, and gender relations among gifted students. *Journal of Counseling and Development*.

Kerr, B. A., Multon, K. D., Syme, M. L., Fry, N. M., Owens, R., Hammond, M., & Robinson-Kurpius, S. E. (2012). Development of the distance from privilege measures: A tool for understanding the persistence of talented women in STEM. *Journal of Psychoeducational Assessment, 30(1)*, 88-102.

Kerr, B. A., & Robinson-Kurpius, S. E. (1999). Brynhilde's fire: Talent, risk and betrayal in the lives of gifted girls. In J. LeRoux (Ed.), *Connecting the Gifted Community Worldwide* (261-271). Ottawa, Canada: World Council on Gifted and Talented.

Kerr, B. A., & Robinson-Kurpius, S. E. (2004). Encouraging talented girls in math and science: Effects of a guidance intervention. *High ability studies, 15(1)*, 85-102.

Kerr, B. A., & Sodano, S. (2003). Career assessment with intellectually gifted students. *Journal of career assessment, 11(2)*, 168-186.

Kinzie, J., Thomas, A. D., Palmer, M. M., Umbach, P. D., & Kuh, G. D. (2007). Women students at coeducational and women's colleges: How do their experiences compare?. *Journal of College Student Development, 48(2)*, 145-165.

Kirk, C. A. (2003). *J. K. Rowling: A biography*. Westport, CT: Greenwood Press.

Kitano, M. K. (2010). Issues in research on Asian American gifted students. In J. Castellano, & A. D. Frazier (Eds.), *Special Populations in Gifted Education:*

Understanding Our Most Able Students From Diverse Backgrounds, (p. 3-25). Naperville, IL: Sourcebooks.

Kitano, M. K., & Perkins, C. O. (1996). International gifted women: Developing a critical human resource. *Roeper Review, 19(1)*, 34-40.

Klein, A. G. (2002). *A forgotten voice: A biography of Leta Stetter Hollingworth*. Scottsdale, AZ: Great Potential Press.

Kronborg, L. (2010). What contributes to talent development in eminent women? *Gifted and Talented International, 25(2)*, 11-27.

Krumboltz, J. D. (2009). The happenstance learning theory. *Journal of Career Assessment, 17*(2), 135-154.

Kuh, G. D., Kinzie, J., Schuh, J. H., & Whitt, E. J. (2010). *Student success in college: Creating conditions that matter*. San Francisco, CA: Jossey-Bass.

Lamb, S., & Brown, L. M. (2007). *Packaging girlhood: Rescuing our daughters from marketers' schemes*. New York: St. Martin's Press.

Langlois, J. H., Kalakanis, L., Rubenstein, A. J., Larson, A., Hallam, M., & Smoot, M. (2000). Maxims or myths of beauty? A meta-analytic and theoretical review. *Psychological Bulletin, 126(3)*, 390-423.

Lawrence, B. K. (2009). Rural gifted education: A comprehensive literature review. *Journal for the Education of the Gifted, 32(4)*, 461-494.

Leonard, H. L., Goldberger, E. L., Rapoport, J. L., Cheslow, D. L., & Swedo, S. E. (1990). Childhood rituals: normal development or obsessive-compulsive symptoms?. *Journal of the American Academy of Child & Adolescent Psychiatry, 29*(1), 17-23.

Lindgren, C. (2010). Last child in the woods-saving our children from nature-deficit disorder. *Acta Paediatrica, 99(1)*, 151.

Lee, S. Y., Matthews, M. S., & Olszewski-Kubilius, P. (2008). A national picture of talent search and talent search educational programs. *Gifted Child Quarterly, 52(1)*, 55-69.

Lewin, T. (2011). Record level of stress found in college freshmen. *New York Times, 26*, A1.

Local School Directory. (2013). Retrieved from http://www.localschooldirectory. com/public-school/25204/IL

Lohman, D. F. (2005). The role of non-verbal ability tests in identifying academically gifted students: An aptitude perspective. *Gifted Child Quarterly, 49,* 111-138.

Lovas, G. S. (2011). Gender and patterns of language development in mother-toddler and father-toddler dyads. *First Language, 31(1)*, 83-108.

Loveland, E. (2010). *Creative colleges: A guide for student actors, artists, dancers, musicians, and writers*. New York: Supercollege.

Lubinski, D., & Benbow, C. (2006). Study of mathematically precocious youth after 35 years: Uncovering antecedents for the development of math-science expertise. *Perspectives in Psychological Science, 1(4)*, 316-344.

Lupkowski, A. E. & Assouline, S. G. (1992). *Jane and Johnny love math: Recognizing and encouraging mathematical talent in elementary students; A guidebook for educators and parents.* Unionville, NY: Royal Fireworks Press.

Lucas-Thompson, R.B., Goldberg, W.A., & Prause, J. (2010). Maternal work early in the lives of children and its distal associations with achievement and behavior problems: A meta-analysis. *Psychological Bulletin, 136(6)*, 915-942.

Maslow, A. H. (1950). Self-actualizing people: a study of psychological health. *Personality,1* 11-34.

Mathis, M. A., Alvarenga, P. D., Funaro, G., Torresan, R. C., Moraes, I., Torres, A. R., .& Hounie, A. G. (2011). Gender differences in obsessive-compulsive disorder: a literature review. *Revista Brasileira de Psiquiatria, 33*(4), 390-399.

Matthews, D. J. (1997). Diversity in domains of development: Research findings and their implications for gifted identification and programming. *Roeper Review, 19(3)*, 172-177.

Matrix, S. E. (2006). "I-Do" feminism courtesy of Martha Stewart weddings and HBC's vow to wow club: Inventing modern matrimonial tradition with glue sticks and cuisinart. *Ethnologies, 28(2)*, 53-80.

McAlister, K. (2009). Linguistic giftedness. In B. A. Kerr (Ed.), *The Encyclopedia of Giftedness, Creativity, and Talent Development.* Beverly Hills, CA: Sage.

McCoach, D. B., & Siegle, D. (2007). What predicts teachers' attitudes toward the gifted?. *Gifted Child Quarterly, 51(3)*, 246-254.

McCrae, R. R., & Costa Jr., P. T. (1997). Personality trait structure as a human universal. *American psychologist, 52(5)*, 509.

McGrew, K. S. (2005). The Cattell-Horn-Carroll Theory of cognitive abilities: Past, present, and future. In D. P. Flanagan, & P. L. Harrison (Eds.), *Contemporary Intellectual Assessment: Theories, Tests, and Issues* (pp. 136-181). New York: Guilford Press.

McMillan, R. (2013). [Personal communication used with permission.]

Mendaglio, S. (2012). Overexcitabilities and giftedness research: A call for a paradigm shift. *Journal for the Education of the Gifted, 35(3)*, 207-219.

Mendaglio, S. & Tillier, W. (2006). Dabrowski's theory of positive disintegration and giftedness: Overexcitability research findings. *Journal for the Education of the Gifted, 30(1)*, 68.

Mendez, L. M. R. (2000). Gender roles and achievement-related choices: A comparison of early adolescent girls in gifted and general education programs. *Journal for the Education of the Gifted, 24(2)*, 149-69.

Moore, F. R., Filippou, D., & Perrett, D. I. (2011). Intelligence and attractiveness in the face: Beyond the attractiveness halo effect. *Journal of Evolutionary Psychology, 9(3)*, 205-217.

National Association for the Advancement of Colored People. (2010) Factsheet. Retrieved 9/1/2014 from http://www.naacp.org/pages/criminal-justice-fact-sheet.

National Middle School Association. (2005). *This we believe: Successful schools for young adolescents: A position paper of National Middle School Association.* Cheltenham VIC, Australia: Hawker Brownlow Education.

National Science Foundation. (2003). *Gender differences in the careers of academic scientists and engineers: A literature review,* (p. 2). Washington, DC: NSF.

Neihart, M. (2006). Achievement/affiliation conflicts in gifted adolescents. *Roeper Review, 28(4)*, 196-202.

Nicpon, M. F., Allmon, A., Sieck, B., & Stinson, R. D. (2011). Empirical investigation of twice-exceptionality: Where have we been and where are we going?. *Gifted Child Quarterly, 55(1)*, 3-17.

Noble, K. D. (2001). *Riding the windhorse: Spiritual intelligence and the growth of the self.* New York: Hampton Press.

Noble, K. D. (1994). *The sound of a silver horn: Reclaiming the heroism in contemporary women's lives.* New York: Fawcett Columbine.

Noble, K., Subotnik, R., & Arnold, K. (1999). To thine own self be true: A new model of female talent development. *Gifted Child Quarterly, 43(4)*, 140-149.

Oden, M. H. (1968). *The fulfillment of promise: 40 year follow up of the Terman gifted group* (Vol. 77). Paolo Alto, CA: Stanford University Press.

Olszewski-Kubilius, P., Grant, B., & Seibert, C. (1994). Social support systems and the disadvantaged gifted: A framework for developing programs and services. *Roeper Review, 17(1)*, 20-25.

Orenstein, P. (2011). *Cinderella ate my daughter: Dispatches from the front lines of the new girlie-girl culture.* New York: HarperCollins.

Orenstein, P. (2013). *Schoolgirls: Young women, self-esteem, and the confidence gap.* New York: Random House.

Park, L. E., Young, A. F., Troisi, J. D., & Pinkus, R. T. (2011). Effects of everyday romantic goal pursuit on women's attitudes toward math and science. *Personality and Social Psychology Bulletin, 37(9)*, 1259-1273.

Parker, W. D. (2000). Healthy perfectionism in the gifted. *Journal of Advanced Academics, 11(4)*, 173-182.

Paul, A. M. (2011). Is pink necessary? *The New York Times, 21.*

Perrone, K. M., Perrone, P. A., Ksiazak, T. M., Wright, S. L., & Jackson, Z. V. (2007). Self-perception of gifts and talents among adults in a longitudinal study of academically talented high-school graduates. *Roeper Review, 29(4),* 259-264.

Perrone, K. M., Webb, L. K., Wright, S. L., Jackson, Z. V., & Ksiazak, T. M. (2006). Relationship of spirituality to work and family roles and life satisfaction among gifted adults. *Journal of Mental Health Counseling, 28(3),* 253-268.

Perrone-McGovern, K. M., Ksiazak, T. M., Wright, S. L., Vannatter, A., Hyatt, C. C., Shepler, D., & Perrone, P. A. (2011). Major life decisions of gifted adults in relation to overall life satisfaction. *Journal for the Education of the Gifted, 34(6),* 817-838.

Pesta, A. (2013). Being Malala Yousafzai's dad. *The Atlantic.* Retrieved from http://www.theatlantic.com/international/archive/2013/03/being-malala-yousafzais-dad/274244/

Peterson, C., & Seligman, M. E. (2006). The Values in Action (VIA) classification of strengths. In M. Csikszentmihalyi, & I. S. Csikszentmihalyi (Eds.), *A life worth living: Contributions to positive psychology,* 29-48. New York: Oxford University Press.

Peterson, J. S. (2000). Gifted and gay: A study of the adolescent experience. *Gifted Child Quarterly, 44(4),* 231-246.

Pew Foundation. (2013). Teens, social media, & privacy. Retrieved from http://www.pewinternet.org/Reports/2013/Teens-Social-Media-And-Privacy/Main-Report/Part-1.aspx

Piirto, J. (2002). *My teeming brain: Understanding creative writers.* New York: Hampton Press.

Piirto, J. (2004). *Understanding creativity.* Scottsdale, AZ: Great Potential Press.

Protzko, J., Aronson, J., & Blair, C. (2013). How to make a young child smarter evidence from the database of raising intelligence. *Perspectives on Psychological Science, 8(1),* 25-40.

Pryor, J. H., Hurtado, S., DeAngelo, L., Blake, L. P., & Tran, S. (2009). *The American freshman: National norms fall 2009.* Los Angeles: Higher Education Research Institute.

Ramirez, J. D., Yuen, S., Ramey, D., & Pasta, D. (1991). Longitudinal study of structured English immersion strategy, early-exit and late-exit bilingual education programs for language-minority children (Final Report, Vols. 1 & 2). San Mateo, CA: Aguirre International.

Raven, J. (2000). The Raven's progressive matrices: Change and stability over culture and time. *Cognitive psychology, 41(1),* 1-48.

Reardon, S. F. (2013). The widening income achievement gap. *Educational Leadership, 70(8),* 10-16.

Reardon, S. F. (2013). No rich child left behind. *New York Times.* SR1. Retrieved from http://opinionator.blogs.nytimes.com/2013/04/27/no-rich-child-left-behind/?_r=0

Reis, S. M., & Sullivan, E. E. (2009). A theory of talent development in women of accomplishment. In L. V. Shavinina (Ed.), *International handbook on giftedness,* (pp. 487-504). Dordrecht, Netherlands: Springer.

Renzulli, J. S. (2002). Emerging conceptions of giftedness: Building a bridge to the new century. *Exceptionality: A Special Education Journal, 10(2),* 67-75.

Renzulli, J. S., & Reis, S. M. (2012). The schoolwide enrichment model: A focus on student creative productvity, strengths, and interests. In C. M. Callahan, & H. L. Hertberg-Davis, (Eds.), *Fundamentals of Gifted Education: Considering Multiple Perspectives* (pp. 199-211). New York: Routledge.

Rhoads, S. E., & Rhoads, C. H. (2012). Gender roles and infant/toddler care: Male and female professors on the tenure track. *Journal of Social, Evolutionary, and Cultural Psychology, 6(1),* 13-31.

Rivero, L. (2002). *Creative home schooling: A resource guide for smart families.* Scottsdale, AZ: Great Potential Press.

Robinson-Kurpius, S. E., Kerr, B. A., & Harkins, A. (2005). *Handbook for counseling girls and women: Talent, risk, and resiliency.* Mesa, AZ: Nueva Science Press.

Roeper, A. & Higgins, A. (2007). *The "I" of the beholder: A guided journey to the essence of a child.* Scottsdale, AZ: Great Potential Press.

Rogers, K. (2002). *Re-forming gifted education: How parents and teachers can match the program to the child.* Scottsdale, AZ: Great Potential Press.

Rotigel, J. V., & Fello, S. (2004). Mathematically gifted students: How can we meet their needs?. *Gifted Child Today, 27(4),* 46-51.

Rowling, J. K. (2008). The fringe benefits of failure, and the importance of imagination. *Harvard Magazine, 5.*

Ruf, D. (2009). *5 levels of giftedness: School issues and educational options.* Scottsdale, AZ: Great Potential Press.

Sabharwal, M., & Corley, E. A. (2009). Faculty job satisfaction across gender and discipline. *The Social Science Journal, 46(3),* 539-556.

Sadker, M., & Sadker, D. M. (2010). *Failing at fairness: How America's schools cheat girls.* New York: Simon and Schuster.

Salmond, K., & Purcell, K. (2011). Trends in teen communication and social media use: What's really going on here?. *Pew Internet & American Life Project.* Retrieved February 9, 2011, from http://pewinternet.org

Sandberg, S. (2013). *Lean in: Women, work, and the will to lead.* New York: Random House.

Santos, F. (2013, May 24). Judge finds violations of rights by sheriff. *New York Times*. Retrieved from http://www.nytimes.com/2013/05/25/us/federal-judge-finds-violations-of-rights-by-sheriff-joe-arpaio.html

Sassaroli, S., Lauro, L. J., Ruggiero, G. M., Mauri, M. C., Vinai, P., & Frost, R. (2008). Perfectionism in depression, obsessive-compulsive disorder, and eating disorders. *Behavior Research and Therapy, 46(6)*, 757-765.

Sax, L. J., & Harper, C. (2005). Origins of the gender gap: Pre-College and college influences on differences between men and women. Paper presented at the Annual Meeting of the Association for Institutional Research, San Diego, CA, May 2005.

Scarr, S. & McCartney, K. (1983). How people make their own environments. A theory of genotype→environment effects. *Child development, 54(2)*, 424-435.

Schlesinger, J. (2012). *The insanity hoax*. New York: Shrinktunes Media.

Seagoe, M. V. (1975). *Terman and the gifted*. Ann Arbor, Michigan: William Kaufman.

Sears, P. S., & Barbee, A. H. (1976). Career and life satisfaction among Terman's gifted women. *Gifted Child Quarterly, 20(3)*, 288.

Shriver, M. (2009). *The Shriver report: A woman's nation changes everything*. New York: Simon and Schuster.

Siegle, D. & McCoach, D. B. (2005). Making a difference: Motivating gifted students who are not achieving. *Teaching exceptional children, 38(1)*, 22-27.

Silverman, L. K. (2012). Asynchronous development: A key to counseling the gifted. *Handbook for counselors serving students with gifts and talents*, 261-279.

Simonton, K. (1988). *Scientific genius: A psychology of science*. New York: Cambridge University Press.

Singer, D. G., Singer, J. L., D'Agostino, H., & DeLong, R. (2009). Children's pastimes and play in sixteen nations: Is free-play declining?. *American Journal of Play, 1(3)*, 283-312.

Sisk, C. L., & Foster, D. L. (2004). The neural basis of puberty and adolescence. *Nature Neuroscience, 7 (10)*, 1040–1047.

Skelton, C. (2010). Gender and achievement: Are girls the "success stories" of restructured education systems?. *Educational Review, 62(2)*, 131-142.

Slaughter, A. M. (2012). Why women still can't have it all. *The Atlantic, 310(1)*, 84-102.

Smith, M. (2012, November 10). Introducing the Malala Fund. *Huffington Post*. Retrieved from http://www.huffingtonpost.com/megan-smith/introducing-the-malala-fu_b_2110875.html

Smutny, J. F., Walker, S. Y., & Meckstroth, E. A. (1997). *Teaching young gifted children in the regular classroom: Indentifying, nurturing, and challenging, ages 4-9.* Minneapolis, MN: Free Spirit Publishing.

Solow, R., & Rhodes, C. (2012). *College at 13: Young, gifted, & purposeful.* Scottsdale, AZ: Great Potential Press.

Sotomayor, S. (2013). *My beloved world.* New York: Random House.

Spelke, E. S. (2005). Sex differences in intrinsic aptitude for mathematics and science?: A critical review. *American Psychologist, 60(9),* 950-958.

Stainthorp, R., & Hughes, D. (2004). What happens to precocious readers' performance by the age of eleven?. *Journal of Research in Reading, 27(4),* 357-372.

Stewart, J. (2013, April 3). *The Daily Show with Jon Stewart.* [Television]. Retrieved from http://www.thedailyshow.com/watch/wed-april-3-2013/sheryl-sandberg

Stone, P. (2008). *Opting out?: Why women really quit careers and head home.* Berkeley, CA: University of California Press.

Stykes, B., Payne, K. & Gibbs, M. (2012). *First marriage rate in the U.S., 2012.* Retrieved 8/29/14 from http://www.bgsu.edu/content/dam/BGSU/college-of-arts-and-sciences/NCFMR/documents/FP/FP-14-08-marriage-rate-2012.pdf

Streznewski, M. K. (1999). *Gifted grownups: The mixed blessings of extraordinary potential.* Hoboken, NJ: J. Wiley.

Subotnik, R. F., & Arnold, K. D. (Eds.). (1994). *Beyond Terman: Contemporary longitudinal studies of giftedness and talent.* Westport, CT: Greenwood Publishing.

Subotnik, R. F., Duschl, R. A., & Selmon, E. H. (1993). Retention and attrition of science talent: A longitudinal study of Westinghouse Science Talent Search winners. *International Journal of Science Education, 15(1),* 61-72.

Subotnik, R. F., Olszewski-Kubilius, P., & Worrell, F. C. (2011). Rethinking giftedness and gifted education: A proposed direction forward based on psychological science. *Psychological Science in the Public Interest, 12(1),* 3-54.

Sundgot-Borgen, J., & Torstveit, M. K. (2004). Prevalence of eating disorders in elite athletes is higher than in the general population. *Clinical Journal of Sports Medicine, 14(1),* 25-32.

Suzuki, S. & Nagata, M. L. (1981). *Ability development from age zero.* Austin, TX: Birch Tree Group.

Swiatek, M. A. (2002). Social coping among gifted elementary school students. *Journal for the Education of the Gifted, 26(1),* 65-86.

Terman, L. M. (Ed.). (1981). *Mental and physical traits of a thousand gifted children* (Vol. 1). Paolo Alto, CA: Stanford University Press.

Torrance, E. P. (1995). Insights about creativity: Questioned, rejected, ridiculed, ignored. *Educational Psychology Review, 7(3),* 313-322.

Torrance, E. P. (1988). The nature of creativity as manifest in its testing. In Sternberg, R. J. (Ed.), *The nature of creativity: Contemporary psychological perspectives.* (pp. 43-75). New York: Cambridge University Press.

Tran, N. & Birman, D. (2010). Questioning the model minority: Studies of Asian American academic performance. *Asian American Journal of Psychology, 1(2),* 106.

Twenge, J. M., & Campbell, S. M. (2012). Who are the Millennials? Empirical evidence for generational differences in work values, attitudes and personality. In E. S. Ng, S. T. Lyons, & L. Schweitzer, (Eds.), *Managing the new workforce: International perspectives on the Millennial generation.* Northampton, MA: Edward Elgar.

UNICEF fact sheet. (2011, November). *Afghanistan Country Office, Education.* Retrieved from http://www.unicef.org/infobycountry/files/ACO_Education_Factsheet_-_November_2011_.pdf

U.S. Department of Education. (2014). *Funding Status—Jacob K. Javits Gifted and Talented Education Program.* Retrieved from http://www2.ed.gov/programs/javits/funding.html

VanTassel-Baska, J. (2010). An introduction to the integrated curriculum model. In J. Van Tassel-Baska, & C. A. Little (Eds.), *Content-based curriculum for high-ability learners,* 9-32. Waco, TX: Prufrock Press.

Wai, J. (2011). *Spatial ability: A neglected talent domain.* Retrieved from http://www.tip.duke.edu/node/940

Walberg, H. J., & Stariha, W. E. (1992). Productive human capital: Learning, creativity, and eminence. *Creativity Research Journal, 5(4),* 323-340.

Webb, J. T. (2013). *Searching for meaning: Idealism, bright minds, disillusion, and hope.* Tucson, AZ: Great Potential Press.

Webb, J. T., Amend, E. R., Webb, N. E., Goerss, J., Beljan, P., & Olenchak, F. R. (2005). *Misdiagnosis and dual diagnoses of gifted children and adults: ADHD, Bipolar, OCD, Asperger's, depression, and other disorders.* Scottsdale, AZ: Great Potential Press.

Webb, J. T., Gore, J. L., Amend, E. R., DeVries, A. R. (2007). *A Parent's guide to gifted children.* Scottsdale, AZ: Great Potential Press.

Webb, J. T., Meckstroth, E. A., & Tolan, S. S. (1994). *Guiding the gifted child.* Scottsdale, AZ: Great Potential Press.

Wessling, S. (2012). *From school to homeschool: Should you homeschool your gifted child?* Scottsdale, AZ: Great Potential Press.

Whitney, C. S., & Hirsch, G. (2011). *Helping gifted children soar: A practical guide for parents and teachers.* Scottsdale, AZ: Great Potential Press.

Wiggs, C. M. (2010). Creating the self: Exploring the life journey of late-midlife women. *Journal of Women & Aging, 22(3)*, 218-233.

Willis, J. (2009). *Inspiring middle school minds: Gifted, creative, and challenging.* Scottsdale, AZ: Great Potential Press.

Winfrey, O. (2013, April). The O interview with Sheryl Sandberg. *O Magazine.* 152-153, 194-195.

Winfrey, O. (2012, October 1). Oprah interviews J. K. Rowling. [Television]. In Oprah Winfrey (Producer), *The Oprah Winfrey Show.* Chicago: Harpo Productions.

Wolf, M. B., & Ackerman, P. L. (2005). Extraversion and intelligence: A meta-analytic investigation. *Personality and Individual Differences, 39*(3), 531-542.

Wojtczak, H. (2004). Pregnancy and childbirth. *English Social History: Women of Nineteenth-Century.* London: The Hastings Press.

Worrell, F. C. (2007). Ethnic identity, academic achievement, and global self-concept in four groups of academically talented adolescents. *Gifted Child Quarterly, 51(1)*, 23-38.

Yewchuk, C., Äystö, S., & Schlosser, G. (2001). Attribution of career facilitators of eminent women. *High Ability Studies, 12(1)*, 201-205.

Yousafzai, M. (2009). Diary of a Pakistani school girl. *BBC.* Retrieved from http://news.bbc.co.uk/2/hi/south_asia/7834402.stm

Endnotes

Chapter 1

1   Kaufman, 2013
2   Seagoe, 1975
3   Both Florence Goodenough and Catherin Cox went on to have significant careers as influential psychologists.
4   Ceci, 2009
5   *A Nation Deceived*, by the Institute for Research and Policy on Acceleration, summarizes much of the relevant research at http://www.accelerationinstitute. org/nation_deceived/
6   Torrance, 1988
7   Torrance, 1988
8   Gallagher & Reis, 2004
9   Raven, 2000
10   Colangelo, Assouline, & Gross, 2004
11   Renzulli & Reis, 2012
12   Olszewski-Kubilius, Grant, & Seibert, 1994
13   Gardner, 1983
14   McGrew, 2005
15   Goleman, 2012
16   Gilligan, 1982
17   McCrae & Costa, 1997
18   Feist, 1998
19   Chamorro-Premuzic & Furnham, 2008. Some researchers have found that more intelligent people tend more often to be introverts. However, their samples are biased toward clinical populations and small classroom samples, rather that large sample sizes. Occasionally, extraversion has been reported to correlate (positively and negatively) with intelligence (Wolf & Ackerman, 2005), but this relation has been moderated by the nature of the test and the context (Bates & Rock, 2004).
20   Kerr & McKay, 2013

21   Feist, 1998

22   Chamorro-Premusic & Furnham, 2008

23   Mendaglio & Tillier, 2006

24   This is somewhat different than the "flow" experience described by Csiksz-entmihalyi (2009), which we will touch on later.

25   Emmons, 2000

26   Noble, 2001

27   Kerr & McAlister, 2001

28   Kerr & McKay, 2013

29   Common tests are the Stanford-Binet 5 (SB 5), the Weschsler Intelligence Test for Children — Revised (WISC-R), the Cognitive Abilities Test (CogAT), the Woodcock-Johnson, and the Raven Progressive Matrices. See http://www.hoagiesgifted.org/tests.htm. The National Association for Gifted Children has called for recognizing gifted as being in the top 10% in any one or more domains. See www.nagc.org/index2.aspx?id=6404.

30   Emotional intelligence has been measured both as an ability and a trait. One ability test actually asks people to interpret emotions in faces and situations and requires a high level of competence in perceiving and reasoning with emotion. Some emotional intelligence tests are being revised for children, but at this point, the best way to find the smart girl with emotional intelligence is to look for the girl that everybody turns to for help and that everybody wants as a leader.

31   Creativity has usually been measured by tests that elicit various levels of fluency, flexibility, originality, and elaboration, most notably, the Torrance Tests of Creative Thinking. Although these tests are expensive and difficult to score, they remain the best way to measure divergent thinking in children. Adolescent students can be identified best using profiles of personalities, interests, values, and accomplishments.

32   Kerr & McKay, 2013. By adolescence, personality testing is possible, and we have tested almost a thousand creative young people using the NEO-PI –R and other measures of the personality factors of Neuroticism, Extraversion, Openness to Experience, Agreeability, and Conscientiousness. We looked for high scores on Openness to Experience to help find creative students, and examined other scores to help us understand the type of creative personality. Our work resulted in a profiling method that, used in combination with checklists of accomplishments, can be helpful into adulthood.

33   Csikszentmihalyi, 2009

34   Mendaglio & Tillier, 2006

35   Webb et al., 2005

36   Csikszentmihalyi, 2009

37   Subotnik, Duschl, & Selmon, 1993; Kaufmann & Matthews, 2012; Arnold, 1995
38   Sandberg, 2013
39   Lucas-Thompson, Goldberg, & Prause, 2010

Chapter 2

40   Terman, 1981
41   Kerr & Cohn, 2001
42   Burks, Jensen, & Terman, 1930
43   Sears & Barbee, 1976
44   Klein, 2002
45   Hollingworth, 1926
46   Hollingworth, 1942
47   Her very interesting life story is described in *A Forgotten Voice: A Biography of Leta Stetter Hollingworth* (Klein, 2002).
48   Friedan, 2010
49   Friedan, 2010, p. 8
50   Hrdy, 1999
51   Drife, 2002
52   Shriver, 2009; Salmond & Purcell, 2011; Pryor et al., 2009; Kerr, Kurpius, & Harkins, 2005; AAUW, 2000

Chapter 3

53   Twenge & Campbell, 2012
54   Ge et al., 2007
55   Csikszentmihalyi, 2009
56   Filippelli & Walberg, 1997; Kerr, 1997
57   NSF, 2003
58   Duncan & Owens, 2011
59   Shriver, 2009
60   Sundgot-Borgen & Torstveit, 2004; Sassaroli et al., 2008
61   Kerr & Robinson-Kurpius, 2004
62   Blehar & Keita, 2003
63   Twenge & Campbell, 2012, p. 109
64   Webb et al., 2005
65   Gnalauti, 2013; Schlesinger, 2012
66   Kerr, Kurpius, & Harkins, 2005
67   Faigenbaum & Myer, 2012; Lindgren, 2010; Singer et al., 2009
68   Pryor et al., 2009
69   Lewin, 2011
70   Colangelo, Assouline, & Gross, 2004
71   Hyde & Mertz, 2009

72   Shriver, 2009
73   Pew Foundation, 2013
74   Pryor et al., 2009
75   AAUW, 2000
76   AAUW, 2000
77   Pew, 2013
78   Shriver, 2009
79   Pryor et al., 2009
80   Twenge & Campbell, 2012
81   Friedman, 2008
82   For the past several years, Robyn had the opportunity to work with many gifted girls and young women at Arizona State University's Herberger Young Scholars Academy and the WiSE Leadership Program. In the following chapters, you'll get to know the smart girls who stand out as leaders and who stand up for what they believe in. In most cases, the names are pseudonyms. Each Smart Girl Profile begins with impressions of each girl, including her demographics, and social, emotional, and career development. Then, in the section titled In Her Own Words, you'll hear from the smart girls themselves as they talk about what it means to be a smart girl, and their thoughts on issues that affect smart girls.

Chapter 4

83   Goertzel et al., 2004
84   Oden, 1968
85   Oden, 1968, p. 325
86   Subotnik, Olszewski-Kubilius, & Worrell, 2011
87   Noble, Subotnik, & Arnold,1999
88   Simonton, 1988
89   Kerr, 1985
90   Csikszentmihalyi, 2009
91   Yewchuk, Äystö, & Schlosser, 2001
92   Kronborg, 2010
93   Kronborg, 2010, p. 21
94   Kerr & Robinson Kurpius, 1999
95   Freeman & Walberg, 1999
96   Lubinski & Benbow, 2006
97   Halpern & Cheung, 2011
98   Kirk, 2003; Winfrey, 2012; Rowling, 2008
99   Fey, 2011
100 Hudson, 2012
101 Local School Directory, 2013
102 Brenner, 2013

103   Yousafzai, 2009

104   Yousafzai, 2009

105   Boon, 2012; Pesta, 2013

106   Ellick, 2012

107   Habib, 2011

108   Ellick, 2012

109   UNICEF Fact Sheet, 2011

110   The Nobel Peace Prize for 2013 was awarded to the Organization for the Prohibition of Chemical Weapons (OPCW).

111   Yousafzai, 2009

112   Smith, 2012

113   Sandberg, 2013

114   Winfrey, 2013

115   Jaschik, 2005

116   Sandberg 2013

117   Sandberg, 2013

118   Sotomayor, 2013

119   Cammermeyer, 2010

120   Goodall, 1996; Goodall & Berman, 1999

Chapter 5

121   Yewchuk, Äystö, & Schlosser, 2001

122   Csikszentmihalyi, 2009

123   NSF, 2003

124   Piirto, 2002

125   Bloom & Sosniak, 1985

126   Other examples of isolated eminent women, as described in *Smart Girls: A New Psychology of Girls, Women, and Giftedness*, are Georgia O'Keefe, Eleanor Roosevelt, Marie Curie, Maya Angelou, and Rigoberta Menchu.

127   Holland & Eisenhart, 1990

128   Kerr & Larson, 2007. Although this study referred to "defendence," we have used the more common word "defensiveness."

129   Sabharwal & Corley, 2009

130   Csikszentmihalyi, 2009

Chapter 6

131   Protzko, Aronson, & Blair, 2013

132   A good resource for developmental milestones for gifted children can be found in *5 Levels of Giftedness: School Issues and Educational Options* by Deborah Ruf.

133   Suzuki & Nagata, 1981

134   Scarr & McCartney, 1983

135 Hyde & Linn, 1988.

136 Silverman, 2012

137 More information about asynchronous development in bright children can be found in the award-winning book *A Parent's Guide to Gifted Children* by Webb, Gore, Amend, and DeVries.

138 Lovas, 2011

139 Stainthorp & Hughes, 2004

140 Stainthorp & Hughes, 2004

141 Halsted, 2009

142 Borland, 2012

143 Gagné & Gagnier, 2004

144 Baron & Leonberger, 2012

145 Haroutounian, 2002

146 Wai, 2011. http://www.tip.duke.edu/node/940

147 McAlister, 2009

148 http://www.cal.org/resource-center/briefs-digests/digests

149 Rotigel & Fello, 2004

150 Lupkowski & Assouline, 1992

151 Wai, 2011

152 Colangelo et al., 1993

153 Gross, 2002

154 Paul, 2011

155 Orenstein, 2011

Chapter 7

156 Kerr et al., 1992

157 Kerr & Colangelo, 2001

158 U.S. Department of Education, 2014

159 Gallagher, 2004

160 Finn, 2012

161 Siegle & McCoach, 2005

162 Kerr & Cohn, 2001

163 Swiatek, 2002

164 Hong, Greene, & Hartzell, 2011

165 VanTassel-Baska, 2010

166 Karen Rogers describes various options and what kinds of gifted children are likely to need those options in her book *Re-Forming Gifted Education: How Parents and Teachers Can Match the Program to the Child*. Another excellent resource to help parents understand the various options is *Helping Gifted Children Soar* by Whitney and Hirsch.

167   Great Potential Press, Free Spirit Press, Prufrock Press, Royal Fireworks, and Corwin Press are examples of publishers with large catalogs of books and resources for gifted students.

168   *Academic Advocacy for Gifted Children*, by Bobby Gilmore, can be a valuable guide for parents.

169   Flanagan & Alfonso, 1995

170   McMillan, 2013

171   Rivero, 2002; Wessling, 2012

172   Webb, Meckstroth, & Tolan, 1994; Smutny, Walker, & Meckstroth, 1997

173   Bes et al., 1991.

174   Lamb & Brown, 2007

175   Reardon, 2013, p. 1. No rich child left behind. http://opinionator.blogs.nytimes.com/2013/04/27/no-rich-child-left-behind/?_r=0

176   Csikszentmihalyi, 1980

177   Bergin, 2002

Chapter 8

178   Brown & Gilligan, 1993

179   Orenstein, 2013

180   Kerr, 1985

181   Dai, 2002

182   Johnson, Roberts, & Worrell, 1999, p. 2

183   Willis, 2009

184   Sisk & Foster, 2004

185   Orenstein, 2013

186   Duan et al., 2009

187   National Middle School Association, 2005

188   http://www.lifepracticepbl.org

189   Lee, Matthews, & Olszewski-Kubilius, 2008

190   Brody & Mills, 2005

191   http://www.duketipeog.com

192   Solow & Rhodes, 2012

193   Mendez, 2000

194   Kerr & Robinson-Kurpius, 2004

195   Johnson, Roberts, & Worrell, 1999

196   Alvarez, 2007

197   Johnson, Roberts, & Worrell, 1999, p. 50. http://www.apa.org/pi/families/resources/adolescent-girls.aspx#

198   Costa & McCrae, 1992; Peterson & Seligman, 2006

199   Hertberg-Davis & Callahan, 2008

200   Durham, 2009

201   www.seejane.org

202 Peterson, 2000
203 Johnson, Roberts, &Worrell, 1999, p. 50
204 Crosnoe, 2011
205 Cross, 2005; Swiatek, 2002
206 Shriver, 2009
207 Webb et al., 2005
208 Arnsten, Mazure, & Sinha, 2012
209 Sadker & Sadker, 2010
210 Aronson, Quinn, & Spencer, 1998
211 www.iseek.org/education/admissions.html
212 Berger, 2006
213 It is important to note that consultants advise on the entire range of schooling from Pre-K through Post Grad, including Gap Years, Therapeutic Schools, and Schools for students with Learning Disabilities. In fact, they advise on schools working with many mental health issues. Families with gifted girls may seek advising for any of these levels of education.
214 Loveland, 2010
215 Kinzie et al., 2007, p. 145
216 Choi & Rhee, 2012
217 Kamenetz, 2010
218 Barnett, 2013. www.forbes.com/sites/chancebarnett/2013/05/08/top-10-crowdfunding-sites-for-fundraising/
219 Brooks-Gunn & Zahaykevich, 2013

Chapter 9

220 Skelton, 2010
221 Bolick, 2011
222 Halpern, 2011
223 Subotnik & Arnold, 1994
224 Park et al., 2011
225 Sax & Harper, 2005
226 Kerr & Multon, (in press)
227 Armstrong & Hamilton, 2013
228 Horowitz, 1987
229 Kuh et al., 2010
230 Kerr et al., 2012
231 Holland & Eisenhart, 1990

Chapter 10

232 Walberg & Stariha, 1992
233 Stykes et al., 2013. http://www.bgsu.edu/content/dam/BGSU/college-of-arts-and-sciences/NCFMR/documents/FP/FP-14-08-marriage-rate-2012.pdf

234 Bolick, 2011
235 Kerr & Sodano, 2003
236 Dijkstra et al., 2012
237 Matrix, 2006
238 Etaugh et al., 1999
239 Hirshman, 2007
240 Hirshman, 2007
241 NSF, 2003
242 Spelke, 2005; Hyde, 2005
243 Hyde, 2005
244 Ceci & Williams, 2011
245 Ceci & Williams, 2011
246 Ceci & Williams, 2011
247 Ferriman, Lubinski, & Benbow, 2009
248 Rhoads & Rhoads, 2012
249 Kelly & Grant, 2012
250 Hirshman, 2007, p. 11
251 Davidson & Edgar, 2003
252 Butler & Schwartz, 2010
253 Streznewski, 1999
254 Belkin, 2003
255 Stone, 2008
256 Sandberg, 2013
257 Winfrey, 2013. http://www.oprah.com/own-oprahs-next-chapter/Sheryl-Sandberg-on-the-3-Biggest-Mistakes-Working-Women-Make-Video
258 Slaughter, 2012
259 Hewlett & Luce, 2006, p. 21
260 Kaufmann & Matthews, 2012
261 Kendzior, 2014, p. 1
262 From an anonymous party speaking during the author's supervision of Blackboard.
263 Holahan & Velasquez, 2011
264 Perrone et al., 2006
265 Perrone et al., 2007
266 Perrone-McGovern et al., 2011
267 Noble, Subotnik, & Arnold, 1999
268 Kerr & McAlister, 2001
269 Noble, 2001
270 Wiggs, 2010
271 Noble, Subotnik, & Arnold, 1999
272 Kaufmann & Matthews, 2012

273   Holahan & Velasquez, 2011

274   Kaufman, 2013

275   Roeper & Higgins, 2007, p. 117-118

276   Roeper & Higgins, 2007, p. 121. Reprinted in the SENGVine, Gifted Adults at www.sengifted.org/archives/articles/growing-old-gifted#sthash.Extq2hxW.dpuf

Chapter 11

277   Much more information on issues of misdiagnosis and dual diagnoses of gifted children and adults is available through the SENG Misdiagnosis Initiative (www.sengifted.org/programs/seng-misdiagnosis-initiative) as well as from the *2e Newsletter* and from books such as *Misdiagnosis and Dual Diagnoses of Gifted Children and Adults* by James Webb, et al.

278   Webb et al., 2005

279   Mendaglio & Tillier, 2006

280   Kaufmann, Kalbfleisch, & Castellanos, 2000

281   Kaufmann, Kalbfleisch, & Castellanos, 2000; Nicpon, et al., 2011

282   Elkins et al., 2011

283   Elkins et al., 2011

284   Elkins et al., 2011

285   Hallowell. Personal communication.

286   Hinshaw et al., 2012

287   Jamison, 1996

288   Schlesinger, 2012

289   Webb, 2013

290   Bekker & van Mens-Verhulst, 2007

291   Two particularly helpful resource are books by Dan Peters, *Make Your Worrier a Warrior*, which is for parents and teachers, and *From Worrier to Warrior*, which is for the worrier.

292   Mathis et al., 2011

293   Leonard et al., 1990

294   www.nimh.nih.gov/health/publications/pandas/index.shtml

295   Parker, 2000

296   Persons with Social (Pragmatic) Communication Disorder show deficits in social communication, such as greeting and sharing information, inability to change communication to match context or the needs of the listener, problems in using verbal and nonverbal signals to regulate conversation, and concrete thinking and difficulty understanding idioms and metaphors.

297   Grandin, 1990. "Needs of high functioning teenagers and adults with Autism" is just one such article. An Internet search will show many other helpful books and videos.

298   Nicpon et al., 2011

299   Baum & Reis, 2004

Chapter 12

300 Davis, 2010

301 Raven, 2000; Lohman, 2005

302 Kerr et al., 2012

303 Erwin & Worrell, 2012

304 Johnson, Roberts, Worrell, 1999

305 Davis, 2007

306 Worrell, 2007

307 Kerr et al., 1992

308 American Association of University Women, 1994

309 National Association for the Advancement of Colored People, 2010. http://
www.naacp.org/pages/criminal-justice-fact-sheet

310 Ford, 1995

311 Begay & Maker, 2007

312 Neihart, 2006, p. 197

313 Ramirez et al., 1991

314 Calderón, Slavin, & Sánchez, 2011

315 Iddings, Combs, & Moll, 2012

316 Santos, 2013

317 Kerr & Robinson-Kurpius, 2004

318 Tran & Birman, 2010

319 Chua, 2011

320 Iddings, Combs, & Moll, 2012.

321 Kitano, 2010

322 The SES online fact sheet of the American Psychological Association summarizes research about the gap of rich and poor. http://www.apa.org/pi/ses/
resources/publications/factsheet-education.aspx

323 APA, 2010

324 Reardon, 2013

325 Himmelstein, & Brückner, 2011

326 Himmelstein, & Brückner, 2011

327 Brumberg, 2010

328 Langlois et al., 2000, p. 390

329 Bailey & Ricciardelli, 2010

330 Moore, Filippou, & Perrett, 2011

331 Bacon, 2013

332 www.seejane.org; http://amysmartgirls.com

333 Kitano & Perkins, 1996

334 Florida, 2012

335 Lawrence, 2009

336 Piirto, 2004

337 Howley, 2009
338 Howley, 2009
339 We are now hoping to test the idea that our Distance from Privilege scale can help educators and counselors to understand their students better so they can help them to overcome the barriers that are most important to them.
340 Kerr et al., 2012

Chapter 13
341 Kaufman, 2013
342 Renzulli, 2002
343 Daniels & Piechowski, 2010
344 Mendaglio, 2012
345 Mendaglio, 2012; Webb et al., 2007
346 Mendaglio, 2012
347 Dweck, 2006
348 Cross, Coleman, & Stewart, 1993
349 Clance & Imes, 1978
350 Dweck, 1986
351 Assouline et al., 2006, p. 294
352 Duckworth & Quinn, 2009
353 Siegle & McCoach, 2005
354 Csikszentmihalyi, 2009
355 Torrance, 1995
356 Maslow, 1950
357 Deci & Ryan, 2004

Chapter 14
358 Noble, Subotnik, & Arnold, 1999
359 Matthews, 1997; Subotnik, Olszewski-Kubilius, & Worrell, 2011
360 Reis & Sullivan, 2009
361 Kerr & McKay, 2013
362 George, Helson, & John, 2011
363 Kaufman, 2013, p. 303
364 Anders Ericsson and Neil Charness (1994) concluded that experts generally had to spend 10 years or 10,000 hours in their area in order to become experts.
365 Kaufman, 2013, p. 305
366 Krumboltz, 2009
367 Jarvin & Subotnik, 2006
368 Subotnik, Olszewski-Kubilius, & Worrell, 2011
369 Kerr & Cohn, 2001

Chapter 15

370 http://fussbudgetyfeminist.wordpress.com/tag/the-bechdel-test-2/
371 Noble, 1994

Chapter 16

372 Digital History, 2014. www.digitalhistory.uh.edu/topic_display.cfm?tcid=70
373 Wojtczak, 2004

Index

20s, 195, 196, 198. *See also* college; marriage
2e (twice-exceptional), 225, 227-228, 237-239, 346
    ADHD, 12, 109, 162, 225, 228, 229-231
    anxiety, 39-40, 157, 161-162, 173, 191, 198, 225, 227, 234-236, 250, 253, 266, 275, 308. *See also* stress.
    autism, 108, 225, 226, 228, 237, 266, 346
    disability, 108, 122-123, 158, 162, 225-227, 229, 238-239, 243, 281, 296, 344
    misdiagnosis, 40-41, 44, 159, 225-226, 228-229, 266, 277
    mood disorders, 39, 229, 231-234
    OCD, 40, 105, 234, 235-237
40s, 29, 35, 211-215. *See also* Generation X; midlife crisis.
50s, 76, 217, 219
60s, 76, 217-218, 219, 222

AAUW, 37, 38, 42, 43, 245, 339, 340
abilities, 2-6, 20, 28, 53, 145, 176, 201, 267-270, 281, 283, 338, 346
    academic, 5, 26, 149, 162-164, 199-200
        See also achievement; college.
    artistic, 98, 112, 166-167, 203-205, 234, 259, 295
    creativity, 4-5, 5-6, 12-14, 17, 19-21, 52, 55, 57, 60, 96, 118, 129-131, 158, 166, 185-186, 203-205, 230-232, 233-234, 259, 265, 282, 303, 312. *See also* flow; Procreator Bees.
    disability, 108, 122-123, 158, 162, 225-227, 229, 239, 243, 281, 296, 344. *See also* 2e.
    general, 8-9, 14, 17, 19, 281

math, 7-8, 42, 53, 100, 111-112, 145, 152, 163, 167, 187, 198, 200-203, 218, 251, 268, 282. *See also* STEM.
music, 65-67, 109-110, 130, 167, 203-204, 208, 252, 259, 293
overexcitability, 13, 21, 228-229, 264-266, 271
spatial, 8, 18, 112, 187, 200, 282
specific, 8-9, 10, 15, 17, 18, 51, 96-97, 109, 279, 281
spiritual, 13-16, 17, 21-22, 118, 214-216, 246, 283, 288, 301, 307, 309. *See also* emotional intelligence; Queen Bees.
verbal, 7-8, 62, 104, 107, 110, 119, 135-136, 168, 237, 249, 268, 282, 346. *See also* writing.
academics, 5, 26, 149, 162-164, 199-200. *See also* achievement; college.
acceleration, 3, 6-7, 42, 83, 107-109, 124, 130, 147-148, 148, 294, 313, 337
achievement, 26, 40, 42, 96, 98, 156, 211, 214-215, 221, 269-270
    barriers
        external
            discrimination, 23, 66, 81, 201, 204, 252, 259, 284, 296, 302
            resources, lack of, 34, 37, 39, 50, 101, 110, 120-121, 156, 176, 178, 186-187, 201, 238, 242, 252, 260, 288, 296
            sexism, 23, 143, 201, 245, 248, 260
        internal, 187, 206
            Imposter Syndrome, 35, 73, 267
    gap
        between races, 244-245, 248, 250, 251-253, 268, 281

between socioeconomic status, 241-
242, 244, 253, 260
gender, 30, 42, 50, 84, 100, 141, 149,
157, 176-177, 199-200, 205-206,
235, 242, 277
in math, 7-8, 42, 53, 100, 111-112, 145,
152, 163, 167, 187, 198, 200-203, 218,
251, 268, 282. *See also* STEM.
in science, 42, 200
on Maslow's hierarchy, 14, 273-274
public, 59, 66, 204, 220, 279, 280, 287-
288, 289-290
tests
AP (Advanced Placement), 151-152,
167, 176, 296, 313
intelligence, 2-5, 7-8, 15-16, 18, 25,
42, 108, 123-124, 127, 147, 163,
176, 263, 338
standardized achievement tests, 7,
18, 25, 78, 147, 151, 163, 167, 242,
244, 293, 296, 338
state assessments, 123. *See also* No
Child Left Behind (NCLB).
adapting, 137, 202, 217, 219-223
ADHD, 225, 228, 229-231, 239. *See also* 2e.
adjustment, 11, 25-27, 29, 32, 72, 207, 232,
308
admissions, early, 45, 107-109, 148
adolescence, 141-144, 146-147, 149-151,
156-157, 254-255
adult life, 18, 34, 51, 146, 195-224
Advanced Placement (AP), 151-152, 167,
176, 296, 313
advice, 47, 122, 157, 174, 205, 234
for parents
college years, 298-299
kindergarten through fifth grade,
293-294
preschool years, 291-292
middle school, 294-296
older adolescence, 296-298
for professionals who work with gifted
women, 308-309
for smart girls
elementary and middle school,
299-300
teens, 300-303
college and graduate school, 303-306
adult smart women, 306-308
advocacy, 28-29, 86-87, 125, 153, 312
affirmative action, 80. *See also* race.

African-American, 29-30, 38, 45-47, 53,
64-67, 91, 149, 209-210, 241, 243-245,
253. *See also* Hudson, Jennifer; race.
agency, 143, 154, 197, 258, 274. *See also*
sexuality.
aggression, 80, 92, 156
aging, 87, 219, 221-223
agreeableness, 11, 72, 182, 308. *See also*
disagreeableness.
alone time, 10, 14, 91, 97-98, 114, 137, 288,
314. *See also* loneliness.
Alyssa, 45-47
American Association for University
Women (AAUW), 37-38, 42, 165, 245,
339, 340
American culture, 27, 30-32, 39, 63, 71,
82-83, 144, 175, 260
American Psychological Association (APA),
142, 150, 156, 215, 239, 253, 347
anecdotes, Barbara Kerr's, 32, 116, 132, 136,
140, 143, 154, 163, 171, 214, 215, 216,
242, 243, 245, 246, 281
animals, studying, 88-91, 93, 138, 168, 303
stuffed animals, 117, 133
Anna, 192-193
anxiety, 40, 157, 159, 161-162, 173, 191, 198,
234-236, 253, 266, 308
AP, 151-152, 167, 176, 296, 313
Arizona State University, 45, 149, 172, 189,
192, 250, 340
Arnold, K. D., 22, 51, 176, 213, 219, 279,
339, 340, 344, 345, 348
Aronson, J., 103, 163, 317, 341, 344
arts, 98, 112, 166-167, 185, 203-205, 234,
259, 295, 302
liberal arts, 164, 186
musical, 65-67, 109-110, 130, 167, 203-
204, 208, 252, 259, 293
performing, 20, 39, 158, 165, 167, 231,
287
Asian American, 8, 243, 250-253. *See also*
race.
Assouline, S. G., 5, 42, 111, 267-268, 337,
339, 342, 348
aspirations, 141, 148-149, 160, 177. *See also*
dreams.
asynchronous development, 38, 104, 109,
142, 342
at-risk girls, 39, 41-42, 53, 96, 99, 144, 149,
241, 297

athletics, 26, 39, 100, 149-150, 158, 234, 283, 287, 295, 302
attitude, 11, 14, 134, 173, 188, 222, 236, 253
  societal, 5, 22, 25, 78, 86-87, 124, 214, 285
attractiveness, 100, 117, 133, 154, 158, 206, 243, 247, 255-257, 276, 300, 305
auditions, 66-67, 135, 167, 204, 287
autism, 105-106, 108, 122, 225-226, 228, 237, 266, 346. *See also* 2e.
average,
  girls, 26-27, 120, 210, 270
  schools, 120, 122-125
awakening, spiritual, 13-16, 17, 21-22, 118, 214-216, 246, 283, 288, 301, 307, 309. *See also* emotional intelligence; Queen Bees
Äystö, S., 261, 263, 340, 341,

babies' characteristics, 28, 103-104. *See also* children, having.
Baby Boomers, 42, 215
babysitting, 41, 133, 296
balancing career and family, 22-23, 35, 52, 54, 62, 75-76, 81, 101, 157, 176, 181, 196, 201-203, 206, 208, 211-213, 219, 223, 252, 285, 301 *See also* dual careers
Barbara Kerr's anecdotes, 32, 116, 132, 136, 140, 143, 154, 163, 171, 214, 215, 216, 242, 243, 245, 246, 281
barriers to achievement
  external
    discrimination, 23, 66, 81, 201, 204, 252, 259, 284, 296, 302
    resources, lack of, 34, 37, 39, 50, 101, 121, 156, 178, 186-187, 201, 238, 242, 252, 260, 288, 296
    sexism, 23, 143, 201, 245, 248, 260
  internal, 187, 206
    Imposter Syndrome, 35, 73, 267
beauty, 100, 117, 133, 154, 158, 206, 243, 247, 255-257, 276, 300, 305
Bechdel Rules, 301
Beehive of Smart Girls, 15-22, 117-118, 162, 281-283, 289
  Forager Bees, 17, 18, 117, 282
  Honey Bees, 17, 19, 117, 282-283
  Procreator Bees, 17, 19-20, 118, 282
  Queen Bees, 17, 21, 118, 283
  Worker Bees, 17, 18, 117, 282-283
belonging, 78, 150, 187, 189, 218, 255, 260, 273-274, 285. *See also* social capital.

Benbow, C., 7, 32, 53, 202, 340, 345
bias, 2, 16, 50, 145, 163, 176, 195, 242, 244, 337
Big Five Personality Theory, 10, 13, 151, 228
biographies, 54
  Cammermeyer, Margarethe, 82-87, 102, 215
  Fey, Tina, 59-64, 95
  Goodall, Jane, 88-93, 98, 102, 137, 215, 341
  Hudson, Jennifer, 64-67, 340
  Rowling, J. K., 55-59, 101, 137, 217, 274, 289, 340
  Sandberg, Sheryl, 23, 71-76, 95, 101, 205-206, 208, 215, 339, 341, 345
  Sotomayor, Sonia, 76-82, 101, 116, 121, 233, 341
  Yousafzai, Malala, 67-71, 101-102, 120, 121, 274, 284, 341
black women, 29-30, 38, 45-47, 53, 64-67, 91, 149, 209-210, 241, 243-245, 253. *See also* Hudson, Jennifer; race.
Bolick, K., 175, 196, 344, 345
books, 77, 88, 106, 109, 117, 124-125, 138-140, 292, 301, 309, 313. *See also* bibliotherapy; reading.
boredom, 42, 44, 119-120, 124, 152, 166, 225, 229, 235
boundaries, 60, 63, 99-100, 157, 159, 295
boys
  boyfriends, 38, 43, 62, 79, 98, 116, 143-144, 154-156, 177, 179-180, 182, 188, 192-193, 196, 212, 254, 285, 299, 302. *See also* romance.
  compared to girls
    differences, 7, 28, 31, 39, 43, 51, 73, 98, 104, 111-112, 115, 124, 133, 136, 142, 145-146, 152, 157, 163, 195, 200-202, 217, 228-230, 248, 267-268
    gender gap, 30, 42, 50, 84, 100, 141, 149, 157, 176-177, 199-200, 205-206, 235, 242, 277. *See also* male privilege.
    similarities, 2, 26, 120, 142
brain, 8, 142, 146, 161, 271
Brain Café, 128, 131
bridal mania, 197-198
Brown, L. M., 133, 141, 343
Brückner, H., 254, 255, 347
bullying, 109, 113, 155, 210, 235, 252, 256

business, 54, 71, 169-170, 216, 283, 288

Cammermeyer, Margarethe, 82-87, 102, 215
Campbell, S. M., 37, 40, 44, 339, 340
capital, social, 187, 260-261, 286, 313
career
    aspirations, 141, 160, 177, 192, 302, . *See also* dreams, goals.
    assessment, 16, 45, 151, 172, 296
    balancing family and career, 22-23, 35, 52, 54, 62, 75-76, 81, 101, 157, 176, 181, 196, 201-203, 206, 208, 211-213, 219, 223, 252, 285, 301
    development, 51, 96, 100, 151, 162, 184, 189-191, 215, 286-287, 289-290, 308, 340. *See also* WiSE.
    dreams, 23, 33, 26, 32, 34-35, 56, 84, 118, 179, 190, 193, 207, 210, 212, 289. *See also* falling in love with an idea; goals; having it all.
    dual-careers, 23, 28, 51, 79, 87, 101, 155, 196, 198, 207, 215. *See also* balancing family and career.
    goals, 11, 23, 34, 45, 49, 50-51, 79, 84, 96, 98, 128, 149, 175, 176-177, 184, 188, 190, 197, 219, 224, 258, 266, 273, 283, 285, 289, 302, 305, 308
    guidance, 31, 74, 151, 153, 286-287, 296, 304, 313
    identities, 96, 98-99, 186
    opportunities, 3, 44, 63, 123, 152, 164, 168-169, 174, 184, 190, 191, 259, 270, 286-287, 303
    opting out, 35, 41, 51, 160, 195, 205, 207-211, 215, 224
    paths, 22, 34, 53, 54, 60, 74, 95-96, 177-186, 203, 282-283, 301, 306, 313
    status, 20, 27, 30-33, 38, 50, 59, 64, 148, 158, 177, 220, 224
    traditionally masculine careers, 199, 201-203, 205. *See also* ceiling effect; STEM.
Carlie, 181-182
Castellanos, F. X., 229, 346
Catholic school, 78, 185, 250
Ceci, S. J., 3, 201-202, 337, 345
ceiling effect, 35, 123, 169, 205
challenge, providing, 2, 6, 34, 41-42, 45, 49, 75, 97, 100, 111-112, 119, 140, 162, 219, 226, 268, 270-272, 275, 301, 313
Chamorro-Premuzic, T., 10, 12, 337, 338

chance, 98, 164, 169, 259-260, 286, 298, 311
change, 21, 31, 37, 43, 71, 74, 76, 87, 217, 294, 306
children, *see also* mothers.
    childcare, 23, 29, 30, 41, 51, 58, 91, 101, 121, 196, 203, 205, 209, 287-288
    childhood experiences, 44, 53, 61, 72, 81, 98, 99, 134, 137, 213, 236
    having children and motherhood, 54, 85, 96, 107, 205, 209, 221
    homemakers, 27, 30-31, 69, 192, 209, 214, 219, 287
    pregnancy and childbirth, 23, 31, 38, 51-52, 58, 60, 65, 85, 143, 149, 188, 198-199, 208-209, 303, 307, 311
chimpanzees, 90-93. *See also* Goodall, Jane.
choices, 23, 32, 51, 57, 98, 189, 195, 201-203, 208-211, 212-214, 285, 287
chores, 131, 137, 205, 207, 248, 288, 302
civil rights, 1, 30, 34, 43, 54, 56, 71, 78, 81, 82, 86-87, 117, 146, 198, 215, 255, 275, 284, 307, 311-312
CJ, 106-107
classes, 57, 121, 122-123, 145, 146, 152, 153, 164-165, 170-171, 190, 195, 235
    classmates, 161, 172, 182. *See also* peers.
Clance, Pauline, 267, 348
CLEOS, 151, 234, 296
clothes, 38, 115-117, 133, 158, 175, 178, 179, 314. *See also* beauty.
code-switching, 261 *See also* race.
coeducational colleges, 148, 165. *See also* women's colleges.
CogAT (Cognitive Abilities Test), 338
Cohn, S. J., 26, 124, 289, 339, 342, 348
Colangelo, N., 5, 42, 112, 121, 267, 337, 339, 342
college,
    admissions, 7, 147, 151, 153, 162-163, 165, 167-168, 193, 202, 248, 286, 313, 344. *See also* standardized achievement tests.
    early, 45, 107-109, 148
    advice, 47, 122, 157, 174, 205, 234, 303-306
    applications, 147, 163, 176
    aspirations, 34, 42, 60-61, 187, 211 *See also* career aspirations.
    campus visits, 149, 164, 285
    coeducational, 148, 165

culture, 78, 83, 166, 175-180, 259
  of romance, 34-35, 95, 98, 100, 175-
    178, 187, 192-193, 212, 284-285
  DIY and alternatives, 169, 171, 186, 298,
    305
  dual enrollment and college level work,
    7, 152-153, 160, 298, 313
  experiences, 41, 42, 57, 166, 169, 175-
    180, 185, 188, 248, 252, 298-299
  first generation, 78, 178, 181, 248, 250,
    259
  gap year, 169, 170-171, 305
  graduates, 2, 30, 122, 171, 185, 195, 245
  graduate school, 3, 42, 80, 91, 141, 149,
    164, 168, 176, 192, 195-196, 199,
    202-203, 286
  guidance and development, 31, 51, 74, 96,
    100, 151, 153, 162, 184, 189-191, 215,
    286-287, 289-290, 296-297, 302, 304,
    308, 313, 340
  liberal arts, 164, 186
  majors, 34, 41-42, 57, 62, 73, 152, 165,
    177-179, 180-181, 183, 185-187, 190,
    199, 304, 313
  planning and preparation, 133-134, 149-
    150, 151, 153, 162, 164-165, 174, 179,
    195, 250, 254, 296-298, 302. *See also*
    career development; career guidance.
  professors and faculty, 74, 78, 126-127,
    164, 166, 181-183, 185, 190-192, 203,
    204, 298, 303-304. *See also* mentors.
  specialized, 166-168
  STEM, 51, 160, 177, 181, 184, 186-189,
    190, 192, 199-203, 287
  tuition and finances, 84, 97, 136, 147,
    152, 164, 167, 178-179, 181, 198, 248,
    252, 253, 286, 296-298, 305
  women's, 52, 165-166, 169, 286
Combs, M. C., 249, 252, 347
comedy, 59, 61-64, 135. *See also* Tina Fey.
communication, 19, 111, 152, 159, 173, 178,
  237
community, 65, 121-123, 127-128, 146, 148,
  149-150, 183, 185, 241-242, 247, 249,
  255, 273
competition, 11, 50-51, 78, 120, 123, 133,
  144, 152, 161, 169, 195, 197, 268, 273
compulsion and OCD, 40, 105, 234, 235-
  237. *See also* 2e.
computers and computer science, 121, 152,
  167, 282. *See also* technology.

conditions
  of eminent women, 52-54
  working conditions, 37, 201, 207, 288
confidence, 45, 47, 141, 147, 156, 160, 174,
  176, 180, 187-189, 201, 252, 261, 267,
  286. *See also* self-efficacy.
conform, pressure to, 22, 95, 99, 141, 146
  nonconforming, 4, 11, 20, 40, 118, 131,
    158, 166, 171, 267, 282
conscientiousness, 12-13, 18, 60, 264, 181,
  251, 271-272, 308, 338
context, 227, 279
conversations, 35, 75, 112, 114, 159, 176,
  190, 313, 346. *See also* communication.
Costa, P. T., 10, 151, 337, 343
counseling, 19, 151, 153, 159, 164-165, 179-
  180, 182, 191, 195, 234, 238, 282, 287,
  296-298, 300, 304, 307. *See also* career
  guidance; disorders; psychological.
Counseling Laboratory for Exploration of
  Optimal States (CLEOS), 151, 234, 296
creativity, 4-5, 5-6, 12-14, 17, 19-21, 52, 55,
  57, 60, 96, 118, 129-131, 158, 166, 203-
  205, 230-232, 233-234, 259, 265, 282,
  303, 312. *See also* flow; Procreator Bees
  Creative Pathway, 185-186
critical events, 96, 98, 109, 111, 132, 253
criticism, 40, 44, 97, 124, 172, 233, 241
Cross, T. L., 156, 267, 344, 348
cruelty, 89-90, 92-93, 138, 155, 212, 227, 252
Csikszentmihalyi, M., 14, 20, 22, 38, 52, 96,
  102, 138, 270, 338, 339, 340, 341, 343, 348
cultural capital, 260-261, 280, 285, 313
cultures, 4, 5, 152, 247-249, 251-252, 293,
  298, 301 *See also* race.
culture of romance, 34-35, 95, 98, 100, 175-
  178, 187, 192-193, 212, 284-285
curiosity, 2, 12, 103, 229, 271-272, 283
curriculum, 125, 149, 153, 185, 189. *See also*
  No Child Left Behind.

Dabrowski, K. 228, 265
danger zones, 34, 157-159, 176, 242, 261
dating, 83, 100, 155, 179, 182, 196, 211. *See
  also* romance.
Davis, J. L., 241, 244, 347
decision-making, 9, 142, 174, 188-190,
  195-196, 198, 203, 211, 303, 313. *See also*
  choices.
defensiveness, 99, 155, 182, 210, 253, 255, 341

demographics, 206, 247, 279, 280, 284, 340
See also race; SES.
depression, 38-40, 73, 179, 191, 213-214,
   225-227, 229, 231-234, 239, 254, 256,
   265-266, 297, 308
development
   asynchronous, 38, 104, 109, 142, 342
   cognitive, 134, 165
   intellectual, 104, 108-109, 165, 183
   optimal, 13, 49, 51, 189, 207, 273, 277,
      280, 289, 291. *See also* CLEOS.
differences, gender, 7, 28, 31, 39, 43, 51, 73,
   98, 104, 111-112, 115, 124, 133, 136, 142,
   145-146, 152, 157, 163, 195, 200-202,
   217, 228-230, 248, 267-268. *See also*
   gender gap.
direction, 9, 170-171, 176, 185, 194, 196,
   220, 283
disability, 108, 122-123, 158, 162, 225-227,
   229, 239, 243, 281, 296, 344. *See also,* 2e;
   misdiagnosis.
disagreeableness, 11, 70, 204, 219, 312. *See*
   also agreeableness.
discrimination, 23, 66, 81, 201, 204, 252,
   259, 284, 296, 302
disillusionment, 207. *See also* depression.
disorders. *See also* 2e.
   ADHD, 225, 228, 229-231, 239
   anxiety, 40, 157, 159, 161-162, 173, 191,
      198, 234-236, 253, 266, 308
   autism, 105-106, 108, 122, 225-226, 228,
      237, 266, 346
   eating disorder, 34, 39, 44, 158, 175, 179-
      180, 232, 255, 257, 297
   mood, 39, 142, 229, 231-234, 266, 275
   OCD, 40, 105, 234, 235-237
dissatisfaction, 31, 214, 216
distance from privilege, 3, 187, 242, 254-
   255, 257-258, 260, 279-281, 339
divorce, 27, 32, 35, 58, 74, 81, 92, 137, 213,
   214, 217, 220, 284, 308
DIY education, 169, 171, 186, 298, 305
doctor, becoming a, 28, 69, 83, 160, 193,
   199, 209
dreams, 23, 33, 26, 32, 34-35, 56, 84, 118,
   179, 190, 193, 207, 210, 212, 289. *See also*
   career aspirations; career goals; college
   aspirations.
dresses, 61, 66, 116, 133, 156, 158, 197, 291.
   See also beauty; clothes.

dual-career, 23, 28, 51, 87, 101, 155, 196,
   198, 207, 215
dual enrollment, 7, 152-153, 160, 298, 313
Dweck, C. S., 266-267, 348

early admissions, 45, 107-109, 148
eating disorders, 34, 39, 44, 158, 175, 179-
   180, 232, 255, 257, 297
economics, 73-74, 130, 219
education. *See* college; schools.
   DIY, 169, 171, 186, 298, 305
   experiences, 41, 42, 57, 166, 169, 175-
      180, 185, 188, 248, 252, 298-299
   goals, 11, 23, 34, 45, 49, 50-51, 79, 84, 96,
      98, 128, 149, 175, 176-177, 184, 188,
      190, 197, 219, 224, 258, 266, 273, 283,
      285, 289, 302, 305, 308
   traditional, 51, 68, 112, 150, 155,
      166,169-170, 192, 258, 285
egalitarian relationships, 43, 75, 79, 95, 101,
   155, 293, 314. *See also* balancing career
   and family; partners.
Eisenhart, M. A., 98, 187, 341, 345
elderly, 27, 87, 104, 137, 201, 221-223, 246
elementary school girls, 44, 124, 299-300
Elkins, I. J., 229-230, 346
Ellick, A., 69-70, 341
eminence, 1, 4, 29, 49-52, 209, 263, 272,
   289-290, 311
   characteristics of, 38, 52, 95-102
      boundaries, 99-100
      connection to a master teacher, 97
      early interest in and time spent learn-
         ing, 96-97
      egalitarian relationships and flexible
         childrearing, 101
      falling in love with an idea, 102, 272
      financial independence, 101
      highly developed career identity,
         98-99
      loss of a parent or loved one, 95-96
      love of solitude, 97-98
      resistance to the culture of romance,
         100-101
      resistance to stereotype threat, 100
   eminent women
      Cammermeyer, Margarethe, 82-87,
         102, 215
      Fey, Tina, 59-64, 95
      Goodall, Jane, 88-93, 98, 102, 137,
         215, 341

Hudson, Jennifer, 64-67, 340
Rowling, J. K., 55-59, 101, 137, 217,
  274, 289, 340
Sandberg, Sheryl, 23, 71-76, 95, 101,
  205-206, 208, 215, 339, 341, 345
Sotomayor, Sonia, 76-82, 101, 116,
  121, 233, 341
Yousafzai, Malala, 67-71, 101-102,
  120, 121, 274, 284, 341
emotions, 11-14, 51, 129, 142, 158-159, 176,
  189, 198, 222, 266, 295, 298, 300. *See also*
  SENG.
emotional intelligence, 9, 19, 21, 117,
  157, 162, 168-169, 265, 338. *See also*
  Honey Bees.
employment, 27, 166, 286
  employer, 170-171, 184, 195
  unemployment, 184, 247
engagement, academic, 12, 96, 131, 179,
  183, 192, 234, 263, 266, 271, 276, 283. *See
  also* marriage.
Engaged Pathway, 182-183, 185
engineering, 18, 54, 167, 186, 188-189, 192-
  194, 199, 218, 282, 292. *See also* STEM.
entrepreneurship, 35, 158, 169-170, 172,
  184, 204, 217, 286, 289-290
equality, 43-44, 75, 145, 154-156, 188, 203-
  204, 211, 288, 300, 301, 305, 306, 307. *See
  also* egalitarian relationships.
ethic, work, 12, 45-46, 62, 160, 181, 204,
  242, 251, 264, 267, 269-270. *See also* task
  commitment.
exhaustion, 157, 199, 208, 214, 226, 231,
  234, 285, 288
expectations, 25, 27, 95, 100, 134, 149, 206,
  223-224, 226-227, 234, 248, 250, 252,
  285, 296, 300, 314
experiences
  college, 41, 42, 57, 166, 169, 175-180,
    185, 188, 248, 252, 298-299
  new, 12, 14, 46, 104, 190, 219
  peak, 14, 49, 185, 229, 277. *See also*
    self-actualization
expertise, 18, 19, 87, 96-97, 237-239, 252,
  259, 270-272, 282, 286-287, 289
extreme jobs, 199, 202, 206-208, 210, 216,
  287

failure, 20, 34, 44, 145, 159-161, 174, 178,
  180-181, 195, 216, 246, 253, 260, 267,
  269, 304

fairness, 3, 5, 16, 125, 163, 203, 245, 256, 260
family
  balancing career and family, 22-23, 35,
    52, 54, 62, 75-76, 81, 101, 157, 176,
    181, 196, 201-203, 206, 208, 211-213,
    219, 223, 252, 285, 301
  dynamics, 60-61, 66, 77, 81, 177, 198-
    199, 209, 251, 301
  life, 43, 45, 76, 82, 85, 114, 128-132, 208,
    268, 293, 295,
  low-income, 41, 89-90, 178, 248, 254,
    258, 297. *See also* SES.
  responsibilities, 23, 35, 41, 51, 54, 75,
    96, 121, 137, 157, 177, 196, 217, 248,
    285, 296
  support, 53, 64-65, 68-71, 89, 140, 150,
    210, 224, 245, 260, 273, 288, 292. *See
    also* cultural capital; social capital.
fathers, 52, 61, 68-71, 76-77, 83-84, 95-96,
  180, 181, 248, 287
fear, 35, 113, 121, 133, 137, 158, 188, 234,
  235, 249, 311
  fearlessness, 70, 188, 231
  of failure, 84, 161, 184, 253
  parents', 43, 85, 118, 216
Feist, G. J., 10-11, 337, 338
female professors, 203
femininity, 2, 19, 22, 26-27, 34, 99, 112, 133,
  155-156, 178, 188, 230, 309. *See also*
  beauty; gender differences.
feminism, 9, 31, 75, 128, 131, 150, 215, 222,
  258, 370
Fey, Tina, 59-64, 95
filters, 279
  educational and career opportunities,
    286-287
  gender role and gender relations, 284-285
  legal rights, 284
  social and cultural capital, 285-286
  STEM, 152-153
  talent domain, 287
finances,
  financial independence, 23, 49-50, 81,
    95-96, 101, 211, 218, 219, 261, 276
  financial issues, 131, 164, 178-179, 198,
    307, 308. *See also* college, tuition and
    finances; family, low income; SES
flexibility, 20, 101, 109, 127, 202, 206, 207,
  210, 287-288. *See also* balancing career
  and family.

flow, 20, 49, 52-53, 102, 151, 191, 230, 233, 270-272, 276-277, 283-284, 303, 313, 338
Forager Bees, 17, 18, 117, 282
freedom, 32-33, 37, 60 131-132, 138-139, 178, 199, 201-202, 223, 311. *See also* financial independence.
Friedan, B., 31, 339
friendships, 43-44, 55-56, 62, 81, 98, 101, 112-114, 138, 156-157, 159, 173, 178, 260, 293, 295-298, 313
frustration, 22, 104, 212, 265, 267
fulfillment, 22, 33, 102, 165, 211, 213, 217, 258, 224, 276-277, 281, 285, 306, 314. *See also* potential; self-actualization.
funding, 6, 8, 41, 101, 123, 149, 241. *See also* college tuition and finances; lack of resources.
Furnham, A., 10, 12, 337, 338

Gallagher, J. J., 5, 123, 337, 342
gap year, 169, 170-171, 298, 305
Gardner, H., 8, 14-15, 52, 337
gender, roles, 99, 166, 196, 224, 230, 261, 284-285, 289. *See also* femininity.
gender differences, 7, 28, 31, 39, 43, 51, 73, 98, 104, 111-112, 115, 124, 133, 136, 142, 145-146, 152, 157, 163, 195, 200-202, 217, 228-230, 248, 267-268
gender gap, 30, 42, 50, 84, 100, 141, 149, 157, 176-177, 199-200, 205-206, 235, 242, 277. *See also* male privilege.
gender relations, 177, 187-188, 280, 284-285, 314. *See also* romance.
generations, 25, 27, 29, 32-33, 35, 38-39, 40-44, 54, 60-61, 75, 76, 186, 188, 215, 251. *See also* college, first generation.
Generation Me, 37, 40
Generation X, 33-35, 71, 74
gifted
    characteristics, 4, 5, 7, 10-11, 13, 22, 26-27, 29, 105-106, 110-112, 119-120, 141-145, 157-159, 166, 176, 211, 228-229, 232-233, 237-239, 241, 246, 263-270, 279, 281
    definition and identification, 1-2, 15, 25, 32
    education, 6, 42, 50-51, 107-109, 114, 123-128, 147-149, 151-153, 165, 169, 195-196, 215, 222

programs, 5-8, 41, 107, 114, 123, 125, 147-148, 153, 164, 189, 243, 250, 295, 296, 313
Gilligan, C., 9, 141, 337, 343
girl power, 115, 133
goals, 11, 23, 34, 45, 49, 50-51, 79, 84, 96, 98, 128, 149, 175, 176-177, 184, 188, 190, 197, 219, 224, 258, 266, 273, 283, 285, 289, 302, 305, 308. *See also* career aspirations; college aspirations.
Goodall, Jane, 88-93, 98, 102, 137, 215, 341
grade skipping, 3, 6-7, 42, 83, 107-109, 124, 130, 147-148, 148, 294, 313, 337
graduate school, 3, 42, 80, 91, 141, 149, 164, 168, 176, 192, 195-196, 199, 202-203, 286. *See also* doctor, becoming a.
grandparents, 25, 65-67, 73, 76, 87, 88, 118, 137, 209, 247. *See also* family.
Grant, B., 8, 203, 337, 345
grit, 269, 271. *See also* task commitment.
Gross, M. U., 5, 42, 113, 337, 339, 342
grouping, cluster, 124-125, 145, 294, 313
growth, 142, 183, 214, 216-217, 265, 266, 288
guidance, 31, 51, 74, 96, 100, 151, 153, 162, 184, 189-191, 215, 286-287, 289-290, 296-297, 302, 304, 308, 313, 340. *See also* counseling.

Halpern, D. F., 54, 176, 340, 344
happiness, 43, 47, 85, 179, 213-214, 219, 221-222, 227, 303, 314. *See also* emotions.
hard work, 12, 45-46, 62, 160, 181, 204, 242, 251, 264, 267, 269-270. *See also* task commitment.
Harkins, A., 37, 41, 339
Harry Potter, 55, 57-59, 137, 274. *See also* Rowling, J. K.
Harvard, 72, 74, 78, 218
having it all, 23, 34, 43, 206-207, 215. *See also* balancing career and family.
healers, 15, 84, 168, 283. *See also* doctor, becoming a; nursing.
health, 3, 26, 37-39, 208-209, 221-223, 236-238, 254-257, 291, 307. *See also* disorders.
Herberger Young Scholars Academy, 45, 148, 172, 340
hierarchy, Maslow's, 273-274
Higgins, A., 223, 346
high school, 7, 18, 65-66, 72, 130, 147, 148, 151-153, 155, 158, 170, 208, 298

higher education, *see* graduate school.
Himmelstein, K. E., 254-255, 347
Hirshman, L. R., 198, 203, 205, 345
Hispanic-Americans, 3, 150, 177, 193, 243, 247-250, 253. *See also* Sotomayor, Sonia.
Holahan, C. K., 211, 222, 345, 346
Holland, D. C., 98, 187, 341, 344
Hollingworth, L. S., 27-29, 32, 232, 339
homemakers, 27, 30-31, 69, 192, 209, 214, 219, 287
homeschooling, 127-130, 132, 287-288
Homework, 69, 157, 161, 177, 210, 301, 312
Honey Bees, 17, 19, 117, 282-283
house wives, 27, 30-31, 69, 192, 209, 214, 219, 287
Howley, C. B., 259-260, 348
Hudson, Jennifer, 64-67, 340
Hughes, D., 105-106, 342
husbands, 27, 30, 32, 34, 51, 197, 202, 205, 208, 214, 285. *See also* romance.
Hyde, J. S., 42, 104, 200, 339, 342, 345,
hyperactivity, 12, 109, 162, 225, 228, 229-231
hypomania, 231-232, 234

Iddings, A. C. D., 249, 252, 347
ideals, 27, 30, 32, 44, 101, 144, 148, 188, 207, 233, 251, 255, 281, 303
identity, 96, 98-100, 150-151, 174, 186, 197, 243, 244-245, 267, 295
imagination, 13, 55, 59, 116, 119-120, 135, 138, 194, 212, 219, 227, 228, 236, 265, 303. *See also* creativity.
Imposter Syndrome, 35, 73, 267
income, 30, 129, 134, 188, 198, 202, 312, . *See also* SES.
 low, 41, 89-90, 178, 248, 254, 258, 297
independence, 33, 37, 53, 81, 95, 205, 245, 293
 financial, 23, 49-50, 81, 95-96, 101, 211, 218, 219, 261, 276
individualized instruction, 125, 140, 164
inferiority, 3, 27, 100, 257
innovation, 11, 19-20, 171, 186, 189, 217-218, 271. *See also* Procreator Bees.
inspiration, 74, 76, 79, 147, 269
intelligence, 1-19, 14, 103, 229, 232, 263-266, 281, 269. *See also* abilities; gifted.
 emotional, 9, 19, 21, 117, 157, 162, 168-169, 265, 338. *See also* Honey Bees.
 multiple intelligences, 8-9, 157

specific, 8-9, 10, 15, 17, 18, 51, 96-97, 109, 279, 281
spiritual, 13-16, 17, 21-22, 118, 214-216, 246, 283, 288, 301, 307, 309. *See also* Queen Bees.
tests, 2-5, 7-8, 15-16, 18, 25, 42, 78, 108, 123-124, 127, 147, 151, 163, 176, 242, 244, 263, 293, 338
intensity, 21-22, 57, 102, 142, 263, 265-266, 298. *See also* emotions.
International Baccalaureate (IB), 151-153, 313
internships, 164, 167, 178, 180-181, 193, 195-196, 286, 304, 305
inverviews, 78, 108, 189, 192, 202. *See also* employment.
intimacy, 38, 99-100, 112, 143, 153, 155, 157, 197, 273, 285, 305. *See also* romance; sexuality.
introversion, 10, 46, 58, 275, 282-283, 337
intuition, 9, 117-118, 190-191, 194, 227, 230, 257, 259, 270, 303. *See also* flow.
isolation, 51, 98-99, 102, 144, 232, 255, 341
IQ, 1, 28. *See also* intelligence.

Jane Goodall, 88-93, 98, 102, 137, 215, 341
Jacob K. Javits Gifted and Talented Students Education Program, 6, 123
Jasmine, 172-173
Jenna, 161-162
Jennifer Hudson, 64-67, 340
jobs, 30, 40-41, 84, 128-129, 134, 183-185, 201, 275, 284, 286-288, 302, 303. See also employment.
 extreme, 199, 202, 206-210, 216, 287
 part-time, 137, 157, 208-209, 217, 247, 285, 297
 secretarial, 57, 89-90
 status, 27, 32, 59, 64, 148
Johnson, N. G., 142, 150, 156, 244, 343, 344, 347
justice, 77, 80, 128, 133, 169, 183, 185, 233, 307. *See also* Sotomayor, Sonia.

Kalbfleisch, M. L., 229, 346
Katie, 184-185
Kaufman, S. B., 1, 2, 222, 263, 266, 283, 286, 337, 346, 348
Kaufmann, F. A., 22, 207, 219, 221-222, 229, 290, 339, 345, 346

Kerr, B. A., 11, 15, 20, 26, 37, 38, 39, 41, 52, 53, 99, 121, 124, 141, 149, 177, 187, 196, 214, 243, 245, 250, 261, 281, 289, 337, 338 339, 340-345, 347-348
  anecdotes, 32, 116, 132, 136, 140, 143, 154, 163, 171, 214, 215, 216, 242, 243, 245, 246, 281
kindergarten, 105, 107-109, 111, 293-294, 313
Kitano, M. K., 253, 258, 347
Klein, A. G., 27, 29, 339
knowledge, 18, 97, 153
Kronborg, L., 53, 340

labels, 2, 12, 63, 103, 106, 178, 226, 229, 237, 241, 264, 266-269, 295, 296
language, 44, 110-111, 122, 183, 242-243, 246-247, 249-251, 292-293, 302, 303. *See also* race.
Latinas, 3, 150, 177, 193, 243, 247-250, 253. *See also* Sotomayor, Sonia.
law school, 34, 79-80, 149, 176
leadership, 6, 32, 45, 73, 75, 149, 168-169, 172-174, 177, 184, 189, 192-194, 206, 219, 246, 283, 302, 303, 306, 307
Leakey, 90-91
lean in, 23, 73, 75, 206, 215, 224, 288
learning, 2, 96, 109-110, 131, 132, 145-146, 161, 226, 228, 268-269, 294
  disabilities, 108, 122-123, 158, 162, 225-227, 229, 238-239, 243, 281, 296, 344
legal rights, 1, 30, 34, 43, 54, 56, 71, 78, 81, 82, 86-87, 117, 146, 198, 215, 255, 275, 284, 307, 311-312
lesbians & LGBT, 62, 83, 85-87, 155-156, 215, 243, 254-255, 260, 281, 295, 302. *See also* Cammermeyer, Margarethe.
Lolita Effect, 154
loneliness, 114, 29, 137, 156, 173, 191, 196
loss of a parent or loved one, 57, 66, 77, 92, 95-96, 236
love of an idea, 52-53, 78, 83, 102, 174, 183, 222, 224, 233, 254, 269, 271-273, 276, 281, 284, 289-290, 297, 301, 303, 304, 306, 308. *See also* boys; marriage; romance.
Lubinski, D., 53, 202, 340, 345
luck, 2, 42, 113, 124, 179, 210, 267

majors, 34, 41-42, 57, 62, 73, 152, 165, 177-179, 180-181, 183, 185-187, 190, 199, 304, 313
Malala Yousafzai, 67-71, 101-102, 120, 121, 274, 284, 341
male privilege, 1, 7, 18-19, 26, 30, 35, 38, 44, 50-52, 73, 75-76, 100, 167, 175-177, 196, 199, 203-204, 207, 242, 284. *See also* gender gap.
Margarethe Cammermeyer, 82-87, 102, 215
marriage, 23, 27, 32, 35, 38, 51, 74-75, 87, 101, 179, 188, 196-198, 199, 208, 299
  See also balancing career and family; romance.
Maslow's hierarchy, 14, 273-274, 277, 348
Massive Open Online Courses (MOOCs), 169-170, 186
Master's degree, 182, 192, 199, 208, 217, 281. *See also* graduate school.
master teacher, 97, 102, 110, 167, 295. *See also* mentor.
mastery, 51, 64, 73, 102, 146, 162, 252, 274, 275, 286, 289, 309
math, 7-8, 42, 53, 100, 111-112, 145, 152, 163, 167, 187, 198, 200-203, 218, 251, 268, 282. *See also* STEM.
Matthews, D. J., 22, 147, 207, 219, 279, 339, 343, 345, 348
maturity, 38, 47, 112, 113, 144, 154, 159, 233, 246
McAlister, K., 15, 214, 338, 345
McCoach, D. B., 124, 270, 342, 348
McCrae, R. R., 10, 151, 337, 343
McKay, R., 11, 15, 20, 216, 281, 337, 338, 361, 340
meaning, finding, 172, 179, 183, 209, 217, 219-220, 233, 236, 269, 276-277. *See also* depression.
Meckstroth, E., 343,
media portrayals, 23, 30-31, 38-39, 44, 70-71, 100, 133, 142, 153-154, 185, 233, 243-244, 257, 285, 294
medical school, 34, 84, 107, 149, 159-160, 176, 195, 203, 208. *See also* doctor, becoming a; graduate school.
memory, 13, 16, 28, 103, 142, 162, 270
men's privilege, 1, 7, 18-19, 26, 30, 35, 38, 44, 50-52, 73, 75-76, 100, 167, 175-177, 196, 199, 203-204, 207, 242, 284
Mendaglio, S., 13, 21, 228, 265, 338, 346, 348

mentors, 56, 75, 78-79, 89, 97, 102, 156, 164, 167, 181, 186, 190, 191, 275, 286, 295, 297, 304
being a mentor, 83, 307
middle class, 2, 8, 23, 26, 29, 37, 123, 133-135, 178, 180, 187-188, 209, 241, 261
middle school, 121, 144-147, 152, 160, 174, 199, 294-296, 299-300
midlife crisis, 211, 214-217
military, 82, 84-87, 215
Millennials, 35, 37, 39, 41-44, 59, 76, 134, 157, 169
mindset, 266-267, 269, 271
minorities, 180
African-Americans, 29-30, 38, 45-47, 53, 64-67, 91, 149, 209-210, 241, 243-245, 253. *See also* Hudson, Jennifer.
Asian-Americans, 8, 243, 250-253
Hispanic-Americans, 3, 150, 177, 193, 243, 247-250, 253. *See also* Sotomayor, Sonia.
lesbians, 62, 86-87, 155-156, 215, 243, 254-255, 302. *See also* Cammermeyer, Margarethe.
Native American, 15, 110, 118, 150, 215, 241, 246-247
religions, 243, 257-258, 296
rural and suburban, 30-31, 121, 180, 243, 259-260, 281, 285
misdiagnosis, 40-41, 44, 159, 225-226, 228-229, 346
models, 75, 79, 56, 75, 78-79, 89, 97, 102, 156, 164, 167, 181, 186, 190, 191, 275, 286, 295, 297, 304
Moll, L., 249, 252, 347
Mommy Wars, 101, 208-209
money
MOOCs (Massive Open Online Courses), 169-170, 186
mood disorders
moral development,
mothers, *see also* children; generations.
absent, 95-96
influence of, 42-43, 56, 61, 65, 75, 76-77, 88, 95-96, 128
single, 23, 37, 41, 43, 65, 134, 137, 210, 244, 248-249
stay-at-home, 27, 30-31, 69, 192, 209, 214, 219, 287
Tiger Mother, 251-252

motivation, 12, 20, 53, 141, 177, 213, 263-266, 271, 273, 283-284
multipotentiality, 8-9, 157
musical giftedness, 65-67, 109-110, 130, 167, 203-204, 208, 252, 259, 293. *See also* Hudson, Jennifer.
myths, 100, 106-107, 110-111, 127, 154. *See also* media portrayals.

name change, 197
nap time, 109, 292
National Association for Gifted Children (NAGC), 238, 296, 338
National Science Foundation (NSF), 37-38, 41-42, 53, 96, 199, 242, 261, 339, 341, 345
Native American, 15, 110, 118, 150, 215, 241, 246-247
nature, 14, 88, 90-91, 93, 138, 288, 294, 308
Navajo, 241, 246-247, 281
neighborhoods, poor, 76, 123, 138, 249, 253, 285
neuroticism, 11-13, 210, 228, 266, 338
Nicpon, M. F., 229, 239, 346,
Nika, 179-180
No Child Left Behind (NCLB), 41-42, 123, 145, 149
Noble, K. D., 14, 15, 51, 213, 216, 219, 279, 280, 308, 338, 340, 345, 348, 349
nonprofits, 128, 169, 210
nursing, 19, 27, 30, 34, 76, 84-87, 159-160, 181, 183. *See also* traditionally feminine careers.

obesity, 38-39, 44, 121, 253, 255-257. *See also* eating disorders; media portrayals.
obsessions, 227, 252, 255, 264, 272,. *See also* love, of an idea; OCD.
occupational status, 20, 27, 30-33, 38, 50, 59, 64, 148, 158, 177, 220, 224
OCD, 40, 105, 234, 235-237
Oden, M. H., 50, 340
old age, 27, 87, 104, 137, 201, 221-223, 246
Olszewski-Kubilius, P., 8, 50, 147, 279, 289, 337, 340, 343, 348
openness, 12-13, 19-20, 47, 60, 157, 228, 265, 283, 338
opportunity, 3, 44, 123, 130, 149, 152, 164, 168-169, 174, 181, 184, 190, 191, 249, 259, 286-287, 303
optimal development, 13, 49, 51, 189, 207, 273, 277, 280, 289, 291. *See also* CLEOS.

opting out, 35, 41, 51, 160, 195, 205, 207-211, 215, 224
Orenstein, P., 115, 141-142, 342, 343
orientation, sexual, 62, 83, 85-87, 155-156, 215, 243, 254-255, 260, 281, 295, 302
overexcitablities, 13, 21, 228-229, 264-266, 271

Pakistani Schoolgirl, 67-71, 101-102, 120, 121, 274, 284, 341
parenting, 42, 60, 62, 103-104, 105-106, 126, 132, 134, 137, 154, 209, 227, 251-252. *See also* advice, for parents; children; family; fathers; mothers.
    school involvement, 108-109, 111, 125, 145-146, 127-128, 171. *See also* advocacy.
    loss of a parent, 57, 66, 77, 92, 95-96, 236
    support, 53, 64-65, 67-71, 74, 81, 89, 117-118, 137, 140, 146, 149-150, 171, 203, 207, 210, 224, 227, 230, 245, 260, 273, 288, 292
partners, 35, 52, 54, 75, 87, 99, 101, 174, 181, 183, 188, 203, 205, 208-210, 273, 285, 295, 297, 305, 306, 314. *See also* egalitarian relationships; romance.
Party Pathway, 177-179, 192, 259, 285, 305
passion, 33, 53, 68, 96-97, 102, 131-132, 139-140, 186, 217, 263-264, 271-274, 283-284, 289-290, 305-306. *See also* love, of an idea.
paths, 22, 34, 53, 54, 60, 74, 95-96, 177-186, 203, 282-283, 301, 306, 313
peers, 6, 8, 26, 98, 114, 120, 145, 148, 153, 164, 185, 186, 226, 232, 237, 293, 296, 297
    pressure, 41, 156, 158, 179, 257. *See also* media portrayals.
perfectionism, 34, 39, 157-158, 163, 181, 232, 236, 253, 272, 308
Perrone, K. M., 209, 211, 345
persistence, 97, 164, 187-188, 208, 264, 267, 269, 281
personality, 10-13, 20, 22, 72, 151, 204, 228, 265, 281-283, 338
Pew Foundation, 43, 340
Ph.D., 85-86, 91, 193, 199, 218. *See also* doctor, becoming a.
Piirto, J., 96, 259, 341, 347
pink, 112, 115-117, 133, 189
planning for college, 133-134, 149-150, 151, 153, 162, 164-165, 174, 179, 195, 250,

254, 296-298, 302. *See also* career development; career guidance.
portfolios, 6, 40, 166-168, 287, 305. *See also* arts.
Post-Sputnik, 4, 32-33, 35, 75
Potter, Harry, 55, 57-59, 137, 274
politics, 50, 63, 69, 75, 81, 87, 169, 205, 284, 305. *See also* civil rights.
poverty, 41, 58, 76, 89-90, 101, 120-123, 178, 217, 247-248, 254, 258, 297. *See also* finances.
power, 3, 9, 62, 69, 71, 72-73, 76, 156, 175, 179, 190, 197-199, 242, 245, 254-255, 257, 260, 274, 280-281, 290, 296. *See also* distance from privilege; girl power; status.
precocious abilities, 7, 104, 105-106, 111, 142, 153, 202, 307
preferences, 163, 186, 201-203
pregnancy, 23, 31, 65, 85, 143-144, 149, 198, 303, 311
prejudice, 201, 249, 256-257, 296. *See also* race; sexism.
preschool, 105, 108-109, 111-112, 114, 117, 254, 291-292
Presidential Scholars, 22, 207, 215, 219, 222
pressure, 29, 34, 38-41, 97, 99-100, 178-179, 196-197, 203, 206, 210, 256, 265. *See also* media portrayals.
prestige, 50, 100, 200. *See also* status.
primates, 90-93. *See also* Goodall, Jane.
Princess Industrial Complex, 114-117, 197, 284, 291, 301, 314
Princeton, 61, 78, 80, 206
private schools, 42, 120, 126, 129, 164, 293
privilege, 6, 78, 209, 242-243, 248-250, 261, 285, 296
    distance from, 3, 187, 242, 254-255, 257-258, 260, 279-281, 339
Pryor, J. H., 37, 41, 43, 339, 340
Procreator Bees, 17, 19-20, 118, 282
professionals, 18-19, 27, 28, 34, 35, 168, 195-196, 205, 221, 228, 282, 286, 289, 297, 305-308. *See also* career.
professors, 74, 78, 126-127, 164, 166, 181-183, 185, 190-192, 203, 204, 298, 303-304
programs, gifted, 5-8, 41, 107, 114, 123, 125, 147-148, 153, 164, 189, 243, 250, 295, 313. *See also* acceleration; AP; cluster grouping; IB; WiSE.
psychology, 3, 4, 8, 9-10, 20, 189, 308

adjustment, 16, 119, 157, 288
pop, 200, 238
seeing a psychologist, 19, 108, 109, 151,
191, 237-239, 296, 297, 300, 307
puberty, 38-39, 44, 141-142, 144, 146, 174,
200, 294
public, 59, 66, 204, 220, 279, 280, 287-288,
289-290
public school, 72, 76, 120, 123-127, 130
Puerto Rico, 76-81, 248. *See also* Hispanic-
American; Sotomayor, Sonia.
punishment, 124, 156, 201, 205, 215, 253-
255, 257
purpose, sense of, 14, 77, 101, 143-144, 150-
151, 171-172, 180, 183, 213, 236, 254,
306, 308

Queen Bees, 17, 21, 118, 283
quitting, 27, 136, 205, 207-208, 210, 222. *See
also* opting out.

race, 3, 243, 247, 296. *See also* minorities.
African-Americans, 29-30, 38, 45-47,
53, 64-67, 91, 149, 209-210, 241, 243-
245, 253. *See also* Hudson, Jennifer.
Asian-Americans, 8, 243, 250-253
Hispanic-Americans, 3, 150, 177,
193, 243, 247-250, 253. *See also*
Sotomayor, Sonia.
Native American, 15, 110, 118, 150, 215,
241, 246-247
white, 1-5, 8, 29, 38, 78, 154, 204, 209-
210, 241, 244-246
Raven, J., 5, 16, 242, 337, 338, 347
reading, 26, 55-56, 58, 77, 96, 104, 105-107,
109, 119, 124, 233, 238, 291, 292, 298, 299
Reardon, S. F., 134-135, 253-254, 343, 347
Reis, S. M., 5-6, 239, 279, 337, 346, 348
rejection, 43-44, 57, 58, 116, 120, 157-158,
230-231, 235, 254
relationships, *see* romance.
religion, 21, 43, 89, 110, 243, 255, 257-258,
296
Renzulli, J. S., 6, 264, 337, 348
resilience, 53, 61, 66, 96-97, 122, 244, 254,
284. *See also* grit.
resistance, 99, 100, 144, 150, 156, 291, 294,
298
resources, 23, 97, 108, 111, 112, 125, 128,
132, 198, 202, 228, 238-239, 296, 297. *See
also* capital; finances.

books, 1, 23, 31, 52, 73, 106, 159, 165, 167,
207, 213, 228, 252, 257, 259, 263, 267
lack of, 34, 37, 39, 50, 101, 110, 120-121,
156, 176, 178, 186-187, 201, 238, 242,
252, 260, 288, 296
responsibility, 30, 41, 85, 188, 207, 212, 269
household, 23, 35, 41, 51, 54, 75, 96, 121,
137, 157, 177, 196, 217, 248, 285, 296
reunions, 208, 214, 217
rights, 1, 30, 34, 43, 54, 56, 71, 78, 81, 82,
86-87, 117, 146, 198, 215, 255, 275, 284,
307, 311-312
Roberts, M. C., 142, 150, 156,244, 343, 344,
347
Robinson-Kurpius, S. E., 37, 39, 41, 53, 149,
177, 187, 241-242, 250, 281, 339, 340,
343, 347
Roeper, A. 222-223, 346
roles, gender, 99, 166, 196, 224, 230, 261,
284-285, 289. *See also* femininity.
romance, 35, 153-155, .
boyfriends, 38, 43, 62, 79, 98, 116, 143-
144, 154-156, 177, 179-180, 182, 188,
192-193, 196, 212, 254, 285, 299, 302
culture of, 34-35, 95, 98, 100, 175-178,
187, 192-193, 212, 284-285
dating, 83, 100, 155, 179, 182, 196, 211
gender relations, 177, 187-188, 280, 284-
285, 302, 314
husbands, 27, 30, 32, 34, 51, 197, 202,
205, 208, 214, 285
intimacy, 38, 99-100, 112, 143, 153, 155,
157, 197, 273, 285, 305. *See also* sex.
marriage, 23, 27, 32, 35, 38, 51, 74-75, 87,
101, 179, 188, 196-198, 199, 208, 299
partners, 35, 52, 54, 75, 87, 99, 101, 174,
181, 183, 188, 203, 205, 208-210, 273,
285, 295, 297, 305, 306, 314
Rowling, J. K., 55-59, 101, 137, 217, 274,
289, 340
rules, 118, 125, 132, 138, 158, 191, 198, 213,
286, 293, 294, 301

sadness, 56-58, 66, 89, 92, 117, 207, 224?,
230-233, 295. *See also* depression.
safety, 68, 121-122, 132, 149, 150, 157, 171,
245, 254, 273-274, 298
salaries, 38, 180, 199-201, 204, 208, 220, 224.
See also gender gap.
Sandberg, S., 23, 71-76, 95, 101, 205-206,
208, 215, 339, 341, 345

Sara, 218
satisfaction, 27, 50, 31, 101, 166, 196, 200, 209, 211, 213-216, 219-222, 271-273. *See also* self-actualization.
Schlesinger, J., 33, 232, 339, 346
Schlosser, G., 52, 95, 340, 341
scholars, 18, 29, 101, 165, 200. *See also* Forager Bees.
scholarships, 8, 101, 126, 163, 167, 180-181, 252, 283, 296, 297, 305, 313. *See also* finances; Presidential Scholars.
schools, *see also* college; education.
    average, 120, 122-125
    best, 120, 125-127, 283, 292
    elementary, 44, 124, 299-300
    high school, 7, 18, 65-66, 72, 130, 147, 148, 151-153, 155, 158, 170, 208, 298
    homeschool, 127-130, 132, 287
    law, 34, 79-80, 149, 176
    middle school, 121, 144-147, 152, 160, 174, 199, 294-296, 299-300
    medical, 34, 84, 107, 149, 159-160, 176, 195, 203, 208. *See also* doctor, becoming a.
    preschool, 105, 108-109, 111-112, 114, 117, 254, 291-292
    private schools, 42, 120, 126, 129, 164, 293
    public and charter schools, 72, 76, 120, 123-127, 130
    worst, 120-122, 126-127
science, 51, 53, 83, 100, 133, 147, 152, 159-160, 163, 167-169, 187, 188-189, 200, 251. *See also* STEM.
secretary, 57, 89-90
self-
    actualization, 21, 49-50, 214, 224, 258, 273-274, 279, 283, 289. *See also* optimal development.
    confidence, 45, 47, 141, 147, 156, 160, 174, 176, 180, 187-189, 201, 252, 261, 267, 286
    efficacy, 175-176, 187-188, 201, 203, 261, 281, 296
    esteem, 34, 40, 53, 141-143, 150, 172, 179, 230, 245, 252, 256, 273
SENG, 228, 238
sensitivity, 11, 13, 21-22, 107, 109-110, 114, 157, 172, 183, 228, 255, 265-266
SES (Socioeconomic Status), 157, 243, 253-254, 281
sex

differences, 7, 28, 31, 39, 43, 51, 73, 98, 104, 111-112, 115, 124, 133, 136, 142, 145-146, 152, 157, 163, 195, 200-202, 217, 228-230, 248, 267-268
    orientation, 62, 83, 85-87, 155-156, 215, 243, 254-255, 260, 281, 295, 302
    pregnancy, 23, 31, 65, 85, 143-144, 149, 198, 303, 311
    sexism, 23, 143, 201, 245, 248, 260
    sexuality, 31, 38, 64, 101, 133, 142-144, 153-155, 157, 178, 231, 258, 284, 305,.
    sexualization, 38, 44, 294. *See also* media portrayals.
    sexual victimization, 175, 178-179, 181, 204, 236, 284
shame, 110, 207-208, 210, 230-231, 257
Sheryl Sandberg, 23, 71-76, 95, 101, 205-206, 208, 215, 339, 341, 345
Shriver, M., 37, 39, 41-43, 157, 339, 340, 344
Sidney, 114
Siegle, D., 124, 270, 342, 348
single, 27, 31, 35, 51, 179, 210, 219, 221, 272, 311, 314
    moms, 23, 37, 41, 43, 65, 134, 137, 210, 244, 248-249
single-sex education, 52, 165-166, 169, 286
skills, 15, 19, 97, 106, 109, 118, 127, 159, 167, 230, 236-237, 246-247, 257, 266, 270-271, 275, 282, 295, 314. *See also* abilities.
Slaughter, 206, 345
Smart Girl Profiles, 45-47, 106-107, 114, 159-160, 161-162, 172-173, 179-180, 181-182, 184-185, 192-193, 193-194, 218, 218-219
social
    capital, 187, 260-261, 286, 313
    work, 181, 183, 217, 282
Socioeconomic Status (SES), 157, 243, 253-254, 281
solitude, 10, 14, 91, 97-98, 114, 137, 288, 314
Sonia, 193-194
Sotomayor, Sonia, 76-82, 101, 116, 121, 233, 341
spatial-visual giftedness, 8, 18, 112, 187, 200, 282

sphere, 279-280
    personal, 287-289
    public, 289-290
spiritual, *see also* Queen Bees.

awakening, 13-16, 17, 21-22, 118, 214-216, 246, 283, 288, 301, 307, 309
intelligence, 13-16, 17, 21-22, 118, 214-216, 246, 283, 288, 301, 307, 309
Sputnik, Post-, 4, 32-33, 35, 75
Stainthorp, R., 105-106, 342
Stanford-Binet test, 2, 29, 338
status, 9, 37, 100, 187, 195-196, 212, 216, 223, 260, 284. *See also* career status; SES.
STEM, 51, 160, 177, 181, 184, 186-189, 190, 192, 199-203, 287
   science, 51, 53, 83, 100, 133, 147, 152, 159-160, 163, 167-169, 187, 188-189, 200, 251
   technology, 43, 74, 122, 127, 152, 158, 166-168, 170-171, 184, 189, 259, 282, 288
   engineering, 18, 54, 167, 186, 188-189, 192-194, 199, 218, 282, 292
   math, 7-8, 42, 53, 100, 111-112, 145, 152, 163, 167, 187, 198, 200-203, 218, 251, 268, 282
stereotype, 1, 26-27, 40, 75-76, 80, 95, 100-102, 111, 127, 133, 163, 229, 237, 244-245, 250-253, 257-259, 296
strengths, 46, 96-98, 144, 173, 191, 244-245, 250, 275, 283-284, 308
Striver Pathway, 180-182, 204, 250
Subotnik, R. F., 22, 50-51, 176, 213, 219, 279, 280, 287, 289, 339, 340, 344, 345, 348
success, 49-51, 73-76, 81, 134, 174, 177, 190, 191, 198, 199, 201, 211, 215, 218, 219, 243-245, 251-252, 267
summer programs, 8, 85, 114, 125, 147-148, 156, 168, 226, 232, 260, 275, 286, 295, 302, 313
support, 53, 64-65, 67-71, 74, 81, 89, 117-118, 137, 140, 146, 149-150, 171, 203, 207, 210, 224, 227, 230, 245, 260, 273, 288, 292
Supporting Emotional Needs of Gifted (SENG), 228, 238
Swiatek, M. A., 124, 156, 342, 344
symptoms, 84, 137, 158, 179-180, 214, 227, 229, 231-232, 235-237, 239, 266, 308

talent, *see also* abilities; intelligence.
   development, 6, 22, 50, 96-98, 149-150, 162-163, 215, 259, 274-275, 279-280, 284, 286, 289, 312
   domain, 53-54, 96-97, 109-110, 241, 274-275, 280, 287, 289

search, 7-8, 18, 147-148, 286, 295
Taliban, 67-70, 120, 274. *See also* Yousafzai, Malala.
Tara, 159-160
task commitment, 5-6, 136, 182, 264, 269, 271
teachers, 11-12, 19, 26, 56, 77-78, 109-110, 121-127, 146-147, 226-230, 246, 260, 264. *See also* professors.
   as a career, 19, 27, 30, 34, 50, 58, 128, 282, 287
   master, 97, 102, 110, 167, 295. *See also* mentors.
teamwork, 83, 136, 144, 145, 283
technology, 43, 74, 122, 127, 152, 158, 166-168, 170-171, 184, 189, 259, 282, 288. *See also* STEM.
teens, 20, 33, 38, 65-66, 72, 141-145, 147, 149-150, 212-213, 244-245, 300-303
television, 30, 43, 63-64, 66, 70, 106, 150, 154, 259
Terman, L. M., 2-4, 22, 25-27, 32, 50, 143, 219, 221-222, 232, 287, 339
Tessa, 218-219
tests
   anxiety, 40, 157, 159, 161-162, 173, 191, 198, 234-236, 253, 266, 308
   AP (Advanced Placement), 151-152, 167, 176, 296, 313
   intelligence, 2-5, 7-8, 15-16, 18, 25, 42, 108, 123-124, 127, 147, 163, 176, 263, 338
   personality, 10, 13, 20, 151, 204, 338
   standardized achievement tests, 7, 18, 25, 78, 147, 151, 163, 167, 242, 244, 293, 296, 338
   school tests, 135, 159
   state assessments, 123. *See also* No Child Left Behind (NCLB).
   vocational, 151, 296
thorns and shells, 99, 203-204, 308
Tillier, W., 13, 21, 228, 338, 346
Tina Fey, 59-64, 95
Torrance, E. P., 4-5, 20, 272, 337, 338, 348
toys, 88, 107, 112, 115-118, 133-134, 292
tradition, 15, 26-27, 82, 112, 150, 162, 169-171, 246-247, 250-251, 257-258, 285
transitions, 74, 83, 108, 203, 249, 269, 298
Twenge, J. M., 37, 40, 44, 339, 340
twice-exceptional (2e), 225, 227-228, 237-239, 346

ADHD, 12, 109, 162, 225, 228, 229-231
anxiety, 39-40, 157, 161-162, 173, 191,
  198, 225, 227, 234-236, 250, 253, 266,
  275, 308. *See also* stress.
autism, 108, 225, 226, 228, 237, 266, 346
disability, 108, 122-123, 158, 162, 225-
  227, 229, 239, 243, 281, 296, 344
misdiagnosis, 40-41, 44, 159, 225-226,
  228-229, 266, 277
mood disorders, 39, 229, 231-234
OCD, 40, 105, 234, 235-237

underachievement, 264, 270
unemployment, 184, 247
universities, 7, 126, 148-149, 151, 164, 168-
  169. *See also* college; dual enrollment.
  Arizona State University, 45, 148-149,
    168, 172, 189, 250, 340. *See also*
    Herberger Young Scholars Academy.
  Harvard, 72, 74, 78, 218
  Princeton, 61, 78, 80, 206
  Stanford, 2, 25, 168, 195
  University of Iowa, 108, 151, 168
  Yale, 78-80, 167

valedictorians, 22, 77, 195, 267
values, 42-43, 49, 52-53, 150-151, 156-157,
  182-183, 174, 200, 220, 251, 276-277, 281-
  283, 288-289, 301, 303, 305, 308, 313-314
variability hypothesis, 28-29
Velasquez, K. S., 211, 222, 345, 346
verbal giftedness, 7-8, 62, 104, 107, 110, 119,
  135-136, 168, 237, 249, 268, 282, 346
victimization, 142-143, 154, 284
  sexual, 175, 178-179, 181, 204, 236, 284
violence, 65-66, 120-121, 150, 170, 200, 233,
  236, 245, 247, 254, 284
visionaries, 21, 46, 312
vocations, 12, 23, 49, 99, 128, 151, 224, 258,
  259, 271, 275, 283-284, 288, 296, 307. *See
  also* career.
voice, 9, 71, 105, 114, 120, 138, 141, 146,
  169, 213, 299, 315. *See also* Hudson,
  Jennifer; music.

Wai, J., 110, 112, 342
Walberg, H. J., 38, 53, 195, 339, 340, 344
war, 4, 29-30, 33, 60-61, 68, 82, 84, 89, 92,
  102, 173, 233
weaknesses, 26, 46-47, 150, 230, 275, 314

Webb, J. T., 22, 40, 104, 132, 147, 159, 226,
  228, 233, 265, 338, 339, 342, 343, 344,
  346, 348
white girls, 1-5, 8, 29, 38, 78, 154, 204, 209-
  210, 241, 244-246. *See also* race.
Williams, W. M., 201-202, 345
Winfrey, Oprah, 55, 72, 206, 340, 341, 345
WiSE, 184, 189-190, 192-193, 340
women's colleges, 52, 165-166, 169, 286
work, 23, 27, 29-31, 41, 52, 57, 73-78, 137,
  183, 198, 203, 205, 209-210, 264, 272
  See also balancing career and family;
  employment.
  conditions, 23, 37, 75, 200-201, 206-207,
    253, 258, 285, 287-288
  ethic, 12, 45-46, 62, 160, 181, 204, 242,
    251, 264, 267, 269-270
Worker Bees, 17, 18, 117, 282-283
Worrell, F. C., 50, 142, 150, 156, 243-244,
  279, 289, 340, 343, 344, 347, 348
writing, 55-59, 63, 68-69, 96, 130-131, 168,
  179-180, 203-204, 211-212, 217, 259,
  299. *See also* Rowling, J. K.

Yale Law School, 78-80, 167
Yewchuk, C., 52, 95, 340, 341
Yousafzai, Malala, 67-71, 101-102, 120, 121,
  274, 284, 341

About the Authors

Barbara A. Kerr, Ph.D. is the Williamson Family Distinguished Professor of Counseling Psychology at the University of Kansas. Her experience as a Post-Sputnik gifted kid led to a lifelong career of research into the development of talent and creativity. She founded laboratories for counseling gifted and creative students at four universities, including many research projects in gender equity for the National Science Foundation. Currently, she directs the Counseling Laboratory for the Exploration of Optimal States (CLEOS), where creative students learn to navigate the invisible pathways to creative careers, and is co-director of the Lawrence Creates Makerspace, where artists and technologists innovate together. She is the author of the first *Smart Girls, Gifted Women; The Encyclopedia of Giftedness, Creativity, and Talent; Major Works in Gifted and Talented Education;* co-author with Sanford Cohn of *Smart Boys*; and has authored over a hundred other scholarly works in the her area. She is a winner of the NAGC Torrance Award for Contributions to Creativity, an American Psychological Association Fellow, and was named one of the 25 most influential psychologists in the study of giftedness by APA.

Robyn McKay is the founder and creative director of she{ology} by dr. robyn mckay, an international leadership and coaching program for bright women. Previously, she was the psychologist at the Gary K. Herberger Young Scholars Academy at Arizona State University and the founding adviser for ASU's Women in Science and Engineering (WiSE) Leadership program. She received her

Ph.D. in Counseling Psychology from the University of Kansas, her M.A. in Psychology from the University of St. Mary, Kansas, and her B.S. in Biology from the University of Kansas. She cofounded the Counseling Laboratory for the Exploration of Optimal States at the University of Kansas. She completed a post-doctoral residency in mindfulness and student health at the University of Missouri. Her mission is to promote economic growth and equality by empowering girls and women to create sustainable businesses using their unique talents and abilities.

CPSIA information can be obtained
at www.ICGtesting.com
Printed in the USA
FSHW020751050719
59725FS